Library of
Davidson College

Aristocrats and the Crowd in the Revolutionary Year 1848
A CONTRIBUTION TO THE
HISTORY OF REVOLUTION AND
COUNTER-REVOLUTION IN AUSTRIA

Josef Polišenský
translated by Frederick Snider

State University of New York Press
ALBANY, NEW YORK

Published by
State University of New York Press

©1980 State University of New York

All rights reserved

Printed in the United States of America

No part of this book may be used or reproduced
in any manner whatsoever without written permission
except in the case of brief quotations embodied in
critical articles and reviews.

For information, address State University of New York
Press, State University Plaza, Albany, N.Y., 12246

Library of Congress Cataloguing in Publication Data

Polišenský, Josef V
  Aristocrats and the crowd in the revolutionary year 1848.

  Translation of Revoluce a kontrarevoluce v Rakousky, 1848.
  Includes bibliographical references and index.
  1. Austria—History—Revolution, 1848-1849.
2. Europe—History—1848-1849. I. Title.
SB83.P5913   943.6'04   79-14765
ISBN 0-87395-398-3

Contents

	Introductory Note	vii
I.	The Long Road Towards the Problem	1
	1. Bohemia, Austria and the European Revolution	1
	2. In Search of the Problem	7
	3. Marxism and the Theory of Revolution	12
	4. New Problems and New Sources	21
II.	Between Two Revolutions	29
	1. The Age of Industrial and Political Revolution	29
	2. What was Austria Before 1848?	40
	3. Prague and Vienna in July 1844	52
	4. The "Czech Question" and European Politics at the Beginning of 1848	61
III.	The Autumn of the Old Order and the Springtime of the Peoples	71
	1. Metternich and the Spectre of Revolution	71
	2. Ficquelmont and Thun on the Eve of the Revolution	84
IV.	The March Revolution in Austria	94
	1. March 13, 1848: The Black Day for the Old Order	94
	2. The Inglorious Flight of Prince Metternich	101
	3. The Revolutionary Crisis in Italy	103
	4. The Social Basis of the Revolution in Bohemia	109
V.	The Retreat of the Old Order: March–May 1848	116
	1. Kolowrat and Ficquelmont	116
	2. The Origins of the Social and Nationality Questions	124
VI.	The First Center of Counter-Revolution	136
	1. Politics and the Army	136
	2. Prague, Vienna and Innsbruck	141
VII.	The First Victory of the Counter-Revolution: Prague, June 12–18, 1848	148

	1. Windischgrätz and Lobkowitz	148
	2. The Six Days	153
	3. The Results of Windischgrätz's Victory	162
VIII.	The Weakness of the Revolution and the Strength of the Counter-Revolution	169
	1. The Government's Unsteadiness and the Army's Growing Might	169
	2. The Bohemian Germans and Their Congress at Teplitz	178
IX.	"The Army Takes Over the Protection of the Court and Government"	185
	1. The Road to Olomouc	185
	2. The Second Victory of the Counter-Revolution: Vienna in October 1848	193
X.	Austria's Future is Decided	199
	1. The Rise of Felix Schwarzenberg	199
	2. Austria and the "Bohemian Question" at the End of 1848	206
	Epilogue: From the Revolution of 1848 to the Paris Commune and the First International	211
	Notes	216
	Index	241

Introductory Note: What this Book is About

The book you have before you is the last of a trilogy of studies about the relationship of Czech society to revolution—more specifically to three of the "early bourgeois" revolutions. *The Thirty Years' War and the European Crisis of the 17th Century* explored the connections between Bohemia and the Dutch and English revolutions of the sixteenth and seventeenth centuries; *Napoleon and the Heart of Europe* traced the divided reaction of Bohemian society to the French Revolution and the dictatorship of Napoleon. This book will describe the revolutionary springtime which eventually arrived, full of twists, in Bohemia itself, and it will focus upon two antagonistic social forces: the retreating aristocracy and the proletariat, scarcely aware yet of its identity but already fighting with its passion and its blood.

At this point it would perhaps be well to warn the reader not to search for things in this book that are not going to be found. First, there will be nothing of that which is available in outline in every textbook. There is no general protrait of society, for that would require an examination of a third social class, the one whose interests were primarily at stake in 1848 in central Europe: the middle classes. This central theme is currently being studied by historians who know far more about it than I, and from them we may look forward to some significant contributions. They include Josef Kočí, author of a valuable biography of Emanuel Arnold; Zdeněk Samberger, author of pioneering studies of the radical democratic movement, particularly in 1849. Both have been most generous to me with their expertise, and without their encouragement this book would not have been undertaken. But they bear none of the responsibility for whatever shortcomings may be found in the present volume.

It will soon be apparent that I have not placed the Czech-German problem at the center of the stage, in spite of its importance—even crucial importance—in the years that followed. It will be apparent, too, I trust, that there are good reasons for this. In any case, Arnost Klima has recently completed a lengthy study which explores this problem far more thoroughly than is possible to do here. On the other hand, I have placed great stress on the relations between Austria and the Czech lands, between Vienna and Prague. In recent years Marxist historians from Slovakia and Hungary have also been reconsidering problems of 1848, which unite rather than divide the history of these two peoples. Since some of their broadly conceived work is readily available,[1] there is no need for me to deal directly with the Hungarian and Transylvanian parts of the Austrian Monarchy in the present study. At the same time, the events in the

Polish part of the Monarchy (Galicia) and the Italian (Lombardy, Venetia, Illyria) are brought in only where necessary. Because the revolutionary struggles of the Hungarian and Italian bourgeoisie reached their climax only in 1849, and because I have come to the conclusion that the fate of the revolution was essentially decided already by December, 1848, I do not go beyond the end of the year. Thus I fear that, against all tradition, I have largely dismissed the Imperial Diet at Kremsier (Kroměříž) as well as the May Uprising of 1849.

What can I offer in place of all this that will be interesting, important, possibly even new? Chiefly, perhaps, the fact that I have not studied the revolution merely in Prague, or merely in Prague and Vienna. I have attempted to establish the wider connections and to suggest why traditional views are often only partly credible. The revolutionary wave of 1848 traversed practically all the European continent, and we should be able to view it in a perspective at least as broad as that offered the readers *Národní noviny*, *Pražský večerní list* or *Občanské noviny*, periodicals published in Prague in 1848. You will see that the "Czech question" was not completely unknown in the rest of Europe before 1848 and that its stormy progress during the revolutionary year placed the Czech nation on the map of Europe with such force that it could not be erased. This is not to suggest that a Czech historian of the latter twentieth century ought to view the events and the politics of 1848 with any particular pride. Rather the reverse, in fact, is true. It seems to me that it should not be our task to defend established legends, however sacred they may be, the actions of the liberal-nationalist "fathers of the Nation" or even those of their radical-democratic opponents. The structure of the society in which we live is quite different from that of 1848. Nor should it be forgotten that at the beginning of this same year the *Communist Manifesto* first saw the light. If the bourgeoisie was already at this time undergoing differentiation, there were also elements on the fringes of society who were living under the pressure of two revolutions, industrial and political. Until now they have been perceived only schematically. But what was the actual strength of the old order, which was able so effectively to mobilize its forces in 1848? What form did the "crowd," the "rabble," the "working classes," the "proletariat" assume in 1848? In other words, who stood on the barricades in Prague, Vienna, or Milan? Who shed their blood in March and October in the streets of Vienna, or in Prague and Paris in June? Was this fighting "crowd" any different in its composition from that involved in the Chartist movement in London?

Perhaps there is another way in which this book is not traditional. It is intended, of course, for readers who are interested in history, but it is not for them alone. I have come to the possibly preposterous conclusion that this book should interest every other kind of reader as well. Is it possible to infuse an in-

Introductory Note

teresting presentation with a certain measure of scholarly reliability? It occurs to me that the history of the year 1848 is so engrossing that the narrative portions almost take care of themselves. But today's historian cannot get by without analysis as well. These portions are essentially probes into the depths of source materials, whose purpose is to recover knowledge which will change our picture of the past. If it is possible to write interestingly about archaeological discoveries, why can it not be done with history? The story of every truly scholarly effort is interesting, and it may be exciting, whether it is a question of archaeology or history. In any case, a famous archaeologist once remarked that although he himself might find Diogenes' cask, he was incapable of reconstructing Diogenes' thought. The thoughts and speculations of people who are separated from us by the space of four or five generations can be presented by modern historical scholarship because it uncovers new problems which generate searches for new source materials and new ways of using them. The first chapter, then, is actually the history of one particular scholarly problem. Should it seem uninteresting to you at first, feel free to pass over it. You might return to it profitably after finishing the rest of the book.

The history of 1848 can be studied in Czechoslovakia more easily than in most other parts of the world. This is because the events of 1945 and 1948 opened to scholars the riches of the former patrimonial and family archives of the nobility. Since the interests of landowners favored the preservation of written documents, which guaranteed their material and political claims, and thanks to the foresight of the archival administration, much documentation has been preserved here which has not been saved elsewhere. With my students and other young people, it has been my privilege during the summer vacations to help the archivists organize and catalogue the collections, and open them to scholars. The work consumed much time, often spent in the most obscure spots in the Republic, but it includes some of the happiest days of my life. If I have anybody to thank for what is new in this book, they are the archivists my friends, and the young people, more or less hard-working but uniformly curious and interested. Should I dedicate this book to anybody, it would be to three friends with whom I have often discussed the fateful significance of 1848 and with whom I can speak no more. They were Karol Goláň of the Comenius University, Bratislava, Alfons Lhotsky of the University of Vienna, and Tibor Wittman of the University of Szeged.

I

The Long Road Towards the Problem

1. Bohemia, Austria and the European Revolution

The Austrian counter-revolution achieved its first decisive victory on the streets of Prague during the Whitsun riots of 1848. The fateful conflicts that erupted in the search for a solution to problems of society and nationality permitted the leader of the counter-revolution General Windischgrätz to pursue his success to an extent greater than he could have hoped. Thanks to Windischgrätz, Prague became the symbol of the triumph of reaction; and thanks to the ill-considered policies of the Czech and German bourgeoisie, Bohemia became the symbol of political conservatism.

This far, at least, historians are in unanimous agreement. But what was the role, in this complicated situation, of the various social elements which repeatedly engaged themselves in the conflict? On this point modern scholars are no nearer agreement than were contemporaries.

The anonymous author of an official report on the "Whitsun-week Events in Prague, 1848," based on the "legal investigations so far carried out," bears eloquent testimony to the confusion of the participants.[1]

> At the time, the June events in Prague were exploited by the press of all parties, and there appeared such varied propaganda from manifold sources, that it is difficult for the impartial observer to distinguish between the true and the false, the just and the unjust, and thus recount these sad occurrences in their true guise ...[2]

Some see in them merely the results of an unfortunate misunderstanding. Others point to the incitement of the students, who provoked the cry for arms. Still others stress the intrigue of those who wished to sabotage the Slavonic Congress, whose aim was to prevent union with Germany. A fourth group blames the restless Poles for the events and interprets them simply as an open rebellion. A fifth view holds that the entire movement was planned and executed by Pan-Slavs, who aimed to remove Bohemia from the Empire ...[3]

Another comtemporary, the historian Anton Springer, viewed the "Austrian

Revolution" and the "June Events" in Prague from a slightly greater perspective. In *Austria After the Revolution*,[4] published at Leipzig in 1850, he wrote:

> It is true that nowhere else and at no other time has a revolution been so enthusiastically welcomed as was the March revolution in Austria. But then at no other time or place were the realities of government so shameful and unendurable. The demise of a system at which even the police poked fun cannot of course elicit even the faintest sigh. But this does not prove that a truly revolutionary mood existed. On the contrary—within a few days of the outbreak of the popular riots, most of the people were seized with an overwhelming desire to contain the flood and restore public order. The National Guard was out night and day against the ominous spirit of unrest, which was expected in the guise sometimes of the proletariat, sometimes of the peasantry. In Vienna some wanted to outlaw every radical word. In Prague the campaign for peace went so far that writers promised each other that for the time being they would not so much as mention the painful issue of nationality—as though an open wound could be rendered less serious by covering it with a cloth bandage.[5]

It is remarkable that until recently the national antagonisms went unrecognized—at any rate, no attention whatever was paid to their political consequences. Austria was regarded as a united state with a quite uniform character and a single set of goals. The censored textbooks spoke only of the Austrian states. At the most there might be mention of the special relationship of Hungary to the rest of the hereditary states. It was quite forgotten that Austria carried within herself the irrepressible seeds of a confederation [*Bundesgenossenschaft*] which would foster the development of the nationalities [*Volksstamme*] by introducing a richly structured political life. In any case, how could one be aware of this, when the spiritual endeavors of the people were everwhere paralyzed by the pressure of a clumsily mechanical method of government, when a simple lack of freedom crushed all manifestations of national individuality and political consciousness? Until 1848 Austria never functioned as a state but only as a power. As a power, she behaved towards her own peoples precisely as she behaved towards foreign countries. She possessed the usual accessories of political power—a large army, an orderly administration, a system of taxation—but she had little of that which creates an organic state. There was nothing like a sense of common interest among her people, nor even any real principles of government. In a word, old Austria consisted of a conglomeration of withered political bodies which led a merely mechanical life within the European balance of power. This is a reality which nobody will dispute who looks at the history of Austria with an unprejudiced eye.[6]

A united Germany, including both Prussia and Austria, would include two distinct great powers. What a political monster! The two simply cannot exist together: which of them would or could yield? Prussia, almost exclusively a German state? Austria, which if she wants to overtake Prussia must do so in terms of German national enthusiasm? That would mean getting rid of the greater part of her own population and suppressing all political freedom within her borders. The Austrian government, like all others, is concerned with its own survival and therefore cannot be seriously interested in a united Germany. Nor have the Austrian Germans shown themselves to be seriously interested in such a union. Had they been, they would simply have refused to participate in the elections for the Austrian Imperial Diet. This divergence in the will of Austria's people, the sad fact that they were trying to build two different states at the same time, divided their forces and set them up against each other, sealing the fate of the March movement. But this was not the only reason for its failure: national confusions and the position of the army also came into play. The old Austria, through its army, confronted the new. Because the two were unable to comprehend one another, they were obliged to oppose each other. The confrontation took place in newspapers, pamphlets, poems, and finally with arms in hand—in June in Prague, then later, in October, in Vienna.[7]

Various aims have been ascribed to the Prague uprising. But it would be difficult to substantiate any of them, particularly if one wishes to make the leaders of the Czech national party responsible. This party was of course concerned primarily with creating a Bohemian Diet, for which preparations had been completed and elections begun. The cause of a Diet was not helped by the uprising, which instead postponed its convocation indefinitely. Or was there the hope that a successful uprising would bring independence for the Bohemian Crown? Certainly the stories that later circulated about a "Bohemian Duke" seem to support this view. But if this were the case, the national party could scarcely have done better than support the provisional government, which was created by the régime itself, and continue warily along the path on which it had already set out, to achieve Bohemian political independence in the shortest possible time. The uncertainty surrounding the establishment of the provisional government has not yet been resolved. It was probably intended to paralyze the revolutionary ministries set up at Vienna and save at least a part of the Monarchy for the dynasty. Whatever the case, if the national party in Bohemia really contemplated the dissolution of old political ties, then it would have been enough to change the rules of the game that it had been playing with Austria and transform itself from a means into an end. In spite of all its difficulties, this path offered a greater prospect of success than an uprising, whose outcome and consequences were at best problematical, could have possibly done. But was there anything else that could have bound the Czech leaders to the revolution?

A mood of excitement prevailed in Prague as everywhere else. Freedom had come as a gift, without a struggle, and there was no time for passions to cool. Just as in Vienna, no amount of progress could satisfy the young people, no freedom went far enough. Tension between the army and the people was maintained now for national as well as political reasons. Was there not then sufficient tinder to make a conflagration likely?[8]

From a still greater distance—nearly twenty years later—J. V. Frič, one of the

3

leading participants in the June uprising, delivered his judgment. In his Paris exile, he edited a collection of essays with Louis Léger entitled *La Bohême historique, pittoresque et littéraire*, in which he included an article about the Slav Congress of 1848.[9] His interpretation here is substantially different from the one he later gave in his *Memoirs*, which appeared between 1885 and 1887.[10]

Around the end of the autumn of 1847, the first stirrings of political life arose among the Czechs—a consciousness of nationality and a resolve to take action. The files of the secret police contained the names of several dozen individuals whom the government called *patriots*. When the remains of Josef Jungmann and later those of the national poet Kalina were borne to the cemetery, twelve thousand people joined in the procession to pay their respects. When they passed by the New Town Hall, where Kalina's friend Arnold had been imprisoned for protesting against the entry of the Jesuits into Prague, the whole crowd bared their heads to honor the martyred writer.

Two parties emerged among the patriots. One could be called the scholars, the other the democrats. The latter wasted no time organizing the middle class and the workers into patriotic clubs, which during Shrovetide 1848 became truly public assemblies; and they arranged patriotic speeches for every occasion.

It should be noticed, too, that the Diet, consisting of the nobility of the land, was also showing signs of life. As early as 1846, when the government demanded that the Diet undertake the erection of a monument in honor of the Emperor Francis, Count Buquoy arose and exhibited a coin with the nominal value of thirty kreutzer but worth in fact just six kreutzer. 'These coins,' he said, 'are a sufficient monument, for they remind us all of the Emperor's fatherly concern as well as the filial gratitude of his subjects.'

There is no doubt that the Bohemian noblemen, those of Lower Austria, were resolved to present a petition demanding freedom of the press and economic reforms. These aristocrats made commendable efforts to get in touch with members of the national party, and together they eventually established a national organization whose goal was the erection of a national theatre.

Then came the news of the February Revolution. Two of the parties, the noblemen and the scholars, were horrified. The former were afraid of the people, for whom they had done nothing; the latter were afraid that it would now be impossible to remain within the limits of their own program: the freedom to speak and write Czech.

Only the democratic party intensified its efforts, and, in spite of the obstacles thrown up by the government, they were able to organize an assembly of ten thousand people who, even in the face of Autrian arms, drafted a petition asking for the renewal of the old rights of the nation, freedom of the press, freedom of assembly and so forth. They also elected 25 delegates empowered to establish a provisional government. Karel Sabina, the last speaker before the assembly, expressed the general mood: Today the Czechs have removed the stain which for two centuries has defiled the moribund body of their country.[11]

Meanwhile the party of reaction gathered its forces and considered how to use them.

Their contacts with the Prague military commander Windischgrätz became daily more open, and the General dispatched his couriers to the court at Innsbruck and to Metternich, who had been expelled from the country. Faced with this situation, the democratic committee sought to strengthen its position against the reactionaries and also against the German party, who increasingly threatened the other nationalities. Therefore, inspired by the zealous Slovak patriot Ludovít St'úr, and in cooperation with the Polish committee at Poznań, they summoned the Slav Congress to Prague on May 31, 1848.[12]

[During the Congress] the forces of reaction—the so-called Bohemian aristocracy in conjunction with the Austrian Camarilla—prepared a bloody conclusion for the meeting.

The Germans from the Frankfurt Assembly, the Viennese students and the National Guard consistently vilified the Czechs for having dissociated themselves from the plan for German unity. Artillery was sent to Prague, and guns were placed on the surrounding hillsides. A coup d'état was expected any day.

"During our meeting," one of the participants wrote, "the German press daily insulted the Slav Congress and accused it of concocting plots to crush the Germans in Bohemia, annihilate the Magyars in Hungary, and bring about the Russian domination of Europe. But our aims were not at all aggressive. We were only interested in defending ourselves against the proposed German union, which had revealed its appetite for parts of Bohemia, as well as most of the Duchy of Poznańand the slavic territories of the Adriatic. We wanted simply to resist the pressure to which the Slavic peoples were already being subjected." The newspapers which defamed the Congress asserted that it had been called only out of enmity toward the Germans. This came precisely at the time when those who had begun the revolution were modifying its direction. In France the leaders continued Louis-Philippe's policy towards the rest of Europe, as though nothing had changed. In Austria and in all of Germany the forces of reaction stood ever more openly against the progress that the revolution had accomplished. The old anti-Slav tendencies which had been temporarily neutralized now boldly reasserted themselves. For some the suppression of foreign nationalities amounted to the fulfillment of a moral obligation. To impose one's language upon others, to deprive an indigenous nationality of its means of livelihood, to deprive it of meaningful political influence and assume control of its property, appeared to some a proper consequence of their own superiority. With incalculable narrow-mindedness they ascribed maturity only to themselves: Frenchmen, Englishmen, Italians and most of all Slavs were to be suppressed. Therefore it is no wonder that during this period of freedom the Czechs decided to oppose these indefensible aims. And even while threatened by Windischgrätz's army, the city of Prague, through its representatives, made clear its awareness of the dangers facing the people. The people would not be satisfied until they were given better security. Therefore the municipal spokesmen requested that Windischgrätz turn over to them 2,000 guns, 80,000 cartridges and one battery of artillery. Windischgrätz, however, received the delegation with disdain. On Whit-Monday, June 12, a vast assembly gathered at the statue of St. Wenceslas, before which Mass was celebrated. Here the students, burghers and workers promised to remain united forever. Many people took part in the festivities without realizing that they were being manipulated by a provocateur. When the crowd passed by the Princes' Palace, a quarrel broke out with the military contingent guarding the Garrison Staff Headquarters, and they fired on the unarmed people.

The heroic struggle lasted four days. It was primarily the courageous Poles who distinguished themselves on the barricades. Only when the last hope of help arriving had evaporated, only when the bombarded buildings began to burn over the heads of the fighters, only when the National Guard threatened to attack the barricades from the rear, did the rebels yield and abandon their positions to escape the revenge of Windischgrätz and Thun. In six days 483 persons were buried, according to the hospital records, two-thirds of them soldiers.

As the reaction gained its victory, the persecution of the patriots began. The prisons and the barracks filled up with the defenders of liberty ...[13]

It is obvious that these three witnesses—the military auditor, the Docent in the University of Prague, and the radical-democrat in exile—recounted the events exclusively from their own viewpoints. For Frič it was important to win over the French public and the democratic émigrés in Paris, most of them Poles. Perhaps he also wished to alter the unfavorable image of Bohemia that prevailed in these circles. Springer rightly emphasized that the revolution of 1848 turned on the solution of two questions, the social and the national. In central Europe the Germans and the Magyars combined a progressive solution of the social and political question with a conservative one for the national. On the other hand, the representatives of the Slavic nationalities justifiably demanded equality, but they pursued a conservative political and social program. The tragedy of the revolution in central Europe consisted in the fact that the struggle in Hungary became a national war in the spring of 1849. Springer compared the military conflict of 1849 to the religious conflict of the sixteenth century, and he hoped that this stage would soon give way to equality among nationalities. The military ispector, by contrast, contented himself with gathering information, and in this he was quite successful. It may be doubted whether he really believed his strange theory about the origin of the Prague Uprising—in any case, his assessment appeared only at a time when General Windischgrätz (who as we shall see was partial to the theory of an international conspiracy) was no longer looking over his shoulder.

Until now we have been rather ill-informed about the relationship of events in Prague and Vienna to European developments. It is widely admitted that the "European Revolution"—the revolutionary wave which innundated practically the entire continent—implied some sort of connection between the events in the various European capitals. Anton Springer, whose views on the Czech and Austrian revolution we have cited, delivered lectures on the "History of the Revolutionary Age (1789-1848)" in the University of Prague in the academic year 1848-49. They reveal him as something of a forerunner of the English historian Eric Hosbawm, who in the 1960's also explored the phenomenon of revolution in a broadly European context.[15] Springer's interest in the study of social and national questions in 1848 grew from his earlier interest in social and political questions. Hobsbawm speaks of two revolutions in whose charmed circle European society lived out the first half of the 19th century: political revolution, inspired by the French Revolution of 1789, and the Industrial Revolution, beginning in England after the second third of the 18th century, then on the Continent in one country after another.

Thanks to Springer, the historical school in the University of Prague has quite a long tradition of interest in the problems of 1848 and their European context. This is not to say that the impulses provided by those who participated in the 1848 revolution have been exhausted. Nor have all the questions that they and their descendants posed been satisfactorily answered.

2 In Search of the Problem

I should like to describe my own pursuit of questions that have not been answered in the many books written by our forebears. The revolutionary year 1848 is separated from our own day by roughly a century and a quarter, or about six generations. My great-grandfather, František Polišenský, householder in the Moravian village of Nová Dědina near Kroměříž Kremsier, was conscripted into the army sometime in the 1840s. According to the evidence of his daughter-in-law, my grandmother Rosalie, who died in the summer of 1945, the "lords" wished to be rid of him at the time. They were the Thun-Hohensteins from the castle at Kvasice, and before 1849 they could manipulate the lives of their tenants in any number of ways. It was said that my great-grandfather remained in the army through two "capitulations"—fourteen years —and that he returned home penniless but rich in adventures and experiences. As a boy I was disappointed that his tales never had anything to do with military action. What seemed to have impressed him were the cities and gardens of Italy. At any rate, he himself was interested chiefly in his own garden—so much so, in fact, that he avoided going to work in the fields. Most of all he liked to tell of the beauty of Lombardy and Venetia and of towns with foreign-sounding names. From two of them, Piacenza and Pescharia, he received his village nicknames. I imagine that my great-grandfather lived out the rest of his life as something of a village Marco Polo, and that his neighbors refused to take very seriously most of what he had to say.

I used to look on the map for the places where my great-grandfather had once been on maneouvers in his long blue coat and military cap, with a rifle over his shoulder. The years of his Italian soldiering became one of the themes of my extensive but chaotic reading—stories of the brave infantrymen from Haná under old Field-Marshal Radetzky, the discreet defense of the Revolution written by Josef Alexander Helfert, Frič's *Memoirs*, Jakub Malý's *Our Renaissance*, and J. Toužimský's *Dawn of a New Era*; then later the works of the Brno historian Hugo Traub, which greatly impressed me, and one of the first history books that I read in German: Brügel's *History of Austrian Social Democracy*.[16] In the latter I first ran across the tragic figure of Wenceslas Messenhauser, writer and leader of the Viennese National Guard. He was born in 1813 in Prostějov, where I, too, was born and spent most of my youth. How was it that the social-democratic mayor of this town of weavers and tailors was unable to have a single street named after Messenhauser? In Toužimský's book I found a lithograph portrait of Jindřich Špitzer, a student at the Vienna Polytechnic, born in Bzenec in Moravia, who was "the first to fall for freedom and his fatherland in Vienna on March 13, 1848."[17] And among the last victims of the Viennese revolution, besides the Frankfurt delegates Blum and Becker, was the former student of Leipzig, Herman Jellinek, editor of a radical Viennese journal, who was born in Uherský Brod. If the German socialists and Marxists remembered Blum, Becher and Fröbel as fighters for freedom, was it not right to remember also Messenhauser, Špitzer and Jellinek?

When, after some complications, I came to study history at Charles University in Prague, I discovered that there were at least three members of the faculty who were interested in the history of 1848: the docents František Roubík, K. Kazbunda and Otakar Odložilík. I read Roubík's *Czech Year of 1848*, his *National Guard in Bohemia in 1848-51*, and *The Czech Movement in 1848* by Oklžilík and Kazbunda. These were works by historian-archivists, based on the official records and conscientiously constructed, even though slightly one-sided.[18] More impressive to me was the study by J. Matoušek, *Karel Sladkovský and Czech Radicalism During the Revolution and Reaction*, with its fascinating description of the meteoric rise of this student who transferred from Vienna to Prague. I returned to Frič's *Memoirs* and attempted a critical analysis of their first volume. Without much difficulty I realized that "truth" and "poetry" were intermingled here, that it was a literary work that should not otherwise be taken seriously.[19] My own sympathies, of course, lay with the fighters on the barricades, but neither Sladkovský nor Frič, and later neither Sabina nor Arnold, seemed able to fill the role of a great revolutionary. I also searched in vain for the type in Vienna. Here the exploits of Hans Kutlich interested me, but his ideas seemed a curious blend of social progressivism, anti-Semitism and German chauvinism. To me the most sympathetic figure was Franz Schuselka, the anti-hero of Havlíček's songs. I was surprised to discover that in his own way poor Schuselka meant well toward the Czechs.[20]

Thus I could find no worthy counterpart to Garibaldi or Mazzini, nor even to Louis Blanc or Albert. Then I began to work under Docent Josef Fischer, the author of a remarkable analysis of the political thought of František Palacký. What was the character of Palacký's "realism" or "Austroslavism?" How was it possible that in the first days of the June Uprising the conservative Palacký behaved sympathetically toward the students, condemned the cowardice of the National Guard and sharply criticized Windischgrätz? Was Palacký's letter to Frankfurt really such a remarkable political document as the textbooks suggested? Was not his faith in the Habsburgs a bit naive? And what was the source of his naivete? Or Havíček's, or even that of the radical-democrats—not to mention the rural populace, who apparently retained their faith in the goodness of their lord the Emperor? Or perhaps Palacký and Havíček simulated naiveté in order to deceive themselves? I decided that Palacký was a much better historian than politician in 1848, and this was as far as I could go at the time.[21]

I have saved two paperback volumes from my student days to which I returned for guidance in the labyrinth of questions surrounding the year 1848. They are the tenth Czech edition of the *Communist Manifesto* and Reiner's translation of Lenin's *State and Revolution*. It seemed to me that these two works might help me to place the 1848 revolution in a new perspective. But where could one find historical work in the tradition of Marx, Engels, and Lenin? I knew of the German writings of Mehring, Lukacs, and Pokrovsky, and had begun to study the essays of V. Cejchan and J. Charvát on the period of 1848.[22]

Josef Fischer, who fell victim to the Nazi occupation, was succeeded by Eduard Bass. It is my honor to have been able to work with him, and in the 1940s, along with many others, I enjoyed his *Readings About 1848*. In some respects this colorful panorama of the age has yet to be surpassed. I realized this during the war when, at the suggestion of M. Novotný, I tried to put together selections from the military diary and the *Bohemica* of the "last Hussite" Jan Jeník of Bratřice. In the course of my work, some "heretical" thoughts occurred to me: how is it possible that Jeník looks at the Prague of his youth—*i.e.* the 1760s and 1770s—still a "Czech" city? I knew from Josef Volf's book that Czech newspapers could not even survive at this time. But what actually was the character and volume of literary production? Jan Jeník of Bratřice only wrote down his recollections as a very old man. But the strength of his memory is shown by the long passages from operas and the countless songs that he knew by heart until his death—and he died only in 1845. According to him there was no concern in the middle of the eighteenth century that the rural population of Bohemia would one day be Germanized. It was a different matter, however, with the burghers and noblemen. But Jeník himself was bilingual, and he wrote in both Czech and German. Was not, then, that process which we usually call the "national revival" really a struggle for national consciousness on the part of the threatened urban population, who to some extent glorified the "patriotic intelligentsia?" Jeník himself doubtless inclined more and more towards the urban middle class, although as late as the 1830s he was still attempting to win the interest and support of his noble friends for Czech history, language, and literature. But we also know that this had occupied him during his military service, when he used to chat for hours in Czech with Major Wallis, who was of Irish descent.[23] Did Wallis perhaps sense that Czechs and Irishmen shared a similar fate? It is certain, however, that Jeník did not blame Josef II for the threat to Czech national existence, and he remained a staunch supporter all his life. Nor is it surprising: Josef II insisted that all important edicts and laws be linguistically comprehensible to all his subjects. He even ordered an investigation once into the possible existence of several Slavic languages in Moravia beside Czech.

I read some of Rosenmüller's Czech newspapers and his appeal in the preface to the *Forerunners of the Bohemian Courier*, addressed to all who feel "love towards my country, that is, the Czech people and their language." It was a pathetic effort to win subscriptions from "all true patriots, as well as the descendants of all old Bohemian well-born families, all old Bohemian towns and communities, all true lovers of our language and all erudite Czechs." Still, the language of this journal does not betray any signs of a "degeneration" of linguistic standards. The same conclusion emerges from a glance at the *Latin, Czech and German Vocabulary* published in Rosenmüller's printing shop by František Ignac Kirchner sometime before 1745. It appears, then, that the "crisis" of the Czech language began sometime after this date and reached its peak around 1772-82, and that the Josephine period reestablished more favorable conditions for the Czech press. By this time subscribers could be found for *Schönfeld's Post-Courier* and its more successful competitor *Kamerius's Royal Bohemian Patriotic Journal* (1789-95), then later for Schönfeld's newspaper which survived until 1848 under the title *Prague News*.[24]

The development—or if you wish, the formation—of the modern Czech nation therefore did not proceed in a linear fashion. There was no sudden morning of rebirth following upon an "age of darkness." But how was the "modern Czech nation" actually formed? How did its social elements come into being and how did their structure and function evolve? I did not know, and therefore I refused a flattering offer, after Bass's death, to edit the materials for a second volume of his *Readings*. It seemed to me that too many of the important questions were not covered by Bass's documentation, and that I should be proceeding just as doubtfully as if I were to write of the politics of the Kremsier Assembly entirely from F. V. Peřinka's papers, with which I became acquainted while working on the military section of the Kremsier anniversary exhibition of 1948.

The centennial brought a flood of writing about the revolution. Most of this work has been forgotten, but perhaps the most significant were the contributions of Czech scholars published in the *Slavonic and East European Review*.[25] Far more interesting, however, is the work done in the 1950s, which considerably altered traditional views. Jaroslav Purš began to explore the difficult problems of the Industrial Revolution. L. Karníková and P. Horská contributed new information about the demographic changes resulting from industrialization and urbanization in the first half of the nineteenth century. M. Novák explored the character of Metternich's police régime; and J. Křížk emphasized the essentially bourgeois character of the National Guard. The radical democrats replaced the "fathers of the Nation" in the interest of the historians.[26] Palacký and Brauner, even Havlíček, became less popular, and the National Committee came to be viewed in a more sober light.[27]

In these circumstances I was faced with the task of lecturing on the fundamental problems of Czech history to students who had been drawn to Prague from all over the world by their interest in the postwar situation, in the historical roots of contemporary society, as well as in Marxism and socialism. Sometimes with genuine interest, sometimes not without a hint of malevolence, my young students asked me for a Marxist interpretation of the events of 1848. Of course, they had in mind Engels's analysis of the revolution in central Europe (long ascribed to Marx), *Revolution and Counter-Revolution in Germany*.[28] Engels based his account on the articles that he and Marx wrote during the revolutionary months in the *Neue Rheinsche Zeitung*. I pointed out that the position of this newspaper was by no means unfavorable to the Czechs and the Poles, that Marx correctly assessed the significance of the Whitsun riots in Prague, and that he identified the workers, of whom the Czech and German bourgeosie grew more afraid than they were of the aristocrats, as the real strength of the revolution.[29] Proceeding from his negative assessment of the middle-class politicians of 1848, Engels concluded that after the defeat of the Prague Uprising, the Slav national movement, influenced by the bourgeoisie and the nobility, was taken in tow by the enemies of revolution. How did the forces of counter-revolution succeed? I could not say very much about that, except to note that the March revolution was unable to break the power of the Camarilla, that the revolutionary bourgeoisie in Prague (and even more in Vienna) were unable to neutralize or even substantially weaken the old administrative apparatus or the army. I fear that I was also unable to explain precisely how there appeared in Engels's work, along with his correct judgments, his mistaken conclusions about the historical development of the Slavic peoples. Engels himself, I knew, later confronted his false prognosis about the future of small nations and revised it. Historians have not yet convincingly demonstrated precisely how the small Slavic nations were able after 1848 to demonstrate their capabilities for independent national development—not only for building their own states but also for placing them among the builders of the socialist order.[30]

I looked for an answer to these questions in the work of Marxist authors who were concerned directly or indirectly with the revolutionary year 1848. But I found only that the number of questions grew. Was Karel Kreibich right when he concluded, like Palacký, that "the Czechs have the Habsburgs to thank for the preservation of their national existence?"[31] "To what extent did the Czech bourgeoisie help defeat the revolution?" Jan Sverma asked in his anniversary article in 1928.[32] Why did a democratic solution to the nationality question prove so elusive, and what prevented the union of all the revolutionary movements of the central European peoples?[33] Five years later Sverma recalled Marx's statement that the Czech nation stood at a crossroads in the spring of 1848.[34] But where did the "nation" reside in a society that was divided into classes? What were the groups and classes that existed within the Czech nation? What was the social composition of Austria?

During another "anniversary occasion", in 1938, Kurt Konrad returned to the problems of 1848 in a series of articles in the periodical *Tvorba*. Like Sverma, he emphasized the need to approach the problems from an international perspective. He also surveyed the views that have been taken about the possibilities for democratic and revolutionary cooperation between Czechs and Germans. Then during the Second World War Jan Sverma pointed to the need for a reevaluation of Slavic thought, in which the Czechs sought support in the Russian nation rather than Tsarist absolutism. At about the same time Zdeněk Nejedlý suggested the need for a reinterpretation of the events of 1848.[35]

A great help to me in my discussions with the students was an article by the English Marxist A. Rothstein, published in February 1948, a thorough comparative analysis of the experience of the English and Czech peoples in 1848, 1938 and 1948.[36] He showed me the way back and the way forward. The way back to Marx and Engels at the beginning of 1848, and the way forward to the formulation of new questions and the search for answers in new, so far unknown sources.

3 Marxism and the Theory of Revolution

Early in February 1848 appeared the first copies of a pamphlet entitled

Manifesto of the Communist Party. It had been written in November the previous year and was to present the new program of the Union of Communists. But the authors, Marx and Engels, accomplished more than they had set out to do. Their *Manifesto* was not to become merely a policy statement of one group, of which there were many. Instead it formulated new conceptions of history and politics. The *Manifesto* is a historic document which ushered in a new era. Its significance begins with its proclamation that capitalism had brought forth a new reality: communism.

> Europe is haunted by a spectre—the spectre of communism. All the powers of old Europe have joined the chase against this spectre—the Pope and the Tsar, Metternich and Guizot, French radicals and the German police ...
> It is highest time that the communists reveal to the world their views, their goals and endeavors, and, against the rumors about communism, publish the manifesto of the actual party.[37]

Marx's and Engels's conception was historical but not antiquarian. Unlike the utopian socialists, who proceeded from the feelings, intuitions and yearnings of individual thinkers, they proceeded from the laws of social development and formulated a suggestion for action on the basis of concrete forces which exist in the real world. Therefore they were able to give a correct picture of the positive accomplishments of the bourgeoisie without hiding the fact that the aim was to end their rule. All human society undergoes a series of stages in its evolution, each determined by economic development, the relations of production. At that time, in 1848, the bourgeoisie was in control, but it would die from its internal contradictions, and already it had given rise to its own antithesis: the proletariat:

> The weapons with which the bourgeoisie crushed feudalism will now be turned against themselves. But the bourgeoisie not only forged the weapons which would result in their extinction, they also produced the people who would use them to rule—the modern workers, the proletariat.
> In the same measure as the bourgeoisie develops, so too will the proletariat, the modern class of workers, who can exist only when they are able to find work, and can find work only so far as their work augments capital.[38]

The struggle between the bourgeoisie and feudalism, like the struggle between the proletariat and the bourgeoisie, is not simply the eternal struggle between the rich and the poor. Instead, it is a class struggle, a contest between two antagonistic classes which hinges upon the relations of production. This struggle is actually the program of the proletariat and its organized defender, the Communist Party.

> The immediate goal of the Communists is the same as that of all other proletarian parties: the formation of the proletariat into a class, the overthrow of the rule of the bourgeoisie, the seizure of political power by the proletariat.
> In a bourgeois society, work for livelihood is only the means for expanding bought labor. In a communist society bought labor is only the means for the enrichment and simplification of the life processes of the workers.
> In a bourgeois society, therefore, the past dominates the present, and in a communist society the present the past. In a bourgeois society capital is independent and personal, while the working individual is dependent and non-personal.
> You are horrified that we wish to abolish private property. But for nine-tenths of the members of your society private property is already abolished. It exists only because for nine-tenths it does not exist. Therefore you reproach us for wanting to abolish property, which necessarily assumes that the vast majority of society is without property.

The revolution of the proletariat and the dissolution of classes is a program that can be realized only by the proletariat. It alone can form a revolutionary class:

> Of all the classes which stand today against the bourgeoisie, the really revolutionary one is the proletariat. The others will decline and disappear with the development of large-scale industry. The proletariat, however, is its unique product.
> The middle classes, the small businessmen, the shopkeeper, the craftsman and the farmer, all struggle against the bourgeoisie to defend themselves against extinction as the middle class. Therefore they are conservative rather than revolutionary. That is not all: they are reactionary because they try to turn back the wheel of history. If they appear to be revolutionary, then it is only with regard to their impending transfer into the ranks of the proletariat. In this case, they are defending not their present but their future interests. They forsake their own perspective in order to take up the perspective of the proletariat ...[40]

The re-formation of the capitalist organization of society into a socialist one is not possible without political revolution:

> Political power in the true sense of the word is the organized brute force of one class for the suppression of another. If the proletariat unites in a struggle against the bourgeoisie as a class, if it incites a revolution against the ruling class and destroys the old ruling class, then at the same time it destroys class antagonisms. It destroys classes themselves and even its own rule as a class.
> In place of the old bourgeois society with its classes and class antagonisms there

appears an association in which the free development of each individual is a condition of the free development of all.⁴¹

The "proletariat," *i.e.* the industrial proletariat, is therefore not automatically the "working class." It must be transformed into a class by the Communists, if need be, in the fire of class struggle. The victorious conclusion of the class struggle will lead to the liberation of the individual.

Communists are reproached for wanting to do away with country and nationality. Workers have no country. What they do not have cannot be taken away from them. In so far as the proletariat must first of all seize political control, rule over other classes and constitute itself as a nation, it is itself still national, although not in the bourgeois sense. National differences and the antagonisms among nations progressively disappear with the evolution of the bourgeoisie, freedom of trade, the world market, the homogeneity of industrial production and the corresponding conditions of life. The rule of the proletariat will quicken this process. The combination of forces, at least those of the civilized lands, is one of the first conditions of the liberation of the proletariat. As the exploitation of one individual by another shall disappear, so too shall the exploitation of one nation by another. And when antagonisms among classes within nations disappear, so shall enmity among nations.⁴²

In a class society, then, nations are divided; hence the possibility of kindling enmity among them. But this must be overcome. Therefore the *Manifesto* concludes with an invitation cutting across all political and national boundaries:

The Communists consider it dishonorable to conceal their opinions and their goals. They declare openly that their aims may be accomplished only through a violent overthrow of the entire existing social order. Let the ruling classes tremble before the communist revolution ...⁴³

It is evident from the *Manifesto* that its authors were addressing communists in western Europe and that by the "proletariat" they meant the urban proletariat, born of the Industrial Revolution. But their thinking was not merely abstract; nor did they forget about the masses of rural agrarian proletariat. Thus in France in the beginning of 1848 they counted on the collaboration of the followers both of Ledru-Rollin and Louis Blanc against the bourgeoisie. In Switzerland they were willing to support the radicals against the conservative Sonderbund. In Poland they looked for allies among those who made agrarian revolution a condition of the struggle for national liberation.

Communists turn their attention chiefly to Germany because Germany stands on the threshold of the bourgeois revolution, and it is carrying out this coup under conditions generally more advanced and with a much more mature proletariat than existed in England in the seventeenth century or France in the eighteenth. The German bourgeois revolution, therefore, may be the immediate prelude to the proletarian revolution.[44]

As we shall see, the *Manifesto's* prognosis was borne out in several ways in the first months of 1848. That its optimism remained unfulfilled in the end may be attributed to several objective realities. The brightest prospects for realizing the demands of the popular masses existed in western Europe, in England and France, where the bourgeois revolutions had already run their course even though remnants of feudalism survived. Therefore some Marxist historians believe that the struggle on the barricades of Paris in June 1848 was the first "proletarian" revolution, while others have called it a "bourgeois-democratic" revolution.[45] Usually it is regarded as a bourgeois revolution with pronounced democratic characteristics—a vague definition at best. More precise is the Marxist conception of bourgeois revolution, which although not universally accepted today is nevertheless employed in practice by most historians—including some who have been at pains to dissociate themselves from Marxism.

The year 1848 brought a series of bourgeois or bourgeois-democratic movements which effected a qualitative change from the old feudal order to a new capitalist one, particularly in the lands of central Europe. Here a political change did occur, but its results were quickly wiped out or at least contained by the power of the feudal ruling classes, whose strength was based upon landed property. Nevertheless, conditions were established for the development of a capitalist society, even where the revolution was only half-hearted or where its progress was prematurely halted.

The Dutch Revolution of the sixteenth century, the English Revolution of the seventeenth and the French Revolution of the eighteenth century possessed a number of traits in common.[46] In the first place, all of them began when the ruling class fell into internal conflict—a struggle within their own ranks involving their ruler—and when those over whom they ruled were no longer able or willing to prolong their accustomed mode of existence. In practical terms, then, the introductory phase of these revolutions was a period of resistance on the part of the Estates against the absolutist behavior of the ruler. Its duration was usually quite brief—only in the Netherlands did a fiction endure of revolt against the "evil counsellors" but not against the ruler himself. In England it ended in the summer of 1642, in France it dissolved by September 1789. After this there usually took place a shift in favor of a new ruling class—thanks to the intervention of the popular masses who enforced a more radical break with the past. This second phase occurred in the Netherlands between 1566, with the iconoclastic struggles, and 1572, when the towns of Zeeland and Holland became established as leaders of the struggle against the Spanish Habsburgs. In England the shift took place during the First Civil War (1642-46). The war that was kindled by the French Revolution was also an indispensable factor. Once the most immediate threats were disposed of and internal as well as external enemies were defeated, a third phase began, in which differentiation occurred within the ranks of the new ruling class. In the Netherlands this resulted in the brutal shattering of the revolution after the successes of 1576. In France there was the struggle for Jacobin dictatorship in 1793-94, and in England the victory of the Independents over the Presbyterians in the Second Civil War. The last stage of bourgeois revolution represents its culmination and also its alienation from its popular allies, the fourth Estate. In the Netherlands this stage was reached in 1576-78; in England in 1649, when the movements of the Levellers and Diggers were defeated and the way was open for the liquidation of the monarchy as well as for Cromwell's dictatorship. In France the final clash, occurring after 1794, had a similar result: the Thermidorian reaction and Bonaparte's dictatorship.

This comparison suggests that the beginning of a bourgeois revolution requires that at least a part of the old ruling class arrive at the conviction that the "old order" is untenable. This is why the representatives of state power hardly ever offered any opposition in the first phase of the revolution. All the early bourgeois revolutions, since they were struggles for political power in the state, were limited geographically to one state. Where conflict with an external enemy was involved, they were "national." But at the same time these revolutions were international in that they had repercussions in other countries. This is true of those which expressed their program in religious terms and also of those which, like the French Revolution, employed a "national" ideology. Revolutionary struggle is impossible without organization, especially military organization. To assure the success of the revolutionary program, therefore, it was necessary that at least a part of the existing armed forces shift to the side of the revolution, to create a new kind of army. This is what happened in the Netherlands, when, thanks to the strength of the towns, the struggle against the Spanish infantry created a new military tactic. This is what happened, too, in England when Cromwell formed his "Independent" heavy cavalry. It happened, finally, in France when Carnot created his "amalgam" of old and new contingents.

The key role of the towns in all three cases is indisputable, even though it is less evident in the Dutch case in the early years of the rebellion than in England, where London occupied the same decisive position that Paris did in

France. In the Netherlands, by contrast, the "agrarian problem" played a much smaller role than elsewhere, since a markedly urbanized territory was at issue. In France, where this situation did not obtain, the rural masses were neutralized by the prompt destruction of feudal remnants and the possibility given them to acquire the lands belonging to the aristocrats who fled. Usually the rural masses ended as neutrals, but sometimes they set themselves up against both sides in the conflict.

We shall see how far this model of bourgeois revolution coincides with what took place in central Europe in 1848. Marx and Engels based their own perceptions upon the historical experience of the English and French Revolutions. Therefore they were not in a position to give full consideration to the significance of the rural masses who inhabited the lands of central and eastern Europe. Perhaps it seemed to them that the problem was never a real one; in any case, it was solved later, both theoretically and practically, by Lenin.

Marx and Engels pinned their hopes on the German industrial proletariat, which in fact was a significant agent only in the industrialized areas of the Rhineland and Westphalia, as well as in two large cities elsewhere, Berlin and Leipzig.[47] For Austria the agrarian problem was still of central importance; a proletariat, in fact, had only just begun to appear—in Lower Austria, Bohemia and Moravia.

Alongside the contradiction between agricultural and industrial production, there emerged another one which was tragic in its proportions and its consequences: the contradiction between the rural masses, bound to the past by the ancient rythms of seasonal labor, and the growing liberal-democratic movement among the bourgeoisie. This contradiction, which was scarcely evident in the lands of western Europe, was of incalculable importance in central Europe. It was especially prominent in the revolutionary movement in Austrian Galicia, which began in 1846 and pursued ambitious goals of national unification. The Austrians suppressed the revolt even without the help of Russia and Prussia. On February 18, 1846, they occupied Cracow, the last remnant of free Poland, and they crushed an attempted uprising at the end of the month. The Austrian provincial government in Galicia, therefore, was the first successfully to employ a recipe that later became common: national passions and fears were used to provide the occasion for imposing again the most extreme forms of dependence—the revolt of the Ukrainian peasants against their Polish landlords was immensely cruel.[48]

It would be oversimplifying to explain this rebellion as a product of the peasants' reactionary outlook, abetted by the propaganda of the government and the clergy. We know that similar troubles arose at about the same time in Lombardy, where the rural masses had the same lack of comprehension of the political aspirations of the landholding *signoria*, who were politically liberal and violently anti-Austrian. In central and eastern Europe feudalism had simply ply not yet died out, and the peasant, who yearned for his own freedom, did not discern in the government the immediate agent of this suppression simply because he had no direct contact with it. His oppressor was his lord, who wielded political as well as economic power as far as he was concerned. As long as the patrimonial system endured, the peasants lived under the pressure of the feudal pyramid, and it did not matter to them whether their lords supported the Habsburgs or opposed them. Thus it was natural in 1848 that the Galician peasants should turn against those whom they perceived as their oppressors and that they should regard the peak of the feudal pyramid, the ruler, as their sole support. This was the way in which the illusion of trust in the central authority had been maintained in Austria ever since the time of Josef II.

It is clear, then, that in the lands of central and eastern Europe the revolutions took place within a socioeconomic structure which was quite different from that of western Europe. Therefore the revolutions themselves were different, and Marxism presented an analysis of western European development. But the existence of industrial centers and of an urban proletariat in the Bohemian and Austrian lands distinguished these regions from the eastern half of the Habsburg monarchy, and this fact invites particular attention.

The social and ethnic composition of the western part of the Monarchy, as we shall soon see in greater detail, was rather complicated, and by the beginning of the nineteenth century the bureaucrats who were heirs of the Austrian Enlightenment and products of the first state schools were well aware of the complexities. The structure of society in central Europe in the middle of the nineteenth century, then, needs some clarification. "Social classes," generally speaking, are groups of people distinguished from one another by their position in the process of production and therefore by their role in the organization of society. We have already noted how Marx and Engels drew a distinction between the "proletariat" and the "working class." They spoke of the class "of itself" when the proletariat did not yet comprehend its social role, and the class "for itself" when the proletariat became aware of its function and its historical mission. Therefore it is not enough to ascertain that before 1848 there were so and so many individuals who may be classified in a particular relationship to the means of production, and then speak of them as a class. A social class is not a concrete object but a historical phenomenon characterized by the awareness and expression of certain interests on the basis of common experience. These interests may be contrasted with those of other groups, which are not only different but also usually in conflict.[49]

This common experience shared by the individuals composing a social class is a result of the relations of production into which the individuals themselves were born or into which they entered during their lives, voluntarily or otherwise. Class consciousness is therefore the way in which class experiences are given form. "Bourgeois" sociology, derived from the work of Max Weber and his pupil Talcott Parsons, uses the term "class" in this "concretized" sense—as a component of the social structure—while on the other hand it considers "class consciousness" to be the unfortunate invention of erring intellectuals: for anything that disrupts the harmonious coexistence of social groups (or "classes") is a regrettable "symptom of unjustified interruption" of the posited harmony.[50] In this view society is composed of groups with different "social functions," and the task of the sociologists, and of the social sciences generally, is to arbitrate among groups and classes, to get them to accept their social roles and, as far as possible, to "rectify and appease" their grievances.

It is obvious that if we understand a class to be a historical phenomenon, we must insist on studying actual class relationships in an actual historical context. We can do this by considering the changes that took place during a particular period within a class—a social and cultural phenomenon whose composition, ideas and institutions may be reasonably understood. From this point of view the simplest task would be to study classes which in 1848 had behind them centuries of development and thus centuries of accumulated class experience and consciousness. This may be found in abundance among the ruling class in feudal society, the landholding nobility. For members of the middle classes within the dominant nationalities the task is also relatively simple; for those of subject nationalities it is more difficult. But the situation is far more complicated, as we shall see, when it comes to the rural and urban masses in the pre-industrial age—*i.e.* for central Europe, before the year 1848.

Certainly it is possible to consider the urban population, anticipate its subsequent development and speak anachronistically of a "working class"—as did V. J. Tarle, for example, or M. J. Thompson for revolutionary France. But it is not possible in dealing with the countryside. Terms such as "rural population," or simply "the people," "the common people," "working people," the "working classes," "lower Estates" are all as imprecise as those employed by Burke or Taine for the driving forces of the French Revolution. Between these terms and others such as "mob," "rabble," "bandits" or "*canaille*" there is a vast difference of judgment. But both groups of words have one thing in common: they are stereotypes. More neutral is the designation "crowd," which today usually suggests a mob which is (still) behaving rationally. It is distinguished from "the people" or "the masses" by the fact that it manifests itself in a particular situation of conflict—during a strike, a street fight, a revolt, an uprising, or a revolutionary struggle. Therefore a crowd is not a collective phenomenon, as is for example a class, a nation, a political party, a "public" or any other group too numerous to lend itself to analysis on an individual basis.[51]

The crowd in the pre-industrial age may be a concrete object of historical study, and it has the advantage that the source materials can offer us important information, on condition, of course, that we elucidate the particular situations of conflict in which the crowd manifests itself. Then we can determine other facts: how large the crowd was; who its leaders were, if any; what kind of people composed it. The answers to these questions will reveal the character of the crowd and its behavior, but they also enable us to identify its members, to isolate individuals and groups, discover their social origins, their position and employment. Another group of questions concerns those who were the object of the crowd's attack. How large and determined were the forces mobilized against the crowd? What were the results of the conflict, and what was its historical significance?

4 New Problems and New Sources

Marx's, Engels's, and later Lenin's work on the problems of bourgeois revolutions, especially those of 1848, possesses several distinguishing features. In the first place, since it grew out of the authors' political experience, it is a prime source for the study of their views. Second, it originated from the viewpoint of "proletarian internationalism", so that all the problems were placed within a general historical frame. Thus the revolutions of 1848 in central Europe are viewed in the context of European, even world history. This by itself offers an antidote to much of the Czech, Austrian, German or Hungarian work which is often isolated and provincial, and at worst blindly nationalistic. Finally—what is most important for historians—the works of these men constitute a school of historical thought, method and technique, and their theoretical conclusions are a valuable aid for the modern historical sciences.[52]

In *The Situation of the Working Class in England*, written in 1844-5, Engels showed how statistical material may be used to illuminate an important problem: the influence of the Industrial Revolution upon the position of the proletariat and its formation as the "working class." Conditions on the Continent were considerably less advanced than in England, but it is no coincidence that this was the first work by the founders of scientific socialism to reach Bohemia and elicit some response. Even after the events of 1848 it attracted the attention of Anton Springer and F. L. Rieger.[53] Engels's analysis of English conditions offered a preview of where society in central Europe was headed. It would be a mistake to assume that useful knowledge about social evolution in central

Europe maybe drawn only from the parts of the classic Marxist *corpus* that are directly concerned with this part of the continent.

Just as history is indivisible, so too is the work of the historian. It is impossible to separate the methods from the techniques of historical scholarship. Methodology represents the theoretical basis of historical work and arms it with its fundamental means of perception; it assigns a scale of values and steers the historian towards particular kinds of problems. The methods of historical work are the concrete functions performed by the scholar; the techniques are the various kinds of special knowledge needed to deal with particular problems and materials.

Engels in the *Situation of the Working Class in England* and Marx in the *Class Struggles in France* and later in *Capital* demonstrated how newly formulated problems can be investigated by using source materials from the state administration and the capitalist entrepreneurs. But obviously they did not exaggerate the value of older historical work, which cannot satisfy the modern historian for our predecessors worked from different methodological principles; they posed different questions and possessed a different scale of values. On the other hand, Soviet historiography especially has shown that opportunities await historians when the old family archives are made available for research.

Between 1945 and 1948 the Czechoslovak government took over the administration of the archival collections that remained on the noble estates. These "agricultural and forest archives" usually included several kinds of materials. They contained documents concerning administrative functions (since the *patrimonia* carried out local administration and justice), as well as records of the economic activities of the estates. They also included personal papers of the noblemen, some of them private, others connected with their official or public functions. Since the estates of the Bohemian lands were generally more lucrative than those for example in the Tyrol or Voralberg, the aristocracy of the whole Austrian Monarchy endeavored to acquire lands in Bohemia or Moravia. Usually the noblemen preserved the papers of their ancestors, which included the original property titles or patents of office, in their urban residences at Vienna, Prague, or Brno. But when space ran out, the archives were often stored in their chateaux in the countryside and joined to the administrative records of the estates. Between the World Wars the State Agricultural Archive took over sixty-nine such archives, and after 1945 it administered all the estate archives in Czechoslovakia.

The organization of the materials was a superhuman task. In Bohemia and Moravia alone there were 1,582 separate domains in the middle of the nineteenth century. On the other hand, the 1,050 estates in Bohemia were distributed among only 187 noble families, according to František Palacký's calculations. In about 800 of the estates which were seats of an administrative apparatus, no archives were to be found because they had been moved to other estates belonging to the same family. The other 750 estates did contain records, and these were deposited in the branches of the State Archive system.[54]

Since most of these archival records have never been catalogued, it would be useless to proceed by attempting to draw up a list of names of the participants in the events of 1848. It would be far more profitable to consider just which problems can be investigated on the basis of the available materials and focus on them. There are about twenty archives which can really contribute something to our knowledge of developments in Austria between 1815 and the 1840s; and about half of these have something to reveal about the events of 1848 and 1849.

One of the most significant archives is one whose owner had a hand in its organization. Chancellor Metternich took a personal interest in his own papers, which later came to be called the *Acta Clementina*, and he kept them close by until his death. He also took the trouble to ensure that posterity would receive from this wealth of written material only what would contribute to what he regarded as a balanced picture. The Viennese archivist Klinkowström, following Metternich's suggestions, made a careful selection from the papers, and thanks to the support of the Chancellor's son Richard (who was for many years the Austrian ambassador in Paris), this is what was presented to the public. The selection included original documents and transcriptions, and it incorporated corrections that were made not very carefully by Richard with a blue pencil. Since the edition did not indicate where portions had been left out or altered, it gives only a sketchy indication of the archive's contents. Yet until the 1950s this set of papers remained the basic source for his biographers—the admiring von Srbik, the critical Bibl, as well as more recent authors such as Breycha-Vauthier, Berthier de Sauvigny, and Henry Kissinger.[55] The first historian to become better acquainted with more of Metternich's papers was the Humboldt University historian K. Obermann, whose work on 1848 drew repeatedly from the Metternich collection.[56] Even Obermann did not use all the material, because the *Acta Clementina* were made accessible only in 1969 with Antonín Haas's guides.[57] Still, it is now clear that Metternich's image as an elder statesman who withdrew from the political stage after March 13, 1848, is quite unreal and that the ex-Chancellor continued to play the mentor to the Court and the governments.

Far more difficult is the search for the papers of Metternich's arch-rival and emphemeral successor Franz Anton Kolowrat Libštejnský. The Kolowrat family archive, once stored at Rychnov nad Kněžnou, has preserved nothing of great significance concerning him; for he did not get on very well with the Kolowrats of Rychnov. At least a portion of his papers ended, through one of his heirs, in the Khuen-Lützow family archive. What has turned up is not very enlightening. Nor do the papers of Kolowrat's colleagues and competitors Mittrowsky, Hartig, and Chotek offer much insight, though all of them are valuable for economic questions, and the Hartig collection includes some documents which are damaging to the reputations of Metternich and Kübeck.[58] Some of the other marginally important family archives are those of Bellegrade, Dyem of Střítež, Kolowrat of Břenice, Lažanský, Nostitz-Rieneck, Waldstein-Wartenberg, Salm-Reifferscheidt, and Berchtold.[59]

Metternich's papers are supplemented by those of his successor Count Ficquelmont, which document his entire career through his journey to northern Italy in 1847, whose purpose according to Metternich was to steal a march on the spreading revolution.[60] Ficquelmont's papers are now in the Děčín branch of the State Archive at Litoměřice, along with some other important collections: Clary-Aldringen of Teplitz, Leo and Friedrich Thun-Hohenstein of Děčín, and General Eduard Clam-Gallas of Friedland. Edmund Clary-Aldringen participated in the events as a supporter of the "Protective Alliance" of the German-speaking bourgeoisie of Bohemia, and he observed their activities with a growing skepticism. Eduard Clam-Gallas considered himself a pupil of Radetzky and a representative of Windischgrätz, both of whose archives still suffer from neglect. The same is true of the papers of Metternich's confidant, the diplomat Friedrich Thun-Hohenstein, who is less well-known than his brothers Franz and Leo. Leo's activities have been studied often in recent years, and the value of his papers was early recognized by J. A. Helfert.

Windischgrätz and his cousin Felix Schwarzenberg were also among the Bohemian landholders. Windischgrätz's papers have been used by the Hungarian historian Erzsébet Andics in her work on Habsburg-Romanov collaboration against the Hungarian revolution. It is quite possible of course that all these documents were subjected to self-censorship, and the suspicion is particularly strong in the case of Windischgrätz, who arranged the material for his appearance before the military tribunal after his defeat in Hungary.[62]

A different kind of censorship may be observed in the papers of Felix Schwarzenberg, who ordered all his official correspondence destroyed after his death. Since his wishes were respected, his activities are more clearly revealed by the papers of Windischgrätz and Metternich than by the fragments of his own, which are preserved in the "Secret" Schwarzenberg Archive at Krumlov. But what remains include some interesting documents from his youth, as well as papers of his colleagues, once collected for a biography which was never published.[63]

The papers of two further prominent actors in the drama of 1848-9 present rather different problems. One of them was Josef Matthias Thun-Hohenstein, of the Klášterec branch of his family, an important figure in pre-March Bohemia. He was a correspondent of the Hungarian politician Széchenyi, a propagandist for Czech culture in German surroundings, and in 1848 the first president of the Slavonic Congress. His *Apology* was found by Václav Chaloupecký in the Lobkowitz Archive, and the rest of his papers are important in spite of their scantiness.[64] The second is Marshal Josef Lobkowitz, from the branch of his family at Dolní Beřkovice, who was not only the commander of the Prague National Guard but also the Military General Command's contact with the Court, where his correspondents included General Grünne and the leader of the counter-revolutionary faction, War Minister Baillet-Latour. After the defeat of the revolution in Prague, Lobkowitz served as Emperor Ferdinand's Adjutant, in which capacity he continued to represent the views of Windischgrätz and Schwarzenberg.[65] Thus he was in a more significant position than Clam-Gallas, who with Felix Schwarzenberg belonged among the collaborators of Radetzky.

The richness of these sources, together with the papers of Metternich's collaborator Hübner and those of the Archbishop of Olomouc Sommerau-Beck, make it easier to accept the fact that for our purposes the papers of the Auerspergs, Lažanskýs, Waldstein-Wartenbergs and Nostitzes are rather scanty, that those of the Stadions are unavailable and that the Lichnowsky archive has not yet been catalogued.[66] What is available amounts to a very rich source for a study of the social character of the Austrian Monarchy as well as the activities of its ruling class in 1848-9. But they are useful for much more than a purely individual approach: they form the basis for a "collective biography" of a power group and its changing role in the course of political events. The landed aristocrats sought to achieve their ambitions in the army, the diplomatic service, the state administration and through economic activity. We may distinguish the position of the old ruling class in some of the situations of conflict—the Prague riots of 1844, the Whitsun rebellion of 1848, the struggles in Vienna in October 1848. But its structure cannot be revealed by the family archives. For this the tax records are more useful—records that go back much farther than the "fifteen fateful years" before 1848.

Methods of quantification may be applied to the aristocracy just as appropriately as to the middle class, and to some extent, at least, they may also be applied to the emerging working class. They are obviously useful in explaining the structure of a society, the formation of its classes, or exploring the phenomenon of the "demographic revolution" from the eighteenth century to the twentieth. In the political history of the pre-industrial age, methods of quantification can be used to study the participants in collective actions: strikes, demonstrations, armed conflicts with the authorities, revolutionary movements. It is of course easier to study questions for which the material has already been collected. Such collections, however, can be used to answer only certain questions, usually the most obvious—how did the electors vote in 1848, or how did the members of the Imperial Parliament vote in 1848-9? If we wish to go further and find out why they voted as they did (why, for example, they voted to abolish the *robota* with or without conditions attached, or what their attitude towards the German Customs Union was), then we must begin to look for other kinds of statistical information. In doing so, moreover, we may wish to make the original question more precise or more comprehensive.[67]

New sources yielding answers to new problems are not usually available on demand. They require prepatory studies. For the present problems, some have appeared in my section of the historical seminar of Charles University in the 1950s and 1960s: L. Neckařová's study of Mazzini and the Bohemian question, the work by K. Novotný and M. Myška on the origins of the working class and the social composition of the workers in certain industries, or M. Hroch's investigation of the formation of the Czech bourgeoisie.[68] In addition, B. Löwenstein worked on the democratic movement in Germany; L. Sumavská on the response of the pre-March Czech press to the events in England and Ireland; M. Churaň and J. Vitula investigated the reporting of the conflicts in the Bohemian and Moravian press.[69] Some of the published work resulted from collaboration between teachers and students. A study of the first Bohemian railroads is an example; a book about the Congress of Troppau came from the historical seminar of the University of Olomouc; and work was published on the study of history at the Universities of Prague and Olomouc around the year 1848. There was also a collaborative translation of Karl Obermann's *Fourth Estate in the Revolution of 1848*, and finally a study of *Austria, Prussia and Germany* in the middle of the century.[70]

Most of these works were frankly polemical, addressed to those Austrian historians who looked back nostalgically to the days of "great Austria." This sort of bias was less evident in the work done for the centennial in 1948 than, for instance, in the popularized treatment by Alexander Nowotny, R. Endres's book on the Austrian revolution, or M. Ehnl's biography of Messenhauser. On the other hand, the studies by R. Kiszling, H. Benedikt, and A. Wandruszka, while displaying a good deal of nostalgia, are nevertheless of high quality.[71] Compared with these, it is difficult to accept the work of H. Hantsch, whose view of the nationality problems in Austria did not progress beyond that of J. A. Helfert. A less extreme view was presented in A. Lhotsky's historiographical essays and E. Zöllner's textbook for university students.[72] The biographical sketches by R. Lorenz, A. Nowotny and L. Jedlicka are scarcely more than anecdotes and reminiscences, but the studies by Austrian archivists have maintained the traditionally high standards: Walther's book on Doblhoff's mission to Innsbruck and the work by R. Neck.[73] The well-meant contributions of the Austrian Marxists E. Priester and E. Fischer strove with only partial success for a scientific investigation of complicated problems.[74]

The west German historiography of the period was similarly diverse. Perhaps the most valuable is the work on the beginnings of the Industrial Revolution in Austria, followed closely by C. Thienen-Adlerflycht's biography of the young Leo Thun, which was partly based on Czechloslovak archival sources, and the studies by Friedrich Prinz.[75] For a long time North American historians—A. J. May, J. Blum, and R. Kann—remained dependent on the Austrian materials,[76] although more recently, R. John Rath's *History of the Viennese Revolution of 1848* and Stanley Pech's book about the Czech revolution have made use of more varied sources, and William Langer has offered an interpretation of central European developments in a broadly continental context.[77] Finally, S. Fischer-Galati, V.L. Tapié, and J. Droz have regarded 1848 as the turning point in the nationality problems of central Europe.[78]

E. Winter's work on the pre-March period should be mentioned with that of Karl Obermann, as one of the best portraits of the age; and the studies by E. Wolfgramm have contributed much to our understanding of Czech-German relations.[79] Soviet historians have continued the pioneering work bby R. Averbuch, and contributions have appeared by B. F. Porshnev, A. Benedik, A. L. Narochnitsky and A. S. Nifontov.[80]

The work by Karl Obermann and Erzsébet Andics comes closest to our set of problems. But there is also some Czech work which is indispensable for an analysis of pre-March Bohemian society. M. Novák's *The Austrian Police and Political Development in Bohemia Before 1848* has not yet been fully appreciated. K. Herman has contributed to our knowledge of Czech panslavism, F. Cervinka has explored currents of Czech nationalism in the nineteenth century, and V. Záček has described the situation in Silesia as well as the activities of Cyprián Lelek and J. V. Frič. Conditions in Moravia have been the subject of work by B. Sindelář, J. Radimský, M. Wunschová, J. Kolejka, and M. Trapl.[81]

The late Ludmila Karníková produced an ambitious demographic analysis of the Bohemian lands from 1754 to 1914, and the studies by M. Hroch and J. Havránek provide the foundation for all further work in nineteenth-century Czech history. E. Arnold has found his biographer in Josef Kočí, whose book also provides the best general portrait of the Czech radical-democrats. Jan Ohéral and Božena Němcová, along with the less well-known Chovanetz and Klácel, have been the subjects of biographies which concern themselves as well with the events of 1848.[82] The same may be said of F. Jílek's work on the Prague Polytechnic and Belda's study of Liberec. The political events have been described by V. Pokorný, J. Lepčík and the tireless František Roubík.[83]

There is no reason to complain, then, that the period has been neglected. Nor is it likely that 1848 will become less relevant in the future. Future work will have to come to terms, of course, with the findings of earlier scholarship. The problems dealt with by the more recent work are so new themselves that there is little danger of the same questions being covered by two historians at once. The study of the two farthest-removed protagonists in the sociopolitical conflict in 1848—the feudal landholding aristocracy on the one hand and the much-feared proletarian crowds in Prague and Vienna on the other—is no simple matter even today. It is perhaps tempting to satisfy oneself with the conclusion that the problem will be better resolved once more sources are made available and when the centers of historical research are better equipped to employ methods of quantification. But the same could be said of any problem at any time. I believe that it is possible to begin the long journey toward solving the problem by gathering the knowledge that is presently available, especially to point the way for young readers. The results of historical work are always provisional, and this is as it should be. What can hope to have lasting significance are not the conclusions of a study as much as the instruction contained in its method of dealing with problems. Because the results which the reader has before him now are in many ways different from a literary or a cinematic image of the pre-March era—most familiar, perhaps to today's audience—it may be hoped that there will be no lack of people who in reading the following chapters will pose further questions.

II
Between Two Revolutions

> Our pardonable dissatisfaction with the flaws and inadequacies of our present situation always diminishes when we cast our gaze toward the future: what a prospect we behold, and what hopes!
>
> K.J. Vietz, *Das Studium der allegmeinen Geschichte*, Prague 1844

1. The Age of Industrial and Political Revolution

The decade of the 1840s has been called a period of hope and a period of poverty. Its culmination arose from dislocations in the lower end of the social spectrum, which in turn resulted from the industrial revolution on the one hand and the social and political revolution of 1789 in France on the other.

The population of Europe in the middle of the eighteenth century has been estimated at 140 million. It had grown to 188 million by 1800, and it reached 266 million by the middle of the century. Therefore the population of Europe rose by 40 percent in the first half of the nineteenth century. In Great Britain the increase was from 11 to 22 million, in Ireland from 5 to 8½ million; at the other end of the continent, in Russia, the figures are 39 million and 60 million. This amounts to a genuine demographic explosion.[1]

But was the growth in numbers accompanied by a change in the composition of society? Certainly the industrial revolution changed the very foundations of the social structure. Yet on the surface little was changed. It is truly amazing how much of the feudal structure survived the French Revolution and Napoleon's régime. Resistance to change was tenacious. In the first place, Europe, with the exception of Switzerland, was a continent of monarchies. The republican movement in the middle of the nineteenth century was a minority movement. Moreover, its effect was to strengthen the position of monarchical institutions: once confronted with new social forces, the monarchies composed their differences with their aristocracies, and the tension that used to exist between them vanished. In most European countries landed property was still the primary form of wealth—and of political power. The nobility was a class of feudal landholders; in many parts of Europe noblemen still exercised much of their feudal authority, and the prestige that landed property carried with it led the more successful middle-class entrepreneurs to invest their profits in land.

Only in France and the nearby areas most directly affected by the Revolution did small holdings predominate. After 1815 there were more than six million landholders in France, and most of them had only miniature holdings. Balzac's novels of rural life give us a concrete picture of the society of the 1830s and 1840s, ruled over by the gentry, wealthy peasants, and officials. In Great Britain, by contrast, 500 noble families controlled nearly half the arable land. To a great extent the holdings of these families had originated in the eighteenth century and were acquired from commerce in east Indian teas, west Indian sugar and African slaves. A number of these families traditionally served the state or the East India Company, and they maintained their leading position in spite of the the parliamentary reform of 1832. The nobility controlled the House of Lords, of course, but also in the lower House there were 100 descendants of lords and 200 members elected at their sufferance. They composed nearly half the lower house. Between 1832 and 1866 there were 64 ministers of aristocratic origin; only 12 were lawyers, and 5 were primarily involved in commerce.[2]

In the Scandinavian countries and in the Netherlands there was a free peasantry, but the noble landholders enjoyed a monopoly of political power. Farther to the east the power of the nobility remained unshaken. In Prussian Silesia nearly half of the land was in the hands of 54 magnates, who also controlled the army, the Church and the state administration. In 1842 9 of the 11 Prussian ministers, 29 of the 30 diplomats, 20 of the 28 provincial governors, and 7,264 of 9,434 army officers came from the ranks of the nobility. The Prussian Lichnowskys and Pucklers were more than equal to the Russian Sheremetyevs and Vorontsovs.[3] In the east of Europe there was also a numerous impoverished nobility along with the wealthy magnates, and they, too, enjoyed feudal privileges.

In the middle of the nineteenth century, then, European society was still predominantly agrarian, and it was ruled by a privileged feudal minority who exploited the mass of the people. The aristocracy of course opposed anything that might threaten its position. The French Revolution had demonstrated that landed property could be confiscated, monarchy overthrown, and that the bourgeoisie could replace the old ruling class. The defeat of France in 1815 did not remove the fear of a possible resurgence of revolution on the French model. The system of great powers associated with the Austrian Chancellor Metternich—the "M System," "Pentarchy," or less precisely the "Holy Alliance"—emerged at the initiative of Britain and Austria as early as 1813, from talks held at Prague and Teplitz, whose purpose was to renovate the "old régime." Metternich of course was too much the heir of the eighteenth century Enlightenment to be unaware that the bourgeoisie was on the rise. Therefore he was not flatly opposed to all change, but he favored gradual change. Still, some of his proposals, at least, were regarded as so dangerous that Francis I and Nicholas I stored them in the secret compartments of their writing tables. Metternich had some success at the Congress of Aix-la-Chapelle in 1818, but at the Congress of Troppau, called at the end of 1820 to deal with the revolution in Italy, he achieved little agreement with the British and French. The Congress of Vienna in 1823 gave France a free hand for intervention in Spain, but British diplomacy opposed intervention in Spanish America. Later the British and Russians opposed Metternich's legitimism and favored the Greek independence movement; and the July Revolution of 1830 in Paris brought a real upset in the country itself as well as a threat to international stability. Metternich's plans were ruined by the opposition of international financiers. The Rothschild concern, which until now supplied resources for the "Holy Alliance" opposed intervention against France or Belgium and now began instead to support the "liberal" Franco-British coalition.[4]

After 1830 Europe expected a revolutionary wave in England, where the bourgeoisie was stronger than in France and where the elements of crisis were abundantly evident. The Reform Bill of 1832 gave expression to the growing community of interest between the landed aristocracy and the middle classes. Of the aristocratic members of the Commons between 1841 and 1847, fully 15 percent were actively engaged in commerce, and 35 percent were involved in the management of industrial concerns.[5]

On the whole, however, the revolutionary threat in the beginning of the 1830s was successfully met mainly by Austria and Russia. In Italy, Poland, and Germany it was crushed chiefly because in these countries the bourgeoisie was not yet strong enough to bring about social and political changes. This did not mean, however, that there was no social conflict. The agrarian question lay behind the "tithe war" in Ireland in the 1830s and the rebellion of 1842 and 1843 in Wales. It lay, too, behind the numerous rebellions in Russia and the mass uprisings of peasants in Galicia in 1846. In Bohemia the Social Question—in other words the poverty of the working masses—led to the rebellion of rural weavers in 1844 and an uprising of railway workers two years later.[6]

From Ireland to eastern Europe we see everywhere the same picture in the countryside. The commons were being destroyed, land was "regulated," and the rural population, for whom there was not enough land, continued to increase. In England and Wales the "agricultural proletariat," the landless peasantry, represented about one-fifth of the entire population. In Ireland, where the situation was worst of all, six to seven thousand English landlords controlled 90 percent of the land. For the most part, the Irish peasant subsisted on a small potato-field in return for which he was obliged to work on his landlord's fields. The Irish duty labour, equivalent to the central European *robota*, had its analogy also in Italy, where the hated *signori* impoverished the mass of the rural population by taking half their yield and extracting other feudal dues. In Germany the land reform of 1807 permitted the peasants to buy themselves free of their feudal obligations, usually by giving up between a third and a half of their lands, and they gained only about 14 percent of the former common lands.[7]

The progressive liquidation of small landholdings, the consolidation of large domains and the appearance of a rural proletariat, assumed explosive proportions with the sharp increase in population. It appears that this increase resulted from two newly arrived realities: first, an increased food production and second, a trend toward earlier marriage, begun with the dissolution of the older feudal restrictions. The growth in food production is accounted for by the potato. However incredible it may seem, English and Irish peasants were able to feed a family of seven, a cow, and a pig from one acre of potatoes. Poor soil, prepared only by a hoe, was sufficient, and its yield was four times as great as an acre of corn. Thus in central Europe in 1830 a young man with only a patch of ground could marry; and since girls could marry much earlier than had been the case before, they produced more children.[8]

These realities enabled some landlords to increase their profits. Some English landlords established a "model" economy on their estates, and they were visited by their Continental counterparts—among them for example the Thun-Hohensteins of Děčín. Societies were founded to improve production methods, and even some peasants tried to learn new techniques: the unfree peasants of the Mělník region sent their representatives to Kent to learn about the kind of poles used there in the cultivation of hops. But a substantial increase in production resulting from new techniques cannot be demonstrated in Bohemia before the middle of the nineteenth century. Until then most of the work continued to be performed by hoe.

Until about the early 1840s food production in Europe kept pace with the rising population, thanks to the potato and the increasing amount of land under cultivation. But then a crisis developed. In some places the potatoes were attacked by blight, and even where it did not appear, overpopulation began to have results in the countryside—overpopulation in the sense that there was insufficient food at a price which an average worker could afford, and that there were not enough opportunities to find work whose wages would support a family. The situation was probably the worst in Ireland, where the numbers of unemployed—those out of work for more than four months out of a year—was estimated at half a million in the 1840s. If their dependents are considered, the unemployment affected three-eighths of the population. The outcome was famine and, for those able to pay passage, migration to America.[9]

The situation was not much better in Scotland and England, in Flanders or southwestern Germany. Everywhere we find seasonal migration, and after 1840 sizable emigration overseas. The same problem appeared even in Russia, where it was solved by the mass transfer of serfs from the overpopulated areas of central Russia to the southeastern regions. In 1843 alone the numbers of people involved came to 171,000.[10]

Were the European aristocratic landowners aware of the immanent crisis? The English example, leading to the discovery of new production techniques and to more enlightened social relationships, already had its Continental admirers. Among them were the future unifier of Italy Count Cavour, the Hungarian progressive Széchenyi, and in Bohemia members of the Děčín branch of the Thun-Hohenstein family.[11] But autocrats like Francis I of Austria and Tsar Nicholas I were also aware of the urgency of the peasants' predicament. Still, no far-reaching reforms were possible simply because no ruler wished to become the target of the aristocrats' wrath. The latter insisted that the feudal relationships were divinely ordained and thus unalterable.

Of course there was no shortage of views about how to deal with impending social conflict. One of them was derived from Thomas Malthus's teaching about the necessity to limit the population—a limitation upon personal freedom which can be seen in practice today only in South African *Apartheid*. The beginnings of social legislation in England, called forth by fear of the revolutionary rumblings of 1830-31, were of a more positive character. Care of the poor was removed from the hands of local authorities. The poor were placed in "workhouses," which was to say that nobody capable of working should live from charity. There was, however, a public outcry against the new system. The London *Times* printed horrifying stories about conditions amounting to forced labor. Charles Dickens's *Oliver Twist*, published in 1836, was a most effective expression of the general revulsion against the institution.[13]

If by industrial revolution we mean the mechanization and concentration of production processes, and the substitution of mechanized power for human labor, then Great Britain was the one industrialized country in Europe in the 1840s. Industrial production already accounted for 35 percent of the gross national product, and the annual rise was an unheard-of 3 percent.[14]

Great Britain, or more specifically England and Wales, were the models of industrialization for the rest of the world. To discover their impact in central

Europe, we must begin with the early years of the century, when F.H. Salm-Reifferscheidt, the founder of an ironworks at Blansko near Brno, went to England to learn the latest methods of iron production. The English industrialist family of Baildon were connected by marriage with the family of J.V. Homoláč of Silesia, who owned ironworks in northern Moravia. In 1814 a member of this family built the first steam engine in the Bohemian lands. After Salm came the professor of the Prague Polytechnic F.A. Gerstner, builder of the first horsedrawn railway between Budweis and Linz, who had visited England three times and made use of his experiences when he wrote his textbook on mechanics in 1831.[15] After him came Franz Xavier Riepl, from 1817 to 1820 director of the Fürstenberg iron works at Nový Jáchymov, who as a pupil of Gerstner began to combine his interest in metallurgy with a lively appreciation of the possibilities of railroads. Beginning in 1820 Riepl taught at the Vienna Polytechnic, but at the same time he served as consultant to various feudal entrepreneurs, including the Moravian governor Mittrowsky, who wished to modernize his ironworks at Sobontína, and the Archbishop of Olomouc the Archduke Rudolf, who had decided to augment his ironworks at Friedland with a new one at Vítkovice. Riepl was well aware of the crucial significance of the Ostrava region with its coal deposits. But since the deposits of iron that had been found in the Beskydy Mountains seemed unpromising, the Vítkovice ironworks began in 1828 to import ore from Styria. As early as 1829 Riepl had devised plans for a railroad to connect the salt deposits of Bochnia in Galicia and the coal mines of Ostrava with Vienna; from here the line would continue to the iron deposits of Styria. Salomon Rothschild immediately recognized the importance of the project, and in 1820 he sent Riepl to England to learn first-hand about steam engines from the Stephenson brothers. Riepl made full use of his stay in England. In Pennydaran in Wales he hired three foundry experts—David Evans, David Thomas, and William Jones—to work for three years in the Archduke Rudolf's Vítkovice ironworks and impart their skills to Moravian workers.[16] The Welshmen blamed the relatively poor quality of the Moravian product on the continued use of charcoal. Therefore in 1835 Riepl left once again, this time for London. The following year a new furnace of his own design was installed at Vítkovice.

From 1837 the Vítkovice works was served by the Northern Railroad, and in the beginning of the 1840s it shifted from charcoal to coke from Ostrava. The Mittrowsky ironworks at Sabotína and Štěpánov were also built after English models. These were taken over by middle-class entrepreneurs, the brothers Klein, who came from a wealthy north Moravian peasant family. The Kleins had acquired engineering skills at the *Realgymnasium* in Brno and had first put them to use in the construction of a dam in the Liechtenstein castle park at Led-nice. In the 1820s they worked on the construction of Imperial roads and in the 1830s became involved in railway construction, chiefly the Northern Line in Moravia. This carried them easily into the manufacture of rails and bridge construction, the acquisition of mining interests in the Ostrava region, and even a brief period of competition with the Rothschilds themselves.[17]

The Fürstenbergs also followed the English model. Their rolling mill at Stará Hut' near Beroun, completed in 1842, was built by Edward and James Thomas. The brothers owned a workshop in Libeň, where Edward moved in 1832 from Reichenberg, where he had been engaged in the manufacture of textile machinery. His partner in this enterprise, Thomas Bracegirdle, later established a machine shop in Brno. Another place where "English" machinery established itself was the Prague suburb of Karlín, where there were factories belonging to Joseph Lee, David Evans, and Ruston.[18] A still wider acceptance of British models was hampered by several obstacles, especially an insufficiency of raw materials. Nevertheless the prevalence of the English model in Bohemia is remarkable. England served at once as a teacher and a warning: the new forest of chimneys plainly meant the end of the traditional forms of craft production.

The immediate repercussions of the technical advances were political as well as economic. The railroads were welcomed also by the army, whose commanders dreamed of a network connecting Vienna, Berlin, and St. Petersburg, making possible a rapid transfer of soldiers and creating a system of defense for the "northern" powers. At the same time, the German political economist Friedrich List suggested a plan to connect the lands of the German Union by a link through Dresden and Prague but excluding Vienna. The strategic possibilities of the telegraph were also being considered, though a telegraph network was still regarded as impracticable.

In this age of rapid progress, the process of economic change moved quite unevenly. Modern research, for instance, has shown that in Britain the years 1833-6 saw intensive development which was followed by a period of stagnation and regression, then a gradual recovery until 1839, followed by another crisis lasting until 1842. The years of prosperity that ensued came to an end with the railroad bankruptcy of 1845, accompanied by famine and other signs of crisis until 1849. All this also brought unforeseen problems for the bankers. In an age still without telegraph communications it was very difficult to predict supply and demand over large areas and gear production to the changing requirements of the market. People were aware that they were living in a new and rapidly changing world—a world which appeared to some to be filled with undreamed of opportunity but which was at the same time inconstant and uncertain.

Continental Europe, as we have seen, was predominantly agrarian throughout the first half of the nineteenth century, and it exported grain, livestock, and raw materials. Nonagrarian production was mainly of a traditional sort, concentrated in the urban centers, but with some crafts distributed through the countryside. The industrial revolution was realized everywhere only with difficulty. One general impediment to more rapid progress was an enduring penchant on the part of the wealthy to invest in agriculture. On the Continent, there was also a lack of the raw materials in which Great Britain was so rich: high quality iron ore and coal deposits. These were plentiful, to be sure, in the Ruhr valley, but their development was only just beginning. In most countries raw materials were imported or exported: rarely did they supply domestic industry on an appreciable scale. Only in Belgium, in fact, could British conditions be approximated, so that by 1850 coal and iron mining here had reached a modern level. In the middle of the century Belgian coal mines produced twice as much as the rest of the Continent together, and half of this was exported. The papers of the Beaufort-Spontin family archive enable us to trace the mining of coal at Florennes and St. Aubin near Namur from its beginnings in the 1760s. During the French Revolution the owners received more from the mines than from the traditional feudal income of the Marquisate of Florennes, and they fought staunchly for exemption from confiscation. The correspondence of the Intendant Paridant with the owners between 1819 and 1843 makes it possible to trace the rise of the mining and iron making enterprises to the middle of the century.[19]

Belgium also served as an industrial model for the rest of Europe, particularly for Germany, where Friedrich List, founder of the German Customs Union, had been trying since the 1830s to establish a railway network. The first connection, between Nuremberg and Fürth in 1835 was the work of Englishmen and had little value beyond publicity. The Berlin-Potsdam line in 1838 was similar, but soon after several important lines were opened: Dresden-Leipzig-Magdeburg in 1839-40 and above all the Cologne-Antwerp line in 1843, which relieved German goods of high Dutch customs duties.

By the middle of the century England possessed a true railway network, but the Continent did not. Nevertheless, it was already possible to travel by train from London, via Calais, Boulogne and Dieppe, to Paris and Dijon; from Antwerp through Brussels or Namur to Cologne or Hanover; or from Hamburg through Berlin and Dresden to Leipzig. From Berlin one could travel to Poznań by way of Stettin, or else to Cracow and Warsaw via Breslau. Galicia was connected via Bohumín and Přerov in Moravia with Vienna and Laibach.[20]

The mechanized manufacture of cotton was edging out the traditional ways of making woolen cloth and linen. The European linen manufacturers could not compete with the factory-made cloth of Britain and northern Ireland. In central Europe the mechanical finishing of cotton was done earliest in small workshops in the mountains where there was sufficient water power. But around 1830 other sources of power came into use, and factories appeared in many places.[21] By 1848 Britain still had no Continental competitor, with the exception perhaps of Belgium, where the textile center at Ghent was truly in a position to challenge Manchester and other English centers. In Europe we can look for the new industrial proletariat only in the centers of the textile industry. But at the same time the position of both the traditional nonagrarian manufacturers and of the poorer peasants who supplemented their income by weaving, was being threatened. It may be said that around 1848 the industrial revolution was sufficiently advanced to threaten the old social order but not yet to bring about any improvement in the lot of the masses of the people.

A counterpart to the rural landless propulation had appeared in scattered areas: the factory proletariat. A new division of wealth had come into being which altered the distribution of power and influence in favor of the bourgoisie or "middle classes." These terms appeared in England and France in the beginning of the nineteenth century, and before 1848 the idea of "social classes" was already very fashionable. In the lands of western Europe the bourgeoisie ceased to correspond to the "burgher" class. In the struggle for political power which was the legacy of the French Revolution, writers, philosophers, historians, and politicians formed a new, idealized conception of the bourgeoisie fighting vigorously against the feudal aristocrats. In this context the "bourgeoisie" originally meant the "middle classes," which stood between the "privileged aristocrats" and the "lower," "working" or "uneducated" classes. As early as 1824 the French novelist Stendhal distinguished the "hereditary" aristocracy from the aristocracy of wealth—the *haute* or *grande* bourgeoisie who had grown wealthy from industry and commerce. They were a new class, different from the earlier middle class and distinguishable from the "investment bourgeoisie"—the *rentiers* who lived without employment from their investments and who until now were a peculiarity of France. Further, there were wealthy shopkeepers and farmers, to whom may be added the craftsmen, the lower clergy, small merchants and landholders, and the intelligentsia—together the "petite bourgeoisie." Stendhal, notably, devoted no attention to the most numerous social group, which included day laborers, journeymen, factory workers, and agricultural laborers—all those who depended upon the work of their hands.[22]

It would be an oversimplification to conclude that members of the aristocracy without exception turned their backs on economic enterprise. Beginning in the eighteenth century we may find everywhere in Europe rulers like Francis Stephen of Lorraine, the husband of Maria Theresa, whose factory at Holice in

Moravia supplied fine china to many of the central European chateaux. In the first half of the nineteenth century Francis' grandson, the Archbishop of Olomouc Rudolf of Habsburg was remarkably enterprising during his short lifetime. Louis Philippe of France accumulated vast wealth and felt most at home among the bankers of Paris. William I of the Netherlands was a political conservative and a ruthless entrepreneur. Belgium provides the examples of Leopold I and his nephew Prince Albert, husband of Queen Victoria, who was responsible for the great industrial exposition in London in 1851.

Even though the Salms, Fürstenbergs or Sternbergs may be cited as central European aristocratic entrepreneurs, the fact remains that most of the economic enterprise here was the work of the bourgeoisie. Very often we find that the first generation of capatalist dynasties were men who had mastered new techology. The second and third generations were of course no longer "self-made" men, and they were likely to move in financial and commerical circles. Entrepreneurs with a background in banking were often liable to embark on the doubtful road toward ennoblement; they acquired titles, bought estates, and transformed themselves into aristocrats. The same process may be observed among some of the industrialist families as well, though usually a generation or so later. On the whole, they were uninterested in politics, which of course is not to say that they wielded no political influence.

There are, of course, only rare cases of entrepreneurs who were fully aware of their responsibilities in connection with the "social question." In 1843 Thomas Carlyle wrote that "from the beginning of human society the condition of millions of working people has never been so intolerable as it is in our own day."[23] Although it is difficult to generalize about an age in which statistics were first being gathered, we are entitled to attempt some judgments, just as Carlyle did. How numerous were the "poor" of Europe? The best estimates suggest that they formed about a fifth of the population in the sixteenth century and about a third in the nineteenth. But we know, too, that in the seventeenth century capitalist metropolis of Amsterdam nearly 90 percent of the inhabitants were counted as "poor"—that is, they were unable to pay taxes or provide decent burial for their dead.[24]

Did the industrial revolution bring about a rise or a fall in the standard of living? A recent discussion by British historians offered no clear conclusion. Was there an improvement in diet when white bread replaced black? The availability of meat may have improved, but certainly the living conditions in the cities deteriorated. Wages rose, particularly those of the skilled workers, but this fact is misleading if we forget to take account of expenses. Day laborers and skilled industrial workers made just enough to live, but weavers were known to be among the very poor everywhere. And what can be said of women and children who worked for a half or even a fourth of the wages of an adult male worker? What can be said of the fact that the introducton of gas lighting meant that work no longer went from dawn to dusk but stretched fourteen or fifteen hours, with an hour and a half off for meals? Work in the factories, moreover, could not be regulated as work at home could, because the machines inexorably required a steady and extreme effort. And over this impoverished existence there hung the threat of uncertainty, unemployment, famine. What can be said of the situation of the forty thousand Silesian weavers, of whom three quarters did not make enough to live on in 1844? The governments of the day were simply unequipped to cope with such problems.

It appears that the "pessimist" historians are nearer the mark than their "optimist" colleagues. So were the observers of the first half of the nineteenth century who concluded that the industrial revolution accomplished no change for the better. Today we know that reality may be more accurately reflected by reconstructing the situation of individual families than by merely tracing wage levels. But such a family situation can be discovered only with the greatest difficulty. If a working-class family spent 60 to 70 percent of its income on food and drink, the fact testifies to an unutterably low standard of living. Friedrich Engels, Mrs. Gaskell, and a legion of other reporters have left descriptions of working-class quarters which may well compete with Dante's *Inferno*. The narrow streets of the large industrial cities, teeming with half-naked children playing in garbage, the insufficiency of water and absence of sewer systems, all created conditions in which a half of all children did not reach the age of five and those who did could look forward to perhaps another 35 years. The deprivations drove people to crime in London or Liverpool, just as in Ireland or Sicily. Dickens's *Oliver Twist* or Eugene Sue's *Secrets of Paris* might be read with profit by the authorities of present-day New York or Chicago, who are fighting so fruitlessly against crime among young people—only the "rough spirits" have been replaced by heroin. Sue modeled his Paris bourgeoisie on J.F. Cooper's portrait of American settlers living among savage Indians. And in England Benjamin Disreaeli gave expression to the reality posited by the *Communist Manifesto*. There was no longer just one nation in England but two, and the traditional one was growing ever more appalled at its desperate and dangerous neighbors.[26]

In the beginning the proletariat reacted to the unemployment, poverty, and misery by destroying the machines. This was widespread in England in the second decade of the nineteenth century, and in Prague it occurred regularly in the 1840s. The proletariat was the driving force behind the struggles of the silk workers of Lyons in 1831 and 1834, of the Silesian weavers and the Prague cartoon-printers of 1844, as well as the "potato war" in Berlin in April 1847.[27]

The uprisings themselves were not usually planned and led by a few daylaborers but rather by skilled craftsmen and journeymen who were educated by travel and experience and were thus in a better position than laborers to establish contacts with bourgeois radicals. Otherwise workers' organizations did not exist at all, and attempts to establish them were severely punished. The state proceeded with the same firmness against strikers, who in Paris and Lyons were dealt with by the army. A certain measure of organization was possible only in England, where the so-called "social novels" of Charles Dickens, Disraeli's *Sybil*, Charlotte Brontë's *Jane Eyre* and Elizabeth Gaskell's *May Barton* coerced the bourgeois public into a certain awareness of the "social question." But since these novels offered no prospect of relief outside better education and gradual reform, they could have little real impact.

The government of Britain was aware of one thing that at least some of the Continental governments learned to accept—they bore responsibility for the entire population of their country. But in England as elsewhere the owners of factories still believed that the best protection against the dangerous proletariat was a high wall around their parks and villas. They were not always high enough to protect their owners from the logical outcome of sharpening class antagonism.[28] The same impasse was also reached in Austria.

2 What was Austria before 1848?

"We stand now where France stood in 1789. Very soon it will be decided whether we are to stand as a warning to those who believe that a mere individual can stop the turning wheel of history." These words come from the second volume of a tract published in 1847 by the Tyrolean baron Victor Andrian about Austria, the "China of Europe."[29] The first volume, which appeared in 1842, had already caused a great stir and become a political textbook especially for the opposition in the Diet. It was followed by a flood of pamphlets by a great variety of authors. In Austria they were bureaucrats, soldiers, noblemen, and middle-class liberals: Bauernfeld, Schuselka, Möring, Koch, and Tebeldi. Others came from Bohemia: the impoverished, eccentric Baron Schirnding, Leo Thun and his cousin Josef Matthias, Count Friedrich Deym, Jacob Malý, and A. Strobach. Even Metternich was drawn into the "pamphlet war," but the authors who wrote for him—J.C. Sporschill, Baron Hügel, Julian Chownitz, Anton Gross-Hoffinger—were not exactly master publicists. Most of the "opposition" authors favored a division of governmental power and the participation of the "people"—i.e. the bourgeoisie—in the government; a minority favored Josephine absolutism. The first group was divided into supporters of the Diets and supporters of modern representative reforms without consideration of the old "historical rights" of the individual lands. The Austrian authors were chiefly interested in a general program for reorganizing Austria, less interested in foreign policy, and were scarcely aware of the nationality question. They ignored the nationalist movements of the non-German and non-Hungarian peoples; at the same time, they exaggerated the danger of Russian political panslavism. One exception was the author of a pamphlet called *Austria and Russia*, who made fun of this spectre, but who was also the only one to put forward a defense of Metternich's foreign policy.[30] Only rarely did the Bohemian authors take note of social problems; instead they focused on the nationality question. Those authors who were noblemen, just like those of the bourgeoisie, fought chiefly for the use of Czech in the schools. Leo Thun and F.C. Kampelík published articles in favor of making Czech an official administrative language of the kingdom. Strobach shared their view but never published it. Taking their cue from the Hungarians as well as the English Parliament, the Estates opposition launched a movement to reform the state administration, but they lacked a clear program. Friedrich Deym, spokesman of the opposition, went furthest in his observations, and he formulated a special kind of federalist solution to the situation. The middle-class writers vacillated between a "statist" conception and a romantic Austroslavism.

The views of the political publicists of the 1840s, suprisingly enough, were not nearly as pessimistic as those of their predecessors in the early 1830s. At that time the President of the Court Chamber Kübeck noted a number of interesting points in his diary. Metternich's propagandist concluded as early as the end of 1830 that revolution in Austria was unavoidable, and in February 1832 he compared the Monarchy to a mosaic whose base had softened and which would fall to pieces at the first blow. In the same year Pillersdorf confided to Kübeck: "The political revolts that presently shake us are but the expression of a larger, deeper revolution in society itself. It is aimed against the noble families—their authority their dominion and their privileges. Were it possible to hold out in Austria for a few more years, then a more gradual change could be effected. But it appears that Providence has decided otherwise. At present we are ruled by three personalities, each moving in a different direction. Metternich is trying to preserve the present situtation, and like a great moth he is choking the life and strength of the state." In May 1833 Metternich himself rebuked his rival Kolowrat for supporting those who favored innovations, thereby eroding the foundations of the Empire. Kolowrat replied in horror:

"I am an aristocrat by birth and outlook, and I agree with you entirely that it is necessary to work for conservative objectives and to act accordingly. Our views, however, differ as to the means. Yours are a forest of bayonets and a shrill insistence on that which is. In my opinion, this attitude merely plays into

41

the hands of revolution. We weaken the government, drain its strength, oppress the masses and destroy their well-being. Thus we create great discontent, along with pressure for improved conditions. We shall provoke the middle classes into hatred of our own class, whom they presently envy and fear. Our task is to take any action and make any concession that will assure the material well-being of the masses—in return for their hard work. We must suppress all abuses and excesses, but we must also welcome among us capable new men, for we can strengthen ourselves only through the acquisition of fresh elements. This alone can save us. Your way will lead us to ruin, perhaps not in a year but sill soon enough.''[31]

Although Kübeck's diary must be used with caution, it appears that this individual example of the "fresh element" in the state administration gave quite a reliable account of pre-March conditions—if we make allowances for his bilious temperament. Friedrich Engels's series of articles in the New York *Daily Tribune* gives a similar impression of the multinational Austrian Monarchy.[32]

The official Austrian yearbook, the *Hof-und Staats-Handbuch des oesterreichischen Kaiserthums* of 1847, provides an ample view of the Monarchy's antiquated organization, fully justifying Kübeck's complaint that the chaotic administration was uncontrollable. In theory Austria was an absolute monarchy. In fact, as we shall see, it was ruled by the aristocracy. The administration consisted of three graduated stages: The Imperial Court, the state offices, and the offices of the various lands.[33]

The monarchy rested with the dynasty of Habsburg-Lorraine, which had won a measure of broad sympathy under Maria Theresa, Josef II and Leopold II. But the government of Francis I, Austrian Emperor from 1804, was revealingly characterized by his Italian subjects as the régime of a "Nero in a bathrobe." His strange mixture of *Volkstümlichkeit*, patriarchalism, and incredible harshness, his incorrigible vacillation and fear of making decisions have startled historians to this day—perhaps they might also interest psychologists. But it is certain that Francis I found his alter ego in his Minister and Chancellor Metternich. It is difficult to decide whether Francis suffered under his Chancellor's influence more than the latter "suffered" from the Emperor's powerlessness.[34] His son Ferdinand was an unfortunate person about whom the most loyal historians found it wiser to keep silent. In the highest circles the offical explanation was that he had been "weakened" by illness. His condition was so dreadful that after meeting with him at Teplitz in 1836, Tsar Nicholas I concluded that he was unfit to participate in the government. The doubts raised by Nicholas resulted in an unseemly scramble, followed by a compromise which satisfied nobody.

It did not do away with the fiction that the feeble-minded Emperor stood at the head of the government, and of course he remained at the head of the dynasty and the Court. His wife Maria Anna of the House of Savoy was a far more astute politician. Since there was no hope of children, the question of succession was a live one, and there was no shortage of claimants. Chief among them were Ferdinand's siblings from the Emperor Francis's four marriages. His last wife, the Bavarian Princess Caroline, was still alive. Several of Ferdinand's relatives died during the year 1847. One of them was his older sister Maria Louisa, once the wife of Napoleon I and Empress of France, and officially a widow after 1821. In fact, however, she was the Duchess of Parma, Piacenza and Guastalla, having been twice secretly married. The first of her secret husbands was her chamberlain Adam von Neipperg, a cavalry officer who was assigned to watch Maria Louisa in 1814 to see that she did not flee to Elba to join her husband. Neipperg suited Maria Louisa so well that by 1821 she had borne him two children. Their son, the Prince of Montenuovo, became the not very popular Master of Ceremonies at the court of Francis Josef I. Neipperg was, surprisingly, a liberal and until 1832, with the death of Mariin and Napoleon's son Aiglon, Parma remained the secret hope of the Italian Bonapartists. Even after the revolution of 1831 was crushed by Austrian troops from Milan, "Maria Luigia" continued to rule with mildness, concerning herself with museums and galleries, education, and hospitals. After Neipperg's death in 1829 she replaced him with another dashing cavalry officer, a French émigré Count Charles Louis de Bombilles, and she remained with him until her death on December 17, 1847. Another sister, Maria Clementina, was married to King Leopold of the Two Sicilies. Then there were two brothers—Francis Charles, married to Princess Sophie Wittelsbach, and the youngest brother, the bachelor Archduke Leopold. Francis Charles had hoped after his father's death in 1835 that he would become the Emperor instead of his feeble-minded brother, but dynastic legitimism prevailed. Francis Charles and Sophie were convinced that the decision had really been made by Metternich, who had his own reasons for preferring the nonentity Ferdinand. Their two sons, Francis Josef and Ferdinand Max, who later became the unfortunate Maximilian of Mexico, were two further candidates for the throne.[35]

Aside from these, there were several brothers of Francis and sons of Leopold II. One of them, Ferdinand, established the Tuscan branch of the Habsburg family, and in 1847 his son Leopold II was ruling in Florence. The Tuscan Habsburgs held estates in Bohemia, where they later transferred the remains of their family archive.[36] Two of Ferdinand's uncles died in 1847: the Archdukes Charles and Josef. Charles was perhaps the most gifted of all Leopold's sons, and he was certainly the most popular. This was sufficient reason for him to be kept firmly in the background during his brother Francis's reign. He instructed his children's tutor to "discourage above all any inclination towards absolutism, for it has become antiquated."[37] But in this he had little luck: his eldest son the Archduke Albert, in 1847 already a Lieutenant Field Marshal and Commander of the army in Lower and Upper Austria, was to become the embodiment of narrow-minded absolutism. Of the other brothers, Charles was also a Lieutenant Field-Marshal in 1847 and commander of a division in Prague, where his sister was head of the school for noble girls in Hradčany. The youngest brother William was also in Prague as an infantry colonel.[38] Charles's eldest daughter Maria Theresa was married to the Sicilian King Ferdinand II, known in history as "King Bomba."

Archduke Josef was for many years Palatine in Hungary, where he was quite popular. His son Archduke Stephen was head of the provincial government in Bohemia in 1847, and we shall meet with him again. Three more of Ferdinand's uncles were still alive: Johann, Rainer, and Ludwig. Johann, born in 1782, did not last long in the army. In 1812 he was even implicated in plans for the uprising in the Tyrol aimed against the French, and from this time he lived far from the Court, in Styria. His Joanneum in Graz became the model for all Austrian museums. According to the *Handbuch*, Archduke Johann was still a bachelor in 1847, but in fact he had been married for a long time to the daughter of the postmaster Plochl of Aussee in Upper Austria. He returned from his obscurity only in 1848.[39] Archduke Rainer was head of the government in the kingdom of Lombardy-Venetia, and he had adapted himself perfectly to the Italian milieu. He was quite popular among several circles in Milan. The youngest was Archduke Ludwig, with whom Francis wished Metternich to share state power.

As we have already indicated, the reality turned out otherwise, because Metternich was not interested in removing his old foe Kolowrat, whom Emperor Francis had somehow forgotten to take account of, and also because he concerned himself chiefly with questions of foreign policy, broadened the "duumvirate" into a "triumvirate," gave Archduke Ludwig the presidency of the "State Conference" and left Kolowrat in charge of domestic affairs. The "State Conference" was the highest advisory body in the Monarchy, and its members included Archduke Ludwig, Metternich, and Kolowrat, as well as the Archduke Francis Charles. Theoretically more men were to be named to the State Conference, especially from the ranks of the "State and Conference Ministers"—among them Ficquelmont, Cziráky and Nadásdy—of whom some were at the same time members of the "State and Conference Council for Internal Affairs." This body, abbreviated to "State Council," was composed of several "colleges," above and beyond which stood Kolowrat. They were supposed to represent the flower of the late Josephine bureaucracy, and more than one of their members achieved prominence in the Revolutionary year—Sommaruga, Hartig, Prohaska, Krauss, to name a few. The final equal component for foreign affairs was Metternich's "Privy, Court and State Chancery."

A shade below came the "Court positions," that is to say the central offices of the Court which corresponded to ministries. The first of them was the Imperial and Royal Court Chancery—*K.k. Hofkanzlei*—a sort of ministry of the interior for the Bohemian and Austrian lands, headed by Count Inzaghi, and whose members included besides Pillersdorf also Jan Krtička of Jaden, a friend of Jan Jeník of Bratřice. Hungary and Transylvania were not within the purview of this department and had their own Court Chancery. Metternich planned to establish five groups of lands for administrative purposes: Hungary; Bohemia with Moravia, Silesia, and Galicia; the Austrian provinces; Italy; and finally Illyria. The plan foundered because of Emperor Francis's opposition, and Metternich did not pursue it very energetically afterwards. In fact, ever since the reign of Maria Theresa there existed the roots of political dualism: the Austrian provinces and the Bohemian lands on one side and Hungary on the other. The whole Monarchy came within the sphere of the Imperial and Royal Court Chamber, whose unenviable task was to deal with finances. At its head stood Kübeck, who also led the Chamber for Mining and Minting and the General Directory for Railways. Kübeck devoted particular attention to the last, which according to the vinegary Hartig was not entirely unmercenary. At the head of the Supreme Court was the deceitful Ludwig Count Taafe; Count Sedlnitzky ran the bureau of police and censorship, where the monitoring of Slavic material fell within the competence of F.K. Hallaschka. Under the United Court Chancery came the Court Study Commission, in charge of education, whose presidium included Inzaghi, Pillersdorf, and Krtička of Jaden. The last "Court position" was the Imperial and Royal Court War Council, or the Ministry of War. Its chief was supposed to be the President of the Council Count Hardegg, who died at the beginning of 1848 and was replaced by the chief of the military section of Metternich's "Privy Court and State Chancery," Count Ficquelmont. Ficquelmont was both a soldier and a diplomat—a combination to which Metternich surprisingly gave precedence—and was considered an expert in Italian and Russian affairs. From 1841 he was regarded as the Chancellor's successor, once Metternich retired or died, eventualities which seemed to recede as time passed.

If we consider the information provided by the *Handbuch* concerning the composition of the central administration at Vienna, we may come to these conclusions: the rise of members of the bourgeois "second society" into the upper levels of the bureaucracy was still relatively rare before 1848. If we look at the names of lower court officials—secretaries and clerks—between 1815 and 1848, it appears that about half were bourgeois. It must not be forgotten, of course, that successful officials of middle-class origin were generally ennobled and "introduced" into aristocratic society. Officials of bourgeois background were not coming automatically to the fore; on the contrary, just before 1848 their number was lower than it had been earlier. Influence and connections were crucial in finding position and advancement. It was also true that bourgeois officials were usually outstripped by noble "unpaid civil servants," who enjoyed an automatic precedence in the competition for promotion. Thus we may conclude that the bureaucracy and the nobility shared the power with the ruler and his representatives, and that the latter often received greater support from the bureaucracy than from the nobility. It is clear that the bureaucracy was by no means monolithic. It included Josephine and post-Josephine reformers, partisans of a rigid centralism, and some who sympathized with the aristocratic proponents of greater autonomy for the various lands. Nor was the bureaucracy homogenous as far as its class composition is concerned. All this was bound to manifest itself in times of crisis.[40]

The situation in the army was simpler. Here, too, the important positions were monopolized by the nobility. The *Military Scheme of Imperial Austria*, published in 1847 at Vienna lists the officer corps on active duty. Taking the highest ranks first and looking down through the colonels, their class origins appear as follows:

	Total	Habsburgs	Nobles	Non-Nobles
Field Marshals	7	4	3	—
Cavalry and Artillery Generals	28	4	24	—
Lieutenant Field Marshals	102	4	94	4
Major Generals	125	4	101	20
Colonels	216	8	169	39

There was of course only one real Field Marshal, Wenceslas Radetzky, Commanding General in Lombardy-Venetia; the Archdukes Charles, Josef, and Johann were commanders only on paper, and the British Prime Minister Marshal Wellington's title was purely honorary. Among the Artillery and Cavalry Generals there were four Habsburgs and five princes, most of them from the Empire. This was the rank held by the President of the Court War Council Hardegg and also by Ficquelmont. Those with lands in Bohemia and Moravia included Max Auersperg, Hohenlohe-Langenberg, Peter Morzin, Emmanuel Mensdorff-Pouilly. Prince Alfred Windischgrätz was only a Lieutenant Field Marshal, as were Charles von Auersperg, Charles Liechtenstein and Friedrich

Fürstenberg. The Major-Generals included three Schwarzenbergs—Felix, Karl and Emanuel—Franz Liechtenstein, Josef Lobkowitz, and Franz Colloredo-Mansfeld.[41]

The officer corps, since 1837 dressed in the distinctive black hats with a golden roseta, stood at the head of a formidable military machine. The army was over 270,000 strong in peacetime, 400,000 in time of war, and after 1845 soldiers were conscripted for eight years of service in the Austrian part of the Monarchy. In Hungary the term was ten years, and the Hungarian infantry and cavalry were distinguished by their uniforms from the rest of the army: the infantry wore long, light-blue coats, the artillery and service units, brown coats. The army was still composed of infantry, cavalry, artillery, and supply units. The rather small navy was more Italian than Austrian. The General Staff, headed by Lieutenant Field Marshal Hess, concerned itself chiefly with cartography.

The army was divided territorially into twelve general commands, two of them in the Czech lands: the Second Command was headquartered at Brno, the Eighth at Prague. The General Commands did not follow the boundaries of the lands; similarly, the peace-time garrisons did not correspond to the "supply districts." Thus, if we say that of fifty-eight regular regiments, nine were Bohemian and five Moravian, this means merely that their "supply districts" were located in Bohemia and Moravia, but not necessarily their garrisons. On the contrary, after 1815 the garrisons were deliberately scrambled, so that not only were Bohemians sent to Italy, and Italians to Bohemia, Austria, and Hungary, but also it was the sons of Ukrainian peasants who generally made up the garrisons in the big cities like Vienna and Prague. Most of the cavalry—at least for the eight cuirassier regiments, the six dragoon regiments and the eight chevaux-legér—were recruited from the Bohemian lands. The four lancer regiments were from Galicia, the twelve regiments of hussars from Hungary, though of course garrisons of both were located in Czech villages from Klatovy through the Elbe valley into northern Moravia. Three of the five artillery regiments were from Bohemia or Moravia; in Prague there was for a long time a garrison with a rocket unit which was sold to the Turks. There were quite a number of Czechs also among the officer corps of the service units, which were commanded by Lieutenant Field Marshal Count Baillet-Latour.

The artillery was divided into five field regiments and into artillery batteries. It was equipped with canons and howitzers with a range of 1,200 paces. The infantry rifles of the Augustin type fired reliably to about 500 paces. The largest military unit was usually one army corps, composed of two infantry divisions and one reconnaissance division. The infantry divisions consisted of two brigades of two infantry regiments and one company of chasseurs. A reconnaissance division contained two regiments of light cavalry and from two to five companies of chasseurs. Each military unit was equipped with artillery, generally between 70 and 96 guns divided into batteries of eight.

Finally, one infantry regiment usually consisted of three battalions. The first two had six companies and the third, four companies. Further, the regiments had two companies of grenadiers—tall soldiers with sheepskin hats. Since the grenadier divisions and companies were used as military police, they were not particularly popular.

The regiments were already numbered; they had their names and "proprietors," who theoretically commanded them and determined the methods of their training. This was an anachronism against which Radetzky protested. After 1830 he trained his north Italian corps according to his own comparatively progressive field instructions, and each year he organized large-scale maneuvers. The Lombard-Venetian General Command was considered to be the most important, because this was the most volatile territory, and Radetzky was given a free hand. Windischgrätz tried to imitate his example in Bohemia, using his close relationship with Metternich. He also won the favor of Tsar Nicholas I, who after meeting him at Münchengrätz in 1833 invited him to maneuvers of the Russian army. Metternich realized that a diplomat-soldier would be most useful at the Russian court; thus wherever he could he established links between the military and diplomatic service. More than one Austrian envoy was actually a military officer who had been released temporarily for a diplomatic assignment. This was the case for example of Major-General Felix Schwarzenberg, in 1847 ambassador to the court at Naples.

The heads of several of the provincial administrations worked to instill some "ésprit de corps" among their subordinates—for example The Stadions in Illyria and Galicia. Together there were eleven of these lands. Two of them, Hungary and Transylvania, were connected with the others chiefly by the person of the ruler. Each land had its own administrative organs, its political apparatus called the Gubernium, its legal system, financial bureau and of course its military General Command. These offices for Bohemia were at Prague, where the "Chief of the Land Administration" was Archduke Stephen, and for Moravia and Silesia at Brno, where the governor was Count Rudolf Stadion. Bureaucrats from the Bohemian lands were to be found also at Vienna and in all the other lands as well. The lists of junior officials in all parts of the administration reveal many Czech names. The number of non-nobles in the land administrations was greater than in the central administration offices. Czech names may be found in quite high positions in the various land administrations. The president of the government of Lower Austria, for example, was Jan Talatzko ofJeštětice, a member of an old knightly family. In Galicia the vice-president of the Gubernium was Leopold Lažanský of Buková, and there are many Czech names among the secretaries—Wodák, Rziha, Wacka, Stránský, Moschek, Jarosch, Uhlík, Dworzák and so forth. Yet it must be remembered that names by themselves meant very little, if it were a question of establishing "nationality." Most of the bureaucrats were bilingual, and whether a particular family was to become "Czech," "German," or "Polish" was often still in the process of being decided in the nineteenth century.

The Bohemian lands, therefore, included two important autonomous administrative units. In the "Austrian half" of the Monarchy, Bohemia was the second largest land in terms of territory after Galicia, and Moravia with Silesia stood in fourth place. Also in terms of population the Bohemian lands occupied a key position in Austria as a whole. Of the roughly thirty million people in the entire Monarchy, Bohemia contained about three and a half million, Moravia and Silesia, nearly two million. In terms of population density, Moravia and Silesia came second, after Lombardy-Venetia, and Bohemia came third. The Bohemian lands also contained quite a thick network of towns, although the city of Prague, with 95,000 inhabitants in 1824, ranked only fourth, after Vienna, Milan and Venice, and Brno was in thirteenth place.

In 1826 G.N. Schnabel, professor of statistics in the University of Prague, published a survey of Austria which is crucial for our knowledge of the political, national, and social structure of the Monarchy.[42] Schnabel attempted a breakdown of the population by nationality and even by social rank. He estimated the Slavic population at 13 million, the Hungarian at 4 million, the German at 6 million, and the Italian at 4,300,000. In Bohemia he estimated the number of Czechs at two and a half million and Germans at one million; in Moravia and Silesia he reckoned that there were 300,000 Germans, the rest Slavs. He also divided the population into "producers" and "consumers." Among the former he included chiefly the peasant population, which he estimated at 7,200,000 persons; to them he added 2,400,000 works in crafts and industries. Among the consumers he counted people who did not work at all—beggars, the unemployed—and those who did not participate in the production process but nevertheless lived from it—estate owners, clergy, teachers, soldiers, administrators.

Thus according to Schnabel's survey Austria was predominantly agricultural. Bohemia, Moravia, and Silesia belonged to the Monarchy's area of industrial concentration. His picture coincides quite well with the findings of modern research: in the beginning of the 1840s the Bohemian lánds accounted for 31.8 percent of the entire industrial production of the Austrian part of the Monarchy.[43] The textile industry contributed 43.6 percent of the total value of industrial production in the entire Monarchy. Nearly a half of the textile production in the western part of the Monarchy was located in the Bohemian lands, where the most lucrative kinds of production at this time were linen, wool, cotton goods, then in fourth place brewing and distilling. The production of sugar and sweets, later an important branch of agriculture, was only beginning to develop. In sixth place came the leather industry, then glassmaking, which was suffering from English competition and was losing its position in distant markets.[44]

In all these branches of industry, with the exception of leather and silk, the Bohemian lands were in first place in the Monarchy in terms of the total value. They lagged in the production of iron, which was led by Lower Austria and Styria, and machine manufacture was still in its infancy. In Bohemia as elsewhere the development of industry had social consequences. It created the conditions in which new social classes appeared—the bourgeoisie and the proletariat. The most advanced part of Bohemia economically continued to be the mountainous northern borderlands, where the textile and glassmaking industries had been concentrated ever since the seventeenth century, and where the first iron and machine workshops appeared. This resulted in the appearance of a German-speaking bourgeoisie first of all. But with continued progress in industrialization after the introduction of the steam engine this German predominance within the bourgeoisie began to recede, because wood and water ceased to be the necessary energy sources for factories. In the 1840s of course, the shift was only beginning, and its slowness may be seen from the data published annually in Section XV of the *Handbuch der Königreich Böhmen*.[45] The emerging Czech bourgeoisie enjoyed bright prospects especially in the expanding agricultural industries—sugar refining, brewing, distilling—which were concentrated in the center of the land, and also in the small textile factories in the north and east as well as in the suburbs of Prague. But the wealthiest Czech bourgeois families continued to invest their profits in landed property.

It must be emphasized that the Czech bourgeoisie was only just beginning to coalesce into a recognizeable social class, even though the process quickened during the 1840s. Their most advanced element were the "patriots," people who, mainly in terms of language, evinced a definite consciousness of their own nationality. Thanks chiefly to the work of Miroslav Hroch, some conclusions may be drawn from an analysis of this group of "patriots"—members of "patriotic organizations" such as the Bohemian Museum, industrial organizations, provincial museum societies. There were also the subscribers to the *Matice Ceská* and the *Heritage of St. John of Nepomuk*, contributors and subscribers to the Czech newspapers, graduates of schools whose language of instruction was Czech. It has emerged, for example, that in the twenty years before 1848 the "patriotic" group was composed of several distinct elements whose relative significance was shifting. At the beginning of the period the Catholic clergy predominated, but their influence waned as the generation of "Josephine" priests died out. By the 1840s the number of clergymen was about the same as the number of students or bureaucrats—especially the estate administrators in the countryside. Besides these members of the intelligentsia, there were small merchants and proprietors of small workshops or factories who were arriving at a consciousness of their Czech nationality. The rather striking participation of craftsmen is important. It suggests that they were aware of the results of the Industrial revolution and were interested in placing checks on the larger industrialists, who were predominatly German, by combining with those members of the nobility who were interested in economic enterprise.

The biographical sketches supplied in the recent survey *History of Czech Literature* show that the legends about the patriotic writers of the nineteenth century born under thatched roofs are only legends.[46] Actually the patriots of these years were active in the towns: in the smaller domain and royal towns in the provinces as well as in Prague. Not all of Bohemia, of course, was included in the "emancipation" movement: it was concentrated in the territory stretching from the northern and eastern part of the country into the center, along with parts of the south as well. In other parts of Bohemia an older kind if patriotism survived to a considerable extent, which was grounded not in language but in the earlier existence of a political state. In these areas the clergy and the teachers were the makers of opinion, and bourgeois influences had not yet penetrated. On the other hand, they were very prominent in the Elbe and Moldau valleys, where most of the consciously Czech intelligentsia came from. A new type of patriot, of middle-class and free-peasant background, began to appear during the 1840s.[47]

The formation of a proletariat from the ranks of the rural poor and also from the class of the small craftsmen, who were being impoverished by the growth of mass production, was also in its early stages in the 1840s. There has not been enough research to allow firm conclusions about the origins of the proletariat, but in outline, at least, the circumstances of their appearance are clear. We can trace in an approximate fashion the numbers of the proletariat, and a few studies have been carried out on the formation of the labor force in several industrial enterprises—above all the Víkovice iron foundries. We now know more than before about the formation of the proletariat around Kladno. But so far there are no analytical studies which compare the scanty archival material from the factories with the information in the official matrices for the Prague suburbs of Libeň, Karlín and Smíchov, or for Liberec or Brno. At the beginning of the 1840s the most industrialized city was Brno, where about 15,000 workers were employed in the textile factories. Since Brno had about 45,000 inhabitants, the workers represented a significant portion of the population, even though most of them lived outside the city center. Prague, with just over a hundred thousand inhabitants, had no more than four to five thousand industrial workers—between 800 and 1,000 of them in the calico factories in the suburb of Smíchov, who were the best-organized group.[48] These are very low figures, particularly if we compare them with the numbers of those involved in domestic production, which was particularly important in the linen industry. In 1847 it was estimated that a total of 350,000 were employed in the linen industry, of whom only 27,000 worked in large factories. In 1841 just over 7,500 were employed in cotton factories, and the ten largest cloth factories employed just over 4,000 workers, out of the total of about 19,000.[49]

These figures go far towards explaining why the growing Czech bourgeoisie did not regard the proletariat as a significant element in the "nation"—not nearly as significant as the peasantry. There were, of course, individuals who recognized the importance of the "social question." Among the older generation there was for example the Czech utopian B. Bolzano; in Moravia there was Jan Ohéral and F.C. Kampelík. From the city of Prague we have a mass of information about poverty at the beginning of the 1840s, gathered by Filip Maximilian Opitz, the son of a "Jacobin" from Čáslav, who for many years interested himself in poor-relief in the parish of St. Gall in the Prague Old Town:

> Poverty and want in the whole world arise solely from our impoverished social organization. If we wish to achieve a happier estate, then society must recognize inheritance according to natural capacity instead of family. Everyone who contributes to labor should receive a proportionate share of the profit which results from it.
>
> If poverty is to be eliminated, it is necessary that those who can work but do not want to should be coerced. And those who are too sick or old to work should be cared for in homes for the poor . . .[50]

The expansion of capitalist production, represented in Bohemia chiefly by the construction of railways in the 1840s, led to the explosive situation of which Opitz gave warning. Thus we arrive at the first situation of conflict, which will help us to uncover the class character of the state, and the class differences: the first cracks in the majestic facade of the Austrian Monarchy.

3 Prague and Vienna in July 1844

In July 1844 the construction of the railway linking Prague with Vienna via Přerov was nearing completion outside Prague. It was to be a branch of

"Emperor Ferdinand's Northern Line" connecting Vienna with Cracow and Bochnia, and other branches made connections with Brno, Olomouc, Troppau, Bilsko, and Biala. Rothschild's bank had been involved in the railway project since March 1836, and it was financed by a stock company whose members also included several other Viennese bankers: Feymüller, Biedermann, Eskeles, Mayer and Sina. It was supported by Metternich, Kolowrat, and the president of the Court Study Commission Mittrowsky. Plans for the construction had been made as early as the winter of 1836-7. The contract was awarded to the firms of the brothers Klein of Brno and the Italian F. Talachini. Construction progressed so rapidly that the line between Vienna and Brno was in operation by 1839. The Břeclav-Přerov line reached Lipník by August 1842, but then difficulties arose, and Rothschild had to subsidize the financially shaky stock company. In the spring of 1844, work was begun on the section between Lipník and Bohumín.[51]

Already during charter negotiations for the Northern Line, a group of entrepreneurs from Prague asked permission to build a railroad from Prague through Moravia to Vienna. But this enterprise collapsed in spite of the support of the Bohemian attorney general Lichtner, the Prague financier Mořic Zdekauer and perhaps even the mayor of Brno Reitschel, and the plan was taken over by the Northern Line Company. Meanwhile the government in Vienna decided that the state should take the lead in railway construction, and an imperial decree of December 19, 1841, stipulated that the government should decide on a case by case basis which lines should be constructed as state railways. Ultimately little was changed. At the instigation of the president of the Court Chamber Kübeck, a general directorship was established for state railway construction, and its chairman was Hermanegild Francesconi, director of the Northern Line. On August 3, 1842, a state line between Olomouc and Prague was approved, and the contract was awarded to the Klein brothers, who also shared the contract for the Prague station. Work commenced in September 1842. The section between Prague and Pardubice was supervised by Chief Engineer Jan Perner, who had worked for a brief period with Gerstner in Russia and was later involved in the formation of Czech industrial unions and efforts to establish a Czech technical school. Thus, he was one of the great hopes of the "patriots," and his death in 1845 was deeply mourned.

As many as 20,000 workers were employed on the Prague-Olomouc line during the next two years. By the spring of 1844 the fate of these workers was unclear because the construction plan had not been completed, much less officially approved. The status of the Prague-Dresden line was equally uncertain. Thus the fate of thousands of workers gathered before the gates of Prague hung in the balance. Neither the Archduke Stephen's land administration nor Mayor

Josef Müller was certain what would become of them. Nor were the authorities of the Kouřim Region, whose jurisdiction extended to the eastern boundary of the capital city. But since the peace of Bohemia was guaranteed by more than 100,000 troops, no great alarm was felt. In Prague itself were substantial portions of two infantry regiments under the Bohemian commander Archduke Karl Ludwig and Lieutenant Field Marshal Prince Alfred von Windischgrätz. Some of Latour's twenty-eighth infantry regiment and Palombini's thirty-sixth were also stationed in the city, as well as three companies of grenadiers. It is likely, however, that only the grenadier companies were at full strength; even the regiments that were not "reduced" or partially disbanded usually had substantial numbers of troops on leave in peacetime. In fact many of these soldiers were working at this time on the railway construction outside Prague. But the forces of order in the city were supplemented by 300 men of the Imperial and Royal Military Police, deployed over five municipal quarters: the first quarter included the Prague Old Town, where the stations were located in the Old Town Hall, the Carolinum, the convent of St. Agnes, Týn, and the former convent of St. Michael. The second quarter was the New Town, with headquarters in the New Town Hall, and other stations in the city gates and on the larger squares. The third and fourth quarters were the Lesser Town and Hradčany, with headquarters at the Church of St. Thomas, in the old Lesser Town Hall, and at the gates. The fifth quarter included the Jewish Town, where the single station was located in the old Post Street. The chief of Police was the city captain Peter Muth.[52]

Surprisingly enough, no violence broke out at the railway construction site. The "hungry forties" were years of economic crisis marked by high unemployment, especially in sectors affected by English competition, and also by a rise in food prices after the disastrous harvest of 1842. Popular resentment found its target in the speculators and the heavy Excise or food tax that was collected at the city gates.

In June 1843 the unemployed of Brno rioted, and the same year military assistance was required against construction workers on the road between Prague and Buštěhrad. The workers' situation was becoming desperate: they received between ten and fifteen kreutzer daily, which may be compared with the thirteen kreutzer minimum daily allotment for the prisoners of Prague, who received only one hot meal and 500 grams of bread. Far more serious were the riots of June 1844 which erupted in Prague and Liberec, the two most industrialized cities of Bohemia. Both cases involved textile workers who were protesting a further reducton in their wages. Between the 17th and 24th of June hundreds of factory workers in Smíchov struck until around 500 of them were seized and interrogated in the barracks on the Livestock Market. Muth's police searched to no avail for "foreign revolutionaries," whom they blamed for the strikes. Although the strikes were surpressed, they had such an impact that on June 28 the Gubernium created a commission to formulate a set of "domestic rules" for factories, which in the end were never approved and never took effect. In Liberec, as in Prague, the hated printing machines became the targets of the textile workers. On July 3 the workers marched toward the Liebig factories. They were halted on the bridge over the River Nisa by a band of armed citizens led by the later famous Mayor Karásek.[53]

On July 6 the bricklayers and laborers on the Karlín viaduct near Prague rioted while they were being given their wages. They charged that they were not being paid enough. Skilled bricklayers received a daily wage of 34 kreutzer, unskilled laborers only 24. Those who worked on commissions also suffered, because the engineers and foremen to whom the Klein brothers subcontracted certain sections of the line were trying to increase their profits at the expense of their workers. They regularly made false reports of the work completed and ordered corresponding reductions in wages. Moreover, the foremen controlled the canteens on the construction site, where they sold bad food at high prices. The workers demanded a wage increase to 30 kreutzers for unskilled workers and 40 for skilled workers. A foreman called Sulc who supervised the Karlín section dealt with his "rebels" by transfering them to a more distant section of the track near Hloubětín.

But the "rebels" were not ready to give up. We do not know precisely what happened at Sulc's site on Sunday July 7; but the following morning at six o'clock some of the "rebels" appeared as usual for work. They were fired on the spot. They and their sympathizers began to march along the track in the direction of Hloubetín, where at about ten o'clock they met with another crowd, which had set out from Kyj towards Prague. At about the same time a further group from Běchovice also began to demonstrate.

At one o'clock the crowd, estimated at at least a thousand, approached Libeň, and the authorities began to betray a justified concern at the "hard-headedness" of the "Czech mob." Chief of Police Muth had been informed of the Karlín incident before noon, and he immediately informed the Gubernium that the workers had stopped work and were marching along the track towards the city. The Gubernium ordered the Kouřim Regional authorities, to whose territory the events were still confined, to send in observers to "discover the aims of the workers and the reasons for their insurrection." Thus the Kouřim Regional captain dispatched Pavel Alois Klar, otherwise remembered as the founder of the Prague Institute for the Blind and publisher of the almanach *Libussa*. Klar got into a carriage, taking with him Perner's assistant, an engineer named Kazda, and reached the workers at about two o'clock near Libeň. Here and later at the Invalidovna on the edge of the city, Klar tried to persuade the demonstrators to disband and suggested that they send representatives to Prague to negotiate. He was unsuccessful, and when he saw that the crowd was moving again, he sent Kazda to warn the police at the city gate.

The Hospital Gate was in any case the boundary of his authority. Following an agreement between the civil authorities and Windischgrätz's General Command, the Hospital Gate was occupied by two columns of grenadiers from Reisinger's eighteenth infantry regiment and Wellington's forty-second garrisoned at Theresienstadt. The troops were commanded by Captains Fiedler and Bruner. The gate stood at the end of Poříčí—then called Schilling Street—and formed part of the late seventeenth century fortifications. To the north near the river there was a sally-port in the walls. To the south, in the directon of New Gate, which stood near the present Central Station, there was a sturdy rampart which had been made over into a garden. Outside the walls was a moat, then open space in the direction of Karlín, which at that time consisted only of one street. At the edge of the suburb were several building sites and also the Excise Office where customs officials collected the unpopular food tax.

The crowd halted on the open space between Karlín and the moat, and at this point Klar achieved some success: he found several workers who were willing to convey their comrades' complaints to representatives of the Kleins' firm. The commanding officer Fiedler was willing to admit the negotiators through the gate but not the mass of angry workers behind them. The meeting dragged, and the crowd began to show impatience. Count Schirnding, author of a pamphlet describing the scene entitled *Prague and its Citizens,* mingled with the crowd out of curiosity, and he believed that his persuasive eloquence could be of some assistance to Klar. But according to the official report, he was "insulted" by the workers. Meanwhile a line of produce carts bound for the city began to pile up behind the crowd of strikers and onlookers. Thus at about five o'clock Captain Fiedler ordered the gate opened, and the carts passed through, along with some of the strikers. Fiedler ordered first one platoon, then a whole column, to move out with fixed bayonets and clear the entire open space as far as the customs house. Fiedler's column left the gate, while the second, under Bruner, waited in reserve. But the soldiers were unable to move the crowd. As the workers shouted "forward" and pressed from behind, the grenadiers approached them with their bayonets. At the flank of the formation several grenadiers were in danger of being shoved into the moat by the crowd. At the same time bricks began to descend on the soldiers from the rear of the crowd. One of the grenadiers opened fire; he was joined by others, and together about eighty rounds were discharged. Most of the shooting was apparently in the air, so that the bullets hit several spectators behind the windows of Karlín, instead of the workers. Klar's coachman, who was still seated on the driver's box, was also hit. The investigation was unable to determine who gave the order to fire; certainly nobody wanted to assume the responsibility.

The shooting did not put a stop to the hail of bricks and stones that fell on the soldiers. It began to come also from the walls, where onlookers joined in the conflict by demolishing the guard house. Thus Captain Fiedler, eleven of whose men had been wounded, ordered an inglorious withdrawal to the safety of the gate, just as the police chief Muth was suggesting that the crowd on top of the walls be fired at. At this point a group of high officers of the General Command arrived on horseback, just in time to witness Fiedler's disorderly retreat. According to Schirnding, this official group was led by Lieutenant Field Marshal Windischgrätz himself and Major General Karl Schwarzenberg. As they watched, half of Bruner's troops drove the spectators from the walls, while the other half cleared Poříčí and the surrounding streets. A detachment under Major Grossman then moved out once again to clear the open space in front of the gate. Meanwhile a unit of hussars from Palatin's regiment issued from New Gate and broke up the crowd of workers at Karlova and by the banks of the Moldau. Although the operation was not accomplished without violence, there were no further casualties, and by about six o'clock "peace and order" had been restored.[54]

* Five were fatally wounded: 22-year-old journeyman Václav Siegl of Radnice, 16-year-old painter's apprentice Jan Bílek, 24-year-old František Nešuta, Klar's coachman, and Anna Mikolejská, the infant daughter of a Karlín shopkeeper, shot as she was being held in the arms of a nurse who was watching the events from a window. Seriously injured were 18-year-old shop assistant Jindřich Niedhart and 21-year-old journeyman potter Vojtěch Pechák. Many received less serious injuries, but their number could not be determined because they avoided hospitals and doctors.[55] The soldiers seized twelve workers outside the gate, among whom were Klar's unfortunate negotiators. None of the grenadiers was seriously wounded, and the hussars reported no injuries at all.

The shooting was described in the official report as a "sad but necessary consequence of the criminal insurrection," and Archduke Stephen hastened to assure Vienna that, with the help of Lieutenant Field-Marshal Windischgrätz, he was determined to maintain order at all costs; he asked only for reinforcements. Thus seven cuirassier squadrons from Ferdinand's and Hardegg's regiments were sent to Windischgrätz at Prague. Two of the squadrons were stationed in the city center, the rest in the industrial suburbs. Klein's firm hastily compiled a list of sixty workers who were identified as the chief instigators of the insurrection, and investigations were begun. Six of them were soldiers on leave—four from Latour's infantry, one from Palombini's and one grenadier. The General Command was requested to cancel the leaves of these soldiers and initiate military proceedings against them. The rest of those on the list were separated into "instigators," "leading rebels," and "willing participants." It emerged, that the Kleins did not know the addresses of any of their workers, and the whole project came to nothing.

The official bodies, however, were more successful in their prosecution, but the events at the gate were followed by further disturbances. On the evening of July 8 there were anti-Jewish demonstrations in the Old Town; they continued the next day but were easily suppressed. On July 9 rumors spread through the city that the workers had regrouped at Úvahy to march once again and that the cuirassiers had been unable to stop them. The following day, in fact, there was an incident at Úvahy: the workers demonstrated against the poor quality of the bread they were given. They turned it over to the bailiff and to Regional Commissioner Klar, who concurred that it was inedible. Nevertheless troops were called in and arrests made. These men were cited merely for disturbing the peace, while their comrades who had taken part in the conflict by the Hospital Gate were considered dangerous rebels. The Gubernium decided that the events of July 8 should be investigated by a special commission named by the Prague magistrate. We only know that this body had twenty persons arrested. Three of them were sentenced at the end of July to eight days in prison, to be initiated and concluded with twenty-four lashes; five received the same sentence with eight lashes, and ten were given twelve lashes and released. Of the twenty who were arrested only two possessed any money; the others carried only the tools of their trade, or at most a porcelain pipe and tobacco pouch.

These "political offenders" got off lightly. Those who were sentenced by the Prague criminal court, meeting in the workhouse in Hradčany, were not so fortunate. They were left in prison until the autumn of the following year. Only then was the chief offender, 18-year-old journeyman bricklayer Václav Hrdina, who had admitted throwing a rock at the grenadiers, sentenced to three months in prison. It was still worse for those who protested against the "truck system" at Úvaly. The most severe punishment was four months in prison, assigned to Vojtěch Zika—though again only in October 1845. The judicial inquiry had dragged on for fourteen months, and the unfortunate prisoners were obliged to pay all losses sustained by the foremen, the bakers, and canteen operators.

The power of the state thus aligned itself on the side of the employers and those who shared in their method of exploitation. Yet it is interesting that the representatives of different groups within the ruling class took different positions on the conflict. The "unfortunate events," whose extent exceeded all previous working-class disturbances, drew the attention of the Austrian and foreign public. The official report of the Gubernium, printed on July 14 in the *Prager Zeitung*, maintained that the riots were sparked by "malevolent agitators." But who were they? The municipal captain suspected "well-dressed people of the better classes" who apparently sympathized with the workers—Count Schirnding and the spectators on the wall. A "well-dressed gentleman" who was circulating before the outbreak of violence was discovered to be an engineer recruiting workers for the east Moravian section of the Northern Line. The Gubernium concluded that the whole affair was an unlucky fluke, an explanation that proved acceptable to Engineer Kazda and ultimately to the brothers Klein as well. The *Allgemeine Zeitung* of Augsburg, a newspaper popular among the liberal public in Bohemia, described the conflict as the result of the "present mood of the lower classes," a clash between the irritated grenadiers who fired without orders and the crowd who refused to recognize the law. The whole affair was blamed on the Kleins, erroneously identified as entrepreneurs of Jewish origin: "in any case it is clear that the motive behind these disturbances was not a political one." An anti-Semitic attitude is also evident in several anonymous pamphlets, particularly one entitled "The Jews in Austria and the Bohemian Disturbances." Here we find the judgment that "it was neither Slavic nor Bohemian nor Communist forces which sparked the workers' riots in Prague; rather it was the pressure applied by Jewish entrepreneurs upon their workers." The author of another pamphlet entitled "The Disturbances in Bohemia" contemplated the deeper causes of discontent and concluded that the blame lay both with the workers and their employers, and ultimately with the government as well, which had done nothing to mitigate the antagonism between them. "It is never a disinterested ideal, but always a material interest" which leads to revolution. Upon this rational judgment the author grafted a highly fantastical portrait of Archduke Stephen as the great hope of the popular masses who shall lead them to a bright future "when we shall travel over iron roads in carriages without horses. Then the Germans shall come out of the mountains to aid their Czech brethren; from Blaník they shall enter the city and destroy the rich and well-born. . ."[56]

Among the "rich and well-born," meanwhile, there arose a learned discussion about the significance of the conflict and the prospects for the future. Windischgrätz and his officers soon drew together and concentrated upon ways to obtain further reinforcements so that they could maintain order in the face of any new trouble. Nothing about the whole affair had been particularly glorious; nevertheless Windischgrätz was able to assume the stance of a firm commander capable of nipping revolution in the bud. We shall see how this was to stand him in good stead at the beginning of 1848.

The position taken by the bureaucracy was not nearly so straightforward.

Some officials believed that with any recurrence of trouble, the worker's grievances would have to be gone into. This was Archduke Stephen's view, and it was shared by many others, including Chancellor Inzaghi in Vienna and the simple Regional Commissioner Klar. Most of these men were believers in the patriarchial Josephine conceptions of the role of the state. They regarded the workers as subjects whose relations with their employers belong within the government's legitimate sphere of interest. On the other side, the president of the Court Chamber Kübeck defended the principle of free enterprise. He was against investigating the grievances of the workers and against all state interference in labor relations. Of course both groups—those who wanted to investigate the workers' complaints and those who did not—were concerned with the same thing—the prevention of future conflicts.

Archduke Stephen asked Kübeck, in his capacity as supervisor of state railways, to give immediate approval to the construction of the section between Prague and the Saxon border, since the work near Prague was nearing completion. Kübeck refused on the grounds that it would be too risky to embark on a further section before the entire plan had been approved. Stephen's proposed special commission to consider the workers' views also drew Kübeck's opposition because "the financial administration has never had any influence upon relations between the entrepreneurs, who have been entrusted with the construction, and their employees . . . For this relationship is a legal one, into which the workers entered without coercion, and they assented, either verbally, or by maintaining silence, to the conditions of their work and wages. . ."[57] If the workers had complaints, they should have settled them by legal means, through the state agencies which had control over the construction project. Their grievances should certainly not be investigated: "such a step can only lead to greater disturbances; it would create the impression that the workers indeed had just cause for their violent action. This view, even if it were true, must not be acknowledged in the present circumstances."

Engineer Perner heartily concurred, and he also protested against Archduke Stephen's intention to ascertain the immediate causes of the conflict. Perner vigorously opposed any "milling about the track to investigate the so-called grievances of the railway workers," because "such behavior would surely cause rioting and insurrection among all the laborers, of whom there are ten thousand."[58] The views of the post-Josephine bureaucrat were thus in substantial agreement with those of this representative of the Czech bourgeoisie—or more precisely the growing Czech technical intelligentsia.

The withdrawal of the workers from the railway site closes the wave of labor movements in 1843-4. The troubles among the textile workers of Brno and Liberec represented an insurrection against the introduction of machines. It appears that in Brno the employers were applying pressure upon the cottage workers. In Liberec the factory owners were letting workers go because they were no longer needed. In comparison with the textile workers' riots, the conflict on the railway site was not very well organized, but it was more elemental, and it was more violent. According to the eventual official findings, the fight at the Hospital Gate, show clearly that the administration was not at all concerned with justice.

The crowd assembled before the Hospital Gate on July 8, 1844, is difficult to identify. We do not know very much about those 10,000 bricklayers and laborers who were then working on the entire section from Pardubice to Prague. We can discover the names and nationality of those who were killed or seriously wounded, but not even the names of all who were eventually tried and sentenced have been preserved. Those whom we know something about can serve at best only as random samples, and there are far too few of them to allow us to reach any firm conclusions. At the beginning of July there do not seem to have been very many of the "agricultural proletariat" present on the construction site. We meet instead with journeymen and apprentices from Prague. Probably there were also a significant number of craft workers, too, whose original occupations no longer provided them with a living. We know that this was the predicament of the nail makers of Hořovicko and Radnicko, and that the construction of the highway in Buštěhrad drew impoverished weavers and lacemakers from as far away as the Erzgebirge; the railway project probably did the same. The original vocations of the soldiers on leave who were involved will probably never be discovered, because the records were destroyed by the military authorities in the last century.

The Bohemian lands thus became the center of European attention. We find a reflection of this in Engels's observation that "the active movement of the proletariat begins with the risings of the Silesian and Bohemian workers in 1844."[59]

4 The "Czech Question" and European Politics at the Beginning of 1848

The term "Czech question" refers to the effort to preserve the existence of the Czech ethnic group in any age, whether we are considering the medieval or early-modern "feudal nation" or the modern "nationality" in the age of capitalism. Generally a "nation" may be defined as a large group or community whose members are bound to each other by a number of relationships—linguistic, cultural, economic and so forth. These must always be understood concretely, in their actual relation to the surrounding world. Not long ago Miroslav Hroch published an essay whose very title—"Patriots without a Nation"—was intended to stimulate thought and discussion.⁶⁰ It contains some judgments which appear to be contradictory; in any case it is not really possible to speak seriously of "patriots without a nation" if we accept some of the author's assumptions—especially his view that the Germanization of Bohemia presented no serious threat to the survival of the Czechs even in the eighteenth century. According to Hroch, the national revival, or national "integration"—understood in terms of language—"potentially restricted the Czech public's immediate contact with the mature cultures of the large nations." This supposedly was as clear to Metternich as it was to the critics of Jungmann's or Mácha's generation. "With each successful step in this direction, contact between the Czech micro-world and the larger civilization of rising capitalism was made more difficult."⁶¹

It is not clear what Hroch means by the "larger civilization of rising capitalism." By civilization we usually mean a stage in the evolution of a society, as defined by Morgan and Engels, by Lucien Febvre and others, which is sufficiently compelling to become the model for other societies. In the late middle ages, Renaissance Italy served as such a model; in the sixteenth century there were two, Spain and the Netherlands; in the seventeenth and eighteenth centuries there were England and France. The "larger civilization of rising capitalism" was that of the English industrial revolution—or was it that of the French revolution? In any case, the struggle that the Czechs mounted against German cultural influence was quite natural, and it was an enormously long process. How else could František Palacký, the "Father of the Nation," have impressed Friedrich Engels as a crazy German professor? Later on Masaryk, too, was to strike his cosmopolitan friends as a typical German academic—and not only in his youth. Jan Neruda's notes from his journey to the Paris World Exhibition in 1877 reveal that he liked the city, but that France represented a foreign world to him. Only at one point does he express any personal partiality, when describing his visit to the grave of Heinrich Heine in Montmartre.⁶²

When during World War Two Gustav Winter contemplated that national revivalists' attitude towards the rest of the world, he concluded that in the 1820s and 1830s they looked to Russia politically, regarded Germany as the land of science and scholarship, and Italy as the land of dreams and romanticism. They looked to England for conceptions of political democracy; and French culture also strongly attracted them, as even the case of Havlíček demonstrates.⁶³

Is this the way it was? Is this all that can be said of the Czechs' efforts to become acquainted with a different world than that represented by Metternich's Austria? Is Hroch right when he concludes that until the end of the nineteenth century the world was unwilling to accept the Czech cultural contribution—except in music? Unfortunately there is very little in the way of conveniently collected information on which to base an answer to this question. No modern studies have followed Tadra's *Cultural Relations of Bohemia Abroad*, a book now outdated which does not allow us to deal with the question as it deserves. It is clear, then, that both traditional conclusions and more recent generalizations rest on a body of knowledge which is no longer entirely satisfactory.[64]

But there were attempts on the part of Czechs to establish contacts with the non-German world and to obtain there understanding for the existence of the Czech nation in the interior of the Continent. Italy was doubtless most accessible to the Bohemian lands. Its northern and central provinces were ruled by the Habsburgs. Since the time of Winckelmann and Goethe an Italian journey was a fashionable necessity. Czech visitors to Italy for the most part did not travel in the same manner as Goethe in 1786-8 or Heine in 1828, and their literary testimony was nothing like Goethe's *Italienreise* or Heine's *Pictures from a Journey*. Milota Zdirad Polák came to Italy as a soldier; Dobrovský, Kollár, and Palacký came as scholars; F.L. Rieger as a young politician.[65] Karel Mensinger, the only Czech whose travel notes were published (in 1845), arrived in Milan in 1844 as chaplain to Reisinger's 18th infantry regiment, whose troops came from the region of Königgrätz. Perhaps they were among those referred to in Giuseppe Giusti's *Cathedral of St. Ambrose*, part of the "army of the North, gathered here from Croatia and Bohemia" and sent to Italy by a ruler who lived in fear of the Italians but was able to "curb slaves with other slaves." Hatred between peoples can be useful only to "Kings who rule by dividing, until the nations fall into their arms." Would not these soldiers who were driven into the cathedral not also wish to "send their ruler to the Devil?"[66]

The Italian public was not entirely unacquainted with Czech literature. It knew the work for example of Dobrovský and Šafařík from two journals, *La Fama* of Milan and the Florentine *Anthology*, which began publication in the 1820s.[67] In 1832 the ideologue of "Young Europe" Giuseppe Mazzini published his discussion of the "Poetic Literature of Bohemia," which was based on the Englishman John Bowring's *Cech Anthology*. But Mazzini quickly left literary conclusions for political ones. He maintained that Czech literature was national, that it reflected the character of a nation; and the future of Europe belongs to its nations. "The European balance of monarchies is doomed to a sudden collapse in the face of the supreme rights of the nations." The growing struggle between Slavs and Germans in Bohemia would lead to the destruction of the Austrian Monarchy: "Austria is an obstacle to civilization, to progress, to the drawing together of Europe. It is necessary to destroy it or to reconcile oneself to the negation of nationality, glory, freedom, independence. Let us not delude ourselves. The time of resignation is drawing to a close also for Bohemia. The hour of the liberation of the people is nigh, and Slavdom will not disappoint us."[68] For Mazzini the Czechs (Tcheki, Ceski) were an important element in the process leading to the destruction of Austria and Turkey. The liberated Slavic peoples would then create a dam against Tsarist despotism and Russian panslavism. Belli's more sober views were published in English and French as part of a geographical and statistical survey of Bohemia. Equally sober were the judgments of the Sardinian politican Desare Balbo, published in 1844 under the title *The Hope of Italy*. Balbo looked for the speedy liberation of Poland; beyond this, however, he hoped that an Austria controlled by the Slavs would be able to protect the rest of Europe against Tsarism.[69] The Pole A. de Gorowski offered an original and "revolutionary" conception of Austroslavism in a study published in French at Florence in 1848. He defended the idea of union between Italian and Slavs, as formulated by Mazzini in his *Slavonic Notes*, and he also believed in a socialist future for Russia. Similarly Ruscalle Vegezzi emphasized that the role of the Slavs was to reconcile the east and west of Europe, as well as to promote social and national progress.[70] The "Czech question" therefore existed for Italian political exiles, for Young Italy, and partly as well for the Carbonari and the writers. For the Italian courts, on the other hand, the existence of Austria was still a necessity.

Just as in this sense there were two Italies, so too were there two Frances. "Restoration" France—the France of the Bourbons, of Chateaubriand and Barrand, which gazed towards Prague after 1830 because it was the seat of ex-King Charles X—knew of Bohemia and Moravia only as the region of Napoleon's campaigns and Metternich's congresses. But in the same year that M. Bignon published his study of the Congress of Troppau, a book by Marcel de Serre also appeared: *Austria, or the Morals, Customs and Ordinary Inhabitants of this Empire*.[71] By the end of the 1820s interest in Austria was quite usual. And from the correspondence of the Spanish liberal Castellano with Baron Jeszenák, we know that in central Europe there was the same keen interest in developments in France. Even the official *Pražské noviny* reported on events in France quite thoroughly, both during the revolutionary period in 1830 and during the risings of the Lyons weavers in 1831 and 1834; the newspaper even commented critically on French expansion in Algeria. In the 1830s A.C. Thibaudeau and Edgar Quinet wrote about Bohemia; the *Revue Britannique* reprinted articles on Bohemia from the British press, and "la Bohême pittoresque" attracted the attention of magazines including the prestigeous *Revue des deux Mondes*.[72]

But French writers showed a special interest in Bohemian history, especially the Hussites, during the 1840s. George Sand's work is a particularly good example. In 1842 she published her novel *Consuelo*, in 1843 *Jan Žižka*, and in 1845 *La Comtesse de Rudolstadt*. Count Albert of Rudolstadt, a "descendant of George of Poděbrady, King of Bohemia," recalls in some ways the unfortunate Count Schirnding, who at this time was nearing the end of his life in Prague.[73] What is the explanation for Sand's interest in Bohemia—an interest so vigorous and well-documented that it sparked scholarly speculation that the author had been in Bohemia incognito with Chopin? These were the years when George Sand was interested in a synthesis of "Christian evangelism, democracy and socialism," when she was influenced by Buchez's history of the French Revolution, by Pierre Leroux and Louis Blanc. The first volume of her *History of the French Revolution*, published in 1847, recalls its threefold prelude: the Reformation, the rise of the middle classes, and the Enlightenment. At the beginning of the discussion of the Reformation there is a section entitled simply "Jan Hus" which speaks of Hussitism as a Driving Force "with which individualism already pressed upon Christianity." According to the Soviet literary historian Reizov, George Sand was concerned with the "poetic actualization" of history. We might add that Louis Blanc's evocation of the Hussite revolutionary movement represented an indirect defense of the French Revolution—and the preparation not only of the political but also the "social" revolution of 1848.

In the nineteenth century the economic and cultural debt owed by the young Czech bourgeoisie to English civilization was enormous. But only at the end of the pre-March period can we find the beginnings of a certain Anglophile element in Czech society, which was still essentially petit-bourgeois. In the discussion of Charles Dickens's work that follwed the translation of his *Christmas Carol* by Mořic Fialka in 1846, there is a plain rejection of German criticism of Dickens, as well as a protest against the Czech's "daily bread of German literature." This sort of thing appeared immediately in the journal *Květy*, and the following year it was also usual in the *Pilgrim* and the *Journal of the Museum Society*. Anglophile opinion was reinforced by M.F. Klácel's study *Shakespeare, Goethe, Schiller*, and Jakub Malý placed the "pure and healthy spirit" of Shakespeare above that of the German poets and urged the translation of all Shakespeare's plays.[74]

The earliest translations were done at second-hand. Josef Jungmann translated Milton's *Paradise Lost* with the help of Jacek Przybylski's Polish version, and it was also through Polish translations that Mácha's rendering of Lord Byron's poems first appeared in Czech. Byron's friend in Italy was one of the Bohemian Taaffes, and another of his friends Robert Bowring tried to modify the usual conception of Bohemia exclusively as the land of Wallenstein, as it was for Coleridge, or of Libuše, as it was for Carlyle. From the middle of the

1820s the *Foreign Quarterly* contained mention of Czech scientific and literary life. The culmination was Bowring's review of Jungmann's *History of Czech Literature* and his own *Cech Anthology* published in London in 1832 on the basis of materials provided by F.L. Celakovský. Bowring's *Poetic Literature of Bohemia*, in its Italian and French versions, acquainted the west European public not only with Hus but also with current Czech literature.[75]

Nor was Bowring alone. In 1831 John Strong published an account of his travels in Germany, in which we find the Czech language described as the "Tuscan of the Slavic tongues," along with the information that the Czechs had their first printed book earlier than the English, and the conclusion that their love of music and their success in industry marked them for a hopeful future. Bowring ceased to concern himself with Czech motifs in the early 1840s and J.V. Frič relates in his *Memoirs* how appalled he was to discover in 1845 or 1846 that the refined "Lord Bowring" did not even know any Czech. What permanent interest there was addressed itself to the romantic chateaux and the west Bohemian spas. And in spite of the preoccupation of a handful of authors, Bohemia, thanks largely to Thackeray, continued to be identified primarily with "bohemianism." But in England as elsewhere there were two parties: here too, the one which interested itself in all the suppressed nations of Europe came to power in 1848.

The Czechs gratefully accepted every trace of interest that was directed towards them. They welcomed Julius Purdo's and John Paget's concern with Kollár and Slavs in general and were perhaps sorry when Paget became more interested in Hungary than Bohemia. J. Mitchell attracted their notice by drawing attention to Albrecht Wallenstein's Czech background. Bowring's book was smuggled into Prague as early as 1832. Jan Jeník of Bratřice took great trouble to procure a copy, and in his *Bohemika* he cited Bowring's works: "Time will remove all that has falsely obscured Žižka, Hus and George of Poděbrady, and will write their names indelibly in history as patriots, reformers and heroes. . . ."[77]

While the efforts in behalf of a "Czech" Shakespeare continued from the early 1820s, Czech periodicals also wrote about English industry and English culture. Between 1820 and 1825 Kramerius published translations of Ossian in *Cechoslava*Celakovský translated Walter Scott's *Lady of the Lake* in 1828; Palacký sent reports from England to the *Journal of the Museum Society; Květy* published Karel Sabina's "Pictures from England" in 1840. Jakub Malý translated excerpts from Byron, Washington Irving, and several recently founded journals published a wave of articles about English society and culture. Several well-known Czech writers began their careers with English themes—among them K.V. Zap, K.S. Amerling, M.F. Klácel, J.J. Malý, and

K. Sabina. Kollár and F. Doucha translated Shakespeare into Czech, and Mořic Fialka, a teacher of Czech at the Military Academy in Vienna, translated *Oliver Twist* in 1842.[78]

Karel Havlíček wrote frequently on Chartism and the Irish question, and he used the antagonism between London and Dublin as an oblique reference to that between Vienna and Prague. Repeal of course became a popular slogan in Bohemia. O'Connell's movement fell apart in 1843; Young Ireland wanted more, and the elections of 1846 meant the end of Repeal. The Repeal Club of Prague, whose existence interestingly enough remained unknown to the usually well-informed secret police, could fasten upon a "Czech Repeal" foreseen in a pamphlet entitled "Political Remembrances from Modern Austria," which was published in 1844. At that time, of course, the author was thinking of the Estates' opposition movement; the Irish and O'Connell were cited only as an example of what can be accomplished by national initiative. According to witnesses as different from each other as W.W. Tomek and J.V. Fric, the forerunner of the Prague Repeal Club was a patriotic society which met in pubs. Only in 1847 did Havlíček publish his articles popularizing the late O'Connell and the moribund Repeal. It was only now that the society, led by Vilém Gauc, František Havlíček and Ludvík Huppert, began to call itself the Repeal Club. In 1848 it met regularly at the "Golden Scale" in Havelská in the Old Town. It appears that Eduard Bass and Karel Slavíček described the society rather too exclusively from the viewpoint of elderly survivors of 1848, and that at the time its significance and uniqueness was largely unappreciated. Vojtěch Náprstek, whom Slavíček regarded as the founder of the original group in 1844, does not accord the "Repeal" Club any special place in his own memoirs; in fact he scarcely mentions it.[79]

The balance of Czech-English contact was not altogether one-sided. Bowring's studies of Czech literature led, as we have seen, to Mazzini's political writings. In 1839 the Scottish military chaplain G.R. Gleig published his account of travels in Bohemia and Hungary, in which there is a chapter about "Bohemia under the Habsburgs." Gleig brought with him to Bohemia an issue of the *Foreign Quarterly Review* with an article about Bohemia. It described how the Germans were suppressing the Czechs, how hard-working and patient the Czechs were, how they fought energetically for their language and their schools, and it concluded that their ultimate aim was the kind of freedom that they saw in England.[80]

Finally, the Czechs' efforts to overcome their isolation was able to span the vastness of the ocean, for some of the writers had contacts in the United States. Of the American writers, Benjamin Franklin and, strangely enough, Washington Irving were known to the Czechs. Irving even visited Bohemia, as did Longfellow. Charles Sealsfield (whose real name was K.A. Postl), once a resident of the Crusaders' Monastery in the Prague Old Town, became an anti-Austrian propagandist in 1828 with his *Austria as She Is*. He also introduced America and especially Texas to the German reading public. America was visited by merchants, especially glass dealers, and Catholic priests sent by the Leopoldine Foundation of Vienna. From 1834 we can trace the appearance of American themes in Czech newspapers and journals, and from the beginning the image of a free republic was clouded by the institution of slavery, conflicts with the Indians, and the expansionism of the young republic.[81]

In the 1840s criticism of American conditions became more and more open. In 1835 Jan Slavomír Tomíček, in his *Origins of the North-American States*, was an admirer of "American popular government," which he believed would soon permeate the European great powers, and he saw in it "the model of a free-thinking system." Nevertheless, he was also aware of slavery and the Indian problem.[82] The struggle for Texas and Oregon and the war against Mexico pushed reports of the Mormons and of female emancipation into the background. "America is the land of all things remarkable," Jakub Malý wrote in 1842 in a bitter commentary on the conflict over Texas, and in 1847 J. Benoni expressed similarly mixed feelings.[83] America represented different things to different people, but it is clear that the picture of a land of freedom was by no means accepted uncritically in the years before 1848. Yet it did represent a concrete alternative to the realities of central Europe.

The work of Charles Sealsfield raises the subject of the "Bohemian" literature written in German. Was it only "Germans" who wrote in German? Did not Katerina Klouczková (1833-58) consider herself a Czech patriot even though she used the German langauge? She is buried in Olšany cemetery among the leaders of Prague Czech society—Vyšehrad having become the fashionable cemetery for the Czech intelligentsia only in the 1860s. Most of them spoke and wrote both languages. All his life Bernard Bolzano considered himself a "Czech" who spoke German; Anton Gindely, who is buried nearby, had a similar view of himself, though in his lifetime faith in bilingual patriotism had become almost utopian. The descendants of Josef Helfert and his wife Anna (who was responsible for introducing the Christmas tree into Bohemia around 1820) became entirely Czech, though their forefathers came from the border town of Tachov, and before than from Bavaria. In the Malostranský cemetery and in Malvazinky are buried the patriots from the Left Bank of the Moldau, and they include nearly all of the first, "antiquarian," generation of "national revivalists": F.M. Pelcl, Ignac Corn, members of the Mánes family, as well as the Prachners, Dienzenhofers and Platzers, the admirers of Mozart, Goethe, and Schiller. The Dušek family of Bertramka, V.J.

Tomášk, and Haas are also buried here. In the second Left Bank cemetery of Malvazinky there is a monument to Egon Ebert, author of the "patriotic" epic *Vlasta*.[84]

Certainly Clemens Brentano's *Foundation of Prague* and Grillparzer's *Libussa* belong to German literature. Perhaps therefore they retain greater credibility than Alfred Meissner's *Vlasta* or Uffo Horn's *Žižka*. Even though their literary achievement appears somewhat faded today, their political impact at the time was powerful. Some of the journals, too, had great political significance. One of them was *East and West*, published by Elbert's brother-in-law Rudolf Glaser. And it should not be forgotten that Elbert's *Vlasta* received praise from Goethe himself. Certainly this literature of the "Czech Germans" is obsolete today, and it was deprived of its political impact by the events of 1848. Yet it was the soil from which came the work of R.M. Rilke (whose ancestors lie in Olšany), Franz Werfel, Franz Kafka, and Karl Kraus. Ebert took over the themes of Vlasta and Libuše from Dobrovský, as did Clemens Brentano. There was no difference yet in the sources from which the Czech and German writers drew their inspiration.[85]

Does the same apply to those journals through which the German-speaking public informed itself of developments in Bohemia? Among the most popular journals was the liberal *Die Grenzboten*, founded in 1841 in Brussels by a native of Prague Ignatz Kuranda, and published in Leipzig after 1842. Among its contributors were liberal aristocrats like Count Friedrich Deym and Baron Doblhoff. There were also young Bohemian German authors such as Moritz Hartmann, Uffo Horn, Alfred Meissner, and Josef Rank, whose difficulties with the censorship and imprisonment in 1845 were given thorough coverage in the magazine.

If we browse through the issues of *Die Grenzboten* before 1848 it becomes clear that this well-managed journal devoted itself to some issues in Bohemian affairs that were consistently neglected by the newspapers. On the whole it assumed a criticial posture towards the Estates' opposition and their demands for political liberalization, because it had concluded that the nobility was interested principally in the survival of feudalism. The *Grenzboten* was staunchly Josephine-Centralist in its outlook. It expressed growing apprehension that the Austrian government was unwilling to undertake the solution of thorny economic and social problems, and in this sense it reflected the viewpoint of the German entrepreneur class and the industrial bourgeoisie. The magazine devoted substantially less attention to the nationality question, including the changing relationship between German and Czech elements in Bohemian society. Whatever comment appeared concerning Czech-German relations was of course from the perspective of the Bohemian Germans.

The *Grenzboten* published thoughtful commentary on the workers' riots of June and July 1844, and it accused Austria of backwardness in its withdrawal from the German Customs Union. It suggested that Josef II had been able to deal with social problems, and it maintained that the disturbances in Bohemia must be blamed on the government's inability to halt rises in the price of food. The magazine admitted that the Czechs had cause to be discontented: they were the ones, after all, who felt the full effects of bureaucratism and clericalism; and it was primarily in the Czech regions where demands for agrarian reform were strongest. On the other hand, the *Grenzboten* suspected the government of supporting Czech nationalism—which must have caused Metternich some perplexity—and maintained that the language measures operated to the exclusive advantage of the Czechs. The Czechs were also identified as anti-Semites (Kuranda and a number of his associates had grown up in the Prague Ghetto). The journal's contributors were uninformed about the political program of the Czechs, thus so, too, were its readers. As early as the autumn of 1847 we read that because of the numerical superiority of the Slavs in Austria, Austroslavism most perfectly corresponds to the interests of the Slavic peoples. And the *Grenzboten* left no doubt that it regarded the Austroslav solution as unsatisfactory.[86]

The *Grenzboten* was unaware of the approaching revolutionary crisis in central Europe, and when it actually arrived, Kuranda and his associates were unsure what to do with their newly won freedom. This did not bode well for the future—either for the revolution itself or solutions to problems in Czech-German relations.

III

The Autumn of the Old Order and the Springtime of the Peoples

> It is now forty years since I first took up my position against revolution; and if I am still far from the goal that I have pursued all these years, I must still confess that, had I swerved even for a single day from from the course which I regard as the only proper one, many things would be far worse in the Empire than they are today.
>
> Metternich to Hartig, July 7, 1843

1. Metternich and the Spectre of Revolution

A detailed study of Metternich's position on the Czech question would be welcome for many reasons. We know that in peacetime Metternich identified "Czech patriotism" as the cause of not terribly dangerous dislocations, but he believed that it could have catastrophic results in a time of crisis. Since Metternich dominated Austria after 1809 and European politics after 1813, we can come to no conclusion about any of the broad problems of the first half of the nineteenth century—including the Czech national revival—without giving this remarkable figure his due consideration.[1]

The notion that pre-March Austria and its government stood behind the demands of the Czechs has little evidence to support it. Not only Metternich but also his critic and associate, the otherwise cultivated and perceptive president of the Court Chamber Kübeck, viewed every advance of liberalism as a serious threat. He trusted neither the Lower Austrian nor the Bohemian Estates, and he believed that they were dominated by "the party which is undermining all of Europe, an alliance between blind appeasement and communist radicalism." Kübeck considered the "liberalism of a new kind," proclaimed by the Bohemian Estates' opposition led by Tocqueville's disciple Leo Thun-Hohenstein, to be the cause of the revolution. In 1850 he noted that "in Austria the revolution devoured the nobility and democracy both, from whose union it had originated, and it ushered the army, the bureaucracy and the Church into power—the three great buttresses of Monarchy, as long as they are handled properly."

But Metternich did not take the internal threat very seriously until the autumn of 1847. In any case it did not come within the purview of his own department, and, like the modern admirers of his "art of statesmanship," he was convinced that foreign policy would always be able to justify his grand conception of a "scale of order." This was Henry Kissinger's argument in *A World Restored*, and he discerned Metternich's greatness as a statesman in his unfailing ability to find the right balance between his "legitimist" convictions and the requirements of Austria's situation. Metternich's principle of "legitimacy" enabled him, together with Castlereagh and Talleyrand, to construct a balance of power in Europe after the fall of the Napoleonic system—a balance in which potentially revolutionary France was neutralized by being thrust into conventional great-power politics. According to Kissinger, Metternich and his colleagues, conservative statesmen from lands with a "traditional" social structure—Great Britain was the exception, making Castlereagh's position particularly difficult—were struggling to implement a counter-revolutionary policy, and they were successful as long as they were able to achieve the "legitimization" of their aims at home and abroad. Since Castlereagh committed suicide in 1822 and Talleyrand died in 1838, only Metternich was left to undergo the test of a statesman: he saw the development of a revolutionary situation, and he took some steps against it.[3]

Kissinger, a profound admirer of Metternich, concluded his book with an account of the last intervention, organized against the danger of revolution in Spain in 1823. Thus he has relieved himself of the obligation to prove that Metternich was indeed interested in "legitimization"—a term evidently borrowed from Max Weber and Talcott Parsons. Aside from a passing reference to the multinational structure of the Austrian Monarchy, Kissinger made no attempt to deal with the nationality question, nor did he even mention Metternich's relationship to the nobility and its political program.

Metternich was the heir of eighteenth-century rationalism, and he cared not a whit for the tradition of the Estates. Neither did he care about "Austrian patriotism" or an "Austrian nation," not to mention the "patriotism" applied to Tyrol, Hungary, Lower Austria, or Bohemia. But there was a good deal of effort devoted to uniting the two. The views of a man who considered himself Palacký's rival are instructive in this connection. Josef Leonard Knoll was a professor in the universities of Olomouc, Prague, and finally Vienna, and his writings reflect the views of a Bohemian German historian concerning the Czech national revival. In 1939 Eduard Winter concluded that the Enlightenment "re-integrated Bohemia into the pan-German spiritual rhythm," and thus encouraged Germans to direct their interest to Bohemia's past "in a Czech frame of mind, and to forget too often about the German tradition in the land." Josef Pfitzner went further by emphasizing that in the period of the

Czech revival the Bohemian Germans were "forced onto the defensive as a result of their historical position in Austria," and he praised Knoll's book as a "portrait of the Sudeten lands and Austria from a German point of view." In 1941 Rudolf Schreiber declared that Germans in Bohemia became aware of their German ethnic character only in 1848: "they penetrated the fog of Habsburg dynastic and patriotic feelings and expressed their will for greater German unity." Ten years later Schreiber concluded that the blame for the drift of events lay with the "good will and benevolence of the Germans," who failed to comprehend that Bohemian political patriotism was being turned into "an agressive ploy on the part of the Czechs to seize the government and make their own nation dominant." Metternich himself shared in the blame because he welcomed "Czechism" as an ally for his own programs.[4]

This picture of Machiavellian Czechs and unsuspecting Germans is of course far from reality. In the first place, Josef Knoll was not consistently the ideological ancestor of the "Sudeten German" historians of the twentieth century. His one published work, *Centers of Historical Research and Writing in Bohemia and Moravia*, which appeared in German at Olomouc in 1821, suggested that "special histories of the individual lands" would provide the best foundation for a "classical history of the whole Austrian political structure."This was a view obviously very close to the "land-patriotism" of the nobility, and it was not very original. It came from J. von Müller's conception of a history of Switzerland, to be synthesized from its cantonal foundations, which was accepted by the Austrian Court historian Baron Josef Hormayr. It was embraced by Archduke Johann, the founder of the Graz Johanneum—the model for the Land Museums at Prague and Brno, which drew stiff opposition from the Sternberg brothers in Bohemia and from the Moravian Lieutenant Governor Mittrowsky.

Soon after the publication of Knoll's book, Müller's and Hormayr's works were withdrawn from circulation, and Knoll began to make plans for a new textbook of world history to "celebrate our Monarchy and our country." While he was in Olomouc Knoll wrote articles against the "system which encourages the darkness of ignorance," which he forwarded to Mittrowsky, and he argued in favor of a public review of teachers and scholars. After moving to Prague in 1832 Knoll propagated quite different views, which he continued to send to Mittrowsky, now in Vienna as president of the Court Study Commission, who he hoped would pass them along to members of the government. In his "Memoir Concerning the Principles which Ought to Permeate a History of the Austrian Empire," written in 1837, he no longer favored the idea of writing a history of the Monarchy from the point of view of the various lands or national groups. On the contrary, Austria's justification was that she perpetuated the tradition of the Holy Roman Empire and formed part of the "unity of German states." Palacký's *History of Bohemia*, as Knoll discovered with the appearance of its first volume, was written from a Czech rather than a "Bohemian" perspective: "vom Standpunkt eines Cechen, nicht eines Böhmen." "The spirit which dominates the first volume of this *History of Bohemia* will lead to the outbreak of national struggles, and these will make it impossible for Austria to fulfil her historical mission of defending Europe against the East."

Thus Knoll properly understood the significance of the nationality question for the existence of the multinational Empire. However, the only solution that he could offer was to "strengthen the German element." Therefore the Royal Bohemian Scientific Society should be reorganized; the cultivation of Czech in the University and the Museum should be halted; the teaching of Czech literature should be restricted and language training should be designed to meet the needs of administrators and merchants. Germans must maintain at all costs their leading position in the Monarchy, and the censorship should be used as a tool to assist them. Thus the universities were no longer to be centers of historical research, as he suggested in 1821, but instead must serve the need for unity within the Monarchy. The Bohemian seminaries should be closed and their students given scholarships to study in Vienna. The same goal of Germanization should be pursued by pensions for girls and the military garrisons.

These ideas were greatly admired by the Nazi historians J. Pfitzner, Heinz Zatschek, and W. Wolfram von Wolmar, but to Mittrowsky they appeared so inane that he wanted nothing to do with them or their author.[5] They were also poles apart from the views of Knoll's liberal successor at Olomouc Karl Johann Vietz, who was later called to Vienna and Prague. In 1844 Vietz published his *Study of Universal History According to the Present State of Historical Science and Literature*, which made no plea for the Germans' right to supremacy in Austria. Vietz gave prominence to the work of Dobrovský, Jungmann and Safařík, and he launched no attack against "panslavism," "russophilism"or "Czechism." Therefore he never received any special praise from Nazi historians. In a memoir of June 1844 Vietz argued that the government should not view historical scholarship with such great suspicion, since on the whole it may be depended upon to take the edge off criticism of contemporary conditions. An Austrian national consciousness can be created only when it is explained to all citizens just what the Austrian nation (*natio austriaca*) in fact is. Since the government refused to foster the teaching of Austrian history, "the public in the provinces turns to its own special history, which is well cultivated in many places through the support of the Estates and the efforts of private scholars. ... Surely a capable and attractive presentation of Austrian history would soon put provincial patriotism on the right track ...."[6]

Just how far Metternich himself was removed from such an understanding of the problem is shown by his letter to Hartig which was cited at the beginning of this chapter:

... Only when people understand one another can they proceed along a common path. The exceptions will be those who do not understand even themselves ... The source of failure to understand oneself is failure to grasp the importance of problems and to lose oneself in details .... The worst of details is cosideration for individuals. It is not individuals' who are the reason for the general decay, but their cult is the source of the present weakness. Hungary offers us a political example of this truth. For all of a half-century they had no real government, and today we are faced with a truly serious problem: it is as though we had to repair a machine whose parts are either broken or else covered with dirt and rust. But the repair is necessary, and therefore we must not hesitate to use all the power at our disposal ....[7]

Metternich's opposition to the reform movement, led by Széchenyi in Hungary, was not expressed in any other way—apparently he was unable to win over the court, as he vaguely promised in the later part of his letter. Széchenyi was friendly with at least one member of the emerging Bohemian Estates opposition. This was Josef Matthias Thun-Hohenstein of Klášterec, whose efforts were regarded with considerable sympathy by his cousin Leo Thun-Hohenstein of Děčín.[8] Josef Matthias worked untiringly for the spread of Czech letters in German surroundings. But neither he nor Leo ever learned the Czech language very well. Leo at least did study assiduously, receiving encouragement from Václav Hanka, and in 1842-3 his German pamphlets about the state of the Czech language and the national movement, as well as his polemics with Franz Pulszky about the situation of the Slovaks, attracted considerable attention. The Thuns' position, however, did not go beyond "land patriotism" focused upon the privileges of the Estates and aiming for a certain measure of administrative reform. If the goal was not precisely a renewal of "Czech" statehood, it did at least include administrative autonomy as well as official parity of the Czech and German languages.

But just how far were the Thuns, the Deyms, Lažanskýs, or the Nostitzes willing to go? The question is not easy to answer, because all of them were so thoroughly shaken by the revolution of 1848 that they promptly severed their connection with the dangerous Czech national movement. Among their papers they preserved only those concerning their involvement in the "cultural effort," and their efforts for the economic improvement of the land. The pattern is clear in the archive of Friedrich Deym, who wanted to raise Bohemia to the economic level of Lombardy-Venetia or Westphalia; or in that of Franz Hartig, who belonged to the circle of Metternich's associates in spite of his occasional reservations about the Chancellor's economic policies—Metternich did not always distinguish very clearly between private and state finances.⁹

Statistics and economics also interested Metternich's rival Count Anton Kolowrat-Liebštejnský, whose most interesting papers are not in the family archive of Rychnov but in that of his heirs, the Lützow family. This previously unknown material indicates that this confidant of Francis I was deeply interested first in the economic problems of the Monarchy, then in the affairs of Italy, Poland, and Hungary; for awhile at least he was in close contact with Archduke Johann.¹² But he left nothing concerning his connection with the Bohemian Estates and the Czech national movement, aside from diplomas of honorary citizenship, membership of organizations and so forth. From the viewpoint of the spokesmen of the younger generation of the aristocracy, who in 1843 listened to Palacký's exposition of Bohemian state rights—members of the families of Deym, Thun, Neuberg, Nostitz, Buquoy—Anton Kolowrat seemed just as much a relic of the past as the Supreme Burggrave Chotek, whom the Estates' opposition had just succeeded in removing from office.

But it cannot be said that Palacký was able to influence the political program of this aristocratic opposition, or that his own position may be equated with it. It is highly doubtful that Palacký felt any sympathy with these individual members of the nobility who like nineteenth-century Don Quixotes struggled in the name of Restoration of Feudal Reaction against revolution, fictitious democracy and industrial civilization: men like Felix Lichnowsky or Frederick Schwarzenberg of Orlík. In his *Notes of the Last Lanzknecht*, published in Vienna in 1844, Schwarzenberg treated revolutionaries like Louis Blanc or Barthes with considerable respect, and the merchant representatives of the bourgeoisie with boundless condescension.¹² Felix Lichnowsky, who like Frederick Schwarzenberg had fought in the Carlist war in northern Spain, was a Prussian Junker whose family also held estates in Silesia with a seat at Hradec near Troppau.¹³ Both men were to play not insignificant roles in 1848, which may be said, too, of Frederick's brothers Karl and Edmund, and of course their cousin Felix Schwarzenberg. The latter, after a stormy youth spent in provincial garrisons, and after a number of quite stimulating scandals, settled down to a serious pursuit of a military and diplomatic career.¹⁴

Felix Schwarzenberg, as his school notebooks show, could regard Czech only as the language of cooks, stable boys, and huntsmen. His attitude towards the problems of the Czechs was very different from that of the Thun-Hohensteins, Sternbergs, and the Choteks. Neither Jungmann nor Palacký could ever come to an understanding with the magnate-military section of the nobility. But if there was such a huge difference of outlook within the Bohemian nobility, it is necessary to determine just who composed this class. This can be done partly with the help of Palacký's *Description of the Kingdom of Bohemia*, compiled from statistics of 1843 but not published until 1848.[18] Palacký's *Description* is not without errors, and it contains no comparative data. Nor did Palacký and his assistant W. W. Tomek even try to sum up all the information they collected, much less analyze it. But it does acquaint us with the owners of the 932 feudal domains in Bohemia. In 1843 this group of noble landholders numbered only 187. In the middle of the eighteenth century, when the Theresian Cadastre was being compiled, there were 1,601 separate domains and 693 individual holders.

But to assess the character of the "Bohemian nobility" at the beginning of the revolutionary year a more precise definition must be found. Thus the "nobility" as a "feudal ruling class" can include only those noblemen who had actually "bought into the land"—those who were inscribed in the *Tabulae regni* as estate holders and who had tenants. This group of people will not be utterly consistent with the "nobility" in a more traditional sense. It will include, ror example, Dr. Jan Měchura, Palacký's father-in-law, who owned two estates in western Bohemia with about nine hundred peasants, most of them Czechs. But it will not include Jan Jeník of Bratřice even though he belonged to an old knightly family. High administrative officials who did not own noble estates did not belong among the aristocrats of the Estates except in a social sense, even though since the middle of the seventeenth century they constituted the primary buttress of the Danubian Monarchy.

The "Bohemian" nobility in the narrower sense can be traced from the middle of the sixteenth century. Its composition may be discovered in the *Tabulae regni* for the sixteenth and seventeenth centuries, the *Berni rula* of 1656, the Theresian Cadastre of 1757 and Palacký's *Description*. The changes which took place over three centuries were dramatic indeed. In the first place, the numbers of noblemen in the realm changed significantly:

	1615	1656	1757	1843
Pre-1620 Families	1,174	308	74	42
Post-1620 families	—	192	48	31
Families arriving 1656-1757	—	—	154	39
Families arriving 1758-1843	—	—	—	75
Totals	1,174	500	276	187

But the changes were still greater than the figures by themselves suggest, chiefly because of the circumstances in which they occurred. Even before the Battle of the White Mountain, nearly a quarter of the Bohemian nobility was "new" in the sense that it had not existed in the land more than two generations. A wave of ennoblements began with the first of the Habsburg kings Ferdinand I, who hoped thereby to strengthen his position in the land, and this policy was resumed by his grandson Rudolf II. The confiscations represented a fundamental change, but they bore little direct relationship to the "revolutionary" activities of noblemen in 1618-1620. In other words, the Habsburgs were trying to avoid the possibility of a revived aristocratic opposition in Bohemia, and at the same time to cut away the economic foundation of resistance. The policy of economic ruin was quite successful, and its effects lasted at least a century. What was important about the "new nobility" after 1620 was not so much their sheer numbers as their quality or character. Thus for example about 40 percent of the "new noblemen" whom the Habsburgs placed in Bohemia during the Thirty Years' War were officers, bureaucrats or military entrepreneurs who failed to establish their families in the land. Those that remained became part of the "Austrian" supranational nobility, who held the entire system together until 1918.[16]

What amounted to a revolt by the Bohemian Estates against the Habsburgs occurred in 1741-2: a minority, though by no means an insignificant one, of the 660 members of the aristocracy deserted Maria Theresa and pledged themselves to Karl Albert of Bavaria, who was supported by the French army. They included great and small noblemen, from old families and more recent ones. The old families included Dohalský, Chotek, Czernin, Kokořov, Kolowrat-Novohradský, Lažanský, Wratislaw of Mitrovice, Sternberg, Waldstein-Wartemberg,. Věžník. Some of the newer ones were Buquoy, Clary, Desfours, Hallweil, Kaiserstein, Königsegg, Khuenburg, Morzin, Nostitz-Reineck, Paradis, Piccolomini, Pötting, Trautmannsdorf. It was chiefly members of bureaucratic families who bore the punishments meted out after 1742. The property of relatives of the Bavarian Elector and that of the leaders of the "rebellion" was sequestered—but not confiscated. The rebels from the petty nobility were not greatly affected because they had little property to begin with, and this was the case for example of Josef Deym. Even in some cases involving an extreme "vacillation of loyalty"—for instance that of Count Rudolf Chotek—Maria Theresa did nothing, because she badly needed the services of capable men. Thus the disturbances in the middle of the eighteenth century did not result in another decimation of the society of the Bohemian Estates, and its economic power remained substantially unaffected. Noblemen's political influence as members of the Diet in any case amounted to practically nothing.[17]

The noblemen associated with the emerging Estates' opposition in the 1840s belonged to a social group which had undergone continuous change in the preceding four centuries. To speak of their "Czech" or "Bohemian" provenance is rather difficult, because only about a quarter of them could claim ancestors who were Bohemian noblemen before the Battle of the White Mountain. A good 40 percent of them came from families which acquired their estates in Bohemia only after 1757.

The property of the various families may be measured by several criteria: the geographical extent of their lands; the number of peasants settled upon them; the amount of the taxes they paid. If we look at the situation according to the second criterion, the wealthiest families were these:

	Numbers of Tenants
Schwarzenberg (new)	269,600
Waldstein-Wartemberg (old)	108,600
Clam-Gallas (new)	97,100
Lobkowitz (old)	96,700
Kinský (old)	95,000
Trautmannsdorf (new)	76,200
Habsburg-Lorraine (Prince of Tuscany)	73,600
Auersperg (new)	71,200
Harrach (new)	70,000
Czernin (old)	67,000

The list of the wealthiest individual noblemen looks slightly different:

Johann Adolf Prince Schwarzenberg	218,700
Eduard Clam-Gallas	97,100
Leopold II of Tuscany	73,600
Ferdinand Prince Lobkowitz	72,100
Dugen Count Czernin	64,400
Karl Duke Rohan-Rochefort	63,800
Ferdinand Prince Dietrichstein	63,100
Ferdinand Prince Trautmannsdorf	60,300
Anton Count Waldstein-Wartenberg	58,800
Rudolf Prince Kinský	57,800

Generally it may be said that control of the land was shared by a small group of noblemen, most of whose families were of post-White Mountain origin. Aside from those families in the lists above, the magnates also included Harrach, Thurn-Taxis, Colloredo, Mansfeld, and Windischgrätz. The younger sons of these families, who had the same titles but small hope of inheritance, searched all the more eagerly for careers in the service of the Monarchy. This was true of the Třeboň and Orlík branches of the Schwarzenberg family, the Clam-Gallases and the Windischgrätzes, all of whom were closely related to each other (Alfred

Windischgrätz's wife, for example, was a Schwarzenberg). They had contacts at Court, where the Dietrichsteins and Liechtensteins were hereditary officeholders. Only sporadically did members of these families associate themselves with Bohemian land-patriotism. Some members of this group had close relations with Metternich, whose family also belonged to the post-White Mountain nobility.

The old noble families appeared to be on the rise in the nineteenth century, at least compared with their situation in the eighteenth, even though their ranks continued to shrink through extinction. The Waldstein-Wartembergs, Lobkowitzes, Kinskys and Czernins were prominent in the cultural life of the land, and they maintained a positive attitude towards the movement of land-patriotism even though they were not active participants. More in the foreground in this regard were Nostitz-Reineck, Kolowrat-Liebsteinský and Kolowrat-Krakowský. Clam-Gallas, Sternberg and Chotek all remained temporarily on the sidelines. The Lobkowitzes were in close touch with the first group, but they were not as committed as the Deyms or the Lažanskýs, who, however, were not very prominent in terms of wealth.

Most of the noblemen who arrived at the end of the eighteenth century and in the nineteenth had been uprooted by the Revolution in France and its echoes in Germany: the Princes of Tuscany, Rohan-Rochefort, Lippe-Schaumburg, Hohenlohe-Sigmaringen, Schonborn, Pourtalés. But there were also successful new men of bourgeois background: Sina, Stark, Nádherný, Geymüller, to name a few.

If we look at the location of the magnate families' lands in the sixteen Bohemian regions (*kraje*), it is clear that between 1757 and 1843 more than a third of them disappeared. Czech and German entrepreneurs were equally active in the process of consolidation: The Princes of Tuscany and the Novák family bought large amounts of land in the Rakovník district, as did Wanke in Boleslav, Svoboda in Cáslav, Veith in Kouřim, Lumbe in Beroun, Daubek in Práchen. Their German counterparts were especially active in Loket, Zatec, and Pilsen. The proportion of aristocratic and non-aristocratic estate owners appears to have been quite propitious for the formation of a capitalist system of lands around Prague and the new industrial centers: in Loket, Kouřim, Zatec, Budweis, Beroun. The German nouveaux-riches who invested the profits of their industrial enterprise in land—men like Lanna, Lorenz, Stark, Wagner, Haas—were more numerous than the bourgeois landholders who associated themselves in some way with Czech "patriotism," such as Veith, Zátka, Safařík or Daubek.

If we view the situation in these terms, then it is indeed difficult to speak of a "Czech" nobility in the pre-March period. Even the most devoted antiquarian can find nothing "patriotic" among the papers of the largest landholders and prominent political figures among the "old" nobility which does not represent an attempt to shore up their own base of power or place limits on the financial demands of the Monarchy: they tried to discourage expensive wars, since Bohemia had to bear part of the burden; they tried to force the other lands, especially Hungary, to assume a more equitable share of the Monarchy's financial requirements. There was no other "Czech" or "Bohemian" policy than this. The defense of the "privileges" and "liberties" of the Estates, however, inevitably led to conflicts with their peers in other lands—again especially Hungary—and it ruined the chances of establishing any united Estates' opposition. At the same time, only the most successful of the wealthy bourgeois were accepted among the nobility, so that the formation of a politically influential bourgeoisie was slowed rather than encouraged by the conditions that prevailed before 1848.

František Palacký was by no means an obtuse observer, and he could not help but discern this situation long before 1848. His suggestions for the organization of the Museum show that at the beginning of the 1840s he had already abandoned the program put forward by the Sternberg brothers, and his emphasis on language and historical research determined the social direction of the Museum in the future. It was a program which did not correspond to the actual state of Czech society but rather anticipated it. After his arrival in Prague in 1823 he became associated with the Vaněk and Brož families through Josef Jungmann. Through Dobrovský he became acquainted with the circle of the Sternbergs, then later also with a basically bourgeois milieu which included members of the administrative nobility and more rarely the landowning nobility. In this way he became acquainted with Baron Stentsch, Ahsbahs, Astfeld, Rittersberg; he got to know Jeník of Bratřice, Dr. Held and the Eberts. With help from his "uncle" Jeník, Krtička of Jaden and Kalina von Jäthenstein, Palacký wooed and married the daughter of the Bohemian attorney-general Leopold Měchura, whose connections included the families of Lankisch, Rosner, Ubelly, Berchtold and Wratislaw of Mitrovice.

It was in these generally German-speaking and "Bohemian-patriotic" surroundings that Palacký prepared his Czech-language *History of the Bohemian Nation*. The last volume of the German *Geschichte von Böhmen* (part one, volume 3), extending to 1419, appeared in 1845 after difficulties with the censors. It is likely that his portrait of Hussite Bohemia would have met with still greater difficulties. Therefore the first volume of his Czech *History* was a translation of the already published German text, done chiefly by K. J. Erben.

The great value of Palacký's *History* sprang from his refusal to be satisfied merely with new facts and his insistence that the history of Bohemia be understood as part of European history. His notion of a Slavonic-Teutonic tension formed an interesting counterpart to Thierry's conception of a Romanic-Teutonic tension in English history. Not that Palacký was aware of Thierry's work: he became acquainted with it only in the middle of the 1840s. On the other hand, his conception of history as a struggle between centralism and freedom—and he recognized clearly that Slavs and Germans, Catholics and Protestants, conservatives and progressives all shared both these antagonistic forces—was essentially formulated by the beginning of the 1830s. Palacký was also unacquainted with Thierry's identification of the "Norman yoke" in England with feudalism and thus with his conception of the class divisions in society. He had no idea of Louis Blanc's high regard for the Hussite movement: his political ideal instead remained the conservative Guizot, one of the first victims of the revolutionary storm at the beginning of 1848.[18]

Metternich was certainly not one of Palacký's friends. In 1843 the Chancellor branded him as an enemy of the Monarchy and the "ideologue" of the Estates' opposition. Metternich wished to proceed against the opposition through the man he had chosen to succeed Chotek as Bohemian governor. But his plan to send Rudolf Stadion to Prague was thwarted by Kolowrat, who secured the support of the Archdukes Ludwig and Francis Charles for his own candidate, the young Archduke Stephen, son of the Hungarian Palatine Josef. Stephen was reported to be well-disposed toward the Estates. At the Diet of 1845 he certainly took no steps agianst the opposition, and the next year he even proposed an overhaul of the tax structure which amounted to the overthrow of the Renewed Constitution of 1627. In 1847 Metternich himself warned against tax changes without the approval of the Land Commission, and he hoped that General Windischgrätz would be able to contain the situation in Bohemia. When Stephen left for Hungary to assume his late father's post, Mettenich turned once again to Rudolf Stadion. In the end, Metternich was willing to enlarge the competence of the provincial Estates' assemblies. But it cannot be said that he ever took them very seriously: their role, in his view, was purely one of consent. On the whole, certainly, he did not consider the situation in Bohemia at the end of 1847 to be especially dangerous.[19]

Nor did he view the Hungarian situation with particular alarm. Here he relied on the help of the older generation of reformers, men like Baron Jóseki and Széchenyi, against the younger liberals and radicals led by Deak and Kossuth. In Galicia Stadion's administration appeared to be firmly in cntrol. In fact Lemberg presented a model of administrative efficiency, and after the occupation of Cracow and the dissolution of the Cracovian Republic in 1846, the threat of military attack from Russian or Prussian Poland appeared to have evaporated. In any case, Austria must take a firm stand with Russia and Prussia, as outlined in the Münchengrätz treaty of 1833, against the revolutionary inclinations of the Poles. The "northern triangle" was to operate automatically against every revolutionary threat. The attitude of Britain and France, of course, was another question. The Entente Cordiale, which emerged as early as 1823 from the decay of the Holy Alliance and the Congress System, now had behind it a quarter-century of stormy history. It was an agreement between the most industrially advanced of the great powers, and it was effective enough to prevent Austrian intervention in Belgium; it also survived several periods of difficulty and stress—the Carlist War in Spain, the two Egyptian crises and the plans to partition Turkey. In the 1840's Prussia consistently held back while Metternich modified the orchestration of the "concert of Europe" to meet each contingency as it arose, most often with the object of isolating France. Metternich probably reacted too strongly to French plans for expansion in North Africa and the Near East, which were defended in Paris chiefly by the Duc de Joinville.[20] Prime Minister Guizot had no fonder ambition than to reach agreement with Austria, and in 1845 France was prepared for military intervention in Switzerland in favor of the Catholic-conservative *Sonderbund*. But in October of 1847 the *Sonderbund* was torn apart—to Metternich's considerable sorrow, for he regarded even a neutral Switzerland as a likely field for dangerous revolutionary propaganda.

Certainly Metternich felt more confident in the diplomatic sphere than in the labyrinth of domestic politics—even thos of Lower Austria, the very heart of the Monarchy, whose Diet had seen the greatest penetration of bourgeois elements because of Vienna's position as the center of finance. A consequence was the emergence of opposition against survivals of feudalism. In the end, Metternich, Kolowrat, and Hartig were obliged to issue a special "charter" to the Lower Austrian Estates. After 1844 the demands advanced by the Diet of Lower Austria—the abolition of the peasants's obligations and a substantial limitation upon monarchical absolutism—could scarcely be contemplated in Bohemia or Hungary. In 1846 the Lower Austrian opposition submitted a sharp critique of the existing structure of the land tax; they demanded *urbarium* reform, the abolition of the excise, and public support for the working people in this year of depression. In 1847 Count Andrian-Wernburg, author of the pamphlet *Austria and her Future*, recommended that the Estates unite with the "fourth Estate" to force recognition of the equality of the bourgeois representatives. None of the opposition's demands was recognized. As late as March 3, 1848, the Emperor (*i.e.* the State Council) refused the Diet's request for control over the finances of the land.

Everyone in the government came in for criticism—primarily Metternich, who was accused of excessive reliance on Russia at the expense of further

Austrian expansion along the Danube. Kübeck was blamed for the financial crisis of 1847 and the growth of the public debt. The bureaucracy, led by Chancellor Inzaghi and Sedlnitzky, was criticized for tying the hands of the younger, more liberal administrators such as Pillersdorf. The authority for the censorship declined vastly, and in 1847 nobody even wanted to hear about it. The polemics between Metternich's press adviser Hügel and members of the opposition resulted in a further erosion of the "Metternich System." The government viewed the University of Prague's approaching 400th anniversary with apprehension, but it was unable even to take steps against the Viennese professor Hye, who publicly criticized the annexation of Cracow as a contravention of international law. In Vienna political societies sprang up which often received considerable support from high officials. One of them was the Concordia, composed of writers and artists; then there was the Legal and Political Society, which Sedlnitzky approved at the suggestion of Counsellor Sommaruga at a moment when Metternich himself was away from Vienna. Finally there was the Lower Austrian Commercial Society which supported the German customs union. In their campaign against the government the leaders of the Estates' opposition Bauernfeld and Doblhoff-Dier made adroit use of the poverty and unemployment which was particularly acute in Vienna in the winter of 1847-8.[21]

In 1847 Andrian-Wernburg declared that Austria had reached precisely the point where France stood in 1788, and Bauernfeld maintained that the year 1848 would bring all sorts of innovations. Metternich also expressed similar views on several occasions. But his remarks cannot be taken entirely at their face value because he hugely enjoyed his self-appointed role as indispensable statesman standing face to face with "the most acute social crisis of the last sixty years." His prophecies of political collapse throughout Europe in default of immediate measures against the "spread of radical and communist ideas" were too often directed to the political gallery.[22]

But he did not doubt the gravity of two problem areas: Italy and Poland. He considred Lombardy-Venetia and Galicia to be such dangerous trouble spots that in the winter of 1847-8 he moved quickly to secure himself in both territories. This is what lay behind the mission of his confidant Ficquelmont to Italy and that of Friedrich Thun-Hohenstein to St. Petersburg.

2 Ficquelmont and Thun on the Eve of the Revolution

Karl Ludwig Ficquelmont, Austrian general, diplomat and statesman, came from a noble family of Lorraine which in the seventeenth century followed Duke Charles V of Lorraine to Austria and already had behind it a tradition of service in Imperial regiments extending several generations. One of Karl Ludwig's father's cousins was executed during the French Revolution and a second fell in the struggle against the French at Verona in 1799. Karl Ludwig began his military career at the age of fifteen in the army of the émigrés; then he entered the Imperial army to fight under General Latour in the Rhineland. As a captain he returned briefly to France in 1804, but he left to serve as a major in Nassau's cuirassier regiment in the campaign of 1806, and after the Battle of Austerlitz he became chief of staff to Archduke Ferdinand d' Este, whose troops were in eastern Bohemia and Moravia. In this way he came into close contact with the Habsburg rulers at Modena.[23]

He left in 1809 to fight against Napoleon in Spain; he served on the staff of General Abadia first as a colonel than a brigadier general. He returned in time to take part in the Austrians' Italian campaign under Field Marshal Bellegarde. After the Congress of Troppau Ficquelmont returned to Italy as an envoy and member of the international commission which was to investigate Austrian intervention in Naples. In Florence he married the young Daria Tizenganzen and was appointed extraordinary envoy to the Kingdom of Sardinia. In Turin he sought to promote harmony with the Viennese Court. In 1829 Ficquelmont became ambassador to St. Petersburg, where he made a diligent study of military, economic, even religious conditions in the Russia of Nicholas I, while his wife opened her house to the leading representatives of Russian cultural life—V. A. Zhukovsky, Pushkin, V. Byazemsky. In 1839 Ficquelmont was recalled to Vienna to represent Metternich at the negotiations on the Eastern Question and the integrity of Turkish territory. He became a Conference Minister and head of the Military Section of the State Chancery. Generally he stood on the side of Marshal Radetzky against the Generality headed by Court War Counsellor Hardegg, and quite reasonably he worked for a reduction in the size of the army.

Mazzini's Young Italy had been Metternich's prime enemy for decades. Although Mazzini did not support attempts by the brothers Bandiera to kindle revolution in southern Italy in 1844, he was still viewed with justifiable suspicion by the Austrian authorities. He was not the only one: two spokesmen of the sober Italian bourgeoisie were little better off: the abbé Vincenzo Gioberti was the author of the *Moral and Civil Constitution of Italy*, and Massimo d' Azeglio wrote a pamphlet about *The Recent Events in Romagna*. Both were liberals who pinned their hopes on King Charles Albert, and they hailed the election of Pius IX in June 1846. In April 1847 the "Liberal Pope" promised to convene an advisory assembly and set up a citizens' militia; at the end of the year he even named a responsible government. The Austrian ambassador to the Vatican Count Rudolf Lützow, who had once arranged for Palacký's access to the Vatican Archives, expressed his fear that the ecclesiastical state was on the verge of anarchy.[25]

In this situation the commander of the Austrian army in Lombardy-Venetia Field Marshal Radetzky urged that the military forces be strengthened. In 1847 they numbered forty-seven companies of infantry and twenty-two squadrons of cavalry, divided into two army corps, seven divisions and seventeen brigades. The units were of varied composition. A large number of the infantry troops were recruited in Lombardy or Venetia. The light cavalry, chasseurs, were mostly Croats. In Lombardy, besides regiments from the Austrian lands, there were some from Hungary and Bohemia (Paumgarten's and Gyulay's). Kinský's infantry regiment in Venetia was from Styria. Besides Milan and Venice they held the famous Quadrilateral, the fortresses at Mantua, Verona, Peschiera and Legnago, and after the summer of 1847 also the bridges across the Po in Ferrara and Commacchio, the latter of which was actually on the territory of the Papal State. Austrian intervention was to be conducted as a "preventive action" against the "great insurrection" that was being planned. However, it called forth a storm of protest in London, and in Rome there was even a partial mobilization.

These were the circumstances in which Ficquelmont was sent to Northern Italy—officially to "advise" the Viceroy Rainer, but actually to determine how well-founded the government's fears of revolution really were. In December he reached a certain compromise in the Ferrara affair, although of course he was not able to halt the anti-Austrian movement in northern Italy. This failure was evident in the Scientific Congress held at Venice, before whose opening Ficquelmont met with the Prussian King Wilhelm IV and the "Pomeranian delegate to the Prussian Diet" Count Bismarck, whom the King greatly respected. The news from Ambassador Felix Schwarzenberg at Naples was ever more disquieting, and reports from Sardinia and even Tuscany were scarcely any better. Austria's policy was to divert attention from pressure for a customs union embracing Tuscany, the Papal States, and Sardinia, by binding Parma and Modena closer to Austria. The situation in Parma deteriorated after the death of the Archduchess Maria Luisa, once the wife of Napoleon I. Ficquelmont hoped to pacify Lombardy and Venetia by administrative reform and economic aid. At the end of 1847, fifty-seven companies and thirty-six squadrons stood on the Po, but they did not prevent the establishment of an Italian customs union, the demonstrative dispatch of Lord Minto to Italy, a boycott of the Austrian tobacco monopoly, or demonstrations of opposition in the coffeehouses, the university lecture halls, and the streets of Milan. In Naples a constitution was promulgated, and there could be no thought of a new intervention here because of the presence of the British fleet, which had been ordered to the Neapolitan coast by the Palmerston government. Ficquelmont sent one memorandum after another to Vienna, but his pleas for immediate reform remained unanswered.

In February of 1848 the President of the Court War Council Hardegg died, and Metternich tried to have Alfred Windischgrätz named as his successor. But since he was a mere Lieutenant Field Marshal, it was Ficquelmont who became the new president, probably to the considerable annoyance of Metternich. Certainly Ficquelmont's memoranda could have been welcomed neither by Metternich nor the more agressive generals such as Radetzky (whom Ficquelmont criticized) and Windischgrätz, nor even by the former ambassador in Naples Felix Schwarzenberg.[26] Ficquelmont was to be replaced in Milan by another of Metternich's diplomats, Hübner. But he, too, was unable to draw the military and civil administration together in concrete measures against the threat of revolution. From January to March of 1848 the revolutionary movement in Lombardy and Venetia steadily widened, and news of the revolutionary uprising in Vienna precipitated a critical situation in both provinces. Windischgrätz followed the political situation very closely, and he was kept well informed by members of Radetzky's circle—General Clam-Gallas, Count Wratislaw, Lieutenant Field Marshal Friedrich Taxis, Lieutenant Field Marshal d' Asprey. They also supplied him with highly secret information about the military situation.[27]

Ficquelmont's realistic assessment of the Italian situation at the beginning of 1848 suggested that Austria would be able to defend only Lombardy and Venetia at best—a bitter pill for Metternich and his aggressive advisers Windischgrätz and Schwarzenberg. But did not the Polish question provide a second point of crisis? When Ficquelmont returned from Milan to Vienna, Friedrich Thun-Hohenstein was just leaving to assume his new post as Austrian ambassador in Sweden. Tsar Nicholas's speech of February 24, 1848, in which he took a stand against British policy, was gratefully received by Metternich.[28] At the end of 1847, after the inglorious debacle of the *Sonderbund* in Switzerland, the Prussian and Austrian governments opened negotiations for reforms in the German Union. At that time Tsar Nicholas was opposed, and the Prussian diplomat Radowitz was to journey once again to Vienna at the beginning of March. Metternich hoped that all three Northern Powers would be brought together by the recent news of revolution in France. On February 28, Rothschild as usual was the first to receive reports of what had happened in France.

It was enough. Princess Melanie Metternich noted that the February Revolution of 1848 was a nearly perfect copy of the July Revolution of 1830.[29] It began as an action of the opposition inside and outside the Parliament, which wanted to force the dissolution of Guizot's government. One of the events was to be a great banquet planned for 22 February. Activists led by Ledru-Rollin convened a popular assembly at the Place de la Madeline, from which the throng was to proceed to the site of the banquet in the more fashionable Champs-Elysées. In front of the Parliament building the demonstrators, most of them students, were stopped by the police. A conflict ensued, and the first barricades were erected. However, they were occupied by the police, and the threat of violence seemed to have been averted.

Princess Melanie noted what she called a recipe for revolution: on the first day there are demonstrations, and barricades are erected; on the second day the revolution is defeated; the third day it triumphs. In Paris the formula was slightly altered: the barricades were flung to pieces on the first day, and on the second day there was fighting. There were tens of thousands of hungry and desperate people in the metropolis, and there were also arms dealers. Against the crowd, which until now demanded only the removal of the hated Guizot, stood the police with its military organization but numbering only 3,500 men. The National Guard was supposed to insure public order. It numbered about 80,000 and was divided into legions by arrondissement. It was a bourgeois organization and was regarded as a solid bulwark of the constitutional monarchy, but at the beginning of 1848 most of its members were opponents of Guizot's government. The military garrison at Paris contained about 30,000 troops, but intervention could be requested only by the National Guard.[30]

In miserable weather on the morning of February 23, many more people gathered than on the previous day, particularly in the narrow streets in the center, to which most of the action had shifted from the wide avenues of the western part of the city. The cries demanding Guizot's resignation were joined by voices raised against the King and the dynasty. The National Guard failed to appear even though it had been mobilized, and some of the guardsmen went over to the side of the demonstrators. The bourgeoisie deserted the Monarchy. In the afternoon the shaken Louis Philippe finally arrived at a decision: he dismissed Guizot abruptly and without ceremony. Yet he still could not bring himself to request one of the opposition leaders—Thiers or Barrot—to form a new government. So the demonstrations continued, and in the evening there was a conflict between the crowds (including the National Guard) and the army. The "massacre," which claimed forty to fifty casualties, led to a general insurrection. During the night about 500 barricades were erected throughout the city.

When on February 24 the King finally authorized Thiers to form a ministry, he also appointed General Bugeaud, who had won fame in the colonial wars in Algeria, as the commandant of the army and the National Guard. But Thiers found that even he was not very popular with the crowds in the streets, and he collapsed. Bugeaud discovered that the army was unwilling to fight and that the National Guard had defected to the insurrectionists. At noon he ordered a truce, and the King, who had made one more attempt to win over at least the "better" part of the National Guard, decided to abdicate. He left Paris for Le Havre, whence he fled to England, one of the first victims of the revolution but by no means the last.

With this all was decided. The fighting had not claimed very many lives: there were eight deaths on the side of the government, and among the revolutionaries in the streets and on the barricades about 290. Finally there was an attack on a symbol of the old order, the Tuileries, and Lamartine, the poet and amateur politician, appeared as the spokesman of "the people" to demand a democratic republic. Thus the afternoon of the 24th brought failure to the Duchess of Orleans, who had planned to present to the Parliament her son, in whose favor Louis Philippe had abdicated. In the general confusion Lamartine succeeded in setting up a temporary government in which he became the Foreign Minister. The new government, composed of members of the moderated opposition, moved into the Hôtel de Ville, where it received a number of delegations. One of them, representing the journal *La réforme* published by the democratic and socialist party, succeeded in having Louis Blanc accepted into the government along with a worker named Albert. This greatly upset many of the members of the government, who decidedly were not radicals. But the crowds became all the more radical, and Lamartine was only barely able to prevent the tricolor from being replaced by a red flag. The crowds wanted a social, if not socialist, republic, which would do someting about unemployment, hunger, and poverty. The "right to work" and the "organization of work" became slogans, and the pressure of the working masses resulted in the establishment on February 26 of National Workshops, a pale reflection of the "ateliers sociaux" envisaged by Louis Blanc. From the beginning the National Workshops were only charity intitutions, and the only measure that Blanc and his "work commission" were able to put through was a restriction on the length of the working day: ten hours in Paris and twelve in the provinces.[31]

If the reaction in Prague and Vienna to what was happening elsewhere can be estimated from the memoirs of individuals and from the police reports, it appears that the news from Italy had a greater impact than that from Paris. The Prague police Commissioner Josef Heyde submitted reports about the confiscation of leaflets urging the Czech populace not to fight against the Italians and instead to fight for a constitution:

Brothers! The Italians have arisen and are now in revolt against the injustices of the Austrian government, which, taking no notice of the powerful and angry voices in favor of improving the administration and strengthening nationality, is trying to crush this noble and just uprising. And other nationalities, including the oppressed Czechs, are asked to sacrifice their strength to this inhuman undertaking. We are asked to suppress liberty by shedding our blood, and to serve as the tool of the blindfolded Austrian court.

Brothers! Let there be no more sacrifices for a throne which regards us as its slaves, which oppresses us and burdens us with cruel taxes. The Italians are our brothers. Let us not fight against them, for they are as unhappy as we. Steel yourselves, and refuse to submit to further conscritption. Arise, unite, arm yourselves; liberate yourselves from all lordly and royal oppression, and create a constitution which shall endure on the basis of equality, justice and freedom. On March 20, 1848 there shall be a general uprising.[32]

According to Commissioner Heyde, the author of the broadside was an educated man—although the composition of the original does not confirm the judgment. In any case, he was never discovered, and the revolution in fact materialized before March 20.

In these circumstances Metternich sent Friedrich Thun-Hohenstein on a secret mission to St. Petersburg. Instead of proceeding directly to his post at Stockholm, he left by train from Vienna, reaching Warsaw on March 27; and he arrived in St. Petersburg on April 1.

We do not know precisely when Thun left Vienna. The Hungarian historian Erzsébet Andics, who was the first to grasp the significance of Thun's secret mission, believed that it represented the first action of the new Kolowrat government and its foreign minister Ficquelmont.[33] However, it appears likely that Ficquelmont planned Thun's mission while he was still Metternich's adviser for Russian and Italian affairs, after his return from Italy. Melanie Metternich noted his appointment as President of the Court War Council on March 4 and mentioned that it aroused some opposition. Among Ficquelmont's papers is a memorandum concerning Russia, written in Vienna on March 12.[34] His papers also include letters from Chancellor Nesselrode, Count Vorontzoff, and the Prussian envoy von Rochow.[35]

Thun's first dispatch to Ficquelmont from St. Petersburg on April 5 reports that immediately after his arrival he was received by Nesselrode and that the two discussed the significance of the recent events in Austria (13 March). Thun was apparently informed by a dispatch that arrived at St. Petersburg by courier. It is likely that at the same time he received Ficquelmont's letter of authorization, in which Thun was invited "to emphasize most strongly that the changes which have taken place modify neither the principles of the alliance nor its objectives ...."[36] Further dispatches, containing information about the aims of the new government, were so surprising that Nesselrode, for his part, informed Thun of the contents of reports that he had received from Fonton, the Russian diplomatic representative at Vienna. Nesselrode was sorry for Metternich because "he was the servant of Austria, even all Europe," and he himself had a higher regard for Austria than for Prussia, whose king, it appeared, had gone over completely to the revolutionaries.[37]

On the day of his arrival at St. Petersburg Thun was invited to an audience with the Tsar for the following day, April 2. Nicholas behaved with great sincerity and suggested that he and Thun speak German instead of French, because it would be more "congenial." The Tsar regarded the Austria of Francis I as his second homeland, though he harbored no illusions about the state of affairs after the Emperor's death. Like Nesselrode, he drew a distinction between the "honorable men" in Vienna and his revolutionary brother-in-law the King of Prussia. What had occurred in Vienna was simply a political coup precipitated by the Estates' opposition—and nothing more.

Nicholas's chief concern was to prevent the liberation of Cracow, for he could "never tolerate" a hotbed of revolution so close to his own borders. If the revolutionary movement in Galacia should prove impossible to contain, he would be forced to intervene and restore peace in Austria, to preserve the traditional friendship between the two monarchies. Thus he had nothing in common with the russophilism which was so greatly feared in Vienna. "I have not always shared Prince Metternich's views. I have criticized his System." But in the present circumstances the Chancellor was being treated less than honorably.

Further news from Vienna dated March 26 arrived on April 2, from which the Russian Chancellor surmised that the Viceroy Stadion had been able to maintain order in Galicia, while in Cracow Deym had freed all political prisoners. On the morning of April 3, Nesselrode gave Thun the bad news of the revolution's success in Italy. Later in the day he was received by the Grand Duke Alexander, his wife, and the Tsarina, and he spent the evening with the Grand Princess Helena. During the afternoon Nesselrode informed him of the contents of a dispatch that he was sending to Medem in Vienna, emphasizing the Tsar's interest in the indivisibility of the Habsburg Monarchy, and the need to strengthen the Russo-Austrian alliance as a bulwark against revolution. Any threat to the integrity of the Monarchy, for example, in Galicia, would constitute a *casus belli* for Russia just as for Austria. The Russian government had no wish to prolong the conflict and desired to maintain a strict neutrality towards events in Europe; it asked the same of the other European states. But along with the principle of neutrality it must also defend the principle of a "territorial balance" of power. This concerned principally Austria, which was placed in a privileged position.[38]

On April 11 Thun wrote out two dispatches to Ficquelmont continuing his account of his reception and outlining the Russian reaction to the "perfidy" of Charles Albert of Sardinia and to the uprising in Milan. In his opinion the Tsar's government did not wish to pursue an aggressive policy, but it was doubtless anxious about Austria's internal complications—in Galicia above all but also in Lombardy and Hungary. The leaders of the Hungarian movement in Russia could be shot as outlaws. Thun sent his first dispatch via Berlin, and a second "lettre particulière" through the Austrian chargé d'affaires at St. Petersburg Lebezeltern directly by courier.[39]

On the evening of April 11 Thun was invited to a "family dinner," after which he had a private conversation with Nicholas about the political situation. He hoped that the Austrian situation would be singular. He hoped that the Austrian army in Italy would be victorious and form a nucleus of strength that would contribute to a renewal of "my poor fatherland." The Tsar spoke with respect of Stadion and the generality; he also mentioned the special mission of General von Pfuel from Berlin. As we know from the correspondence of the Prussian ambassador Rochow, the Prussians' hopes, like those of the Austrians, were soon to be fixed upon the "elements of unity and strength," the army and the high bureaucracy.[40]

The last of Thun's papers concerning his secret mission is a letter that he sent to Metternich in London on May 2, 1848, from Stockholm. He declared his agitation at the events of March 13—which confirms that he was not present in Vienna at that time—and he assured the former Chancellor of his devotion. On May 13 Metternich replied, expressing the hope that they continue to correspond.[41]

Thus the aim of Thun's mission was not simply to inform Nicholas that the Emperor intended to grant certain constitutional privileges and administrative reforms. He was also to assure the Tsar that the Austrian government would attempt to renew order and uphold the existing structure of society. Nicholas demonstrated a certain understanding of all these necessities. As far as earlier commitments were concerned—and these were just as important to Ficquelmont as they were to Metternich, whom we may regard as the initiator of the whole affair—Nicholas had already expressed his views at the beginning of April. He would do nothing to threaten the unity of the Habsburg Monarchy—particularly anything involving the use of russophilism or panslavism. On the contrary, he and Chancellor Nesselrode had decided that the Tsar's government—by intervention if necessary—would defend order in the Polish, Italian, and Hungarian provinces of the Empire.

Just how far Metternich's successors were able to implement the general policy of a "renewal of the social order" in the face of the revolutionary outbursts can be judged after we turn our attention once again to the center of the continent—to Vienna, Prague and Pressburg.

IV

The March Revolution in Austria

"To all relatives and friends: I announce that my dear wife, née 'Svoboda' was delivered with some difficulty of a daughter on 15 March last. Mother and child are alive but very, very weak."

First Post Office Declaration for 1849, Prague

1. March 13, 1848: The Black Day for the Old Order

At the beginning of 1848 Vienna had nearly half a million inhabitants. It consisted of the inner city, still surrounded by the massive walls that were begun during the reign of Ferdinand I against the Turks, with ten ramparts, twelve gates and a deep moat, and many suburbs which in the eighteenth century were still surrounded by substantial earthworks, pierced by thirteen gates at which the hated food tax was collected. In the center of the city were the Court, the administrative offices, the palaces of the nobility, banks and shops, as well as the houses of the well-to-do bourgeoisie. Outside the center was the *Glacis* which served as a military exercise field, for which barracks were built in the suburbs. Partly because there was sufficient space, and partly because the workers lived there, the suburbs also contained the factories and workshops—with the exception of a few "better" areas—for example Leopoldstadt, where most of the Jewish population was concentrated.[1]

Besides the Court and the central administration, the center also contained the Lower Austrian provincial offices. The administration of the city itself was in the hands of the "Magistrate of the Royal and Imperial Capital and Residential City," whose members were appointed by the government. The burgomaster Ignatz Czapka was also a colonel and commandant of the urban militia. Under him were magisterial counsellors and secretaries, actuaries, adjuncts, and other municipal officers. In addition there was a so-called Wider City Council composed of wealthy bourgeois loyal to the state. The labor office was attached to the welfare office, the administration of justice was connected with that of the prisons. The maintenance of order was the reponsibility of the police administration, the burgher guard (*Bürgerwehr*), and the General Command for Lower Austria.

At the head of the police administration stood our old acquaintance Peter Muth, who was head of the Prague Police in 1844. The paramilitary police (*Militär-Polizeiwach-Corps*) numbered about 1,200 men, distributed among the municipal districts. Public order was the job of the burgher guard, with about 14,000 men, most of them from the upper and middle bourgeoisie. In contrast with the Paris National Guard it was rather poorly trained and equipped, and it turned out together only on such ceremonial occasions as the feast of Corpus Christi and the Emperor's birthday. The army's commanding general for Austria was Archduke Albert, whose rank was Lieutenant Field Marshal. The commandant of the Vienna garrison, consisting of about 15,000 men, was Major-General Josef Matauschek von Benndorf, whose headquarters were the barracks in suburban Salzgries.[2]

With the exception of the home-based Vienna regiment, the composition of the garrison betrayed the usual diversity, with most of the infantrymen coming from Galicia and Hungary. The composition of the city itself and its suburbs was equally varied. According to some estimates a quarter (perhaps actually closer to a fifth) of the population were Slavs, whose presence can be traced from the end of the seventeenth century in the ecclesiastical records—and of course also in the municipal records, which nobody has yet done. Aside from the Czech craftsmen organized into guilds, the liveliest group were the Czech students from Bohemia and Moravia. The diary of one of them, Vojta Náprstek, who came from the bourgeois house "U Halánskū" on the Bethlehem Square in Prague, helps us to understand how things stood in Vienna at the beginning of 1848.[3]

Náprstek's diary begins in June 1844, but it interests us only from 1848, when Náprstek was a student at the University of Vienna, highly dissatisfied with the situation in Austria and therefore yearning for the far-away lands of Asia or America. At the beginning of this section stands a declaration: "Meditation on the New Year: I fervently hope that I shall celebrate the First of January 1849 in Baltimore, or New York or Philadelphia." In Vienna Náprstek belonged to a circle which included A. Rybička and K. Schneider. In the winter they were responsible for organizing the posthumous demonstration in honor of Josef Jungmann, which took place on January 20, 1848, and which was a huge success—"We Slavs celebrated a triumph," Náprstek noted. He and his friends had previously become acquainted with the leaders of "Czech" society in Vienna. At this time he worked as a tutor for the landed Bergauer family and was in contact with Palacky and Havlíček. He was most impressed by Hanuš Kolowrat-Krakovský, the idealized type of Bohemian nobleman to be found in the pages of Božena Němcová's stories, and by Schwarzenberg's agricultural economist František Horský, who greeted the students with the remark that he, too, "had the honor to be a Czech." Horský was able to secure them the support of Prince Schwarzenberg (Fleix's father) who, although he did not declare himself specifically a Czech, nevertheless corresponded with the students in Czech. They received financial support from Coloredo-Mansfeld, Harrach, and Nádherný of Borutín, a director of the Austrian National Bank. Among these men Náprstek worked to propagate Czech language and literature.[4]

Strangely enough Náprstek makes no mention of Professor Hromádka, who taught Czech at the Philosophical Faculty and at the Realgymnasium which was part of the Vienna Polytechnical Institute. At the University, whose legal and medical faculties alone maintained a high level, the language was taught by Prof. Hallaschka, who as Court Counsellor in the Study Commission and Censor of Czech literature, still had a certain influence. Czech was also taught at the military academy in Wiener Neustadt by Lieutenant Colonel Matyáš Polák, who under the name Milota Zdirad Polák had earlier achieved note as a revivalist poet and writer. He was shortly to be succeeded by the younger Captain-Major Tomáš Burian, a pupil of the late Jan Jeník of Bratřice. The University was a good deal less lively than the Polytechnical Institute or the Medical Academy, both of which were located not far from the industrial suburbs.

At the end of January the Czech students joined their Serbian and Croatian colleagues to celebrate the anniversary of the Croatian poet Vuk Karadžićthey also celebrated the 500th anniversary of the foundation of Charles University, and they made plans for an excursion to Kroměříž, Prostějov, and Olomouc, which later took place in greatly changed circumstances. They made arrangements for a Slavonic ball at Prague, and sent their congratulations to Havlíček upon his marriage. But above all they were interested in news from abroad. Náprstek, who still had not made up his mind whether to remain in Vienna and accept the position of tutor to the pretty Countess Seilern or to leave for America, who discussed patriotism and cosmopolitanism far into the night, made it a point always to refuse the offer of a cigar in order to express his solidarity with the Italian patriots. On March 2 came news of the revolution in France; Náprstek already saw that France would be followed by Italy, Poland, and Bohemia, and together with America these lands would become islands of true democracy. "How do things stand with our homeland?" he asked himself on March 3, even though he still discerned his own future and that of his generation as lying somewhere overseas. On March 11 Náprestek heard from Schneider about the threat of reaction, a renewal of the censorship, about strange machinations at Court; but all this was to be decided at Prague on March 13. At the same time, Kossuth's proclamation at Pressburg raised doubts whether the Germans in Austria would really tolerate other nationalities. In any case, he concluded, Vienna would be the center of political activity by the Slavic peoples, and therefore it would be necessary to unite all the Viennese Slavs.[5]

The news from Italy, the events in France, and finally the meeting of the Hungarian Diet at Pressburg, all served as catalysts of reaction. On March 3 Kossuth proclaimed before the Hungarian Parliament that the nationalities were still loyal to the dynasty, but that it was time to put an end to absolutism, centralized bureaucratic government, and the repressive methods of the "Metternich System." All the parts of the Monarchy should have their representative institutions; but Hungary deserved to occupy a unique position, with complete autonomy and an entirely separate government. Princess Melanie Metternich (even though she was born a Zichy-Ferraris) viewed this as high treason and was in favor of decisive action—but who was to undertake it? Perhaps Prince Windischgrätz, who remained in Vienna even after his failure to obtain the post of President of the Court War Council. Officially he was waiting to receive command of some army unit in Germany. Melanie took comfort in her conviction that the bourgeoisie would be essentially afraid of a republic, and she relied on the loyalty of the German burghers of Pressburg, who, it was said, wanted to have the gentlemen of the Parliament arrested.[6]

But uneasiness grew even in the neighborhood of the chancellery itself. Its supporters among the great financiers were shaken by a pamphlet written by Karl Beidtel, consultant to the Moravian provincial administration. Under the pseudonym Albert Tebeldi he wrote about the financial affairs of the Monarchy and provoked panic. From Hungary came reports that the radical "Poor Lads" (*Szegény legények*) had taken over the government of the counties; and in Vienna the opposition organizations became steadily more vocal. On March 6 in the presence of Archduke Francis Charles, still the official heir apparent, and of Count Kolowrat, the commerical organization declared its loyalty to the Emperor in a lengthy address which urged a greater understanding of the needs of the German bourgeoisie. Even the articles in the *Wiener Zeitung* inspired by Metternich and pointing out the dangers of Babeuf-style communism elicited not the slightest reaction. On March 8 the Viennese booksellers requested an end to censorship. The lawyer Bauernfeld, along with one Dr. Alexander Bach, demanded the regular implementation of "popular representation" and asked that this proposal be considered by the Lower Austrian Diet.[7]

The University students, too, drew up petitions, and on Sunday March 12 in the Universiy Aula a text was agreed upon which called for academic freedom, equality of all religious confessions before the law, and general popular representation. At noon the Rector Janull and two other professors—one of them the popular University Archivist Hye, who had criticized the occupation of Cracow—called at the Hofburg to deliver the document. They were received by Archdukes Ludwig and Francis Charles and they asked that Sedlnitzky be removed and that Metternich be sent on leave of absence. In the evening they were even received by the Emperor and dismissed with an assurance that their proposals would be studied.

The same day Metternich and the Marshal of Lower Austria Count Montecuccoli worked out a program for the session of the Lower Austrian Diet, convened at the *Landhaus* in the Herrengasse. Metternich was already trying feverishly to avoid a "debilitating concession" by putting together an iron front with the help of Russia and Prussia against the revolution which was spreading into Germany from France. Metternich's correspondence with the Austrian ambassadors Appónyi in Paris and Trautmannsdorf in Berlin, as well as his voluminous correspondence with Ficquelmont, show that he pinned his hopes on a decisive military offensive to be undertaken principally by the Prussian Crown Prince and Tsar Nicholas.[8] But in Vienna itself there were few who thought that Metternich could survive long in office after the fateful events of March 13.

Princess Melanie wrote that on the evening of Sunday March 12 there were more guests than usual at the official residence in the building of the State Chancellery on the Ballhausplatz, and that most of them had probably come out of curiosity, since, like the naive Felicia Esterházy, they were convinced that the Metternichs would move out the following day.[9]

The morning of March 13 was clear and crisp. The Lower Austrian Estates assembled in the *Landhaus*, located a few hundred paces from the State Chancellery at the other end of the Minoritenplatz. It was essentially a feudal assembly presided over by the head of the Government Talatzko of Ještětice, a bureaucrat considered to be Kolowrat's spokesman and therefore scarcely sympathetic to Metternich, whom he had already written off as had the rest of Vienna's "better society." Many of them were present at the assembly, but there were also students from the University and the Polytechnical Institute who wished to protest the suppression of their petition of the previous day. The students Böhm and Burian delivered far more firey speeches in front of the *Landhaus* and called openly for Metternich's removal. Their audience gathered in the Ballhausplatz, and while trampling the garden they chanted "Away with Metternich!" The Chancellor, who had been meeting with the Prussian Ambassador Radowitz about reform of the German Union—and measures to be taken against revolution in Germany—discovered that the revolution was now just outside his own windows.[10]

The danger was also made plain to Talatzko of Ještětice, and he requested Archduke Albert to call out his military units, especially those in the neighborhood of the castle and the State Chancellery. But Albert thought that

The March Revolution

it was all up. From the gate by the Scottish Monastery he moved at the head of the cavalry towards the center of the city—not the most effective means to deal with a crowd thronging narrow, crooked streets. Thus the magnificent cavalry and the Archduke's retinue began to be harrassed by flying bricks, and it was not long before shots were fired. The first victims fell upon the pavement, and the angry gathering, which now began to include workers from the suburbs, grew even larger.

The Hofburg was protected by infantry units from Wasa's Hungarian and Ceccopieri's Italian regiments, commanded by Major-General Count Mittrowsky. Covered by these soldiers and accompanied by his faithful followers Jósika and Hügel, Metternich proceeded to the Hofburg at about one o'clock, where a delegation from the Diet, headed by Montecuccoli, was also arriving. The delegation was received by Archdukes Ludwig and Francis Charles and members of the State Conference and State Council. Then, on the advice of Metternich and Kübeck, the delegates were informed that the Emperor intended to create a commission to review the situation and forward its recommendations to the Diet. In Metternich's opinion even the Emperor had no right to make concessions. On the contrary, what was needed was decisive action in the neighborhood of the Landhaus and the Hofburg.

But by this time, around two o'clock in the afternoon, the first casualties of the fighting were already lying in the Herrengasse. Among them was the technical student Jindřich Spitzner, born in Bzenec in Moravia, "the first to fall for freedom and the fatherland." Among the participants were also Vojtech Náprstek and Václav Tieftrunk, who in the next days published the *Zpevník slovanský* as well as Burian's speech on the steps of the *Landhaus*.[11] During the afternoon barricades appeared in the streets, and troops stood at the gates to stem the tide of workers pouring into the center of from the suburbs. The result was that the suburban police headquarters and factories were attacked. One of the targets was Metternich's summer house in the Rennweg.

In the afternoon Mayor Czapka mobilized the burgher guard and requested the military command to withdraw from the streets. Archduke Albert complied, apparently with some relief, and for several days the military units stood in clusters before the walls of the inner city. However, the burgher guard behaved exactly as the Paris National Guard had in February; instead of defending the régime it joined its enemies. A deputation of guard officers even called for Metternich's immediate removal and suggested that the students be armed to help repress the worker's unrest in the suburbs. Metternich was called to another meeting of the Conference at about 6:30 in the evening. He tried to persuade the guard officers to undertake a joint offensive with the army against the demonstrators, but they flatly refused.

Thereafter sentiment in favor of dealing with the popular movement by force gained a temporary ascendancy. Metternich suggested that the command of all military and civil affairs be turned over to his protégé Windischgrätz, whose great asset was his victory over the Prague workers in 1844. Windischgrätz, who did not wish to accept the supreme responsibility in civilian clothes, went home to change; on returning in his parade uniform, he discovered that Metternich had submitted his resignation.

It appears that the officers of the burgher guard had presented the State Conference with an ultimatum; Metternich must be dismissed by nine o'clock that evening and the students were to be given arms. Archduke Johann, Kolowrat, and also the Archdukes Ludwig and Francis Charles eventually succeeded in persuading Metternich to submit his resignation. Windischgrätz still tried to prevent the utter capitulation of the government. It was said that on the same evening Metternich urged Windischgrätz to continue in office. Thus—as few realize—he became the "Plenipotentiary Chief of the Government" from March 13-20 and therefore the last State Minister of Austria.[12] During the night Metternich is also supposed to have persuaded the "reigning Empress" Mariana to prevent her husband from abdicating. At all events, it would be better that he rather than his successor should succumb to the revolution.

In spite of predictions, the conflict in Vienna lasted only a single day. The success of this completely unforeseen revolution, which quickly changed from an aristocratic revolt into a movement led chiefly by the middle classes, students, and workers, resulted from the government's incapacity rather than the opposition's strength. On March 13 it was only the students and workers who behaved with any decisiveness, and it was they who actually forced the government to succumb. The Court was obliged to consent to the formation of a National Guard on the French model and an "Academic Legion." The National Guard was to incude only 10,000 reliable burghers, but it quickly grew to three times that number, while the Academic Legion had 7,000 members. It is true of course that the revolutionary enthusiasm of the bourgeoisie soon evaporated, so that within a month the National Guard shrank to only 7,200—but this did not save the Court from being forced to new concessions. And in fact the growing indifference of the bourgeoisie led to the enhancement of the radicals' influence.[13]

Basic civil rights were acknowledged almost automatically. On March 15 the Emperor promised to issue a constitution, and on March 20 he named the first responsible government. The five thousand students of Vienna, led by two physicians Adolf Fischof and Josef Goldmark, and by the Slovene priest Anton Füster, together with the workers from the suburbs, were the driving force of the revolution in the next weeks and months. Through the Students' Committee and the Central Committee of the burghers, the National Guard and the students assumed control and actually constituted a second government of Austria. Democratic clubs and radical journals attacked the government, the Court, the aristocracy, and the heirarchy of the Church. To many, it seemed as though the end of the world had begun.[14]

2 The Inglorious Flight of Prince Metternich

Princess Melanie Metternich was certainly one who shared this view, and Tuesday March 14 was no less unsettled than the previous day had been. All Vienna welcomed Metternich's removal, and he was plainly going to have to move out of the State Chancellery building. Accompanied by his family, by Jósika and Hügel, he left for the home of the former President of the Supreme Court, Count Ludwig Taaffe. He could not continue long even here, for neither Windischgrätz nor anyone else could guarantee his safety. But the representatives of high finance and the landed aristocracy did not disappoint him. Salomon Rothschild sent the fallen Chancellor a thousand thalers, and the Princes Charles, Alois and Rudolf von Liechtenstein, whose family was said to own a quarter of Moravia, transported Metternich from Vienna in their carriage and accompanied him through the whole day's journey to their chateau at Feldsburg on the Moravian border. They left at about five o'clock on the morning of March 15. Later in the day Princess Melanie and three of Metternich's sons, accompanied by Count Rechberg, recently returned from his diplomatic mission to Brazil, travelled by train from Vienna to Břeclav, thence by carriage to Feldsburg.[15]

Metternich and his family remained here an entire week, during which he sent in his written resignation and wrote as well to Tsar Nicholas. He also learned of Windischgrätz's resignation and the succession on March 20 of his old rival Kolowrat as Prime Minister. At seventy years of age, Kolowrat to be sure was only five years younger than Metternich, but he and the members of his government were reputed to favor substantial reforms, without being by any means "revolutionaries." The average age of Kolowrat's government, which lasted only until April 5, was a rather high sixty-two. It included Karl Ludwig Count Ficquelmont as Foreign Minister, Franz Baron Pillersdorf as Interior Minister, Franz Baron Sommaruga as Minister of Education, Ludwig Count Taaffe as Minister of Justice, Peter Zanini as Minister of War, K.F. Kübeck as Minister of Finance; later Anton Baron Doblhoff-Dier joined the government as Minister of Commerce and Andreas Baumgartner as Minister of Public Works.[16]

Metternich was not safe even at Feldsburg under the protection of Liechtenstein's militia and a detachment of hussars from the Nikolsburg garrison. According to Count Rechburg, he was requested by the Town Council of Feldsburg to leave within twenty-four hours since his presence jeopardized the safety of the chateau and its inhabitants. At the head of the local government stood the still loyal burgomaster Alois Hübner, who certainly was not acting on his own initiative—he was later forced to resign. The minutes of the meetings of the Council of Feldsburg for 1848, however, have not survived, so that Rechberg's information cannot be checked.[17]

At first Metternich considered going to Plasy in western Bohemia, but he changed his mind. In the interval he learned of the events in Prague, which began on March 11, and he ceased to believe in the good faith and loyalty of his Plasy tenants. Brno, which was still loyal, appeared to be safer, or even better, Olomouc, the seat of the conservative Archbishop Sommerau-Beeck, which contained a strong garrison under Lieutenant Field Marshal Sunstenau, who had served under Windischgrätz in 1844 at Prague and was considered to be his collaborator. On the evening of April 22 Metternich left by train for Břeclav with his wife and eldest son Richard (the other children having returned to Vienna) and his colleagues Rechberg and Hügel. Ficquelmont gave Rechberg the task of organizing Metternich's departure. The train arrived at four o'clock in the morning at Olomouc, where the refugees discovered that neither the Archbishop nor the garrison commandant was willing to guarantee Metternich's safety.

Beyond that, they feared that they had been recognized in the train. It was said that Burian, the notorious student who had incited the Viennese against Metternich on March 13, had left by train for somewhere in Bohemia. But Rechberg and one Major Vernier, with the help of a Prague police commissioner who was already fitted out with a red and white "national" cockade, were able to obtain an emergency passport in the name of "Herr von Mayer, landowner from Styria, with entourage." Still, they were not bold enough to travel by way of Prague. They disembarked at five o'clock in the afternoon at Bechovice, the last station before Prague, rode through the city in a closed carriage, spent the night at Doksany, and on March 23 reached Teplitz. Here the municipal administration was very conservative, and the lords of the town, the Clary-Aldringens, relatives of Ficquelmont, ensured that proper respect was paid the former Chancellor even by the newly established National Guard.[18]

Metternich reached Dresden on March 24, where according to the Chancellor's plan the meeting of the German states was to have begun the same day. In Dresden Metternich received more money from Rothschild, as well as a new passport made out to "Herr und Frau von Manteux." With this they traversed Germany without incident and on March 30 reached Arnheim in the Netherlands. After a brief sojourn in The Hague, which impressed Princess Melanie as a prerevolutionary paradise, they arrived in London on April 20, 1848. London already contained a growing colony of refugees from the revolution which was soon to include besides Louis Philipee and Metternich also the Prussian Crown Prince.

Metternich himself entitled the appropriate chapter of his Selected Writings "Voluntary Exile and Return Home." With his son Richard and his publisher Klinkowström, he attempted to create the impression that he had already assumed the role of elder statesman who from the heights of wisdom could observe the futility of everyday endeavors. In fact the situation was quite different. When he wrote from Feldsburg congratulating Ficquelmont on his appointment as Foreign Minister, Metternich also requested regular reports of the latest developments. The same day he received Ficquelmont's first letter, with information about the intentions of the new government. Through the British ambassador in Vienna Ponsonby, Ficquelmont remained in contact with Metternich until the fall of his government in May. Other officials and diplomats were also in touch with Metternich. Rechberg wrote to him from Frankfurt, Prokesch-Osten from Berlin, Hübner from Paris; Metternich himself continued to write to Hügel, Pilat, Lebzeltern, Trautmannsdorf and Münch-Bellinghausen. From London Metternich advised Salomon Rothschild to bide his time: "You should not altogether write me off just yet; I am still alive and well."[20]

3 The Revolutionary Crisis in Italy

According to Antonín Dobroslav Vyšek, an official of the Royal and Imperial Police Directorate and at the same time an Czech revivalist writer and dilettante artist, the first news of the Viennese revolution reached Milan, capital of the Kingdom of Lombardy-Venetia, on March 17.[21] On the morning of the eighteenth the Milanese Podestà Count Gabrio Casatia informed the Vice-Governor Count O'Donnell that demonstrations in favor of a constitution and of independence, organized by a group of liberal burghers and noblemen, would take place the same day.

Casati requested the Vice-Governor to convince the military commandant Field Marshal Radetzky not to call out his men against the manifestation.[22] Around noon approximately ten thousand people, some of them armed, gathered before the Town Hall and forced Casati to lead them to the government palace, bearing a petition which contained not merely the usual liberal demads but republican ones as well: freedom of the press, removal of the police, the creation of a citizens' militia, and the convocation of a national assembly. When Casati reached the palace, the first victims of the fighting already lay in the street. O'Donnell, who was terribly confused, agreed to all the demands, and he accompanied the demonstrators back to the Town Hall as a hostage.

In the narrow streets of the inner city barricades sprang up and the government buildings were surrounded, including the police headquarters. One of those detained within was Antonín Dobroslav Vyšek, who thus became an involuntary witness to the bloody conflict, to the death of his friend Major Standejský, and to the hopeless resistance offered by the Croatian contingents. A counter-attack by the Imperial infantry (chiefly from the Bohemian regiments of Reisinger and Paumgartner) was able to reach the Town Hall, to be sure, but ultimately not even Radetzky with his twelve to thirteen thousand troops could control the city of about 170,000 inhabitants. All the less since the Milanese themselves were more than ready to fight against the hated "Germans." Arms were collected even from the celebrated Uboldi collection, as well as from the wardrobe of La Scala. Although the Milanese lacked fire power—at the beginning of the struggle they had only 600 guns—on the evening of March 19 they formed a central committee headed by the energetic philosopher, economist and republican theorist Carlo Cattaneo.

Thus the struggle, which claimed many victims among the Bohemian infantrymen, lasted the whole of the following day, and its fury was dampened only by a sudden spring storm. Just after midnight on Sunday March 20 Vyšek took the opportunity to leave police headquarters. He was soon captured by the insurgents, but when he declared himself a Pole—who thanks to their revolutionary past were much more highly regarded than the Czechs—he was given arms and participated with them in the fight against his countrymen in Imperial uniforms, until he was able to escape on March 21. Vyšek returned to Prague via Switzerland and Bavaria, and he published his account of the Italian revolution first in Havlíček's *Národní Noviny*, then later as a pamphlet under the title "The Revolt of Milan . . . by a Czech Eye-Witness." But one Czech who remained in Milan was the military chaplain Karel Mensinger, who with Vyšek had published Czech books for the soldiers. He did not want to leave the wounded, and in the end he became a traitor by taking the side of the Italians in their struggle for independence.[23]

Radetzky, who transferred troops to Milan from neighboring garrisons, discovered that he was unable to hold the city. Therefore he ordered the troops into the Castello and satisfied himself with holding the walls of the Old Town and cutting it off from the outside world. But on March 22 he decided reluctantly to evacuate the city. His soldiers were hungry, all of Lombardy was engulfed in the insurrection, and there were justified fears that Sardinia would take the opportunity to declare war on Austria. On March 23 the Austrian army marched out of Milan. The Milanese *cinque giornate* became the model of successful popular insurrection against a military force.[24]

On April 1 the Austrians reached Verona in poor condition, having lost most of their arms and supplies along the way. Radetzky lost around 11,000 men, many of them Italian deserters, but he concentrated his remaining forces at Verona, Legnago and Mantua in the so-called Quadrilateral fortresses, while a further 7,000 troops remained in isolated garrisons. The narrow strip of land between Lake Como and the Po River proved to be the only territory which the Austrians were able to hold on to. The populace of Venice had also risen in revolt on March 17, and by the 22nd the Austrian garrison was obliged to evacuate, whereupon the lawyer Daniele Manin and the writer Niccolò Tommaseo proclaimed the Republic of St. Mark.[25]

Radetzky was left with 35,000 men at most, and in all probability he was soon going to have to face the army of the Sardinian King Charles Albert, which numbered 45,000 men. The provisional government of Lombardy made a prompt appeal for Sardinain aid—not so much against Radetzky as against the radical revolutionaries of Milan. These circumstances, however, gave pause to Charles Albert, who had no wish to involve himself in a compromising alliance with the Milanese revolution. His hesitation at this juncture probably saved Radetzky. By the time that Charles Albert finally decided upon war, Milan was in the hands of a liberal provisional goverment under Casati, and Radetzky was gathering his army into the safety of the fortresses. On March 26 the first Sardinian contingents reached Milan, and in the first flush of enthusiasm Charles Albert struck a medal bearing the motto "Italy shall liberate herself!" He had in mind the possibility of French intervention, which he was not eager to witness a second time. This did not mean, of course, that he despised all military assistance. On the contrary, he welcomed the Tuscan government's contribution on March 29 of 7,000 troops and a similar action by the Duke of Parma at the beginning of April. Even the Papal government sent 7,000 of its regular troops and 9,000 militiamen and volunteers to defend the Po border. Ferdinand of Naples, even though his wife was the daughter of Archduke Charles, succumbed to the spirit of the times and dispatched 14,000 men to the north.[26]

The whole carefully planned network of Austrian positions on the peninsula was destroyed at once. The Austrian ambassador to the Vatican Count Rudolf Lützow, who had been insulted in Rome on March 21 and who concluded therewith his diplomatic career, protested in vain in his *Apologia* that he was just as powerless against the Roman revolution as the commander of the Imperial Army had been against the Milanese.

Nor could any of the other Imperial ambassadors accomplish anything. In Turin it was impossible to prevent Charles Albert from continuing with his treacherous and perfidious plans against Austria. In Florence the Tuscan Grand Duke could not be dissuaded from becoming the willing ally of his own family's and country's enemies. In Naples King Ferdinand could not be induced to punish the perpetrators of a scandal similar to that in Rome, nor discouraged from sending his troops to Po.[27]

What actually occurred in Rome and above all in Naples? On March 25 there was a demonstration before the Austrian Embassy in Naples, during which the Imperial double-headed eagle was torn down and burned on the Largo Santa Catarina. The Imperial ambassadors at Rome and Naples met with very different fates. By the beginning of 1849, when Lützow had been pensioned off and was at work on his *Apologia*, Felix Schwarzenberg was Prime Minister of Austria.

If we encounter in this way the man whose government would soon set the seal on the triumph of counter-revolution, then surely he deserves a fuller introduction. Felix Schwarzenberg (1800-1852) was the perfect reactionary, and he earned the respect of his teacher Metternich. Yet he was not a blind reactionary, and in spite of certain deficiencies in his education, he was an able diplomat, an energetic soldier, and a man of remarkable intelligence. As a younger son of the main branch of the Schwarzenberg family residing at Krumlov and Třeboň, he was bound by tradition for a military career.[28]

As a cadet he entered the regiment of the eighth cuirassiers, where his commander was Colonel Alfred Windischgrätz, who was also his brother-in-law. It cannot be said that the two were very fond of each other. With the execption of a brief sojourn with Emperor Ferdinand's hussar regiment, Felix remained under his brother-in-law's command until the end of 1822, when he was posted to the Second "Ulan" or "Schwarzenberg" regiment, which was scattered throughout Moravia. Here Felix amused himself after the fashion of his fellow officers and was soon heavily in debt. In 1824, probably through Metternich's associate Hügel, Schwarzenberg was introduced to the Chancellor. He appears to have measured up to Metternich's ideal of the soldier-diplomat on Ficquelmont's pattern, for he was sent to the Austrian Embassy at St. Petersburg as a military attaché, probably to the great relief of his brother-in-law. Felix's correspondence with his father Josef and with his sister Mathilde enables us to trace in considerable detail his singular career.[29]

His primary duty in Russia was to study the organization of the army. He took part in its maneuvers, but he also visited Nizhni Novgorod and even distant Astrakhan. He was present at the coronation of Nicholas I, but also became friendly with the brother-in-law of the Austrian ambassador Lebzeltern, Sergei Trubetzkoy, a colonel in the Preobrazhensky Guards, who took part in the Decembrist Uprising. After its defeat his friend Felix Schwarzenberg was no longer *persona grata* in St. Petersburg, in spite of his probably honest protest that he was much more interested in the Decembrists' sisters than in the Decembrists themselves. But in 1826, decorated with the Order of St. Vladimir, he was sent by way of Paris to London. Here he was awaited by another of Metternich's intimates, Baron Neuman, who had just been ordered to Rio de Janeiro to press the claims of the absolutist Dom Miguel. The Brazilian Emperor Dom Pedro was married to the daughter of Francis I, so that Neuman could expect an affable reception, and some of Metternich's economic advisors even predicted a burgeoning commerce with Brazil. But when the British frigate *Forte* arrived at Rio on February 7, 1827, the Empress was dead, and the mission returned to Europe after only ten days. Following a brief sojourn in Bohemia, Schwarzenberg was sent to Lisbon to prepare Dom Miguel's return, and here he was slandered by the latter's political opponents. In the spring of 1828 Schwarzenberg was named military attaché in the Austrian Embassy to the Court of St. James. The attractive ulan officer enjoyed huge social success and fell in love with one of the leading beauties of London, the daughter of Admiral Digby, Lady Jane Ellenborough. The single difficulty was Lady Jane's husband Lord Ellenborough, Keeper of the Privy Seal.

The lovers decided to provoke a scandal and oblige Lord Ellenborough to sue for divorce. The scandal went off perfectly, but there were difficulties with the divorce. Many members of the House of Lords concluded that in view of Ellenborough's own reputation, no grounds for divorce could possibly result from any fault of his wife's. The trial dragged on, and the lovers had to leave the Norfolk Hotel in Brighton. They went to Paris, where Schwarzenberg had been transferred by Metternich, who was always full of sympathy for this kind of predicament. After all, just ten days earlier the Chancellor himself had journeyed to Spa in Belgium for a tryst with Princess Lieven, wife of the Russian ambassador in London. The liaison was only ended by Princess Lieven's determined efforts to make a liberal of Metternich. But Schwarzenberg's affair survived even a journey by his sister Mathilde to England, where she acquired a huge admiration for Tudor gothic, which was fully indulged later in the reconstruction of Hluboká castle in southern Bohemia.

A daughter was born to Felix and Lady Jane, and she was christened Mathilde after her aunt, who brought her up. She was Felix's darling, and eventually she became the wife of Anton Bešín.[30] Lady Jane, however, had long since grown tired of waiting for her divorce. She disappeared to Munich, where she beguiled the Bavarian King Ludwig I. Later she married a German, then a Greek nobleman, and she finished her amorous career in the harem of a Bedouin sheik. Shortly before her death in Damascus in 1881 the still beautiful, foolish "Ianthé," the Lady Arabella Dudley of Balzac's *Lily of the Valley*, completed her truly romantic autobiography.

Upon Lady Jane's departure, Felix's handwriting deteriorated badly and became practically illegible. In Paris he experienced not only the end of his affair but also witnessed the Revolution of 1830 and the succession of Louis Philippe. In 1831 he returned home on holiday, underwent a religious crisis, was promoted to the rank of Major and sent to Berlin for six years. It was not until the autumn of 1833 that he undertook his first independent diplomatic mission—to The Hague, in order to mediate in the conflict with Belgium.[31] In Berlin he witnessed the formation of th German Customs Union, and at about this time he was promoted to Colonel. He accompanied the King of Prussia to his meeting with Francis and Nicholas I at Münchengrätz in 1833, an encountered Metternich, Ficquelmont, and his brother-in-law Windischgrätz. His friendship with the Decembrists appeared to have been forgotten, and Schwarzenberg, following in Ficquelmont's footsteps, was to combine a military and diplomatic career focused upon Russia, Germany, and Italy.

In 1839 he was sent as ambassador to the courts of Turin and Parma, but at the Sardinian Court he was no longer the lion of the salon; his social life was centered in the rather more discreet milieu of Milan.[32] He was promoted to Major-General, and in 1844 he left Turin with some relief for Naples. Here he was again *persona gratissima* at the court of Ferdinand II and his Austrian wife; he became acquainted with Friedrich Thun and accustomed himself to Italian surroundings. In 1846 he was able to conclude a trade agreement that was highly favorable for Austria. He met with Tsar Nicholas, and at the end of the year he went to Vienna for talks with Metternich. On the journey back in January 1847 he contracted typhus in Trieste and barely survived. He changed physically and became an old man, though he lost none of his energy. Upon his return to Naples he discovered that the situation had changed for the worse. He was no longer warmly welcomed at Court; he was unable to agree with members of the government; and after the incident of March 25 he did not need much time to come to a decision. He sent Ficquelmont a telegram informing him that he would wind up his embassy and on his own initiative sever contact with the Neapolitan Court. With this his diplomatic career came to a temporary end.

On March 28 he left Naples on board the Austrian ship *Vulcano*, and after some difficulties, including a mutiny by the Italian sailors, he reached Trieste and travelled to Vienna. He remained only a few days, however. By April 17 he was back in northern Italy, and as a Major-General and brigade leader on Nugent's staff, he crossed the Venetian border. The same day his troops encountered battle near Palmanuova. At Bisnadello his brigade joined the so-called Reserve Army in which three of his cousins were serving: Frederick, the "last Lanzknecht;" Charles, commander of the brigade at Brescia; and Edmund, who had fought at Milan.[33] In Radetzky's army were many of their fellow noblemen from Bohemia and Moravia. One of them, Colonel Teofil Coudenhove, had distinguished himself by suppressing the uprising at Vicenza.[34] Schwarzenberg stood before the city on May 20 and directed its bombardment. On May 29 he led an attack on Curtatone; the next day at the Battle of Goito he was wounded in his left arm. Radetzky, who did not greatly care for his "diplomatic generals," nominated Schwarzenberg for the highest Austrian honor, the Order of Maria Theresa. After a convalescence of several weeks he was chosen by Radetzky to lead political negotiations with the Austrian government, which had fled with the Emperor to Innsbruck. The Austrians were reportedly willing, through British mediation, to give up a substantial portion of their Italian holdings in return for peace with Sardinia. Radetzky hoped that Schwarzenberg would be able to cancel these plans and persuade the government to adopt an agressive policy in northern Italy, to include sending reinforcements up to 25,000 men. After some discussion with the Foreign Minister Wessenberg, with whom he had worked at The Hague in 1833, Schwarzenberg succeeded in establishing the outlines of a decisive policy. He was helped by the Court Camarilla, which included J.A. Helfert, the entire retinue of Archduchess Sophia, the Generals Radetzky and Windischgrätz—and now Schwarzenberg himself. He was also helped by Hartig, who was sent to Radetzky as a commissioner. In London Metternich read a copy of Hartig's correspondence with Radetzky and drew the conclusion that only a short time was needed for the "elements of strength and order" to reestablish themselves.[35]

4 The Social Basis of the Revolution in Bohemia

Just as in Lower Austria, Hungary, and Lombardy, the revolution in Bohemia began with a demonstration by the Estates' opposition. On March 2 a group of noblemen led by Friedrich Deym demanded that the government summon a parliament which would include representatives of the "middle classes." But the authorities reacted with characteristic suspicion, and the demand of the noble opposition remained unanswered. The public learned of their unsuccessful efforts only at the end of the month.

Quite independently of the noblemen, a group of the borgeois opposition met to plan a public assembly at the St. Wenceslas Baths in the Prague New Town, which was set for the evening of Saturday, March 11. The text of the invitation, in Czech and German, was the work of two members of the Repeal group, Vilém Gauč and Ludvík Ruppert. The invitations were sent out on March 6, and two days later the announcement was printed on posters:

> Citizens of the Capital City! The Parisian events have awakened all Europe from her slumber. Germany is preparing for a struggle and is arming her burghers. Citizens of Prague, our own country is watching you. Shake off your lethargy and proclaim that truth which now stands revealed. From this day you must participate actively in affairs of state. You must take a stand to protect what is yours against every threat. And above all, you must do your utmost to insure that the entire Nation shall be aroused to undertake the free and honorable management of its own affairs, in order that 'national consciousness' shall become the property of all levels of the population. It is only in this way that a people can arrive at patriotism based on intelligence and morality, so that, worthy of the government's trust, it might become also its chief support.
>
> Citizens! You shall obtain this by the following: 1) a coherent and comprehensive constitution for the land; 2) an assembly which includes representatives of the towns and the peasantry; 3) the arming of the entire population; 4) the abolition of censorship, which like a moth smothers and destroys all free thought.
>
> Think, consider everything, citizens of the Capital City, and assemble on March 11 at six o'clock in the evening in the St. Wenceslas Baths. This deed is legal, citizens, because it is necessary![36]

At first glance, it appears that the authors of this invitation were taking their cue from the earlier demands of the Estates' opposition. The content was not particularly radical, but its publication anticipated one of its own demands, the abolition of censorship, because the text was given to no one for offical approval. The invitation speaks neither of the Czech nor the German nation, and it makes no direct attack on the government. The authors were clearly trying to win the support of the Czech and German bourgeoisie. Nevertheless, their deed was a bold one; it represented a successful effort in behalf of the first public assembly in the history of modern Bohemia. Most of those responsible for its convocation are only names today. There were the students František Havlíček and Vilém Gauč, an innkeeper Petr Faster, a lawyer Ferdinand Viták, a tailor Bernard Banzet, two roofers František Jaroš and Antonín Sulc, a miller Matěj Vávra, a coppersmith Josef Mencl, and the writers Karel Sabina and Bedřich Peška.[37]

Petr Faster represented a circle which met at his tavern the "Golden Goose" in the Horse Market. The organizers of the assembly had asked them for their help, and they prepared a petition twenty points which they wanted to lay before the assembly. The most important of these included a demand for the teaching of Czech in the schools, abolition of the *robota* and the patrimonial organization. The most radical was article 18, which called for the "organization of work and wages" and which reads like a citation from Louis Blanc. This was the first such demand in Czech history, and the first attempt to give the state responsibility for looking after the needs of the working classes.[38]

They turned over the draft of the petition to the liberal advocate František August Brauner, who edited it thoroughly. He reduced the number of articles to twelve, removed everything that struck him as excessively radical, and gave emphasis to the demands of the Czech nation. Thanks to him the question of the working class disappeared entirely; the peasants were promised abolition of the *robota* now in return for an indemnity; the demand for the abolition of the food tax was added; it was emphasized that the armed middle class militia would protect society against disorder caused by the poor (the "proletariat" in the German version); and prominence was given to a demand for the union of the lands of the Bohemian Crown—Bohemia, Moravia and Silesia—by means of a common Diet. While the first draft called for the introduction of Czech into the schools, Brauner demanded "complete equality of the Czech and German nations in all Bohemian schools and offices."[39]

In Prage public order was the responsibility of the Viceroy Count Rudolf Stadion, the Police Director Josef Heyde, and the burgomaster Josef Müller. They replied to the posters of March 8 with a bilingual edict the next day, warning against all public disturbances. On March 10 Burgomaster Müller called together the "Merchants' Casino," prominent burghers, most of them Germans, to ask their help. They suggested that Müller simply forbid the assembly. Neither Stadion, Heyde, nor Müller himself wished to take this step, and the assembly was actually allowed to take place. Not very many workers were present; nor were there any noblemen, or "better people" at all. Even Palacký and Havlíček were absent, nor did the highly prudent František Brauner make an appearance. F.L. Rieger might have come, but he was in Italy. The audience was composed mainly of Czechs. The text of the petition was read aloud in Czech and German by the innkeeper Faster and a civil servant named Alois Pravoslav Trojan, who demonstrated great courage, for he was truly risking his career. According to police reports, the assembly consisted "chiefly of young people, writers, sons of burghers, artisans, even officials. All the Czech party, even the peasantry, was represented." They accepted the text of the petition and also called for the acceptance of several of the radical demands which Brauner had excised—including the article about the "organization of work."[40]

The final version was entrusted to a committee of twenty, later dubbed the "St. Wenceslas Committee," which included only two radicals, Gauč and Ruppert; the others included several Germans, a Jewish banker, and the rest were middle-class Czech liberals. The radical Karel Sabina wished to conclude the assembly with a reminder that after 230 years the results of the Battle of the White Mountain had finally been overturned, even though the demand for a common Diet had no historical precedent but instead pointed towards the future. Sabina, however, was unable to secure recognition from the chairman Trojan. The lights were lowered, and the people went out into the rain from the St. Wenceslas Baths, remembered now only in the name of the street, for the building was torn down long ago.

The administration's wish that the St. Wenceslas Committee suspend its meetings was not fulfilled. It did continue to meet, sometimes even in the Old Town Hall. Immediately the next day, on Sunday March 12, in spite of Müller's vigorous protests, it elected as its president the popular Count Vojtěch Deym. On March 13 the burgomaster placed the Old Town Hall at the Committee's disposal, and its members gathered there to edit the petition into an even more conservative form. There was less that was radical in its remaining eleven articles, but the protests of the radicals evoked a response as feeble as a suggestion put forward by Palacký, who was now about to make his first public appearance, that the petition be sent to the Emperor through the Estates. Müller called together his conservative German burghers, and together they produced a rival petition. But at this point the students became active, the police received information that there was to be a workers' uprising, and Burgomaster Müller grew fearful. Finally on March 14 he appeared with his own group at a meeting of the St. Wenceslas Committee, put his signature to its petition, and offered the alliance of his conservative burghers. It was doubtful that the radical members of the Committee were very much heartened by this "victory," but the upset that came the next day made everything else appear insignificant. In the morning the petition was presented for signatures, and in the afternoon passengers on the train from Vienna brought news of Metternich's fall and the abolition of the censorship. In the evening there were processions, and Prague noisily welcomed the advent of a new era.

The next day brought news of the Emperor's promised constitution, and suddenly the word became fashionable: everything was "constitutional"—hats, umbrellas; there were even "constitutional" pastries and a "Constitutional Polka." Songs appeared ridiculing Metternich, Sedlnitzky, the police. People began to take an interest in newspapers; new clubs sprang up. So did rumors and terrifying reports that Prague was being threatened by a march of peasants, or of Germans from the mountainous borderlands. Viceroy Stadion and Burgomaster Müller began to consider the possibility of resignation. New candidates appeared for various offices. The advocate Josef Frič, father of the young radical J.V. Frič, suffered a nervous collapse. There was greatly increased travel between Prague and Vienna because the students obliged railway officials to issue them free tickets.

A National Guard appeared on the Viennese model, a good bourgeois affair, and also a slightly more radical Academic Legion. The organizations "Slavia" and "Slovanská Lípa" appeared without any model. "Svornost" took its name from the Viennese "Concordia," but it was exclusively a Czech organization. In the meantime, the final watered-down version of the petition was signed by thousands of citizens, most of them Czechs. The radicals continued to point out how greatly the final text differed from what had been agreed upon on March 11, and they obliged the St. Wenceslas Committee to retreat: on March 17 it announced that the Emperor would be given the original version of the document as well as the "official text." Through the mediation of Prime Minister Kolowrat and Minister of the Interior Pillersdorf, some members of the St. Wenceslas Committee were received by the Emperor on March 22. The expectations expressed by Kolowrat in a cabinet memorandum of March 23 were not fulfilled, and the future remained uncertain. When the delegation returned to Prague, where celebrations had been planned in advance, the disappointment was boundless, and the consequence was rioting in the streets. The mood of the spectators at the assembly on March 28 was highly agitated, and there were calls for the proclamation of a republic against the aristocracy. Even Brauner concluded that the Emperor's reply had been unsatisfactory.[41]

The St. Wenceslas Committee was empowered to draw up a further petition which repeated the demand for a union of the Bohemian lands and issued an emphatic call for a parliament with the broadest base. The present Estates' Diet was rejected as a survival of feudalism. A delegation from the assembly forced its way into Stadion's presence and obliged him to sign the petition. This was too much for the proud bureaucrat. He did not intend to follow Burgomaster Müller's example and remain in his post at all costs.[42] On March 29 Stadion offered his resignation to Pillersdorf. As his replacement he suggested the young Count Franz Thun-Hohenstein, with his brother Leo second in command. In Stadion's opinion, his successor must be an acknowledged Bohemian ("ein böhmischer Name muss es sein.").[43]

Meanwhile, the government had other worries. On March 28 in a cabinet memorandum the Emperor promised to abolish the *robota*, a move which brilliantly neutralized the rural masses. On April 8 another cabinet memorandum was issued in reply to the second Bohemian peititon. Stadion advised that it be accepted as far as possible, warning that otherwise Bohemia would follow the example of Italy and Hungary. Archduke Charles Ferdinand, provisional chief of the General Command, concurred, and on March 30 he armed the National Guard. Perhaps he hoped to win over the soldiers, who had been warned by leaflets against becoming the instruments of reaction and letting themselves be used especially against the Italians.[44]

The cabinet memorandum of April 8, 1848, was regarded as the maximum which the Czechs would be able to obtain from the Viennese government during the revolutionary situation.[45] But even now it was impossible to achieve the union of the Bohemian lands into a single administrative unit. Such a unit had in fact existed before the Theresian administrative reforms, even though there had never existed a single parliament for all the lands, except for the rare convocations of a General Diet in the years before the Thirty Years' War. The proposal was staunchly opposed by the Bohemian Germans, as well as by the Moravian Diet. This predominantly feudal and German body pronounced its view publically only on April 14, and its Czech spokesman was Alois Pražák.[46]

Stadion made one more effort to ease the task of his successor. Since he had been unable to dissolve or control the St. Wenceslas Committee, he created his own "Gubernial Commission." Its membership was announced on April 1, mainly highly conservative Czechs and Germans, among whom Palacký and Borrosch stood out. Needless to say, there was not a single real radical on Stadion's Commission, which met only twice, in closed session, on April 3 and 4. Here, surprisingly enough, Palacký spoke quite strongly against attempts to call the old Estates' Diet. Ernest Nostitz and Francis Thun suggested that the Diet be called but that its composition be altered, or else that it give way immediately to an elected assembly. There was no agreement about just how such an assembly should be elected. Palacký was certainly not in favor of universal suffrage, since the popular elements were under the influence of "malevolent people." Borrosch defended the position that the "common people" were not themselves malevolent; they were simply more subject to their passions. Palacký imagined that "popular representation" meant voting for representatives from among the intelligentsia, the landholders, and the professionals. Thus he excluded landless peasants and workers, but against Thun and Morzin he recommended the inclusion of landed peasants—which in fact later occurred in the "reformed" Diet of Moravia. The subcommittee considering the question of the *robota* consisted exclusively of large landholders.[47]

On April 10 a new assembly gathered at the St. Wenceslas Baths, at which Stadion's Commission was denounced as unrepresentative. Karel Havlíček Borovský's resolution was adopted that the St. Wenceslas Committee should be merged with Stadion's Commission to form a "National Committee." Stadion could not oppose this suggestion. The National Committee met for the first time on April 13, presided over by Stadion himself.

The radicals protested with reason that all this amounted to a further step away from real revolution. But it can hardly have been pleasant for Stadion to find himself at the head of a body which had usurped authority belonging until now exclusively to the state administration. The National Committee, referring to the cabinet memorandum of April 8, was to make plans for the election of a Bohemian parliament. But in the beginning of April nobody knew just how this was to be accomplished. The fact was that in the next six to eight weeks the National Committee became the center of political life in Bohemia. And it remained limited to Bohemia proper; nothing like it existed in Moravia or Silesia.[48]

On the other hand, since its membership was mainly Czech, the National Committee served to crystallize the opposition of the German bourgeoisie. They saw in it an institution which was dominated by Czechs, and therefore, as we shall see, they began to boycott it. Within a month of the first assembly at the St. Wenceslas Baths, it was clear that two serious questions loomed for the future course of the bourgeois-democratic revolution: the social question and the nationality question.

Spokesmen of the liberal intelligentsia and the bourgeoisie feared an alliance with the "proletarians," but they could not ignore their existence. They could not accept the nobility wholeheartedly, either—even Borrosch and Palacký did not want this. Various groups among them were already pursuing independent policies which were determined by class, not nationality, as perhaps some of the more conservatively inclined liberals imagined. In any case, these tendencies were strengthened by the events of April and May. We may concur with the anonymous author of the citation at the beginning of this chapter. "Svoboda" or "Freedom" grew from the bourgeois revolution which was sparked by the street fighting in Vienna, Milan, and Venice and spread to Pressburg and Budapest, as well as to Prague, Brno, and Olomouc. It was very weak because the social base of the institutions that it created was weak, and in the conditions prevailing in the multinational Monarcy, it became progressively weaker. At this point the crucial question was whether these institutions would be able to take over the functions of the old administrative and military apparatus, whether they would be able to guide the foreign and domestic policies of the Monarchy. The answers to these questions should tell whether the Monarchy could survive and in what form.

V

The Retreat of the Old Order: March–May 1848

> "Many times in the past, and even before this rioting in Vienna began, we have held to our justified views, if only we had been able to lay our humble requests before your lordships, gathered in general assembly. Never before has the opportunity presented itself as now, when events have breathed new life into our old requests. Accept, noble lords, our humble and earnest petition, which we present to you. Abolish this source of manifold evils, this ruination of people, of livestock, of bread, this encouragement to theft and all manner of falsehood, this source of bondage . . . so little useful to merciful landlords and so greatly damaging to the rural people . . . this so-called Natural Robota."
>
> Petition of All the Peasantry, Presented to the Moravian Estates, Assembled at Brno, 19 April 1848

1. *Kolowrat and Ficquelmont*

Franz Schuselka, born in Budweis, who was the model for Karel Havlíček's caricature of a liberal, a member of the Left in the Frankfurt Parliament and in the Viennese Imperial Council, left his personal memoir of the "revolutionary year"—from March 1848 to March 1849. Here he came to the remarkable conclusion that, with the possible exceptions of the struggles in Berlin, Austria, then in Vienna, there was really no revolution at all in the German lands, only the threat of impending revolution.[1] The fear of revolution was responsible for the concessions that the government made, but it also influenced the policies of the bourgeoisie. In Schuselka's view, the concessions were won too easily.

Unfortunately, we have no documentation telling us just how much the fear of revolution influenced the actions of the Austrian government between March and May 1848. Certainly it did not influence Chancellor Metternich's negotiations in the last days of the "old order," and it hardly influenced the stance taken by his opponents, for they were all convinced that it had become impossible to govern in the old way, and to them the old Chancellor represented the greatest obstacle. Therefore Metternich fell as a symbol of the old order, as did Police Commissioner Sedlnitzky and Mayor Czapka of Vienna. The casualties of the fighting on March 13 were buried publicly, and on this occasion the chaplin of the new Academic Legion, Professor Anton Füster, made his first public appearance. On March 14 the censorship was abolished, and on the 15th the Emperor issued a cabinet memorandum in which he promised a constitution which was to be drawn up by "representatives of all the Provincial Diets." Kolowrat's diaries from the period of his government—March 20 to April 5—have not been found. But we do have the papers of his Foreign Minister Count Ficquelmont, who succeeded him in the Premiership on April 5.[2]

The cabinet memorandum of March 15 of course was the work neither of Kolowrat nor Ficquelmont, and the members of the government were unable to agree on precisely what it meant. Kolowrat was placed at the head of the cabinet because he was an open opponent of Metternich. It was presumed that he would be more welcome to the Viennese public than Metternich's heir apparent Ficquelmont, who had been decided upon as early as 1840 by a conference of state ministers. And we know that Ficquelmont's attitude towards Emperor Ferdinand's "purportedly free decision to allow his peoples whatever they wanted" was at best ironical.[3]

Ficquelmont's papers inform us about the position of Kolowrat's government on the most serious issues. The Viennese revolution, to be sure, did not evoke much of an echo elsewhere in the Austrian Provinces. Provinces, with the exception of Graz and Linz. In Bohemia it appeared that the government could always rely upon the tension between the Czech and German bourgeoisie. In Hungary, on the other hand, the Palatine Archduke Stephen named a government under Count Batthyány, in which Kossuth played a leading role from the beginning. Things looked even worse in th Italian provinces of Lombardy and Venetia. Faced with the Sardinian threat, it was necessary to play for time, to permit Radetzky to prepare for a defensive war. Therefore Ficquelmont, through the British ambassador to Vienna Ponsonby and the Austrian ambassador in London Dietrichstein, offered Great Britain the role of mediator in the conflict. The British Prime Minister Palmerston, of course, had no intention of trying to save Lombardy and Venetia for Austria, and Ficquelmont ought to have realized this. Peace in Italy and eventual withdrawal from most Italian territory was also supported by part of the Viennese bourgeoisie, who also won over Count Ferdinand Colloredo, President of the Chamber of Commerce.[4]

Ficquelmont was driven onto the defensive, and he tried to prevent any final decision. This was also the case in the question of the future status of Germany, where professors at Heidelberg were agitating for convocation of an all-German National Assembly. At Frankfurt between March 31 and April 3 gathered the so-called Pre-Parliament, set up by the "Committee of Fifty," which was to prepare for the National Assembly. It met on May 18 in the Frankfurt Paulskirche.[5] Ficquelmont declared to a delegation from Frankfurt that "the Austrian government has always been German," and that the German subjects of the Monarchy were of course at the same time Austrians. The government therefore was not against the elections for the Frankfurt Assembly, but it also intended to give its German citizens the choice not to take part. Ficquelmont objected to the fact that the Frankfurt elections were to be carried out practically by universal suffrage on the French model, and that the liberals would demand the same in Austria.[6]

Ficquelmont collaborated at least passively with the military commission of the Committee of Fifty. He sent two infantry regiments into Germany from Bohemia—Wellington's to Rastatt and Latour's to Ulm, ostensibly to protect the border with France. The Frankfurt "revolutionaries" were afraid of the French because of rumors that they were preparing to invade Germany with contingents of Polish and German émigrés. But when the local people complained about the Austrian troops, Ficquelmont very willingly sent them through Bavaria to the Italian battlefields, just in time for Latour's regiment to take part in the attack on Vicenza. The "March to Italy" of course did nothing to raise Ficquelmont's popularity either in Frankfurt or in Vienna.[7]

On April 2 the Great-German tricolor was raised over St. Stephen's Cathedral in Vienna and hung from the balcony of the Hofburg. The next day elections were held in the University of Vienna for the Frankfurt Pre-Parliament. On April 4 a group of Viennese burghers demanded that the Imperial Crown and other insignia in the Schatzkammer be delivered to Frankfurt.[8]

In the meantime the Finance Minister Kübeck submitted his resignation on April 1; Kolowrat followed suit on the 5th. Officially he requested to be relieved for reasons of health. Ficquelmont replaced him at first temporarily, then permanently when Kolowrat was pensioned. Since Kolowrat died only in 1864, his illness in 1848 was probably not very serious. it is more probable that the Court had come to the conclusion that the situation had quieted sufficiently for Kolowrat to give way to Metternich's original heir. The 71-year-old Ficquelmont maintained close contact with both Metternich and the military leaders—especially Windischgrätz, who at this time was staying at his estate Jablonica in Upper Hungary. We do not know how far the discussions of the military leaders of the Prague General Command concerned contingency plans for dealing with unrest in Prague or cooperating with political counterrevolution. But in any case, it was already decided by the end of March, in light of the experience of Vienna and Milan, that no attempt would be made to defend the entire city of Prague. The Old and New Towns would be cleared by troops, and the city would be held in check by artillery batteries on surrounding hillsides—Hradčany, Letná, Petřín and Vyšehrad.[9] Ficquelmont's government was similar to Kolowrat's; its average age was even higher—sixty-seven as against sixty-two. Pillersdorf continued as Minister of the Interior. Sommaruga, considered to be a liberal, remained in the Ministry of Education. After April 2 Krauss replaced Kübeck as Minister of Finance; Taaffe continued as Minister of Justice; Minister of War was Peter Zanini, who was regarded as the representative of "popular"—or bourgeois—elements.

Ficquelmont, then, was partly responsible for the cabinet memorandum of April 8 in which the Emperor granted a kind of acceptance to the petition of the end of March: he pointed out that he had already accepted the earlier demands of March 15; he referred to his patent of March 28 abolishing the *robota*; and he suggested that the actual realization of the demands depended entirely upon the next Imperial Parliament.[10] Kolowrat and Ficquelmont, probably against their better judgment, accomplished an overhaul of the institutions of central government which outlived the revolution itself and indeed survived in its essential features until 1918. Instead of the Court Offices (Hofstellen) and Court Chambers, there were now Ministries. In place of the State Councils and State Conferences there appeared the Ministerial Council. Its minutes reveal vacillation bewtween acquiescence and resistance to further demands from the revolutionary Viennese.

Ficquelmont's government formulated a program of elastic defense which represented a step backward. In situations of conflict—of which there was no lack even in April—serious differences arose among the members of the government. The one great power on whose support Ficquelmont could rely was Russia, but Russia was primarily interested in securing its western border and most concerned with the maneuvers of the Poles (or the Polish noblemen) in the Poznań region of Prussia. During March there was great enthusiasm in Prussia and all Germany for the Polish patriots. Mieroslawski was released from the Moabite prison in Berlin. On March 24 the Prussian King Frederick William IV received a Polish delegation; and there was even talk of reconstituting Poland. As late as April 18 Minister von Arnim-Suckow still spoke in favor of the Poles. But neither France nor Britain was interested in the matter, and after April 13 they purposely kept their distance. The Polish National Committee, established at Poznań on March 20, came up against the opposition of the German minority in the region, and it was opposed even more vigorously in East Prussia and Silesia. On April 26 General Willisen submitted a plan for dividing the Poznań region into Polish and German parts, and in the beginning of May most of the territory was annexed to the German Union. The military resistance of the Poles was broken by May 9, when Mieroslawski laid down his arms before General von Pfuel, who was thus able to claim the first victory for "order" against revolution and anarchy. Pfuel was the representative of military opinion which regarded conflict with Russia over the Polish question as the grossest "stupidity." And it is not surprising that the sentiments of the German bourgeoisie also changed. The journal *Grenzboten* emphasized the importance of bringing both Prussias and the entire Poznań district into the German Union and thus into the purview of Frankfurt. Schuselka even supported the annexation of all Istria—of course out of economic and strategic considerations. Frankfurt's attitude toward the annexation of Schleswig was identical.[11]

Hecker and Struve were the first members of the Frankfurt Assembly to become dissatisfied and leave. From April 8 to 27 there was fighting in Baden. Hecker and Herwegh, a revolutionary poet and organizer of the Legion in France, were defeated; the Baden Republic collapsed immediately upon its proclamation. Karl Marx and Friedrich Engels followed the developments critically, because they considered Hecker's actions to be premature. On April 1 they produced a sketch for a German revolutionary program and planned the publication of the *Neue Rheinische Zeitung*, whose first issue appeared on June 1.[12]

The revolutionary movement suffered another serious blow in April. In Great Britain during March there had been massive demonstrations in the industrial cities of Glasgow, Manchester, and Hanley calling for "Bread or Revolution". In April a manifestation by the Chartists was expected, to lay their third petition before Parliament. But since they already knew how Parliament dealt with their petitions, they planned to convoke a National Assembly. On April 10 a crowd gathered on Kennington Common which was estimated at a quarter of a million people. The government mobilized the army, the police, the frightened middle classes, and both sides backed off from a bloody conflict. The episode amounted to a bitter defeat for the Chartists. Their National Assembly had failed, and from this day Chartism went into irreversible decline.[13]

The next day in Prague František Palacký published his famous letter to the Frankfurt Assembly. There is nothing about this letter in Ficquelmont's papers, nor is it mentioned even by one of the most recent historians of the German Revolution, the Frenchman Jacques Droz. As we shall see, Palacký's letter was more important for the shaping of relations between Czechs and Germans than it was for the Austrian government. The government could conclude from it that it had nothing to fear from the Czech national party, and that therefore it need not concern itself for the present with Czech affairs.

Certainly it had more pressing problems, some of them involving its own members. Because of his quarrels with Ficquelmont, Pillersdorf submitted his resignation on April 19; he was followed the next day by the Minister of War Zanini and on the 21st by the Minister of Justice Taaffe. Ficquelmont did not accept Pillersdorf's resignation, probably because he feared the reaction of the Viennese public. He did not greatly care about Taaffe and entrusted his Ministry temporarily to Sommaruga. But he accepted Zanini's resignation with positive delight, and had a replacement already picked out: Field-Marshal Theodore Baillet-Latour, of a Lorraine family related to Ficquelmont. In fact the Latours had helped Ficquelmont to launch his career in the service of Austria. Baillet-Latour was born in 1780, so that he was ten years older than Zanini, and on October 6, 1848, he became a "victim of the revolution." He did not die, according to Ficquelmont's diplomatic formulation, because he was an aristocrat; "he fell, rather, because his professional activity created forces which everywhere stood firm against the enemies of the Monarchy." In other words, the Minister of War had organized the military forces which enabled Radetzky to win in Italy and Windischgrätz in Prague and Vienna.[14]

As soon as he took office, Latour, widely regarded as the spokesman of thee extreme right, ordered th filling of the third—skeleton—battalions of all infantry regiments and also the reserve squadrons of the cavalry. This meant raising the number of troops by 80,000, and hence new conscriptions. Surprisingly enough, his action provoked no immediate resistance, and the troops from Bohemia, Hungary, and Galicia marched through Austria on their way to the southern battlefields without the slightest hindrance. The Viennese radical democrats, in fact, were on the whole happy to have these soldiers removed from the capital. It escaped them that strong military contingents remained in Galicia and Bohemia.

Ficquelmont knew that Latour's appointment had prompted talk of the "danger of reaction." In his *Apology* he only pointed out that "reaction" was not the same as "aristocracy" and that his bitterest opponents were people who themselves were members of the old ruling class but not supporters of "reaction"—*i.e.* a return to the pre-revolutionary situation. Here he was thinking chiefly of the opposition which coalesced within his own government. He feared these men more than the burgher of Vienna and Budapest, whom he regarded as the bearers of revolutionary thought.

This "internal opposition" manifested itself at the beginning of May. On the evening of May 2 members of the Academic Legion and the National

Guard staged a noisy demonstration before his house in the Herrenstrasse and demanded his resignation. At the cabinet meeting the next day Ficquelmont discovered that he did not have the support of the majority of his government. Since he could be sure of Latour, it appeared that Sommaruga and Krauss had joined Pillersdorf. In the afternoon there was a mass demonstration in front of Ficquelmont's office. The Commander of the Viennese National Guard Lieutenant Field Marshal Hoyos, resigned, and his successor General Sardagna could not bring himself to move against the armed crowds thronging the Ballplatz and the Minoritenplatz. Ficquelmont asked in vain for protection. His house and that of his nephew Prince Edmund Clary-Aldringen were occupied by armed demonstrators, to whom he handed over his written resignation at two o'clock the following morning. According to his version of the events, he had not submitted it to the people, but to the government which had denied him its trust and support.[15]

Why did it happen this way? Ficquelmont had insisted that any constitution must be proclaimed by the Emperor, that it must be accepted as his gift, even if somewhat forced. If the parliament, consisting essentially of feudal elements, could not issue it in time, then it must be given from above. The assembly was to consist of two chambers, one of them automatically reserved for the nobility. This, in any case, is how the constitution looked which was promulgated on April 25, 1848, by Pillersdorf and which Ficquelmont signed. It was derived largely from the Belgian constitution and did not include Hungary or the Italian provinces. Elections to the lower chamber were tied to a tax census; the upper chamber was to be composed of the large landholders and members appointed by the Emperor. In any case, the Emperor had the right to veto any action of either chamber.[16]

It was opposition to this decreed constitution which led to Ficquelmont's resignation and which obliged the counter-revolution once again to slow its pace. It took Pillersdorf an entire fortnight to form a new government. During this time the old government continued to rule, and it had to breast a new wave of discontent as soon as Pillersdorf announced the election procedures in conformity with the constitution of April 25. The moderates among the Viennese burghers were prepared to swallow the bitter pill and reconcile themselves to the constitution, even though it had originated without their influence and did not conform to their expectations. But the students, influenced by Füster, Fischhof, and Goldmark, immediately protested against any limitation upon electoral rights on the basis of wealth. On May 15 there was a large demonstration, before which the government had to capitulate once more. By occupying the Hofburg, which was left without military protection, the students with their "Sturmpetition" forced the government to withdraw the constitution and to promise universal suffrage for the male population, as well as a one-chamber parliament. In addition, the government promised that no military units would be sent to the center of the city unless requested by the National Guard itself.[17]

This was the greatest success to date of the revolutionary minded students, whose efforts were supported chiefly by the population of the industrial suburbs. The Students' Committee controlled the much more numerous Central Committee of the Burghers, National Guard, and Students, which had represented the actual government of Vienna. Democratic clubs and radical journals led by individuals who were understandably unacquainted with politics either in theory or in practice. It was not difficult to direct their attacks not only on the government but also on the Church hierarchy and the aristocracy.

The Court "Camarilla," as the remains of the Imperial Court began to be called, effected a counter-move which was not without a certain success: they left Vienna secretly with the Emperor for the relative quiet of Innsbruck. News of the flight aroused the fears of the constitutional liberals, who thought that the radicals would proclaim a republic in the capital. Particularly among the "kaisertreu" petite bourgeoisie of Vienna there was open hostility to the students. But the Court missed the opportunity to dominate the situation.

In any case, the Court had left behind the government, which after being enlarged was finally formed on May 19 by Pillersdorf. He had been Foreign Minister since May 8, when Ficquelmont was replaced by his older colleague J.P. Wessenberg-Ampringen, another diplomat of the Metternich school. Of the former government there remained Sommargua at the head of the Ministries of Education and Justice; Krauss with the Ministry of Finance, and Latour with the Ministry of War. There were two new Ministries: Commerce, under Anton Doblhoff-Dier, who was forty-eight years old; and Public Works, under A. Baumgartner, who was fifty-five. The average age of the government had declined, but it was still nearly sixty-two years.

On May 25 the government, which miscalculated by concluding that the students had lost all their influence, issued decrees closing the university and joining the Academic Legion to the National Guard. This step only led to further catastrophe. The populace rose in favor of the students; shots were fired and barricades erected. Thousands of workers arrived from the suburbs to support the students' stand against the government. But even before the barricades appeared, which were intended to isolate the government and force it to negotiate, Pillersdorf capitulated utterly. A committee of burghers, National Guardsmen and students was created in defense of rights. It was called the Committee of Safety (*Sicherheitsausschluss*) and led by Dr. Fischhof, who since the beginning of March had been in the vanguard of the radical student movement. The Committee of Safety was the only functioning government of Vienna, and its existence represented a complete victory for the radicals. It also meant the beginning of efforts to end unemployment, which had risen in Vienna, as in Paris or Prague, with the growing political uncertainty. Organizations to assure at least the bare necessities of life were set up somewhat on the model of the French National Workshops. Thus were launched the first efforts to solve social problems.

2 The Origins of the Social and Nationality Questions

The papers of members of Austrian governments from March to May of 1848 suggest that they considered the revolution of students and workers in Vienna to be far less dangerous than the threat of a peasant war. This was probably because the memory of the Galician uprising of 1846 was still fresh. As we have seen, it lay behind the government's decree abolishing the *robota* and all other feudal obligations in Bohemia, Moravia and Silesia, which was to take effect at the end of March 1849. The *robota* was abolished immediately upon payment of indemnity in Styria, Carinthia and Carniola, as well as in Galicia, which was regarded as an especially volatile region.[18] It appears today that these measures actually did produce the effect intended by the government. The peasants of course expected far more from the abolition of the *robota* than they eventually received, but they promptly lost interest in revolution and were increasingly willing to oppose the restless and dissatisfied "city folks." But this was not quite the situation in Bohemia, where the villages were far more differentiated socially. The tensions which were the automatic consequence prevented the peasant population from becoming an independent political force.

In Hungary, where the agrarian problem was just as painful, the frightened Pressburg parliament decided to abolish the *robota* unconditionally as early as March 15. But Kossuth's own program pursued a primarily political aim: the creation of an independent kingdom of Hungary, expanded by the inclusion of Transylvania, Croatia, Slavonia and the so-called Military Frontier. The enlarged and reformed kingdom was to be a national and constitutional state with a goverment responsible to parliament, which was to sit at Budapest. Batthyány's government and the parliament approved the approximately thirty "March Laws" which created a modern bourgeois-liberal state from feudal Hungary. But it soon became evident that the nobility had acquiesced in Kossuth's program only out of fear of a peasant war and that they wanted nothing to do with the Budapest radicals who controlled the municipal administration. The March Laws were signed by Emperor Ferdinand on April 11.

Those around him, however, refused to accept the incorporation of Transylvania, Croatia and the Military Frontier into a united Hungary. Nor did they accept the principle that taxes collected in Hungary should serve primarily domestic needs, · or that the Budapest government should control the Hungarian regiments, of which six were serving in Italy, five in the Bohemian and Austrian lands, and only four in Hungary.[19]

Following its wise old formula for neutralizing centrifugal forces by placing them opposite each other, the Court began to extend its support to the Croats, the Serbs and the Rumanians against the Magyars. On March 23 a new Bán (governor) was named in Croatia: Colonel Josef Jellačić, a friend of Ludovit Gaj, leader of the Illyrian movement which aimed for a union of the Balkan Slavs under the aegis of the Empire. At the beginning of April Jellačić was named commander of military forces in Croatia and in the Military Frontier, and on April 19 he forbade administrative offices in Croatia to have any contact with the Budapest government. Kossuth was able to halt the transfer of Hungarian contingents to the Italian front; by May 7 Jallačić was brought to heel by the Hungarian Viceroy and his military forces placed under the control of the Budapest War Ministry. As soon as the Court arrived at Insbruck, negotiations began with Hungarian delegations. In exchange for a promise of further troops for Radetzky against the Italian revolutionaries, the Court allowed Jellačićto fall. On June 10 he was formally stripped of all authority.[20]

The Serbs and the Rumanians were dropped out of similar policy considerations. The Serbs had made a formal request for independence from Hungary on May 13 at Karlowitz; and the National Committee of Tryansylvanian Rumanians protested against the decision of that country to proclaim union with Hungary.[21]

In the spring of 1848 there could be no doubt about the double-faced policy of the Austrian Court. It is most unlikely that the Czech and German population of Bohemia, Moravia, and Silesia could have been unaware of this, but in the end they behaved as though they were. It happened because among the Czechs and Germans both there were serious internal conflicts of which the leading politicans—on the Czech side Palacký, Rieger, and Havlíček, and on the German Löhner and Uffo Horn—were aware, but about which they were able to do little. In fact, both sides inflamed the situation. Only in their opposition to the "old order" was there no difference between the Czechs and the Bohemian Germans, between the Estates opposition, the grande and petite bourgoisie, the students and the workers. As soon as concessions were wrung from the Government, as soon as the aspirations of the newly rising bourgeoisie

125

were at least partly satisfied, the shaky coalition collapsed, and its individual components began to agitate in favor of their own particular interests. Thereby they created, even against their own will, a situation highly favorable to the counter-revolution.

We have already seen how, in the struggle over the two petitions to Vienna in March, the noble-bourgeois opposition separated into three camps: the democratic, which gave the impulse for the first petition; the bourgeois-constitutional or "liberal," which produced its own version of the first and eventually the second petition; and the Estates. The last sent to Vienna a separate petition of its own with the first petition of the St. Wenceslas Committee. While the second petition—doubtless influenced by the example of Hungary—was being formulated, the Czechs and Germans drew together briefly once again: radicals like Uffo Horn and the excruciatingly cautious Pinkas. On April 2 their text was even supported by a group of Bohemian noblemen, largely followers of Kolowrat, including his nephew Count Lützow. Even after Lützow's disappearance, this essentially tractable "Bohemian Movement" could count on support from the ranks of the bureaucracy. This was manifested in the collaboration between Rieger and Trojan and Count Counsellor Josef Kleczansky, formerly captain of the Leitmeritz region, who in Vienna helped formulate the demands which were incorporated into the text of the cabinet memorandum of April 8. It is very doubtful that Palacký was correct in his description of this memorandum as a "Bohemian Charter," nor was the Czech bourgeoisie very wise later when it tried to establish its policy upon it.

In spite of all the real or imagined successes of this policy, which led chiefly to the creation of the National Committee as a significant political force (although its role should not be exaggerated), it lacked a mass organization until the end of April. This could be provided only by the organization Slovanská Lípa, which, however, necessarily excluded the Bohemian Germans, just as its Jugoslav namesake excluded the Magyars.[22] We have seen that in Vienna the real force of the revolution was provided by the students and workers. Unlike Vienna, Prague still possessed no large industrial quarter, and the number of workers was estimated at only four thousand. The number of students did not even reach this level. In the Polytechnic there were about 1,500 students, in the University perhaps a third more.

Still the administration feared them, and the 500th anniversary of the foundation of the University of Prague was awaited with trepidation. But on April 7, 1848, nothing at all spectacular occurred in Prague. The festivities were subdued, and two days later a "Constitutional Festival of Conciliation" was held in the Stromovka park. The strength of the student movement was sapped by tasteless squabbles about whether the Polytechnic was really on the same level as the University, whether it should be incorporated into the University or remain independent. Essentially its students, though not its professors, were closer to the popular masses; its section of the Academic Legion was the first to have a Czech leadership. It appears that as far as breadth of social composition of the student body is concerned, it was most nearly approached by the Philosophy Faculty of the University, while the professional Faculties, Law and Medicine, were far more restricted. The arrival of some of the Czech and Moravian students from Vienna in Prague provided a certain stimulus. The Prague students admired their more successful Viennese "colleagues."[23] Among them were Vojtěch Náprstek and Karel Sladkovský, who quickly became the students' spokesman and was more influential than the young J.V. Frič, whose *Memoir* is perhaps the least reliable description of the events of 1848. Though only fragments of Náprstek's diaries have survived, it is clear that he hardly had the right to send greetings to Prague in the name of all the Viennese students. We know, on the other hand, that the "Slavonic" students of Vienna had a reputation as great radicals.

At the end of April the Archbishop of Olomouc Sommerau-Beeck complained to the Ministry of the Interior about the conduct of Czech students from Vienna, led by Vojtěch Náprstek, in his peaceful town of Kremsier. The Archbishop, who had begun his career as a cavalry officer, then spun it out through the military chaplaincy to the wealthiest see in the entire Monarchy, was used to a better class of guest. In 1845 there were the Archdukes Stephen and Francis Charles, and a year later Chancellor Metternich. None of them had agitated the Slavic population; but on the night of April 29, 1848, the students staged a "caterwauling" under the windows of an unnamed worthy, probably the Archbishop himself.[24]

By the beginning of May the student organization Slavia began its operations, which were soon halted, however, by dissention within the leadership. Frič, in the thick of the fray, certainly did not distinguish himself. Towards the end of the month he worked in Slavia's military section but was unable to procure sufficient arms, not to mention devise a coherent plan of action in case of an armed conflict. The best organized element in Slavia were the students from the Polytechnic, who were represented politically by A. Bradka, exposed to the ideas of Emmanuel Arnold by Jan Krejčí and Pavel Václav Kleinert, and given military instruction by Maximilian Maux.[25]

On the whole, we know almost as little about the students of Prague as we do about the workers. There exists no detailed analysis of the composition of the working class, but it would be wrong to exaggerate the relations that existed between the students and the workers, as J.V. Frič for example does in his memoirs. After all, the students' point of view was fundamentally alien to the workers. A closer relationship with them was maintained by a member of the St. Wenceslas Committee Dr. C.V. Kampelík, who on March 19 was entrusted with the task of drawing up a petition for Prague textile printers, who were burdened by unemployment. At the end of March Kampelík gave up his public defense of the working class, after being accused of communist tendencies, as we know from the single issue that appeared of his *Hlásník* (*Announcer*), the first newspaper for workers.[26]

Otherwise the St. Wenceslas Committee and later the National Committee treated the workers in a stepmotherly manner. The National Guard was created expressly as an instrument against the proletariat; the electoral statute of the end of May excluded the workers from suffrage—a marked contrast with the situation in Vienna, where there was more or less universal male suffrage. The workers received no reply to the petitions which they submitted throughout April, and their poverty grew. Thus there were strikes and violent conficts—in Königgrätz, Brno, Ostrava; and in the first days of May in Prague there were attacks on Jewish shops which recalled the events of 1844.[27] The Prague typographers, who were the best organized of the workers, carried out a two-day strike in May when their petition was ignored. At the end of the month the workers distributed leaflets asking the public for their support. On June 3 the textile workers demonstrated, and the hussars were sent in to deal with them. It seemed that all was as it had been in 1844, including the presence of Windischgrätz. The Prague Municipal Council did not regard the workers any more favorably than had the old magistracy. On June 10 it advised them to emulate the textile workers of northern Bohemia, who were much worse off but had not yet shown overt signs of restlessness.[28]

These conflicts were not widely reported in the Czech and German newspapers; they were only of peripheral interest to the reading public, who were beginning to take up the rather tame slogan "We want no revolution, we defend only the Constitution!" and were busy arguing about whether inhabitants of the Bohemian lands should go to Frankfurt.[29] It has become a part of historical convention that František Palacký accomplished a momentous act with his letter to Frankfurt; it has been largely forgotten that much of what he had to say here was not new, and that Palacký was not even the first to raise the entire question.

As early as April 2 an anonymous article appeared in *Neue Zeit*, pointing out the difficulties inherent in Austria's relationship to a united Germany. It prompted the professor of Olomouc Adolf Fischer to write his pamphlet "Germany without Austria?" As a "Moravian who loves his country," he opposed a union of Bohemia, Moravia, and Silesia, but on the other hand, he favored the absorption of Austria into Germany. The historical analogy of the Union of England, Scotland, and Ireland, strangely enough, did not dampen the fervency of his argument.[30]

The Olomouc history professor published his pamphlet just as the Committee of Fifty at Frankfurt was addressing invitations to six "Austrians," for whom it reserved places in its ranks, including Palacký and the Moravian German Schwarzer. We do not know whether the invitations were issued before or after April 8, the date of the cabinet memorandum which Palacký came to regard as the "Bohemian Charter." But we do know that the next day a group of Germans from the Bohemian lands, including von Löhner, Josef Rank, and Franz Rössler, protested in person to Pillersdorf himself against the provisions of the cabinet memorandum. They opposed efforts to unify Bohemia, Moravia, and Silesia and favored union with Germany. They disputed the principle that administrative posts be occupied exclusively by natives of the particular land. Thus from the outset the contest was one for places, position, the material safety of the German intelligentsia who sensed that their dominance might be at an end. The contemporary West German historian Prinz regards this protest to the Minister of the Interior as the first official act of the *Verein der Deutschen aus Böhmen, Mähren und Schlesien, zur Aufrechterhaltung ihrer Nationalität*. But it was made in the name of all Bohemian Germans, and even at the end of April this Viennese society did not possess what later became its official name.[31] Prinz describes the *Verein* as "the first democratic self-help organization of German bourgeois nationalism" against Czech bourgeois nationalism; the characterization does not conform to the realities. On April 22 the society proudly announced in the journal *Volksfreund* that its membership included aristocrats—several counts, in fact—and we shall see how Löhner did everything in his power to attract some princes as well. On April 10 the cabinet memorandum was also formally opposed by conservatives meeting in the so-called Central Committee of the Estates.[32] Thus the effort to win allies from the ranks of the old ruling class was by no means peculiar to the political leaders of the Czech bourgeoisie.

On April 11 František Palacký read aloud the text of his letter to Frankfurt (in Czech, let us hope) at a banquet of the Prague Municipal Meeting (*Měšťánská Beseda*), celebrating the twenty-fifth anniversary of this notably mixed society. According to W.W. Tomek, some of those closest to Palacký were present: Jan of Neuberg, Count Vojtěch Deym, Erben, Gábler, Havlíček, Vocel, Tomek, and Palacký's son Jan. His letter reached a wide audience after being printed as a leaflet under the title *Hlas k připojení Rakouska k Německu (Eine Stimme über Österreichs Anschluss an Deutschland)*, and it would be interesting to discover who bore the printing costs for the Czech and German versions of this document of 1848.³³

Palacký's letter consisted of three parts: in the first he proved that from a historical point of view, Bohemian participation in the Frankfurt Assembly was unjustified. In the second he opted for Austria and pointed to its meaning for the Slavs of central Europe. In the final section of his letter Palacký took a skeptical view of earlier attempts to organize all of Germany. His legal and historical analysis was not altogether accurate, since the relationship of the Bohemian ruler to the head of the Empire was in fact determined by considerations of power, so that it constantly changed. He could perhaps have presented an argument based on natural law to the gentlemen of Frankfurt with much greater effectiveness—although we know that representatives of the Assembly in Vienna had tried to acquire the old Imperial insignia. In any case, the Frankfurt Assembly itself argued according to natural law or historical precedent, whichever suited its particular purpose. Franz Schuselka, who like Kuranda was at least in favor of inviting Palacký in the first place, did not comprehend the pathos of Palacký's letter. It appears that what bothered him most was Palacký's reference to Bohemian representation at Frankfurt as "suicide." Two years later he was obliged to admit that Palacký's doubts about the Assembly's viability were justified, but he remained convinced that "Bohemia will nevertheless remain within the frame of Germany."³⁴

Schuselka of course soon left Frankfurt, where he sat on the Left, and in the spring of 1848 he was back in Vienna working in favor of a German Austria. Certainly he did not deserve to become the target of Havlíček's scathing song "Suselka nám píše" (Schuselka writes to us), which in any case does not belong among the brillant successes of Havlíček's literary career. According to Prinz, Palacký's letter is an expression of his "nationalist conservatism," and this is why it was so sympathetic to Josef A. Helfert, who, however, already in 1849 realized that Palacký's inclination towards Austria was not so disinterested as it appeared in the spring of 1848—to the detriment of the Czech cause. Surely it represented nothing new. In May of 1846, Havlíček had written a reply in *Pražské noviny* to Jakub Malý's article "Slovan a Cech" ("A Slav and a Czech"): "Austria's strength is the best guarantee for us and for all Slvas. The stronger the Austrian Monarchy, the greater our security." On March 12, 1848 *Pražské noviny* editorialized: "Our nation is chiefly Austrian, to which we belong along with our other Slavic fellow-nationals . . . We Austrian Slavs shall firmly hold to our Empire, which assures our future." And on March 19 Havlíček wrote in *Národní noviny*: "We are a part of Austria," and he concluded that "complete independence" would in the present circumstances lead to a disaster.³⁵

At the beginning of April it might have appeared that the way to transforming Austria into a federation was truly open. Indeed, on April 17 the Ministerial Council, still under the presidency of Ficquelmont, met to consider the suggestion of the Galician Viceroy Franz Stadion that that land be given an autonomous administration. The Minister of Finance Krauss, chief of a department which nobody else thought about during the entire period of the revolution and who had remained very much on the sidelines until now, suggested that the whole nationalist movement might be neutralized simply by abolishing the *robota*; and the instructions drawn up for Stadion actually did recommend support of the peasants against the landholding nobility.[36] In Hungary and Galicia, therefore, the government was able to make use of national antagonism—but in the Bohemian lands the situation was far more complicated. The government neither encouraged nor forbade the elections to Frankfurt; and for the time being it decided to regard the Czech-German conflict as an affair of little importance.

Löhner's *Verein* claimed 800 members in the second half of April, some of them highly influential, and it continued its efforts to recruit new members. While the National Committee in Prague busied itself with quarrels over what kind of cockade the police ought to wear and whether they should be allowed to wear the Great-German colors, the *Verein* was printing and distributing propaganda in favor of the Frankfurt elections. On April 18 the President of the Lower Austrian Government Jan Talatzko ofJeštětice, whom we have already met, issued a directive concerning these elections, which was quickly reprinted by the *Verein* under the title "To the Germans in Bohemia."[37] At the same time Löhner was in the midst of an interesting campaign to win the high aristocracy over to the German cause. On April 20 he wrote about this to Prince Edmund Clary-Aldringen of Teplitz. He assured him that pro-Frankfurt propaganda presented no threat to Austria's sovereignty; he pointed out that since the *Verein*'s membership already included such luminaries as the Counts Colloredo and Breda, Baron Fries and Baron Doblhoff, it stood as a bulwark against republicans on the one hand and reactionaries and Slavo-maniacs on the other; and finally he thanked the Prince for having offered his palace in Vienna as the *Verein*'s first refuge.[38]

Clary-Aldringen actually joined Löhner's organization, albeit with some reservations. He even prepared a speech for the *Verein*, which however was probably never delivered. Here he considered the position of Germans in the predominantly Slavic provinces of Austria. It would be dangerous, in his view, for the *Verein* to oppose the large landholders—especially since the German population in the Bohemian lands was scattered: its single center of concentration was Vienna. Therefore the German inhabitants of Bohemia, Moravia, and Silesia had no choice but to become convinced Austrians—unless they wished to move away and allow all border regions to become amalgamated with Prussia, Saxony, and Bavaria.[39]

Most of the members of the *Verein* would probably not have agreed with Clary-Aldringen, but it is true that he did win some of his fellow-noblemen over to the cause. In a letter to Johann Adolf Schwarzenberg he opposed Austria's isolation from Germany, the "moral terror" of the Czech elements, and the principle of equality among nationalities, because the Czechs wanted nothing less than political autonomy and national dominance. The "Russian party" among them, moreover, pursued republican and communist aims. All this was enough to persuade Schwarzenberg to join Löhner's *Verein*.[40] Eventually relations between Clary and Löhner became clouded: it emerged that members of the *Verein* were among those who forced their way into the Clary palace in Vienna on the night of May 3 to force the resignation of Clary's father-in-law Count Ficquelmont. This probably meant the end of the hospitality at the Clary palace, but it did not induce Clary himself to resign from the *Verein*. Apparently he shared Löhner's view that in the present circumstances, the integrity of the "German cause" should prevail over extraneous "differences of opinion."[41]

The elections to Frankfurt, which the Moravian Diet had opposed, were approved by Pillersdorf at the advice of the new Bohemian Viceroy Leo Thun, who argued that this was an affair to be decided by the inhabitants themselves. The National Committee in Prague was opposed, and even Ficquelmont was not happy with this solution. On May 9 Dr. Löhner was received by Pillersdorf, who assured him once again that the Government had done all it could for the success of the elections. Löhner, together with J. Machanke and H. Suttner, published more leaflets offering help to qualified candidates. But in the end participation in the election turned out to be minimal in Bohemia and Moravia. There were representatives of Bohemian, Moravian, and Silesian Germans at Frankfurt, but how far they represented the German population, or what part of it they represented, we do not know. There was also one Czech present—Cyprián Lelek of Hlučín, who represented the Prussian United Diet, and he sat on the Left. To the very end there remained in Frankfurt delegates from some Moravian towns (for example Tišnov) whose German character is open to grave doubt.[42]

Once the elections were over, the activities of the *Verein* appear to have subsided, but they received a fresh stimulus from the events of May. The students of Prague rioted on May 10, following the arrest of printer Groll. As in Vienna a few weeks later, the students' intervention was not welcomed by the burghers, who were by now far removed from this kind of revolutionary activity. The burgomaster Anton Strobach and the commander of the National

Guard Colonel A. Haas both submitted their resignations. This was about the time that Stadion left Prague and Palacký refused the post of Minister of Education even though the appointment had already been signed by the Emperor. Palacký declared that he did not wish to complicate matters for Pillersdorf's government, and that furthermore he could not countenance the government's half-hearted stance on the Frankfurt elections. Thus he was behaving in a more "Austrian" way than the Austrian government. But at a meeting of the Ministerial Council, the Minister of War Baillet-Latour advised his colleagues that Palacký's refusal may have been fortunate: according to his information the Minister-designate had become involved in plans to convoke a meeting of the Slavs in Prague, to take place on May 31. The Minister of War, who was now urging that the "discontented elements" among the students and workers be conscripted forthwith into the army or the paramilitary "Freikorps," was certainly no friend of the Slavs. For some time, in fact, he had been issuing warnings about the dangers of panslavism, which has led Prinz to credit him with notable farsightedness. That Latour was the true representative of reaction in Pillersdorf's government is attested by his correspondence with Windischgrätz, which bagan in May.[43]

Windischgrätz's own position at this time was rather interesting. The "extraordinary mission" with which he had been charged on March 14 was cancelled on April 3. Neither Kolowrat nor Pillersdorf wanted him in Prague. Stadion advised against it; Ficquelmont was expected to dissuade him; and Latour was supposed to find him a place in the army in northern Italy. But this was not precisely what Windischgrätz had in mind for himself. Eventually on May 19 he came to Prague from his Upper Hungarian estates, and the following day he took over the General Command, probably to the dismay of the Viceroy Leo Thun-Hohenstein, who could not even have been aware of a letter which Windischgrätz had sent Latour before leaving Hungary. Here he expressed in unambiguous terms his conviction that in Prague he would be in a position to uphold the "interests of the ruler, the dynasty and all honorable men, which hang in the balance."[44] All the members of the Government except Latour were uneasy about Windischgrätz, and on May 23 Pillersdorf rejected Latour's proposal that he be named Field-Artillery General.

The events in Vienna on May 15 and the flight of Ferdinand and his Court to Innsbruck on the 17th called forth varied reactions. According to information received by the Ministerial Council, the response in Prague and Brno was pro-Monarchical and anti-Viennese; in reality it was more complicated. Löhner's *Verein* in Vienna was wholly on the side of the revolution, because May 15 completed the work begun on March 13; it was a demonstration in favor of a constitution but at the same time against machinations aimed at getting

Palacký included in the Government.⁴⁵ In a leaflet dated May 18, the *Verein* opposed the Court and supported the government. The *Verein's* campaigns for the Imperial Court and the Bohemian diet took the same line. Their view was that after March 1848—that is, after the victory of the Revolution in Vienna—the Germans in Bohemia, Moravia, and Silesia were placed in a dangerously exposed position. Their interests at present were bying defended only be the *Verein*, which also endeavored to help realize the unification of Germany. It supported the attempt to increase Germany's territory, for example by including Istria, and also wanted to include Austria within Germany economically and administratively while at the same time defending the basic rights of citizens. Besides the fourteen points which outlined this program, there was one more which called for universal, equal and direct suffrage.⁴⁶ On July 4 in a pamphlet addressed to "Friends and Countrymen" the *Verein* declared that the "ultra-Czech party" oppressed Germans by forbidding them to wear the Great-German colors in Prague and referring to them as "immigrants"—even though it was actually the Viennesse revolution which had given them their freedom in the first place. The Czechs had succeeded in forming a "Provisional Government" in Prague and were preparing a pan-Slavic congress. On May 19 the Hungarian government also lodged a protest against the Slav Congress in Prague, but it received a cool reply from Pillersdorf. The *Verein* organized meetings of Germans from Bohemia and Saxony, supported the foundation of a *Sächsisch-Böhmisch Verein* in Dresden, and eventually under the slogan "Deutschland über Alles" began to plan for the creation of a "Verein der Deutschen in Österreich" as a direct response to the attempts at cooperation among the Slavic nationalities.⁴⁷

The attitude of the Czech population towards the events of May was not quite as united as it might appear. On May 17 the students' spokesman in the National Committee A. Bradka (to the horror of Emmanuel Arnold) signed a letter to Innsbruck inviting the Emperor and his Court to Prague to be "among his faithful Czechs." But two days later the students, meeting in the Carolinum, supported Vienna and opposed the Emperor. They forced Bradka to change his position, but they did not recall him. At the end of May, two to three hundred students of Prague were said to have left for Vienna, which in their eyes was the great model for successful political action.⁴⁸

But here we have jumped somewhat ahead of the events. At the end of May 1848 the Czechs and Germans had not yeat squared off—only the Czech and German publicists and politicians, the one speaking for the predominantly petit bourgeois Czech society, and the other for the substantially stronger German-speaking bourgeois society. The lines dividing them were not yet sharply drawn. The rebuke which earlier historians directed at Karl Marx for referring to Palacký as a "German professor" is paltry, for according to his son Jan, Palacký himself was tolerant in matters of nationality, and until 1860 the language spoken in his household was German.[49] What was more serious was that neither side was interested in dealing with the social question—with the exception of the issue of land reform, which in any case had already been decided in March.

The existence of a dual government—with the Court sitting safely in Innsbruck and relying more and more on the army, and the ministries continuing to function in Vienna—opened up attractive prospects for ambitious men hoping to exploit the situation. One of them was Windischgrätz, who returned to Prague convinced that with a base in Bohemia he would be able to remove the revolutionary danger threatening the dynasty, the Monarchy and the old order. His civilian colleague Leo Thun-Hohenstein, on the other hand, intended to apply the tenets of his teacher Stadion of Galacia and create a situation in Bohemia which the Court and the government would simply have to accept. In the game begun by these two gentlemen, neither the Czech nor the German politicians, as we shall see, played a very distinguished role. Public opinion—that of the students, the petite bourgeoisie and the working population—suspected that something was afoot, and certainly there was no sympathy at all for the cause of counter-revolution, personified by Windischgrätz. But public opinion was a force which continued to lie dormant.

VI

The First Center of Counter-Revolution

> In your camp is all Austria;
> The rest of us are merely its wreckage.
> Out of selfishness or vanity
> We have furthered our own ruin.
> But in those whom you shall lead into battle,
> The old Austria lives.
>
> from Grillparzer's Ode to Radetzky, 1848

1. Politics and the Army

Until the end of May 1848 the forces of counter-revolution, entrenched in the bureaucracy and the army, and representing essentially the interests of the landholding and military aristocracy, were decidedly on the defensive. But even during Ficquelmont's government, as we have seen, their highly flexible defense placed them in a good position to seize every opportunity for counter-attack. The flight of the Court from Vienna to Innsbruck certainly meant a weakening of the "old order", because a dual government automatically came into existence, and the tension between Vienna and Innsbruck could be used to the advantage of the revolution. Yet in the following weeks it turned out to be the revolution rather than the old order which began to disintegrate.

In the first place, the military units which Vienna had so gladly sent southwards to fight against the Italians began to have some success. In April Radetzky was still obliged to hold his two army corps, led by Wallmoden and d'Aspre, on the defensive, behind the protection of the Quadrilateral. But his task was immeasurably lightened by the passivity of his Italian adversaries. The Sardinian King Charles Albert, strengthened by reinforcements from central and south Italian governments, did not involve himself in further conflicts once he had occupied Lombardy. After winning a battle at Goito he crossed the River Mincio and laid siege to the fortress at Peschiera. But it appears that he relied chiefly on France and Britain to help him, by their diplomatic exertions, to liquidate the rest of the Ausrian holdings—primarily Venetia—without struggle. At the same time, pursuing a narrowly dynastic policy, he was interested in effecting a union of Lombardy and Piedmont. In Lombardy there was a republican minority which strongly mistrusted Charles Albert and favored a federal union of all Italy. But throughout April their leader Cattaneo was unable to win over the republican ideologue Giuseepe Mazzini. Thus the whole matter was decided by a plebiscite on May 29 which resulted in a clear victory for union with Piedmont. Plebiscites in Parma, Modena and Venice had similar results.[1]

But this did nothing to improve the military situation, and it was of greater diplomatic advantage to Radetzky than the Italians. Sardinian expansionism was no more welcome than Austrian rule in the view of the Italian governments which had been pressured by public opinion into sending reinforcements for Charles Albert. Pope Pius IX, with whom the Austrian government interrupted diplomatic relations on May 4, came into conflict with General Durando, the commander of the Papal forces which had been sent to northern Italy and at that time were positioned in Vicenza, blocking Radetzky's supply lines across Venetia. In Naples the tension between King Ferdinand and the radicals in Parliament led to street fighting, in which the King, with the help of Swiss mercenaries and the National Guard, crushed the radicals on May 15. Following upon the defeat of the English Charists, the defeat of the revolution in southern Italy was a further blow to hopes for a "European Revolution".[2] King Ferdinand then recalled his forces from the north. Just as Durando did not listen to the Pope, so the old revolutionary Guglielmo Pepe, who had once lived in exile in Brno, refused to obey King Ferdinand. But both generals saw a large proportion of their troops return home from the front anyway. The contingents led by Charles Albert, Durando, and Pepe, in fact, were reduced by nearly 150,000 men, while Radetzky was beginning to receive some help—the First Reserve Contingent under Nugent, made up chiefly of Croatian and Serbian companies, numbered about 70,000 troops. With these reinforcements Radetzky fought a defensive battle at Santa Lucia on May 6 which strengthened his position in Lombardy, but even more importantly raised the morale of the officer corps, who succeeded in preventing the Italian and Hungarian contingents from deserting.[3]

Charles Albert continued to believe that French Foreign Minister Lamartine would be able to clear the Austrians out of northern Italy, and he failed to perceive that the unification of northen Italy under his rule could be acceptable to France only if she were given certain "concessions" in return—Savoy or perhaps Nice. But Charles Albert had no wish to provoke direct intervention by France, and this view was heartily shared by Palmerston. British diplomacy was attempting to halt and neutralize the republican movement throughout Italy, but it had no wish to see the expansion of French influence in the peninsula. Therefore Palmerston was in favor of mediation, and in this spirit he met with the Austrian diplomat Karl Hummelauer in London between May 23 and 25. Hummelauer proposed certain concessions—chiefly the formation of an administratively independent kingdom of Venetia-Lombardy as a new Italian state to be ruled by one of the Habsburg archdukes; he was even willing to consider withdrawal from Lombardy. But the British government of Lord John Russell demanded the cession of both Lombardy and Venetia. On May 24 the National Assembly, convened shortly before, adopted a resolution in favor of the Italian independence movement. An Imperial commissioner was sent to negotiate with Charles Albert for a truce.[4]

But Radetzky was hardly willing to abandon the position that he had gained with his victory at Santa Lucia. According to his modern biographer H. Kerchnawe, he got in touch with two of his colleagues—Windischgrätz, recently returned to Prague, and the Croatian bán Jellačić. They promised each other support against the "revolution fomented by international Freemasonry and Jewry but cloaked in national colors wherever necessary."[5] The military triumvirate (called WIR after their initials) agreed to a sort of mutual assistance pact in the struggle against revolution. Radetzky was certainly not going to give up Lombardy. In an attempt to aid the besieged garrison at Peschiera, his troops engaged the Italians at Curatone on May 28 and at Goito two days later. But Peschiera surrendered in the meantime, and Radetzky, having received news of the struggles in Vienna and the flight of the Court to Innsbruck, embarked on no further offensives but decided to conserve his strength. In any case Charles Albert continued to rely on the diplomatic assistance of France and Britain. Radetzky took advantage once again of his inactivity, and on July 11 by taking Vicenza, where the Papal troops and their allies capitulated, he reestablished his lines of communication through Venetia to the Austrian lands.[6]

In 1948 Karel Kreiblich pointed to the significance of the "Generals' Fronde." In Windeischgrätz's connection with Radetzky and the Cracow commandant Castiglione he discerned the origin of what became the tragedy of the revolutionary movement in Austria. Castiglione prevented the spread of the revolution in Cracow by simple police measures, but it does not appear that such a solution would have been possible outside Galicia. The military garrison at Lemberg, as we shall see, played a greater role in the counter-revolutionary efforts than its counterpart at Cracow. Among Windeischgrätz's papers there is no lack of evidence concerning his connection with Radetzky and the "Italian" army. From the beginning of the revolutionary movement in Italy he had devoted a great deal of attention to that country. Through the corps commander d'Aspre he was informed of the army's strength from the end of

February; he also received copies of orders and military bulletins. His son Victor wrote to him regularly from Italy, as did the Division Commanders Schwarzenberg and Clam-Gallas. But the surviving fragments of his correspondence with Radetzky and Latour prove little. Nor do the rest of the papers from May 1848 reveal anything of significance about the military or political activities of the leader of the Prague General Command. From Latour's correspondence it may be inferred that Windeischgrätz was to be entrusted with the creation of a "northern" army which was to act in cooperation with Radetzky's "southern" army. Thus it appears that the idea of using the army as a political instrument originated in Latour's (and Ficquelmont's) circle at Vienna, even before Windeischgrätz returned to his post at Prague. In Radetzky's vicinity, as we have seen repeatedly, there were plenty of officers who were in close contact with Windeischgrätz's military-feudal group.[7]

Certainly from the very beginning this group included Major-General Prince Josef Lobkowitz, commander of a brigade stationed at Prague in the spring of 1848. This member of the Beřkovice branch of the magnate family counted traditionally among the "old" Bohemian nobility, became commander of the National Guard in Prague and all Bohemia on May 13. His appointment was signed by Leo Thun, who remarked that after the incident in which Colonel Andrew Haas was insulted by a group of Polytechnic students, it was important that the new commander be a high military officer, or at least an individual not likely to put up with such treatment. It should be noted, however, that Lobkowitz's new post had been offered first to Karl Schwarzenberg, who decided in favor of the Italian front.[8] Among Lobkowitz's papers there is a draft version of service regulations for the National Guard, decorated with caricatures of burghers playing at being soldiers. It may be assumed therefore that Lobkowitz did not view his appointment as a particularly great honor. Under his leadership the National Guard could scarcely be expected to transform itself into an active agent of revolution; in fact, the opposite occurred.[9] In this regard Lobkowitz was in perfect agreement with Windeischgrätz, who on June 2 requested the return of rifles and swords which had been lent to the National Guard from the military stores. Windeischgrätz was of the opinion that the members of the National Guard ought to acquire arms at their own expense.[10]

The author of a confiscated pamphlet which helped spark the unrest in Prague on May 10, one "Štěpán Donovský"—a pseudonym—who addressed his "Czech Brothers," stated the situation quite openly: "The King's servants, the soldiers, maintain their old rights and and their old weapons. They do not believe, o my nation, that you are able to defend yourself. Show them, my Czechs, show them in time!"[11] There were vigorous efforts to win over the soldiers. The pamphlets "Attention, Soldiers!" and the bilingual "Soldiers of the State, Our Countrymen and Brothers," warned the troops against becoming the tools of reaction. "The Cry and Lamentation of the Bohemian Crown," a pamphlet which probably appeared in the first half of May, took the side of the Italians who were fighting against Radetzky. Its author, "an old Taborite," defended the Italian independence movement and protested against the fact that Czech and Slavic regiments had helped suppress freedom in Italy. "Czecho-Slavs" had let themselves be confused by "mercenaries' pride," but they ought to follow the example of the French, whose army had helped overthrow Louis Philippe. Czech soldiers have no right even to be in Germany, much less in Italy.

> And you, dear, noble Italian nation across the Alps, be assured that from our great distance we have observed you with heavy hearts, sympathized with you and defended your cause. But in the press of events we have been unable to do anything for you. waiting for the time when we should be free of our shackles. You shall be victorious, and the tyranny of the Germans, who are taking over the Austrian Empire, shall be smashed by you, for your cause is just, sacred, anchored upon the rights of nations.
> And you, Slavic regiments, you our brothers and sons, we weep for your blindness, your barbarity; you are the executioners for the enemies of freedom, and with forged iron you have become henchmen of the Germans. You shame the name and glory of the Slavs. Take courage and return over the Alps to your homeland, where we shall forgive you and embrace you, and you shall risk life and limb instead for the freedom of your own nation. Whoever would prevent you, bring him down, and extending your hand to the Italian nation, entrust yourselves to God, who shall open the way homeward for you. Who then can stand in your way? The chronicle of nations shall eternally remember you as worthy Warriors of God.[12]

At any time when Havlíček's *Národní Noviny* was advising parents of soldiers headed for Italy to regard their sons with pride, these pamphlets could not have elicited much of a response, and in fact desertion not only by Czechs but also by Hungarian and even Italian troops was minimal in 1848-9. Attempts to win over the Ukrainian soldiers from Hohenegg's infantry regiment stationed in Prague, Hungarian hussars from the Palatine's regiment, and Galician ulans, also ended in failure. A similar immunity was shared by the "Bohemian regiments of Baillet-Latour and Wocher in Lombardy, the Fifty-fourth or "Moravian" regiment of Lieutenant Colonel Sunstenau, the chasseurs of Colonel Copal's Tenth Company serving in Radetzky's army, Palombini's infantry regiments under Windeischgrätz, and the grenadiers from Reisinger's regiment, who were mostly Czechs. Therefore Bohemia and northern Italy, rather than Vienna or Hungary, became the army's basic sources of strength. As early as May its commanders could quietly ignore the orders of the

Government at Vienna and the Court at Innsbruck and still be confident of the support of Minister Latour himself.

Thus the military-aristocratic clique had a powerful spokesman inside the government, which in any case was only tinged with liberalism. The situation was quite different from that which prevailed in Germany, especially in Prussia, were the liberal bourgeoisie, for a time, were actually in control, and where the government of Campenhausen-Hansenmann was able to issue orders to the army. But the outcome was the same. From the beginning of April members of the government were already preparing to resist the "demands of the crowd." Their firm action against the Poles at Poznań, where General von Pfuel earned the sympathy of Tsar Nicholas I and a reputation as an effective enemy of the revolution, as well as their measures against the student radicals, gave sufficient indication of the trend. Not even Windeischgrätz on his return to Prague was greeted with such opposition as the Prussian Crown Prince on his return in May from exile in England. And if the rebellion in Prague during the Whitsun holidays was crushed, it must also be recalled that on June 14 a march by the people on the Berlin Zeughaus was bloodily halted in Unter-den-Linden. The government of Hansenmann-Auerswald, which then took over, already had a reputation as a "government of action." Developments in Germany outstripped events in Austria, and therefore some perceptive observers in Germany, among them Karl Marx, could judge certain trends in Austria better than anybody living there.[13]

2 Prague, Vienna and Innsbruck

If we read through the newspapers and pamphlets of 1848, we are left with the impression that the situation was clear to nobody. The people (and the journalists) took a sudden interest in all sorts of new things—their horizons had been broadened in a remarkable way. But at the same time, the pace of events was so rapid that they could not be reported coherently. The development of the revoutionary movement and of the counter-revolution was uneven, and this played into the hands of those who wanted to freeze the process of social and political change.

In May the issues dividing Germans and Czechs, liberals and radicals, had not yet become obvious to everyone. The chief problem remained Frankfurt and the relations between Prague, Vienna and Innsbruck. There were differing views about the solutions to these questions. Elections to the Frankfurt Assembly were carried out in only 18 of the 68 electoral districts in Bohemia; on the other hand, 25 of the 28 Moravian districts participated. In Moravia a Diet was convened which sat from May 31 until the following January. Of its 253 members, 110 were from the countryside, 82 from the towns, and 55 were representatives from aristocratic domains. But this "peasant parliament" betrayed no signs of radicalism, and in general it followed in the steps of its forbear the Moravian Estates.[14]

In Bohemia elections were delayed primarily because of the Vienna government's apprehension that once the Czechs elected their own Bohemian parliament, they would refuse to take part in the Imperial Parliament. Was this view justified? The "Main Principles for a Draft Constitution for the Kingdom of Bohemia," drawn up by the National Committee, does, in fact, speak only of a Bohemian parliament and its relationship to the central government (the Ministerial Council) and to the Governor or Viceroy and the government of the land (the Governor's Council). The dilemma of whether to summon a Bohemian or an Imperial parliament—or both— drove firmly into the background the question of the Frankfurt Assembly, whose members from Bohemia met in Prague between April 29 and May 5 to discuss how to improve relations between the Czechs (and Bohemia generally) and the Frankfurt assembly. But the prospects for accomodation were not very bright, since it was already known that plans were under way to call an assembly of all Austrian Slavs, which was regarded automatically as a counterweight to Frankfurt—and Budapest. Thus from the outset the spokesmen of German and Magyar bourgeois nationalism were opposed to the Slav Congress.[15]

But this does not mean that in Bohemia itself there existed only German or Czech chauvinists. On May 18 the poet K. E. Ebert, a friend of Palacky's, published an appeal for concord, and on May 25 in the Stromovka park in Prague there was a festival of "brotherhood and cooperation" between the two nationalities. It is true of course that there were individuals on both sides who considered such efforts to be mere comedy. The German liberals left the National Committee, but we do know that some of them, for example Borrosch, were still willing to cooperate with it. If we compare the Czech and the Bohemian or Austrian German electoral literature of May and June, we find no expressions of fundamental antagonism. The difference lay rather in priorities, and of course, in the attitude towards Great Germany. The assumption of the Central Electoral Committee at Frankfurt was that Austria belonged to Germany. This principle was contradicted by the fact that more than one delegate to Frankfurt—Franz Schuselka himself, for example—gave priority to the Imperial Parliament. But the Frankfurt program at the same time recognized the demand that all the nationalities within Austria be equal.[16]

The head of the administration in Bohemia Count Leo Thun was also convinced that relations between Czechs and Germans would improve. At least this was the gist of the reports that he sent to the Minsterial Council at Vienna. From about May 20 the Council objected with increasing frequency to these reports, and sometimes to their lateness. On the 20th the newspapers published Thun's edict, issued the day before, reporting that the Emperor had left Vienna and had appealed to his "faithful Czechs" for their continued loyalty. When the Government sharply demanded where Thun had received such information, he replied that it had come to him in confidence from a "highly-placed source" in the closest proximity to the Emperor himself. Pillersdorf and his associates probably knew, and Latour certainly knew, that the Prague Commander Windeischgrätz had written to the former Minister President Ficquelmont on May 11 that it was highest time to put an end to concessions and that it would be wise for the Emperor to move to Prague. And they began to suspect that Thun and Windeischgrätz both were proponents of a conservative separatism. When they learned on May 22 that a deputation had been sent from Bohemia to Innsbruck, they decided to send as their own representative Minister Doblhoff-Dier, known to us as a supporter and member of Löhner's *Verein der Deutschen in Böhmen, Maähren und Schlesien*. Similar delegations were sent to the Court by the Magyars, then the Croats, Serbs, and Rumanians.[17]

The same day the Ministerial Council discussed a letter which Vojtěch Deym wrote to Latour, describing the resentment felt by the people of Prague against the ungrateful Viennese. Thun described the reaction to the events in Vienna of May 15-17 in similar terms in a report sent to Pillersdorf two days later. As a result, Latour was against any concessions to the students, but he particularly opposed issuing any arms to the National Guard, and in this way he precipitated a new crisis.[18] Thun's reports of May 27 and 28 provoked the first real consternation, convincing the Ministerial Council that the governor aimed to make himself entirely independent of Vienna. The document of May 28 was a "protocol" written by the heads of the Bohemian judicial department and approved by Windeischgrätz, concerning the creation of a provisional Bohemian govenment, to consist of eight members besides Thun. Four of them were Czechs (Palacký, Rieger, Brauner, Strobach), and four were Germans, (Borrosch, Herzig, and the aristocrats A. Nostitz and A. Wurmbrand). Thun asked the Emperor to summon the Bohemian Diet, which was to concern itself with writing a constitution, the redemption of the *robota*, and the taxes for 1849. Furthermore, he requested the Emperor to approve a "provisional governing council" and to grant him full powers.[19] On May 29 Thun informed the National Committee, which he hoped to get rid of by these measures, of the creation of a provisional governing council. Nostitz and Rieger were sent to Innsbruck, but Doblhoff was already there, and he immediately warned the Court and the Government at Vienna that Thun's action would surely stand as an example for other lands, and that central government would soon become illusory. Thun apparently overestimated the influence of his connections at Court and underestimated the agility of the Viennese ministers. It is certain too that Doblhoff, and later also Wessenberg, were more than a match for Nostitz and Rieger.[20]

On June 1 the Ministerial Council discussed an article appearing in the office *Pražské Noviny*, according to which the Provisional Government in Prague had been created because the Viennese government was unable to operate freely. Pillersdorf wrote Thun a sharp rebuke and lodged a protest against his conduct with the Court. On June 2 he urged the Emperor to dismiss Thun and institute proceedings against him. By the next day Minister Krauss was able to inform the Council that in Prague the Court Counsellor May had refused to participate in Thun's enterprise. And Minister Latour, who otherwise could only have welcomed the Prague initiative, questioned Windeischgrätz sharply about why he supported the governing council.[21] Thun attempted to explain his initiative, but the furious Pillersdorf informed him once again on June 4 that the "interruptions of order" which had taken place in the capital could not alter the fact that it was only in Vienna—not in Prague or even in Innsbruck—that the central government resided.[22] The circumspect Windeischgrätz meanwhile deserted Thun, declaring to Latour that he continued to be his subordinate, without mentioning his insubordination to the government of which Latour was a member. In view of the mounting pressure, Thun began to plan for an orderly retreat. On June 6 he wrote Pillersdorf that his measures of course would go into effect only when they received the Emperor's approval. Pillersdorf, who saw in Thun and Windeischgrätz the danger from the right, perceived the danger from the left in the Viennese Committee of Safety and (quite mistakenly) in the National Committee at Prague. In Innsbruck Doblhoff succeeded in cultivating Archduke Francis Charles and set the seal on the failure of the mission of Rieger and Nostitz.

Thun lost out with his experiment, although the Ministerial Council did not issue a public proclamation of censure against him as it had threatened, nor did it for the time being dismiss him. Doblhoff and Wessenberg recommended that Thun be allowed to summon a Bohemian parliament, but in no case before the Imperial Parliament.[23] Then it developed that the Czechs in Bohemia to a significant degree boycotted the elections for the Imperial Parliament, while the Germans boycotted those for the Bohemian parliament. Doblhoff and Wessenberg were resolutely opposed to the establishment of Thun's provisional government, and they placed him under orders of the Interior Minister. The government, which was at odds over enfranchising the workers (Pillersdorf, Sommaruga and Baumgartner were in favor, Latour and Krauss opposed), was completely united when it came to Thun's "separatism". On June 11 in Innsbruck Doblhoff extracted a decision from the Emperor which withheld approval of Thun's measures. The news reached Vienna on June 14, while the Ministerial Council was in its second day of meetings about the Prague Uprising. Nevertheless it forwarded the document to Commissioner Kleczansky as a guideline.[24]

With this, Thun's efforts to create an independent or semi-independent political center at Prague were defeated, and Thun surely had no illusions about his own position in the eyes of the government. Whether he was particularly upset we do not know. In any case, he had more than enough at the present to keep himself occupied. In Prague on June 2 the Slav Congress opened which had originally been scheduled for May 31 to coincide with the opening of the Frankfurt Assembly. It had been discussed ever since the middle of April as a reply to the efforts for German unification. The intitiative appears to have come simultaneously from Prague, Zagreb, and Poznań.[25] The original program was outlined in four points: 1) Discussion of the Austrian Slavs and the possibilities for their unification; 2) Relations between Austrian Slavs and the other nationalities of the Monarchy; 3) Relations between the Austrian Slavs and other Slavs; 4) Relations between the Austrian Slavs and other European nationalities. The delegates began to meet at the end of May, and after some delays the assembly itself was convened. Nearly 400 delegates were present—the most complete list contains 385 names: 317 official delegates, the rest invited observers. They were divided into three sections: the South Slav (42 members, Slovenes, Croats, Serbs); Polish-Ruthenian (Poles, Ukrainians, together 61 members); and the Czecho-Slovak (Czechs, Moravians, Slovaks, with 237 members). The meeting was officially inaugurated by Pavel Josef Šafařík, while Palacký delivered the opening address and was elected president of the Congress. It is not true, as Fric asserted, that the various nationalities understood each others' speech without diffculty; but neither is it true that the delegates had to use German to make themselves understood, though the resolutions adopted by the sections were announced in German. The written testimony makes no mention of any of the discussion having been conducted in German.[26]

Differences of opinion arose as soon as the meetings opened. The Czechs were afraid of Frankfurt, the Slovaks of Budapest. The Poles supported the Magyars and wanted to mediate. The Polish question was for them a European one, and not at all a matter concerning Austrian Galicia. There were differences between the representatives of Austroslavism and those who wanted to be primarily Slavs. The outstanding figure among the Polish delegation, which included the heaviest proportion both of feudal aristocrats and democratic radicals, was Karol Libelt of Poznań.[29] The original intention of limiting the meeting to Austrian Slavs was overriden from the beginning: Libelt came from Poznań and Michael Bakunin from Russia. In the minutes of the actual sessions there are passages which recall Kollar's "Daughter of Slava" and others showing real interest in the creation of a federal Slav state. All this was enough to cause the President of the Preparatory Committee Count J. M. Thun to fall ill. The majority of the delegates were liberal intellectuals of bourgeois background. The radical democrats attempted to add the questin of social reforms to the agenda, but they were unsuccessful. There was not even any discussion of the peasant question, so that nationality considerations completely dominated social ones. The Congress had an "Economic Committee," to be sure, but its only function was to provide for the material comfort of the delegates during the Congress.[28]

In the midst of the meetings Libelt proposed a change in the program, and he was able to carry it through. In his view, the Congresss should 1) prepare a manifesto of the Slavs to the European nations; 2) draft a petition to the Emperor expressing the demands of the Austrian Slavs; 3) discuss how to maintain permanent connections among the Slavic nationalities. This of course meant broadening the Congress considerably beyond the bounds of Austroslavism. The final text of the Manifesto, written by Palacký, was based on drafts submitted by Libelt, Frantisek Zach and Michael Bakunin. Bakunin's draft has not turned up to this day, and we do not know just what was in it. The others have survived. Libelt began with a romantic view of the Slavic past, but he included a number of suggestions concerning social problems; he even defended what he called "socialism," or a system of social justice. Palacký incorporated nothing of this in the final version. Zach's draft was not so socially oriented as that of Libelt's, but his tone was not so anti-German as that of Palacký's text. Zach was in favor of civil liberties and universal male suffrage. Palacký's version substituted a nationalist note for the social one. It was eloquent and it served the aims of the Congress better than Libelt's or Zach's original proposals. It expressed very well the mood of the liberal bourgeoisie who made up most of the delegation.

The petition intended for the Emperor had been prepared but was not yet approved when the meeting was broken up. The Czechs, Moravians, and Slovenes took a united stand against Frankfurt. The qusestion of the unification of the Austrian Slavs had not yet assumed concrete form by June 12.[29] There were about 100 delegates from Moravia, and they asked the Emperor to give them a "charter" similar to that which they believed Bohemia to have received in the cabinet memorandum of April 8. They were in favor of cooperation with Bohemia but not union. There was not a single Czech delegate from Austrian Silesia, and the Polish delegates from Silesia went to sit with the

Polish-Ruthenian section.

The Congress was to continue until June 14, but the outbreak of the Prague Uprising on the 12th meant its premature end, for most of the foreign delegates were sent away by the army. During the uprising the city was placed under curfew, and the Congress was postponed indefinitely, never to meet again.

The Slav Congress created many illusions, and it helped to get rid of others. Its significance does not lie in any of its concrete measures. Instead, it demonstrated that the Czechs were not alone, that the Slavic peoples did have at least something in common, and that they had a right to exist. Therefore the Slav Congress is a milestone in the history not only of the Czech nation but of the other Slavic nations as well. The *Manifesto of the Slavic Congress to the Nations of Europe* was not merely an oratorical or stylisticc exercise. It was of great moral and political significance in that it emphasized the equality and democratic rights of all nationalities, the need for peaceful coexistence, and it took up the cause of the oppressed nationalities. The *Manifesto*'s efforts in behalf of peace joined the long line beginning with Hus's *Sermons on Peace*, continuing with the Hussite manifestos, the Peace Project of King George of Poděbrady, and Comenius's *Apostle of Peace*.

This is confirmed by the closing words of the *Manifesto*:

> As we, the youngest but by no means the weakest of nations, appear once again on the political stage of Europe, we offer this suggestion of a general European meeting of nations to discuss all international questions. We are convinced that the efforts of free nations are worth more than those of paid diplomats. We hope that our proposal will be heard before the regressive policies of individual courts succeed in leading the nations to destroy each other out of spite and hatred. In the name of liberty, equality and brotherhood of all nations![30]

Palacký did not suspect how near the day was when the "regressive policies" of courts and generals would succeed in setting the nationalities of Austria at each other's throats.

VII

The First Victory of the Counter-Revolution: Prague, June 12–18, 1848

> The wanton nobility, the ignoble nobility
> Thus began its insidious game,
> A game more treacherous than Prague has known
> Since Pagan days;
> The army has always kept power within itself,
> Which soldiers like impoverished slaves must respect.
> Thus Czech was gathered from Czech for a contest of strength:
> Brothers annihilated brothers!
> The soldiers, seduced by the criminal nobility,
> Deluded by the rigor of their oath to the King,
> With devilish cunning implanting in them
> The thought that the Czechs have planned a coup—
> The soldiers who ought to protect lives, defend their Nation
> Against its enemies,
> Have instead destroyed, murdered, plundered in Prague.
> But some day, the nobility shall be made to pay dearly for it.
>
> Jan Sekavec, *The Twelfth of June,
> or A Warning to the Czechs* (1849)

1. Windischgrätz and Lobkowitz

Jan Sekavec, author of *The Twelfth of June*, was twenty-four years old in 1848. Besides this indictment of the Bohemian nobility, he wrote a novel, *Žižka*, which appeared in 1848, and another entitled *Murderer of the Nation*, which remained unpublished. He sent his poems to Havlíček's *NárodníNoviny*, but in July 1849 he was imprisoned, and he died on June 15, 1851, in the Hradčany military hospital after much suffering, truly a victim of the counter-revolution.[1] He wrote on behalf of the "millions of people," the

The First Victory of the Counter-Revolution

poor and oppressed, against their spiritual and secular rulers. And of course also against the lords, the aristocrats, the "traitors" who concocted "fatal plans" against the Slav Congress and all the Slavic peoples.

Understandably, Sekavec never named names, and we can only guess whom he regarded as the traitors among the nobility. Leo Thun-Hohenstein, as we have seen was fully occupied at the beginning of June defending his ambitious plan to set up a provisional government and at one stroke rid himself of interference from both the National Committee and the Government at Vienna. His plans did not coincide with those of the military chief Windischgrätz, who presently found it expedient to avoid becoming too closely associated with him. Before Windischgrätz returned to Prague, Thun had named Josef Lobkowitz as commander-in-chief of the National Guard. But for a long time Lobkowitz had been Windischgrätz's collaborator, most recently as commander of a brigade stationed at Prague. it may be said of both that they were "Bohemian" noblemen only to the extent that their lands were located in that country.

Did Windischgrätz follow orders from Innsbruck, as some of his subordinates supposed? He appears to have followed his own convictions, which he might reasonably have supposed to be in harmony with the views of the Court. They were also shared by his colleagues in Lombardy, Galicia and elsewhere, and the common denominator was hatred of the "Viennese streets," the "Vienna Boys." This impression is confirmed by the Lemberg garrison's letter to the Prague garrison of May 23, 1848, just after the suppression of the unrest in Cracow. "We are bound by our oath to defend and protect our imperial dynasty and our country even against domestic enemies," the letter reads. "It is highest time that in spite of our separation we entreat our generals to station us where we shall be in a position to protect our Emperor and our country. It is not yet too late. We still stand ready. Let us speak plainly, in soldierly fashion: we want order." The military spokesmen made it clear where they wished to restore order. They urged their commander to "rectify with the utmost firmness the chaotic situation in Vienna as well as the demagoguery of those who rule there."

The Prague garrison's reply on June 5 assured the officers of Lemberg that their feelings were shared and that they were entirely loyal to their commander Windischgrätz: "It is our honorable duty to ensure that law, freedom, order and security be preserved wherever they are threatened, to protect them and restore them where they have been overturned."[2]

Following a plan agreed upon at the end of March, guns were placed on Petřin Hill and on Vyšehrad at the beginning of June. The watches in the city were strengthened, but only with soldiers, since Windischgrätz did not wish his men to mix with the National Guard. On June 6 he held a review of the Prague garrison at Invalidovna, which the people of the city regarded as a provocation. Lieutenant Colonel Langenau, Archduke Charles Ferdinand's adjutant who had stood in for Windischgrätz until May, prepared a statement to be issued in case of excessive protest, declaring the Windischgrätz merely wished to review troops that he had not seen for several months. The garrison's jubilant outburst on being reminded of Radetzky's example in Italy was taken as an expression of its determination to "manifest its loyalty in action and to place life and limb at the service of the Emperor and the country." Therefore all attempts to drive a wedge between the troops and their commander must end in failure. The demonstration of military might was underscored by the removal of a canon immediately after the review to the Josephine Barracks in the center of the city.[3]

Thus on June 8 Karel Sladkovský, who became the leader of the students soon after his arrival from Vienna, spoke sharply against Windischgrätz at a meeting in the St. Wenceslas Baths. On June 10 in the aula of the Carolinum the students formally demanded that Windischgrätz supply the National Guard and the Academic Legion with 2,000 rifles, 80,000 rounds of ammunition and one battery of canon. They appear to have been acting upon the example furnished them by the Viennese students in May, and they threw down a challenge to Windischgrätz's determination to disarm the National Guard and the students. At a time when Windischgrätz was announcing his "rigorous measures" to restore order, the students' petition was like a red cloth waved before a bull. And when a student delegation appeared before Archduke Charles Ferdinand, he sent them along, of course, to Windischgrätz.

On Whitsunday, July 11, a new student assembly convened at ten o'clock in the Carolinum, at which Sladkovský repeated his request for arms. Palacky's son Jan was the only one to raise the realistic question of what the students would be able to do with the weapons. The students sent forth another delegation to Windischgrätz which included Sladkovský, the Polytechnic students Vodka and Bradka, Dr. Bruna, and the burgher Jaroš. They were joined by Mayor Wanka and the German alderman Borrosch, who only wanted to persuade the Commander to remove the artillery from the heights around the city. Windischgrätz of course rebuffed the deputation, and the students reacted by distributing copies of a "red poster" signed by Sladkovský, Dr. Bruna, Jaroš, Cermák and the Polytechnic student Noak, which warned the public of the military preparations and asked support for their demands.

The commander of the National Guard Major General Lobkowitz and Governor Thun ordered that the posters be torn down, but the students pasted them up again. The aula of the Carolinum resounded with cries for barricades, incited by Tieftrunk, a member of Náprstek's Seven who had come from Vienna. Borrosch expressed reservations, and Sladkovský himself advised moderation.⁴ Mayor Wanka, who valued the students chiefly as a counterweight to the "proletariat" of the suburbs, wished to avoid a confrontation with the army, and his concern was shared by the University professors who met the same evening. At 5 o'clock there was another meeting at the St. Wenceslas Baths which was addressed by Sladkovský and Kampelík. Both urged calm and an orderly participation in the Slavic Mass which was to be celebrated on Whit-Monday in the Horse Market as a festival of brotherhood. However, by Sunday evening the atmosphere was charged. On Zofín Island a student, later identified as seventeen year-old František Korbel of Bechyně, fired a pistol. It was an accident, but for the German paper *Bohemia* it was the "signal for revolution." The students' prospects in any kind of conflict were doubtless bleak.

Most of the students had left Prague for home or for Vienna because the lectures had ended early. Today the student population is estimated at 800, including Polytechnic and gymnasium students, and most of them were from the Polytechnic. The military section of Slavia had between sixty and eighty members, but it had only recently been established and was already riven by the quarrels among Frič, Maux and Nebeský. Besides the 2,000 rifles which the National Guard received from Charles Ferdinand, the people of Prague could have had at their disposal some of the weapons left by the five disbanded companies and a squadron of sharpshooters and grenadiers, but these amounted to no more than 750 rifles. The weapons in the hands of the National Guard were neutralized, except those belonging to Svornost, which numbered only four companies or 600 men. Meanwhile some of the National Guard, chiefly the German units or those led by noblemen like Francis Thun, took orders from Lobkowitz—and therefore indirectly from Windischgrätz.⁵

Windischgrätz's opponents were far from organized. The radical students were aware of the dangers presented by Windischgrätz's measures, but their only example was the struggle on the Viennese barricades. The documents allegedly seized in the offices of Slavia, which the auditor Ernst published as an appendix to his *Whitsuntide Events in Prague*, contained information about the artillery on Vyšehrad, part of Hradčany, in the Castle, the New Town, as well as a sketch of the barricades around the Clementium. But the way in which these papers were reproduced does not inspire confidence in their authenticity. From the testimony of students arrested afterwards, it appears that the plan was for Dr. Bruna to mobilize the Malá Strana, Bradka the technical students, Frič to occupy the Clementium, while the Carolinum was to be held by law and medical students. But this information, too, is vague and unreliable.⁶

By the most optimistic reckoning, Windischgrätz's opponents could not have had more than 3,000 rifles. It is also true, of course, that Windischgrätz himself did not have as many soldiers as the records indicate. There were normally five or six infantry brigades in Bohemia, or ten to twelve regiments and one cavalry division. Of the brigades stationed outside Prague—at Pilsen, Budweis, Josefstadt and Theresienstadt—only the last could reach the capital easily in time of crisis. Actually, it was easier to bring troops to Prague by railway from Moravia, which appears to have been done with Khevenhüller's 35th "Bohemian" infantry regiment.

Otherwise the official documents mention only the names of infantry regiments actually garrisoned in Prague. Of these, only Hohenegg's Twentieth, under the command of Colonel Mainone, was at full strength. Latour's Twenty-eighth, Wocher's Twenty-fifth, Reisinger's Eighteenth and Palombini's Twenty-sixth can have been represented only by their Third companies and a grenadier division (two companies from each regiment), for, as we have seen, the rest of their men had been ordered to Italy. This means that Windischgrätz had seven infantry companies, for the most part composed of Poles, Ukrainians, Czechs, and Bohemian Germans. They were supplemented by two companies of chasseurs, several squadrons from Palatin's hussars, most of them Hungarians, and several squadrons of ulans mustered in Galicia. The Third Field Artillery Regiment, recruited in Moravia, was in the MaláStrana. Together there may have been five to six thousand infantrymen and 2,000 cavalryment—or, counting Khevehnuller's Regiment and the cavalry contingents that were shifted from Brandýs, Nymburk and elsewhere in the Elbe Valley, something over 10,000 troops. This meant that for every defender on the barricades armed with a rifle there were three well-armed, well-trained soldiers. To engage in armed conflict against these odds was of course foolhardy. But among the students there were plenty of firebrands like Maximilian Maux, who urged violence, walked about with a rifle probably taken from the house of his gamekeeper father, and in the lecture halls demonstrated how to manufacture bullets which he called "Widischgratz pills." At his interrogation on July 3 he made the simpleminded admission that "we assumed that we could achieve what the students of Vienna had achieved, and that we must do as they had done earlier."[7]

If we can sometimes predict the outcome of a conflict with mathematical certainty, then we must add that the variables in Prague and Vienna were quite different. Maux was persuaded of this in the end, and so too shall we be. It is true that Windischgrätz never succeeded (if he tried at all) in separating the Czech liberal bourgeoisie who controlled the Prague Town Halls from the students (Wanka, after all, regarded only the workers as a menace). But the German bourgeois "casino" hastened to establish a *Verein für Aufrechterhaltung der öffentlichen Ordnung*, and, as we shall see, they played a willing role in Windischgrätz's plans.[8]

2 The Six Days

The night of Sunday June 11 was uneasy. At Thun's request, Windischgrätz retreated to the extent of complying with the Town Council's request that the artillery be removed from the city center, and in the morning the orders were issued. But in the watch houses and barracks a state of readiness was proclaimed. Lobkowitz meanwhile sent his National Guardsmen on a sweep of the inns to round up the delegates to the Slav Congress and expel them from the city.

There were several assemblies in Prague on the morning of Whit-Monday. Some committees of the Slav Congress continued to meet in the building of the National Museum on Kolowrat Avenue (now Příkopy). The students met at the Carolinum, whence they were led by Sladkovský to the Horse Market. Finally, in the Riding Hall in Bredovská street in the New Town, members of the Verein met. At about half past eleven they sent a deputation to Windischgrätz to assure him of their support. Later he praised them as "right-thinking Prague burghers" with the courage of their convictions, for after their exit from the General Command Headquarters in Celetná Street, they were pursued by a large crowd of students, National Guardsmen, members of Svornost, and unemployed workers. Windischgrätz's report maintains that they had encountered trouble earlier as well, having been shot at at about ten o'clock.[9] But this is nonsense, because the first conflict could not have occurred long before noon. The Mass probably began shortly after the arrival of the celebrant Father Arnold at 10:30. At its conclusion the students led a crowd of workers up to the Horse Gate, then moved towards Karlín, probably to avoid encountering the grendiers, who stood ready in the New Town Watch House in the middle of the Horse Market. At the lower end of the Market the onlookers at the Mass parted. Some moved along Kolowrat Avenue towards the Museum and the Powder Tower. On the other side of the street were the hotels where several prominent delegates of the Slav Congress were lodged. Others went by way of Můstek, Rytířska and Zelezná past the Carolinum into the Old Town Square. The first conflict occurred when a squadron of grenadiers, leaving the Královdorský barracks under the command of Lieutenant Jablonowski, collided with the crowd moving away from the Powder Tower. With fixed bayonets Jablonowski's grenadiers cleared the way to the General Command Headquarters, then proceeded against the second crowd, now moving out of the Old Town Square into Celetná Street. One company of National Guardsmen led by Franz Thun and one company of the German Concordia under Professor Ruben stood in the vicinity of the Powder Tower, and their attitude towards the demonstrators was decidedly unfriendly. The latter apparently aimed at nothing more than a gesture of protest against Windischgrätz. But the several casualties on both sides, as well as the prisoners rounded up by the soldiers, proved that the conflict which Windischgrätz was expecting had finally erupted.

The six days of fighting that followed have been recounted many times, both from eye-witness accounts like that of Frič and from the official reports, and all the descriptions have been influenced by the kinds of sources on which they were based. We shall look at two which have not yet been used: the journal of Vojta Náprstek and the Prague parish register.[10] Both are valuable for a number of reasons. Náprstek reveals the mood of the students, for which we have hitherto had to rely on Frič, who represented himself as the commander of the Clementium and the moving spirit behind the entire conflict. The reality was far more modest. In the Clementium Sladkovský, Bradka or Dr. Bruna were all more influential than Frič. Moreover, Frič himself reports that on Monday he spent the night at the St. Wenceslas Baths, went home on Tuesday night, and by Friday saw the wisdom of joining the deputation to Vienna.[11]

What, then, did Náprstek, the 22 year-old student in the Law Faculty of the University of Vienna, do in Prague during Whitsun Week? We have already seen that he headed the group of Viennese students who called themselves first the ''''Hydropathic Potato Society,'' then The Seven (Náprstek, Pelzl, Tonner, Tieftrunk, Sourek, Dobrovský, and Sverák), finally the Bohemian-Moravian-Silesian Union. This small group had maintained links with Prague even before March, and most of its members arrived from Vienna to attend the Slav Congress. As the author of greetings from Vienna to the students of Prague, Náprstek gained a certain authority. On June 11 in the Carolinum Tieftrunk urged that barricades be setup up and offered to teach the Prague students the techniques. But it is not likely that any of The Seven were involved in preparations for the conflict.[12]

Náprstek's journal informs us in some detail of the students' activities from Monday July 12. On Monday morning Náprstek hurried to the Museum, attended the Mass in the Horse Market, then returned home for dinner to his family's house in the Bethlehem Square. At half past twelve he learned that barricades were being erected in the Old and New Towns, and he helped set them up in the Bethlehem Square, Dominikánská, the Old Town Square, in Zelezná, and somwhere "near the River." That afternoon he attended a meeting in the Clementium at which Petr Faster appeared, as well as Frič, who aired bloodthirsty views about the fate in store for the captured head of the government Thun. He returned home sometime after one o'clock in the morning with a guest, a "Pole called Bagunin."

On Tuesday morning Náprstek went to the Clementium, where he met with ''some Poles''—those who had avoided the National Guard and had not been put on the train to Olomouc or the steamboat to Dresden. By nine o'clock he was present at negotiations for Thun's release, along with Sladkovský, Frič, and Tieftrunk for the students; Palacký and Neuberg, who had just met with Windischgrätz; Havlíček and Mayor Wanka. Náprstek and Havlíček favored Thun's release, and Sladkovský, too, inclined to the view that "the demands of the burghers must be our orders."[13] According to Náprstek, the release was decided upon over Frič's objections. Náprstek accompanied Thun through the barricades, across Charles Bridge to the barricades in Mostecká which were commanded by members of the Pinkas family. From here Thun reached the Headquarters of the Gubernium in the Malá Strana Square.

On Wednesday morning Vojta's mother suggested that he and his friends dismantle the barricades. Instead, he went to the Clementium, were Frič, whom Náprstek does not seem to have liked very much, was riding to and fro on horseback. Along with Tieftrunk, Vojta delivered a group of eighteen soldiers who had been captured the day before and incarcerated through the night at the inn "u Hulanků" where they gorged themselves on bread and beer, to the Old Town Square to be exchanged for captured students. The talks were shifted from the Clementium to the Old Town Hall, where members of the Government Commission, General Mensdorff and the Court Councillor Kleczansky, were negotiating with representatives the burghers. Náprstek was not present, but he was present "at Havel's"—perhaps at the convent of St. Gall, or perhaps at Havlíček's meeting where Bakunin, Zach, Bloudek and several others discussed the military situation but were unable to agree upon a "plan of action." Zach and Bloudek believed the uprising's chances to be nil. The soldiers were confined to barracks in the neighborhood of the General Command, but with the exception of the Charles Bridge, they controlled all lines of commounication with the Malá Strana, all the city gates and the station, and with the help of Lobkowitz's National Guardsmen they were rounding up prisoners and taking them to the St. George Barracks in the Castle. Among the first to be captured was the leader of Svornost K. D. Villani.

That afternoon Náprstek visited a printing shop, probably in the convent of St. Agnes, to pick up fifty copies of the students' proclamation, which he pasted up around the city with the help of Podskalský. In the pub "At the Golden Tiger" he met Frič. That evening he learned that the soldiers had partially destroyed the Chain Bridge on their way out of the New Town. He spent the night on a billiard table in the coffehouse in the St. Wenceslas Baths.

On Thursday he distributed further posters and leaflets, then met Zach and Bloudek "at Havel's" and accompanied them to discuss with Safařík the possibility of dismantling the barricades. While Náprstek resumed his distribution of posters, the others went to Windischgrätz in the Castle. The Litomysl

155

National Guard arrived in Prague to offer their help—an occurrence unusual enough to warrant special mention even if they did not precisely distinguish themselves.

At seven o'clock Friday morning Náprstek arrived for another talk with Bakunin about defense measures, or rather their lack. Bloudek, Bradka and Frič all favored the creation of a Political Committee on the Viennese model which would supercede the city council, but the meeting degenerated into "terrible confusion," and Frič began to defend the view that "the barricades must be dismantled." Náprstek and most of the other students agreed.[14] In the end it was decided to send a delegation to Vienna, and Vojta Náprstek became one of its members. They left Prague at half past five that afternoon as the barricades were beginning to be taken down. Nevertheless there were "speeches at every stop along the way until Vysoké Mýto."

The delegation arrived in Vienna at four o'clock Saturday morning. They were met by the National Guard and received by Pillersdorf at seven. On Monday there were further negotiations, and Vojta's mother and older brother arrived from Prague. On Tuesday Vojta conceded that the delegation had "accomplished practically nothing." Two days later Frič passed through Vienna on his way to Zagreb; on the 24th Vojta took part in a meeting of the Union, and on the 26th he began to discuss with his mother the possibility of going to America. By this time the Náprstek house in the Bethlehem Square was occupied by soldiers; there were searches and arrests in Prague, and among the victims was "Friedland"—probably Tieftrunk. Náprstek thought it wise to disappear from Vienna, and he accompanied Pelzel to his home town of Rychnov nad Kněžnou.[15]

We shall return later to Náprstek's fate in the summer and autumn. His diary provides some insight into the students' view of the Whitsuntide events, especially those whose horizons were broader than usual. They do not appear to have believed that they could do very much to stem the rising tide of counter-revolution. It is by no means an idyllic picture which the journal conveys; instead it approaches tragicomedy.

On the other hand, the parish registers reveal an unrelievedly tragic picture. They record the deaths and burials of forty-three victims of the fighting.[16] Ten died in the first bombardment on the 15th, and three died in hospitals on the 16th. The rest died, or were found, only later. The eleven victims in the Old Town are recorded in the registers of SS. Simon and Jude, St. Francis, St. Gall, Týn, and St. Haštal. There are twenty-six in the New Town, since the General Hospital, the largest in the city, was located there, and they were distributed among the parishes of St. Apolinare, St. Henry, Our Lady of the Snows, St. Peter's in Poříčí, and Holy Trinity in Spálená. No deaths appear in the registers of Holy Trinity in Podskálí, or in the parishes in Vysehrad, Karlín or Smíchov. The workers from the suburbs therefore reached the center only rarely, and even those from Podskálísustained few losses. But there were five deaths in the Malá Strana, recorded in the registers of Our Lady of Victory and St. Thomas.

In some cases we are informed not only of the names, ages and occupations of the victims, but also where and when they were killed or injured. The heavy fighting apparently took place only on Monday and Tuesday morning. The registers reveal the direction of the soldiers' attack, who unlike the rioters proceeded according to a definite plan. Windischgrätz's first impulse was to concentrate the troops around the General Command Headquarters to prevent the insurrectionists from capturing the artillery and the communications center. On Monday morning there were four main lines of communication linking the Old and New Towns with the Malá Strana and Hradčany. The shortest led through the Royal Way—from the Powder Tower and General Command along Celetná Street to the Old Town Square, the Little Square, through Charles Street and across Charles Bridge. This line was interrupted by barricades at the bottom of Celetná, in the Little Square, and in Charles Street by the Clementinum. The second line led from the Powder Tower along Kolowrat Avenue to New Street and across the Chain Bridge to Ujezd. Here the students, Guardsmen, people whom Windischgrätz called "proletarians," and members of Svornost, whose headquarters were in the Museum on Kolowrat Avenue, had erected barricades in front of the Museum, at Můstek, in New Street, at Perštejn by the ruined Schlick Palace, and in front of the Ursuline convent. The third and fourth communication lines crossed the river beyond the city gates and thus required control of the gates: the old Water Gate on the site of Těsnov Station, Poříčí Gate, New Gate at the end of the Hay Market, the Horse Gate where the National Museum now stands, and Zitna Gate. Vysehrad was occupied by soldiers and guarded communications with the south. Invalidovna, were the cavalry was concentrated, lay outside the gates, and nearby was a temporary pontoon bridge to Bubny and Holešovice.

Clearly the barricades made sense only where they interrupted these lines of communication. Everywhere else they were useless, and Windischgrätz himself reported that only fifteen of the approximately four hundred interested him at all. Most were constructed of materials which could not withstand artillery fire, and this is why Zach, one of the few rebels with practical military experience, opposed their haphazard erection from the beginning. At the first reports of fighting, the soldiers evacuated the main watch houses on the Old Town Square and in the Horse Market, and, covered by the cavalry, they moved armaments to the Josephine Barracks, where artillery reinforcements were sent from Hradčany. Trinity Barracks in Spálená were also evacuated and the garrison—two columns under Major Muller—marched to the Fruit Market between the Estates Theatre and the Carolinum.[17]

Franz Thun's National Guardsmen helped by occupying the hotels across from the Powder Tower, and they were followed by Major Lang's and Van der Mullen's soldiers who drew up in front of the Museum. The Hotel Blue Star, the Museum and the barricades in front of it were all taken without resistance. At about the same time the gates, the Station and the viaduct to Bubny were also occupied. The army's shock troops consisted of a grenadier company from regiments of the "Bohemian" forces (Wocher's, Wellington's, Latour's, Palombini's, Reisinger's) and two companies of Hohenegg's regiment, led by Colonel Mainone. It was at this time that the Uprising's real center—the streets around the Carolinum, Clementinum and the Polytechnic—was just becoming clear. An attempt to capture the headquarters of the government and control the MaláStrana failed, and a procession of farmers moving towards the city from Střešovice was broken up. Marshal Khevenhüller temporarily withdrew troops from Malá Strana Square to Hradčany, so that a few barricades appeared there, too.

Around two o'clock in the afternoon Windischgrätz and Lobkowitz decided that they would secure communications in the city with an offensive from the Powder Tower along Kolowrat Avenue to Můstek. Then one detachment would proceed through Horse Market up to the Gate, while the rest moved against the barricades blocking the narrow entrance to Ovocná street. The commanders were Major Generals Lobkowitz, Rainer, and Schütte and Colonel Mainone. Captain Demuth led the advance to the Horse Gate, which was accompanied by artillery bombardment of the rickety barricades in Vodičková Street and Štěpánská. His soldiers accomplished their tasks with few losses and reached the Livestock Market (later Charles Square). With this, all the city gates from the Moldau to Vyšehrad were in the hands of the army.

Meanwhile troops had launched an attack on the Carolinum, which was defended by fifty to sixty students of the Medical and Law Faculties. They had no chance against Glasser's grenadiers and Major Muller's infantrymen, and they surrendered. There were probably no deaths here. The first death recorded in the registers was fourteen-year-old Josef Schurin, son of a tracteur, who was shot in Ovocná Street just before four o'clock in the afternoon.[18] There was fighting in Ovocná and in New Street almost until dusk. The offensive units—a company of chasseurs, a company from Hohenegg's infantry, two squadrons of Palatin's hussars and three canon, took one barricade after another. The sharpest struggle came with the capture of the strong barricade on Perštejn which had been constructed by Polytechnic students under Bradka's supervision. Major van der Müllen was killed here; a bit farther on Captain Beránek of

The First Victory of the Counter-Revolution

Hohenegg's regiment was mortally wounded; other casualties included Windischgrätz's son and Major General Rainer. With the removal of this obstacle, the two barricades at Voršilky were defenseless, the troops reached Chain Bridge and cut off the New Town from the Old. Several noncombattants were killed in the fire—75-year-old retired army officer Jan Auermann and 'Josefa Brtinská, an innkeeper's wife, as well as 17-year-old shoemaker's apprentice František Válek and 48-year-old journeyman carpenter Jan Köhler, both of whom fell near Our Lady of the Snows.

The soldiers who attempted to reach the Old Town Square met with greater difficulties. Grenadiers under Captain Rauher and Lieutenant Fischhof were active here, and the victims included a 30-year-old commercial traveler Josef Sehner, a 17-year-old carpenter's apprentice Jan Kosta and two unidentified victims about 50 years old, who continued to lie under a barricade until June 17.[19] Josef Cermák, a 54-year-old day-laborer, was mortally wounded. 24-year-old textile worker Jan Karlitz and 41-year-old Josef Slavík died in General Hospital, but it is not known where they fell.

Fighting cotinued into the evening in the Malá Strana, where soldiers from Újezd Barracks and Hradčany under Khevenhüller attacked the barricades in KarmelitskáStreet. The casualties among the defenders included 44-year-old journeyman bricklayer Ignac Zižka.[20] Next to fall were the barricades in Mostecká. Here the soldiers were supported by the Malá Strana National Guard funder Karl Auersperg. Eleonora Windischgrätz, née Schwarzenberg, died quite separately from this conflict. She was shot at about half past four in the afternoon near the General Command Headquarters, when that neighborhood had been in the army's control for some time. During a house to house search for the assassin, the Pole Lubomerski and Helcelet were arrested in the inn "At the Golden Angel;" Maximilian Maux was wounded at the "Black Madonna:" the soldiers suspected him and treated him accordingly as long as he could not prove that the bullet, which is still in the Windischgrätz Family Archive, could not have come from his gun. By the end of the first day, then, Windischgrätz had secured the communication lines and could issue an ultimatum demanding the evacuation of the remaining barricades by two o'clock the following afternoon. But a brief calm ensued when the grenadier offensive by Palombini's regiment halted in the Old Town Square and the Little Square. It can probably also be traced to the fact that Thun was still being held in the Clementinum. The Transporthaus in Jirchaře was taken when its garrison surrendered; at ten o'clock the military hospital in the Livestock Market was besieged briefly, but the attack was repulsed. The only other activity was the steady shooting along the banks of the Moldau. Most of the dead recorded for Tuesday were therefore probably victims of Monday's fighting. The General

Hospital listed eight of them, including a 40-year-old cook Elizabeth Ryšánková, 40-year-old accountant Pavel Reiter, a medical student Jan Kafka from Silesia, 26 years old. The rest were workers—25-year-old laborer Stěpánek, a glover Brosch, 53, an unidentified worker who fell in the Coal Market, and Jan Kraft, a 52-year-old factory worker who died of his wounds on June 19. Master carpenter and New Town Burgher Emanuel Schulz was "shot in a cart by maddened soldiers in front of New Gate" as he attempted to smuggle Petr Faster, innkeeper at "The Golden Scale," out of the city. This "warlord," no longer in the fantastic costume in which Hellich painted him, tried to leave Prague—perhaps, as it was said, to raise the countryside. We know, however, that his flight ended only in Domažlice on the western border, from which he could not possibly have contemplated recruiting help for the Prague Uprising.[21]

On the whole, the serious fighting was over by ten o'clock. After Thun's release, soldiers began bombarding the Clementinum from across the river, though with little effect. The demands of the Clementinum's defenders, proclaimed that evening by Havlíček and Sladkovský, were scarcely "revolutionary:" Windischgrätz's resignation, withdrawal of troops, and the proclamation of a provisional government. These were also the demands with which they entered negotiation with the "Court Commission" consisting of Kleczansky and Mensdorff on Wednesday in the Old Town Hall. They scarcely suspected, of course, that Kleczansky's chief objective in Prague was to prevent the formation of a provisional government.

The talks led to the soldiers' return to barracks and a lull in the fighting. Those who died on Wednesday, therefore, had been wounded earlier: 28-year-old Barbara Hájková, journeyman printer T. Woytek, 24, blacksmith Petr Schubert, 55, Josef Hansdorf, 54, and 28-year-old coffeehouse proprietor Jan Muttig, who had been hit by artillery fire from Zofín Island.[22]

Just after midnight Thursday troops were withdrawn from the center of the city. The smaller contingent left via Kolowrat Avenue, New Street across Chain Bridge to the MaláStrana. The larger passed shortly after half past one through Poříčí Gate into Karlín. From here some crossed the temporary bridge via Stvanice Island, while others were ferried across to Holešovice. Then they all proceeded to Hradčany and Malá Strana. The gates remained in the hands of the National Guard, and the army controlled all the outlying territory. The chasseurs and Palombini's grenadiers controlled the left bank of the Moldau from StřeleckýIsland all the way to Campa, were the chasseurs and infantrymen from Latour's regiment were positioned. At seven o'clock in the morning Windischgrätz's batteries began their bombardment of the city. The defenders' artillery was utterly ineffective across the river. The heaviest fire came in the area of Stvanice Island and Helmovy Mills and near Střelecký Island. Here 18-year-old laborer Anton Radtner was shot, while Konstantin Rester and a 12-year-old schoolboy naMed martin Herzen were killed in the bombardment. At midday a 50-year-old gardener F. Adamovský was killed during the occupation of the Malá Strana: "He treacherously shot one of the soldiers from a window, quite calmly, and was immediately bayoneted by other soldiers."[23]

How much hatred accumulated in the mind of the elderly gardener before he decided that he, at least, would continue the hopeless struggle? His act took place just as Windischgrätz and the Commissioners were agreeing on a withdrawal of troops. The news was delivered to the Old Town Hall by Mayor Wanka and Jan Neuberg on their return from Hradčany at half past one in the afternoon. It is doubtful that it was the formulation of the proclamation announcing this questionable success of negotiations that caused Windischgrätz to reconsider the situation. He could point to the continued shooting (from both sides) along the river. But at five o'clock in the afternoon the situation still appeared quite hopeful.

By Friday morning, June 16, it was all over. Windischgrätz announced that he was resuming his command and that all barricades must be cleared by Saturday morning. The stakes had changed, but Thun, who had moved to the Castle and fell completely under Windischgrätz's influence after his release from the Clementinum, proclaimed a curfew in the Malá Strana. At two o'clock it was decided in the Old Town Hall that the situation could be saved only by a delegation sent to the government at Vienna, and this led to the utter collapse of the uprising. Moreover, at half past eight that evening, Windischgrätz's batteries resumed their bombardment of the city, concentrating upon the Old Town Mills, where the defenders were shooting at the troops across the river on the Campa. The provincial National Guardsmen who had arrived from Litomyšl and Kolin made themselves scarce, and they were joined by defenders on the barricades.

New patients arrived in the Prague hospitals during the day. At General Hospital were 38-year-old Captain Josef Beránek of Hohenegg's regiment, from Stanislawow in Galicia, who died the following day, and 46-year-old journeyman blacksmith Josef Tobias.[24] Others died as well: 26-year-old railwayman Josef Pátek of Orlík, journeyman cabinetmaker F. Muschik, 27, innkeeper and burgher of Chrudim Karel Cerný, who was shot "by accident," baron Hartasi, who died of a stroke in the Old Town Bridge tower; an unidentified body with bullet wounds was fished from the river. The last of the victims was buried fourteen weeks after the uprising, when he was found among the ruins of the Old Town Mills.[25]

On Saturday, June 17, Rieger and Nostitz returned from Innsbruck to

Prague with the news that the Court still assumed that elections for the Parliament would take place. But the situation had changed so radically that this was unlikely. The Government Commission returned to Vienna on Sunday, though it was to have remained longer. On Saturday it had been "reinforced" by an official delegation from Vienna which during its journey witnessed a massacre at Běchovice performed by a hussar squadron under Reitmeister Windischgrätz during a search of the trains. Two companies of Latour's infantry assisted, one of which was led by Captain Mořic Fialka, a Czech patriot and translator of Charles Dickens. The delegation was stopped by soldiers at Invalidovna, then taken under guard to Hradčany, where it learned that while the revolution had triumphed everywhere else, Windischgrätz had crushed it in Prague. Won over by Windischgrätz and impressed with his "restoration of public order," the delegates returned calmly to Vienna. On June 18 martial law was proclaimed in the Old and New Towns, and Khevenhüller's infantry marched to band music over Charles Bridge into the city center. On the 21st the Governors announced the defeat of the Revolution.

But it would have been more accurate to say that the counter-revolution had triumphed. it triumphed over an untried, ill-prepared and disorganized attempt by the revolutionaries to employ the means that they had acquired in March. Given the example of Windischgrätz's success in Prague, the various elements supporting counter-revolution were able to overcome their profound differences and arrive at a common stance, and in time a common program. The chief "buttress" of the regime, however, remained the army.

3 The Results of Windischgrätz's Victory

The picture of the Prague "troubles" sketched by the registers is rather astonishing. What can be said of an uprising during which the trains continued to run on time? During which funeral processions carrying the victims to the cemetery at Olšany passed daily through the gates unhindered by the guards? W. W. Tomek's memoirs reveal how the author of the *History of Charles University*, a participant in the March Revolution, avoided duty on the barricades and in the midst of the fighting left with his wife to stay with relatives in Broumov—where the German National Guardsmen tried to arrest him as an escaped organizer of the uprising—a vivid indication of the confusion and uncertainty that reigned on both sides.[26] Petr Faster's flight from Prague and his anabasis among relatives in the neighborhood of Domažlice is even less edifying. Nor do Frič or Vojta Náprstek come across precisely as heroes. Even their radical colleagues Maus, Tieftrunk, or Sladkovský fail to make a very good impression.

Therefore let us return to the question of who fought on the Prague barricades. The registers reveal just one victim who was a student: Jan Kavka, single, 26-years-old, a native of Domaslovice in Silesia. It is quite possible that the registers are incomplete and that students in particular were not always recorded, but it is not likely. In the list of the wounded treated at General Hospital there appear eleven students, and it is possible that there were more who did not go to public hospitals. Yet the fact remains that the information from the registers coincides quite closely with a contemporary estimate, published in the *Prague Medical Journal*, according to which forty-three were killed and sixty-three wounded in the fighting.[27]

The dead included five women (two laborers, a cook, an innkeeper and a servant), and nine women were wounded (three servants, four laborers, a waitress and one of undetermined occupation). The registers also confirm some facts about the male victims. It is true that no far-reaching conclusions may be drawn from a few dozen cases. But even this figure may be accepted at least as as sample of the participants in the conflict. Most of them were between twenty and forty years of age. Five were under twenty and twelve over forty. Most of the victims in the first two days of fighting were young apprentice craftsmen, an equal number engaged in construction trades—bricklayers, metal workers, carpenters; there were five factory workers, three bureaucrats, four shopkeepers and two army pensioners, as well as six of unknown occupation.[28]

The list of the wounded reveals a similar pattern: they included twenty-seven journeymen, nine day laborers, seven master craftsmen, merchants and officials. There were only a few solid burghers: Emmanuel Schulz, a citizen of the Prague New Town and a master carpenter, and the innkeeper of Chrudim Karel Cerný. A Mass was said for the victims, as the *Národní Noviny* informed its readers in September, and on June 26 the studens remembered their fallen comrades, but unfortunately all the reports are terribly vague. The monument which once stood near the Emausen Monstery disappeared in 1968, and in the military cemetery at Olšany there is a small memorial to the "brave soldiers who fell during the June Days" of 1848.[29]

It is instructive to compare our figures concerning the struggle on the Prague barricades with those touching the slightly later struggle in Paris, from the 22nd to the 26th of June, which was the precursor or "model" of all later nineteenth century bourgeois revolutions. The February Revolution in Paris had claimed 340 victims, but we do not know very much about them. We do know that most were wage laborers, master craftsmen and journeymen, students, journalists and Guardsmen. The June conflict, of course, ended differently. As early as April there were demonstrations by the unemployed in Paris. In the elections, the moderate republicans won with 500 delegates; there were 300 monarchists and only 100 supporters of a "social republic." The demonstrations in support of the Poles which erupted in the middle of May were quelled by the National Guard, and a wave of arrests followed which disposed of the leaders of the "socialists."

On June 21 the Government issued a proclamation abolishing the National Workshops, which employed more than 11,000 people. Negotiations with the Government proved fruitless, and the first barricades appeared on June 22. By evening there were 135 of them. In contrast with Prague, where they were far more numerous, the Paris barricades were all occupied, and their defenders possessed a definite program—renewal of the National Workshops and the establishment of a democratic and social republic. The program was supported by a hundred thousand Parisians, against whom stood 30,000 soldiers, 16,000 members of the mobile guards, 2,000 men of the Republican Guard and National Guardsmen from bourgeois districts. General Cavignac, who like Windischgrätz elicited Nicholas II's accolade, could of course count on the support of the traditionally conservative countryside.

The struggles claimed 2,000 dead and wounded, or twenty times as many victims as the Prague Uprising. More than 15,000 were arrested, sometimes only because they wore workers' blouses, and 11,693 were indicted and placed on trial. The records of the Prague investigative commission of 1848 yield no comparable figures. The backbone, or at least an important element, of the Paris uprising was formed by construction workers: carpenters, metal workers, the eighty railway workers, and the 257 "mechanics" of large workshops or factories. The railways played as large a role in Paris as they did in Prague—and they represented a major source of strength for whoever controlled them—in Paris Cavignac and in Prague the National Guardsmen, who scarcely helped the Uprising because they were confused and hardly able to distinguish what was at stake. But here the railways, in 1848 just as in 1844, were the magnet for the proletariat—those whom Frič accompanied to the Horse Gate after the Slavonic Mass. At that time these workers were being sent by the firm of the brothers Klein to build railways to Dresden and Slaný.[30]

Karl Marx and Alexis de Tocqueville both discerned conflict between the proletariat and the bourgeoisie in the June struggle for the Paris barricades. The fighting in Prague, by contrast, represented a more primitive form of conflict—one between an essentially "popular" crowd on the one hand (since the "proletariat" of Prague was far less evolved than that in Paris) and the force of the army on the other. Thus in Prague, too, a majority of the barricades' defenders were wage laborers, journeymen, and apprentices. And since there were railroads in Prague as there were in Paris, the railway workers were also involved.

What was the significance of the Prague Uprising for the revolutionary movement in Vienna and in the rest of Europe? Tsar Nicholas sent Windischgrätz a letter of sympathy for the "catastrophe" that resulted when he turned his "noble energy" to the task of upholding "conservative principles ... for the salvation of monarchy and country."[31]

The government at Vienna was not so certain in its assessment. The first reports of the fighting in Prague reached Vienna from Windischgrätz through Latour. The government regarded the events as a conflict between the army and the populace of Prague. But the press astonishingly published false reports of firing on the German citizenry, and even though it had little sympathy with the aims of the *Verein*, it suggested that a real struggle between Czechs and Germans had begun. On June 13 the government decided to send Mensdorff and Kleczansky to Prague, the latter charged with watching Thun and preventing further deterioration of the central government's authority in Bohemia. When Mayor Wanka turned to Kleczansky the next day as a possible ally against Windischgrätz, he was only partly justified. Certainly Vienna wished to replace Windischgrätz, but the political aims of the Czech bourgeoisie, insofar as they coincided with Thun's plans, were quite unacceptable.[32]

It was not until June 16 that the Council of Ministers began to consider the events in Prague, and then on the basis of reports announcing Windischgrätz's resignation, while Pillersdorf repeated to the press Windischgrätz's incorrect assertion that the trouble had begun when members of Svornost attacked a delegation of German burghers.[33]. In the minutes of the Council of Ministers there appears not the slightest suggestion of sympathy for Windischgrätz. For his part, however, he was far more interested in winning over the Court, to which on June 17 he sent a report of the events in Prague. He emphasized that "armed proletarians from Vienna" on their way to aid the uprising in Prague had been stopped and dispersed at Pardubice. This information, too, was incorrect.[34] The complaints of the Prague delegation which arrived at Vienna on June 17 were forwarded by the Council of Ministers for arbitration to the Commissioners, whom they believed to be in control of the situation in Prague. on June 18 the government was still willing to eject both Thun and Windischgrätz. But the latter received unexpected support from the German bourgeoisie in Bohemia, and their spokesman Löhner firmly opposed the General's transfer from the city, while holding the government responsible for "every drop of German blood" which Windischgrätz was supposedly protecting. Löhner was aware of a "great conspiracy which is preparing a St. Bartholomew's Eve for all Germans." It did not matter to the government that Ignaz Kuranda was saying the same thing at Frankfurt.

The more rational members of the Frankfurt Assembly, to be sure, warned against a glorification of Windischgrätz, but they had little influence.

Schuselka regarded the Uprising as the work of Czech "ultras" who, like the Hungarians, harmed the revolution in Austria, but he correctly identified Windischgrätz as the champion of reaction. J. N. Berger expressed the same conclusion: "The victors were neither the Germans nor the Czechs: both stood face to face with reaction, and it is not inconceivable that soon both will have to be mobilized against a third, far more dangerous, force."[35]

In the meantime, however, Pillersdorf's government continued to press for the prompt convocation of a Bohemian national parliament, while also urging the postponement of elections for an Imperial parliament. All this must have aroused Pillersdorf's deepest suspicions. The Council of Ministers did give perfunctory support to the government Commissioners, who were under attack from both Windischgrätz and Thun, but they dared voice no objection to Windischgrätz's loudly articulated recognition of the Court Camarilla and the German bourgeois nationalists. On the contrary, Pillersdorf rather gleefully repaid Thun by expressing doubts about his control of the situation. Thun again accepted Windischgrätz's ridiculous conception of the uprising as part of "a far more pervasive Slav conspiracy," and the Council of Ministers, in spite of all their reservations about the Governor, had these views printed in the *Wiener Zeitung* as an official report. Perhaps they were prompted by Schmerling's announcement in Frankfurt that the Assembly was considering a request that the governments of Bavaria, Saxony, and Prussia intervene in Bohemia in favor of the Germans. Pillersdorf at least temporarily maneuvered Thun into position against the Vienna Committee of Public Safety, which urged that the governor be dismissed and placed on trial.[36]

On the whole, the government acted on the basis of Kleczansky's and Mensdorff's unpublished assessment of Windischgrätz and Thun. They believed that the former wished to crush the revolution in Prague, and he was successful. In these circumstances his recall was certainly inappropriate. Opinions about him varied, but it was certain that "at the present, he is indispensable in Prague." He might be removed only when the situation quietened. They regarded Thun as the representative of "Czechism" who had placed all his cards on the convocation of a national parliament. But a revolution had broken out, and the National Committee, Svornost, and also the Germans, all opposed his project for a national Government.[37] Thun's requests for a national parliament thus remained unheard, nor was his report about the Prague Uprising entirely believed.[38] This description of the Whitsun week, preserved among Thun's papers, is most of all testimony to how the insulted "Czech" aristocrat was made to swallow Windischgrätz's nonsensical theory. Equally depressing is the memorandum by J. M. Thun, President of the Slav Congress, who on June 19 rushed to dissociate himself from the Czech cause by issuing a condemnation of "Czechomania." The one reasonable word comes from a report by Court Counsellor Komers, sent to Prague at the beginning of July, who asserted that Windischgrätz ruled Prague as he wished, and that he would lift the siege only when it suited him.[39] By this time, the days, even the hours, of Pillersdorf's government were numbered. On July 8 the presidency was taken over by Doblhoff-Dier, already known to us as Löhner's sympathizer. The government's composition was unchanged, but it was transitional, lasting a mere ten days.

The June uprising dealt the death-blow to Thun's plan for reorganizing Austria from the top, and at the same time it utterly dissolved the sympathy which a part of the Bohemian German nobility had harbored for the Czech cause. In any case, the disenchantment was mutual: the nation and the nobility parted company, and even Clam-Martinitz's well-publicized and passionate Czech anitquarianism in the 1860s could make no difference. But a distorted picture of the struggles—in which both Czechs and Germans died at the hands of German officers, Czech and German infantry and artillerymen, soldiers from Galicia and hussars from Hungary—set the pattern for relations between Czechs and Germans for the next years, even the next century. And the European public uncritically accepted Windischgrätz's thesis of a conspiracy.

Much has been written about the false picture that was presented in the German press. But it has escaped attention that this also gave the rest of Europe its standard account of the events in Bohemia in the spring of 1848. Let us look, for example, at the pages of the most serious newspaper of the period, the *Times* of London. Beginning in March the paper carried reports from German newspapers: the *Schlesische Zeitung, Österreichischer Beobachter, Wiener Zeitung*. Prominence was given reports of anti-Jewish outbreaks in Prague and fighting on the barricades at the beginning of May.[40] Palacký was described, on the basis of a story in the *Kölnische Zeitung*, as a "fanatical Czech, an enemy of the German nation," and Doblhoff-Dier as the hope of Austrian liberalism. Emphasis was placed on Thun's monarchism and on reports that Windischgrätz was ready to march on Vienna.[41] Reports of efforts to mediate between the two nationalities received grateful comment, but there is no doubt that the Germans, rather than the "Tschechish nation" were observed with the greater natural sympathy. This too, is the source of the reserved tone evident in an article about the Slav Conress, in the well-informed reports of the imminent abdication of Emperor Ferdinand and the accession of Francis Joseph, and of Doblhoff's and Wessenberg's activities in Innsbruck against Thun.[42]

The *Times* reported the Whitsun events from German sources. On June 14 it carried stories from the *Könische Zeitung* about the beginning of the student uprising against Windischgrätz which was joined by the Czech inhabitants of

Prague. Reports of crowds of peasants hurrying to aid the uprising were also reprinted.[43] Here, however, fact was overtaken by rumor. According to German informers the Czechs had crucified one Vincenz Weiss, a German burgher. The Germans had fled Prague or were slaughtered, and Windischgrätz was presented as a "bulwark against the wrath of the Czech party," which in any case conformed to the government's report appearing in the *Wiener Zeitung* on June 18. In Prague a civil war had broken out between the two nationalities which was joined by the peasants. The *Times* reprinted *Bohemia*'s stories of a conspiracy aimed at the creation of a Czech empire with Russian help. When "order" was restored, there did appear some doubt whether the conspiracy had not existed only in the minds of the government, but in general the end to bloodshed and the return of peace were greeted with praise. The Czech leaders were identified as Faster (who was still in hiding near Domažlice), Villani and Count Buquoy, whose ally was supposedly Thun himself. Windischgrätz alone prevented the worst. After all, National Guardsmen who had killed two students had been punished by crucifixion, captured soldiers had been tortured to death, not to mention the twenty-three German merchants who had been flung into the Moldau. In 1848 the Hussite Wars were revived in Prague.[44]

It should be added that this represents the view of most of the German press, including Kuranda's *Grenzboten*, and that the reports appearing in the *Economist* and the *Morning Chronicle* closely resembled those of the *Times*. The exceptions were some of the working-class newspapers (*Democratic Review, Northern Star, Labour, Cause of the People*), and the only journalists to write rationally about the Bohemian question were those, like G. J. Harney and E. Jones, who reported the facts of the Whitsuntide events and for whom the journalistic gaffes of the bourgeois press offered welcome targets.[45]

Against the prevailing view, Marx's words were lost:

> The bombardment of a city such as Prague would fill any other nation with the most implacable hatred against its oppressors .... Revolutionary Germany ought to be bound, particularly in relation to its neighboring nationalities, to renounce its entire past. Along with its own freedom, it ought to have proclaimed also the freedom of all nations, including those which it oppressed. And what did revolutionary Germany do? It ratified the old oppression of Italy, Poland and now Bohemia by German armies. Kaunitz and Metternich have been entirely vindicated.[46]

VIII

The Weakness of the Revolution and the Strength of the Counter-Revolution

> Rich, conservative embellisher,
> or poor, wanton destroyer!
> Hear my words:
> The old stone which you have taken from its place
> Hides no other treasure than that of historical memory.
> It was put here three years after the revolution of 1848,
> Which tried in vain to destroy the nobility
> Along with the stony remains of a strong and aristocratic age,
> But which succeeded only in annihilating the last
> Remnants of feudal privilege: robota, tithe and patrimonial court.
> Let this reminder and this historical example
> Be a lesson and a treasure
> To you, rich, conservative embellisher.
>
> Note by Claudius, Fifth Baron of Bretton, placed above the entrance of Zlín Castle in Moravia (1851)

1. The Government's Unsteadiness and the Army's Growing Might

Vojta Náprstek's diary in the summer of 1848 gives us some idea of the mood of the defeated revolutionaries. Náprstek left Vienna on June 25. He could not return to Prague, where his family's house was occupied and most of his friends imprisoned in the St. George Barracks in Prague Castle. He accompanied Ludvík Pelzl, another of the Seven, to his home at Rychnov nad Kněžnou in eastern Bohemia. By the beginning of July he was bold enough to venture out into the neighborhood. On Saturday July 8 he came into conflict with the city fathers of Žamberk, who still placed their hopes with Thun or even Windischgrätz rather than the students. Božena Němcová's husband tried in vain to calm the studens and finally advised that they had best disappear from Žamberk—and Rychnov as well. Thus on July 11 Náprstek crossed the frontier into Glatz, at that time under Prussian control, and remained there until the end of the month. He never moved far beyond the border, but he became acquainted with some of the local inhabitants. He was most impressed with one Geissler, an admirer of Bakunin and a convinced republican. Under his influence Náprstek began to sketch his "Draft for a Democratic Union"—aiming at the establishment of a republic. "It has haunted my mind for a long time; now it should be realized," he wrote in his journal, and after a further week of considering the advantages of a republican constitution he returned to Bohemia, reaching Zábřeh by mail coach.[1]

On August 3 he was in Vienna, and at "the coffeehouse" he wrote that he was welcomed as a lost son. At the pub "Bei Eichhorn" he met with the Bohemian delegates who had come to Vienna for the Imperial Diet. "Such men are deputized for democracy," he noted after meeting the "aristocrats" Rieger, Stroback, Trojan, and Tomek. The next day he met Havlíček, who had been imprisoned in Prague, though only for five days, in July. On August 7 Náprstek witnessed a "celebration for the victory in Italy," which, unlike the "aristocrat" Tomek, he heartily disapproved of. That evening during a meeting of Viennese Czechs at the inn "The City of Prague," where most of the delegates lived, he spoke sharply against celebrating the defeat of the Italian revolutionaries. While the delegates considered national conflicts and the former head of Slavia D. Lambl concluded that "our nation is dying," Náprstek concerned himself with his own organization, the Union. At its meeting on August 20, when more than three hundred artisans gathered, Náprstek denounced Thun and Windischgrätz as the representatives of reaction, and he found himself in complete agreement with the popular Viennese orator Grünwall. His fame grew. On September 1 the Viennese students invited him to join the Academic Legion and to assume command of its Sixth "Slavonic" company.

At this time Náprstek regarded a standing army as the greatest danger to democracy, and he wrote a pamphlet urging the necessity of dissolving the army. He also drafted new, patently republican, by-laws for the Union, which were considered at a meeting on September 3. That evening at a pub he met with Havlíček, Rieger, and Brauner, all of whom he now considered "philistines." He was in closer agreement with members of a "female delegation" from Prague whom he met on September 5 in a reading room. Mmes. Amerling, Jelínková, Thannenberg, and Miss Mařinka Petrová had come to Vienna to plea for the release of students who had been conscripted into the army after the Whitsuntide Uprising. He and Sladkovský accompanied the ladies in Vienna and saw them off at the station on September 10. He found his next duty there far more onerous; on the 16th he went to the station on behalf of the Union to welcome a delegation of Prague burghers, accompanied by eighty Municipal Grenadiers, which included Náprstek's older brother Ferdinand. They had come to Vienna to recover their weapons. The sight of the Prague Municipal Grenadiers standing guard outside the Riding Hall where the Imperial Diet was meeting made Náprstek uneasy, and he stepped up his plans to depart not only from Vienna, but from Austria and Europe altogether.

Although Rieger now behaved more "sincerely" toward him than before, Náprstek could not bring himself to share with him his dream of a "Slavic republic." At the Union he spoke about the "duties of the Female Sex in the present day," collected contributions for the Slovaks and the recruitment of volunteers to liberate them; along with Palacký, Rieger, and Brauner he was elected to a committee to draft a proclamation on the subject, and he met with the Slovak leader Hodza. But his real interests lay elsewhere. The Prague banker Zdekauer introduced him to the Viennese deputy Schütte, who "cursed our own deputies." Náprstek did not agree with all that Schütte had to say, but they shared conviction that the future belonged to a republic and that the army was contemplating treachery. Would the Czech delegates act to perpetuate slavery? Would they be regarded as charlatans, as madmen and bring upon themselves the curse of posterity? "A Slavic republic is our goal, but its precondition is the perfection of an organization."[3]

Vojta Náprstek's path toward political maturity was probably far from typical. But it is noteworthy that after the Whitsuntide events it was not only Viennese students who poured back into the capital, but also students from Prague, who sought safety there. But at this time few had ventured with Náprstek to republican conclusions. Still, it is clear that at least some of the young people were turning away from the "leader of the nation" in the summer of 1848 and that the public perception of Vienna was also changing.

Náprstek considered the chief enemy to be not the Vienna Government but Windischgrätz and Thun. Windischgrätz doubtless had a hand in Thun's dismissal from office on July 17, which provoked little public sympathy. But Windischgrätz himself remained in Prague and continued to rule even after he lifted the state of martial law on July 20. Relations between Thun and Windischgrätz, which had already undergone a complicated evolution, now worsened, and Thun, now out of favor with the Court as well as the government, attempted in letters to acquaintances to distance himself from Windischgrätz's policy, especially his military Committee of Inquiry. The committee rounded up people indiscriminately, and since it was unable to uncover any evidence of a "widespread conspiracy," it operated solely from the testimony of the suspicious informer M. Turanský, until it was dissolved at the end of July. Thun had not taken leave of his senses and could not credit the accusations leveled against Palacký and Šafařík, or Buquoy, Deym and Villani.

But if Widischgratz stuck by his idea of a Slav conspiracy, it did not mean that he planned to pass himself off as a German national hero. For him the determinant of loyalty was class, and although he welcomed the support of the German party, he made distinctions here, too. On July 5 he was certainly happy to receive the support of the German patriciate of Prague, the "Sixty-seven" recruited from the ranks of the *Verein*, but the sympathy of the Viennese bourgeoisie was not very useful to him. Unlike the Vienna government, he was willing to rely solely on force to preserve order. Therefore he cooperated with Thun in getting rid of the remains of revolution. At the end of June the National Committee was dissolved; the "Provisional Governing Council" (the late "Provisional Government of the Land," which in fact never governed) was dismantled; the parliament was not convened; the National Guard was disarmed, and Svornost abolished.[4]

Windischgrätz was unable to prevent the creation of a new government in Vienna under Wessenberg in the Emperor's absence, and it succeeded that of Doblhoff-Dier on July 18. The latter retained the Interior and Education Ministries and thus continued to be highly influential. The new premier, 75 years of age, was an old collaborator of Metternich, with whom he was also in touch at the beginning of August.[5] Wessenberg, of course, did not share the views of Metternich, Kübeck and Windischgrätz about the usefulness of military dictatorship, but as Foreign Minister he resolutely defended the interests of the Monarchy against Great Britain and France; through his ambassador Schmerling he also upheld Austria's position at Frankfurt.

He left domestic affairs entirely in the hands of Doblhoff and his three new associates, all of whom were popular with the Viennese public: the Minister of Justice Alexander Bach, Minister of Trade Theodore Hornbostel and Minister of Public Works Ernst Schwarzer. Bach was a successful lawyer, much admired by R. Cobden, acquainted with the works of Louis Blanc and Robert Owen, and one of the founders of the Legal-Political Reading Club of Vienna. He was Doblhoff's ally in March; he worked for the establishment of the National Guard and had a reputation as a radical. According to A. Hübner, in July he was like "Saul on the road to Damascus" and suddenly turned into a pro-Government Paul—at first still "constitutional" but tby the end of the year absolutist—simply an idealistic revolutionary transforming himself into a hard-nosed Minister of the Interior.[6] Hornbostel was a successful entrepreneur and a less successful politician; Ernst Schwarzer, from Fulnek in Moravia, had made a brilliant career as a publicist.[7] The remaining members of the old guard were the Minister of Finance, whose recall interested nobody, and the War Minister

Latour, who was retained out of consideration for the wishes of the Court. The new Government was considerably younger, with an average age of 51 years: Hornbostel was the youngest at 33; Bach was 35 and Schwarzer 40.

Wessenberg's government lasted until November 21, though it really ceased to function in October. It was a government of the conservatively inclined Viennese bourgeoisie, and it contained two or three real reactionaries in its midst. From its predecessors it inherited the Imperial Parliament elected at the beginning of July, which was opened on the 22nd by Archduke Johann, the newly elected German Administrator. The Parliament had 383 members elected by male voters above the age of 24 who were independently employed. Each delegate had a constituency of about 50,000 people. There were 138 delegates from the Bohemian lands, 100 from Galicia, and the rest came from the Austrian lands. Hungary and Croatia had their own parliaments, as did of course Lombardy and Venetia.[8] There were 92 "peasant" delegates from the countryside, chiefly Ukrainians from Galicia, and they were controlled by the former Galician Governor count Franz Stadion, who was also a delegate himself. Stadion generally supported the government, and "his" delegates buttressed the "black-yellow" center, while the sixteen "peasant" delegates from Bohemia and Moravia belonged either to the "red-white" right or the "black-red-gold" left. The "rightists" with their solidly petit bourgeois and mainly Czech composition, were actually in the center, and they were also called "federalists." Stadion's "center" was centralist, while the leftists were "Frankfurtists" in that they favored the annexation of Austria to Germany.[9]

The most important issue before the Imperial Parliament was a proposal to abolish serfdom, presented by the Silesian German Hans Kudlich on July 26. On August 31 there was a stormy vote on the question of whether to abolish serfdom with compensation or without (which carried 174 to 144) and whether or not to organize the machinery according to the old provincial boundaries (224 to 125). On September 7, 1848, the "Law Concerning the Abolition of Serf and Feudal Obligations" was promulgated. The debate had been enough to provoke the landowners to demonstrations of sometimes uncontrollable anger, and, as we shall see, they attempted to organize their own pressure group.[10] The Parliament's second task was to draft a constitution. Palacký had a special role within the constitutional committee, made up of three delegates from each of the lands, thus conferring special influence upon the "German Austrians." Palacký's first text of September 1848 shows that his views at this time did not diverge widely from those of the German bourgeoisie, at least as far as the guarantee of basic civil rights was concerned.[11]

But he took quite a different view of the "Second Government" at Vienna, the Committee of Safety. At the beginning of August a delegation of Prague students attempted to establish contact with this organization, and the following month the Prague students drew up new statutes, based on the Viennese pattern, governing the Academic Legion, which they now regarded as a political organ for the defense of what remained of the revolution.[12] This development corresponds to what we have already noticed in the evolution of Náprstek's views. But as early as the end of August, Bradka was protesting against the decision of the Prague students to send delegates to the meeting of German students at Breslau. The clash of views about revoutionary Vienna was completely in the open in October, when at least some of the students began to resemble Náprstek in their thinking and came into conflict with members of the older generation.

A far more complicated question was the attitude of the Czech students at Vienna and Prague toward the Hungarian revolution, which had been looming since June. On June 10 Emperor Ferdinand issued his famous patents from Innsbruck which gave preference to Budapest over Zagreb and stripped Jellačić of his power. Croatian-Magyar negotiations produced no agreement. When the Emperor returned to Vienna on August 12, the Court was in a position to alter its policy in Hungary, since the Italian campaigns had begun to yield decisive victories. On September 4 Jellačić was restored to his functions, and on September 11 he launched a military offensive against Budapest. The Jugoslavs, as we have seen, had many enthusiastic friends among the students of Vienna as well as Prague. They also found allies in the Slovaks, who were equally in opposition to Kossuth's Budapest. Here too the divisions were clarified only in October.[13]

The attitude towards the army, at least among the student elements, was unanimously negative. For some time they had been subject to conscription as soon as their "morals" or their academic performance aroused suspicion. Various institutions were taking advantage of the situation to rid themselves of certain students—it was the practice, for example, of the Prague Old Town Gymnasium under the direction of Josef Jungmann. But after the Whitsuntide riots, students were pressed into the army indiscriminately, and this was the reason for the visit of the women's delegation to Vienna. it was not entirely fruitless, because Windischgrätz's measures embarrassed the government. Doblhoff and Bach in particular were concerned about the Government's public image. They might not have needed to worry about Jellačić's treatment, since it was exclusively the affair of the Court, but everybody knew that Radetzky's Southern Army had an enthusiastic supporter in Minister Latour.

The Southern Army and its seventy-one year old commander became popular only when they began to win victories in July. They were also helped in a certain measure by the blunders of the King of Sardinia. While his army besieged Peschiera and reinforcements were pouring into Italy from Austria, Charles Albert could think of nothing better than to initiate a shortsighted policy of political annexation in northern Italy which was resisted only by Venice. The Sardinian failures began in June. On the 11th Vicenza, defended by General Durand, capitulated. One month later Radetzky's forces were already more than 130,000 strong, and on July 23 he attacked the overextended Sardinian line. Three days later the Sardinians were defeated at Custoza and retreated in confusion towards Milan. On August 4 they were beaten again near Milan. Mazzini and the Lombard republicans wanted to defend the city, but Charles Albert and his generals were convinced that the situation was hopeless. They surrendered Milan over the protests of the populace. More than a hundred thousand Lombards left with the soldiers for Piedmont, and on August 6 the Austrian army entered Milan once again.[14]

Three days later Radetzky concluded a truce with the Sardinian General Salaski by which the Piedmont contingents withdrew beyond the River Ticino. The land between was occupied by the Austrians, who marched to Florence under Archduke Charles. Venice, where Daniele Manin had proclaimed a republic, was abandoned. Only Giuseppe Garibaldi and his handful of men continued to fight, but after the battle near Morazzone on August 26 he was forced to seek asylum in Switzerland.

In the interval the international situation also shifted because General Cavignac, now head of the French Provisional Government, and his Foreign Minister Jules Bastide, had no wish to involve themselves in a conflict with Austria. On August 8 they offered Britain mediation on the basis of the Hummelauer memorandum of May 24, by which Austria should cede Lombardy and grant Venetia administrative autonomy. This was the proposal which Radetzky had effectively blocked in June by sending Marshal Felix Schwarzenberg off to Innsbruck and Vienna. Therefore, especially after Charles Albert's cruel defeat at Custoza, it was useless to expect that the Austrian government's behavior should be any more accomodating than it had been earlier. Wessenberg procrastinated over his reply until August 22, when he announced to Britain and France that the Hummelauer memorandum could no longer serve as the basis for discussions.[15]

The Austrian government was still proceeding cautiously, to be sure, but the battle of Custoza had demonstrated even more forcefully than the defeat of Prague that, as long as it had the army behind it, the government would sooner or later be able to crush the revolution. For obviously it could count on at least the passive cooperation of the liberal bourgeoisie, which had never been really revolutionary and naturally took fright at the radicalism of the "lower classes" in the cities and the countryside. The same was true in Northern Italy were, just as in Bohemia, the liberal bourgeoisie evolved and implemented a policy of reform before March, but not one of revolution. Against this, the urban petite bourgeoisie supported democracy and republicanism, and the organized mass demonstrations in Milan which erupted into revolution. But here too, according to Italian scholarship, the struggle on the barricades was chiefly an affair of the workers (predominantly artisans, since factories were only making their first appearance here) and unemployed laborers whose lot was aggravated by high prices. Once the Austrians were expelled, the liberals easily took over the government and allied themselves awith Charles Albert in order to defend themselves against the radicals. The propertied classes—as well as some individual radicals such as Cattaneo—feared a peasant uprising, and they opposed the inclusion of rural folk in the defense of Milan.[16]

We may conclude, then that in the spring and summer of 1848 the revolution in Lombardy ran its course within the limits that obtained elsewhere. Its only exceptional quality was its connection with the war against Austria. The latter, of course, ended in a complete fiasco, thanks partly to the coolness and the considerable military talents of Marshal Radetzky and his Chief of Staff Hesse, partly to the awkward and foolish policies of King Charles Albert. Once Radetzky overcame the defeatism of the Austrian Court, he decisively defeated his traditional opponent—and a new one, in the form perhaps of a Mazzinian united Italy, had not materialized.

On August 12 the *Neue Rheinische Zeitung* published an article—possibly by Engels—about the Italian situation.

> The greatest of all the domestic enemies of Italian liberty was and is Charles Albert. He assumed that he could harness the entire popular movement of 1848 to his own aims. Filled with hatred for all truly free-thinking men, he surrounded himself with men devoted to absolutism and willing to support his royal ambitions. As long as the union of Piedmont and Lombardy remained undecided, as long as there was still a possibility of republican government, he remained in his fortress and did nothing against the Austrians even though they were comparatively weak. He allowed Radetzky, d'Aspre, Welden and the rest to conquer town after town and stronghold after stronghold in the Venetian provinces.

Along with d'Aspre and Welden there were also several landowners from Bohemia and Moravia in the Southern Army. The reactionary Archduke Albrecht arrived as commander of a division in northern Italy from Židlochovice in Moravia, where he had taken refuge after the March events in Vienna. Felix Schwarzenberg arrived from Krumlov, Karl Schwarzenberg from Orlík, and Eduard Clam-Gallas from Friedland.[17] These noblemen created an automatic link with the commander of the Northern Army Windischgrätz, who got into contact with the Court Camarilla through Baron Langenau at the end of July to suggest that the Imperial family not return to Vienna: instead, he offered them asylum in Prague. On August 14 he sent a letter to Empress Maria Anna in which he spoke freely of the "triste nécessité" for her husband's abdication and the accession of his nephew Francis Joseph without any constitutional promises. On September 6 Langanau was given two drafts of the appropriate proclamations, to be delivered for the Empress's scrutiny.[18] We learn more about the emerging union of the Northern and Southern Armies and the reactionary elements at Court from the correspondence of individuals who occupied key positions in the negotiations: Windischgrätz, Eduard Clam-Gallas, and Josef Lobkowitz.

In the Windischgrätz family archive there is a letter of Eduard Clam-Gallas, at that time cavalry General and Commander in Bohemia, dated February 20, 1866, in which he described his relationship with the late General Windischgrätz. After the fall of Milan, Radetzky sent Clam-Gallas to Vienna with news of the victory at Custoza and the fall of Milan. From here he was invited "by the Prague garrison" to Hradčany to Windischgrätz's headquarters. The officers gave him a tumultuous welcome, and Windischgrätz received him with the declaration that "I am resolved not to let the victory that I have gained over the revolution slip from my hands, but on the contrary to capture Vienna, then defeat the Hungarians."[19] We find similar accounts in Clam-Gallas's papers as well as in his authorized biography, written by M. von Angeli.[20] "The Emperor must leave Vienna, but it must not happen, as it did the first time, secretly and at night, but instead in the midst of his loyal contingents." Clam-Gallas thought that Windischgrätz already had the plans worked out for a march on Vienna. With the Empress's knowledge, instructions were prepared for the Emperor's adjutant-general Prince Josef Lobkowitz concerning the army's "Protection for the Imperial Court." Gallas was to inform Radetzky and Hesse of all this and explain to them that in the circumstances it would be impossible to send reinforcements to Italy. Gallas believed that this "deed of historical significance" amounted to a fundamental change in the situation. He reported that Radetzky was in complete agreement with Windischgrätz, and in October, after Latour was lynched, he declared: "Now Windischgrätz shall march upon Vienna and establish order. And if necessary, we shall go to his aid." According to Clam-Gallas, this was how the Bohemian commander became the savior of Austria.

The assembly in Prague Castle took place sometime around August 12. Josef Lobkowitz's appointment as Ferdinand's adjutant-general belongs to the same period. Before his departure for Vienna Windischgrätz received him and gave him the following advice: "You are getting yourself into a most uncomfortable position there in Vienna. Many mistakes have been made; the government is in a position so dangerous that a new revolution must soon break out."[21] His task was to get the Emperor to a place of safety and prevent any further concessions, even should Latour prove willing. The Emperor must leave Vienna "under the protection of his army—but not as if in flight—through Krems to Olomouc. Then I shall take Vienna, after which we shall let the Emperor abdicate in favor of his nephew Francis Joseph. Then we shall concquer Buda." Lobkowitz arranged that the Emperor be given nothing to sign without the Empress's knowledge; since she knew no German, she had Lobkowitz translate everything. When riots broke out on October 6, Lobkowitz, following the plan, sent a "chamberlain disguised as a proletarian" to General Auersperg, who then ordered the Fourth cuirassier regiment and one battery to Schönbrunn. Just as had been agreed, the Court, escorted by these contingents, departed between three and four o'clock on the morning of the 7th for Krems, Znojmo, and Olomouc.

Of the "military triumverate" composed of Windischgrätz, Radetzky, and Jellačič, the victor at Prague was the most active. By the end of August the initiative had shifted entirely to the side of the counter-revolution, whose leader had been correctly identified as Windischgrätz by Náprstek and his friends. The German bourgeoisie from Prague and northern Bohemia, however, continued to regard him as their protector against the "Czech ultras." This brings us back to Bohemia, where alongside Windischgrätz's Hradčany there appeared a second center of political activity at Teplitz.

2 The Bohemian Germans and Their Congress at Teplitz

A highly interesting assembly took place between August 27 and 31 at Teplitz, a town which in 1813, 1819, and 1835 had been the scene of talks which influenced the development of the European state-system. This meeting of representatives from German communities, towns and constitutional associations has been described several times before—although usually on the basis of the minutes which were published in September 1848.[22] Today, however, far more extensive materials are available. Among them are the Memorial Book of the Teplitz town council, the memoirs of the Mayor Eduard John, and finally the journal of the lord of Teplitz Prince Eduard Clary-Aldringen, whom we have already met as an admirer of Löhner, a member of the Viennese *Verein* and the promoter of this organization among the Bohemian noblemen.[23] Edmund Clary-Aldringen was born in 1813; his wife was Elisalex Ficquelmont, so that the Lord of Teplitz was the son-in-law of the former Prime Minister.[24]

One of the impulses for the convocation of the Teplitz Congress came from the center at Vienna, although the actual organization was undertaken by the German Constitutional Society of Prague, founded sometime in June 1848. of those involved in plans for the meeting, the merchant Eduard Strache came from Vienna; the attorney Klier, once a member of the National Committee, and Dr. Tedesko from Prague; Dr. Johann Stradal from Leitmeritz; the physicians Dr. Küttenbrugg von Schonau and Dr. Stoltz, and the attorney Franz Stradal fróm Teplitz. There was a large delegation from Reichenberg, led by Dr. Fischer and the merchant Schirmer, and from Trutnov came the former student leader Uffo Horn, who had once been a member of the National Committee. On August 28, sixty-nine delegates gathered, representing fifteen constitutional societies, forty-one towns and communities in an area extending roughly from Eger to Trutnov and penetrating the interoior of the land as far as Prague. Western and southern Bohemia were unrepresented, nor were there delegates from Moravia or Silesia; but two guests appeared from Leipzig: Dr. Göschen and Prof. Haupt. It appears from the minutes, however, that only about half the delgates remained in Teplitz until the end of the congress.

The first session was opened by Dr. Küttenbrugg in the Garden Hall decorated with the colors of Great Germany, Austria, and those of the individual lands. The official minutes supplement the colorful impressions recorded by Edmund Clary-Aldringen, a founding member of the Teplitz Constitutional Society and honorary commander of the local National Guard, who was, moreover, a highly ambitious young man with plenty of time to keep a detailed journal. The assembly elected Strache of Vienna as its President—a deputy of Löhner, who was too occupied with the Imperial Parliament at Vienna to come himself. The vice-president was Tedesko of Prague, a Jewish banker according to Clary-Aldringen. Both guests from Leipzig were accepted as full participants. The assembly received suggestions and set up three committees to find ways to accomplish its three chief tasks: 1) adopt a stand on a customs union with Germany; 2) establish a permanent organization of Bohemian Germans (Deutschböhmen); 3) formulate political demands and draft the appropriate petitions.

There were several noblemen besides Clary-Aldringen at the opening meeting, and they included members of the families of Schönborn, Nostitz, Lažanský and Kokořovec. Clary-Aldringen wrote that the worse the delegates' German was, the wider the patriotic sashes that they wore. In the afternoon there was an excursion into the countryside, and that evening the local National Guard staged a festive review in honor of the Congress.[25]

The discussions continued at seven o'clock on the morning of the 29th. The Prague delegate Dr. Klier proposed the formation of a network of constitutional societies with a central committee. In the discussion that followed,

Tedesko used the term "German foreign countries" and was reprimanded by Göschen. Uffo Horn upset not only Göschen but most of the assembly when he expressed his views: he favored a union of all the Bohemian Germans, but he was not an opponent of all Czechs, and he favored active cooperation with the Czech "progressive party," since this was the only hope of halting the rising reaction. On the other hand, nothing could be expected from the Frankfurt Assembly, where the progressive party had been defeated. There followed a free-for-all on the contributions of Frankfurt and the German societies of Prague and Vienna. To restore tranquility, greetings were read from the Imperial Council at Vienna and from three delegates to Frankfurt from the Bohemian lands. Clary-Aldringen had been most upset at Uffo Horn's remarks, and he noted with satisfaction that Horn was not recognized afterwards unless absolutely necessary. At luncheon Clary-Aldringen and Lažanský summoned a meeting of landowners, who decided to form a society for the protection of their own interests.[26]

The third session of the congress took place in the afternoon and discussed the question of whether the society's central committee should sit at Prague, Vienna, or Reichenberg. They failed to reach agreement, and the decision was postponed until the following day. Instead there was a debate on Löhner's proposal for the centralization of Austria, which included the abolition of existing land boundaries and institutions. In favor were Stache, Stradal, and Uffo Horn, and thus it was unanimously approved. The creation of "Imperial Regions" and the abolition of land institutions appeared to Clary-Aldringen to be unconscionable. We do not know if he discussed the problem with anyone that evening at the ball in the shooting-gallery—certainly not, however, with Uffo Horn, who on this occasion revealed himself as a prodigious ladies' man ("ein grosser Cour-macher").[27]

At the fourth session the next morning, it was decided that the Reichenberg Constitutional Society should assume the role of a central committee until the time of the next congress. In competition with Prague, Reichenberg won 38 to 8, seven of the delegates having already disappeared. It was further decided that the next congress should meet in three months' time at Eger. The delegates realized that the extent of participation at Teplitz had not been particularly encouraging. Then the discussion turned to the German customs union. As might be expected from an assembly with a strong commercial element, a majority favored the customs "Ausschluss." The incorrigible Uffo Horn and his comrade from Broumov, however, pointed to the necessity of doing something for the impoverished inhabitants of the Giant Mountains, since the traditional lacemaking and linen industries of the region had been practically obliterated. They blamed England and France, but implicitly they also expressed fear of competition from Germany in other traditional industries. It was agreed to urge upon Frankfurt and Vienna the necessity of giving temporary assistance to some of these crafts, and of assuring the endangered German artisans that they could rely on help from their fellow-nationals.

The landowners met for the second time at noon in the chateau. They decided to hold their first formal meeting on September 17 at Teplitz for fifty invited guests, about half of them noblemen. A banquet followed that evening in the Garden Hall, where Clary-Aldringen, who made no secret of his opposition to the "Austrianization" of Bohemia, made the opening toast "to the unity of nations and Estates;" Dr. Göschen of Leipzig drank to the success of German shipping.[28]

At the fifth session there was further debate on the economic and social consequences of the customs union. Since conditions in various industries differed widely, no agreement could be reached. J. Kirchberger of Heinrichsgrün veered from the general line by proposing that the Congress attempt to come to an understanding with the Czechs. Stradal was opposed, but he remained in the minority. The delegates could not decide who exactly was the spokesman for the Czech nation—the Prague city council, or, as Uffo Horn concluded, the Czech delegates to the Imperial Parliament. Tedesko believed that it would be sufficient to advertise in the newspapers; Stradal remained opposed to all attempts at reconciliation. Dr. Göschen inveighed against the "ultra Czechs," who at the Slav Congress had opposed all Germany and had plotted against it in secret. Equality should entail no prejudice to the Germans—and that was the view that endured for generations. Uffo Horn objected to the conspiratorial view of the Slav Congress, pointing out that it had met publicly, but Göschen replied that the point was irrelevant, since German had not been spoken there. Strache finally presented a request of the Vienna German Society that it be empowered to act on behalf of the entire German population of Bohemia. He reminded the delegates of all that Löhner's organization had done for the Bohemian Germans, particularly after the June events, when it prevented the convocation of a Bohemian Parliament.

> The Whitsuntide disturbances in Prague were not entirely unexpected by the *Verein* because it had reports of the intolerable situation in the city. Unfortunately the population of Vienna was badly misled by numerous members of the Czech party about the real aims of the uprising. Where we saw the efforts of Czechism to breathe life into an unconfirmed provisional government, Vienna saw a struggle between democracy and reaction. The activity of the Union thus had to be aimed at explaining the real character of the situation, and many of its members were able effectively to change the mood in Vienna. The *Verein* undertook equally successful activity with the government. The weak Pillersdorf wanted to make concessions,

and Windischgrätz was to be releived at the request of the Prague deputation. Thus it was fortunate that Löhner, Dr. Kuh and myself arrived just before the deputation's departure for the meeting with the rest of the government. Pillersdorf told us of the measures that had been agreed upon, and he was startled when Löhner, with characteristic firmness, shouted that he would be held accountable before all Europe for every drop of German blood shed because of Windischgrätz's dismissal. Our detailed report convinced Pillersdorf. Not only did he withdraw the decree, which had already been published, concerning Windischgrätz's dismissal, but he also dismissed Mensdorff and Kleczansky.[29]

Dean Krombholz of Česká Lípa moved the acceptance of the Viennese proposal, and nobody was willing to speak out to place Strache's impassioned description of the *Verein*'s services in its proper perspective. Uffo Horn perhaps went unrecognized; certainly he could not have agreed with what was being said.

The sixth session on the morning of August 31 brought unexpected difficulties. Only after the speeches, intended for Vienna and Frankfurt, about the dissolution of the lands and the establishment of Imperial Districts, did opposition materialize. The Prague delegates Klier and Tedesko protested against the "sacrifice" of Germans in the Bohemian interior, and they believed that the situation was not ripe for so far-reaching a reorganization. Strache, on the other hand, said that "population of Prague may speak German, but it does not consider itself German," as the poor response to the Frankfurt elections demonstrated. Tedesko replied by describing how in May and June there had been efforts to unite with free-thinking Czechs in Prague against rising reaction, represented chiefly by Thun. Eventually a committee was formed to draft a modified declaration. Kirchberger, who advocated the abolition of old titles, was silenced. Uffo Horn and Sperling-Dauscha again unsuccessfully demanded that the resolution on the customs union be amended to include measures in support of the linen and lace makers. They were put off with a decision to take up a collection for them at the end of the Congress. Otherwise, Strache stressed that "Prague is the center for German trade and industry in Bohemia" and therefore cannot be given up to the Czechs. Dr. Göschen declared that the task of the Congress was to defend the interests of Germany and thus of Bohemia. "As far as Prague is concerned, we must not forget that, when we consider the matter properly, the city is actually German. It is not merely a question of numbers; other things are more important. Who made Prague rich? The Germans! The German factory owners and German merchants insure our industrial interests. For us, Prague must remain a German city!" Nobody rose to answer him; even Uffo Horn favored the acceptance of this addition to the minutes. Only the factory owner N. A. Hirsch of Úštěk perhaps had reservations, but we know nothing of his views because he was not recognized by the chair.³⁰

Clary-Aldringen asked Strache, Stradal, Göschen (all wearing the Great German tricolor) and Dr. Küttenbrugg, to lunch in the chateau. Later these gentlemen made speeches (full of repetition, Clary-Aldringen noted with impatience) at the festival of brotherhood in the shooting-gallery; "At this point I have had enough of German unity to satisfy me for a long time."³¹

The closing session began at seven o'clock in the evening. This time all went smoothly. Dr. Stradal proposed a not very realistic resolution that the Imperial Parliament at Vienna organize supplementary elections to the Frankfurt Assembly. Dr. Göschen urged everyone to appear at the next Congress in "ur-deutsch" Eger. Strache embraced Stradal and Küttenbrugg, and the Congress ended with a cheer and a shout for "Great, united Germany." It had lasted past midnight, to the considerable annoyance of Clary-Aldringen, who noted that "the German brothers are holding a farewell orgy at Hallwich's, yelling and marching."³² Then, in an article published on September 6 in the *Prager Zeitung*, he dissociated himself from the whole affair. Mayor Eduard John of Teplitz noted that only 52 of the delegates were present on the last day, and that from this time the Teplitz Constitutional Society fell into an irreversible decay. In any case, 800 men of Haugwitz's Italian infantry regiment were soon sent to Teplitz, as a kind of punishment, it was said.³³

In October something further was heard from the Teplitz society, when according to John it transmitted to envoy Umlauft incorrect information about Czech-German relations. The Teplitz town council opposed Umlauft, received a friendly communication from the vice-president of Slovanská Lípa František Havlíček, and a rebuke from members of the Prague Consitutional Society, including Tedesko and Klier. Eduard John was a sincere supporter of cooperation between Czechs and Germans, chiefly out of economic considerations.³⁴

On September 18 the Reichenberg Constitutional Society organized a great celebration. On November 20-24 a second assembly of German societies in Bohemia actually met. This too was a social as well as political affair, and Strache was once again prominent. Then in Eger representatives met from seventeen towns, including Olomouc but not Teplitz or Leitmeritz. The program was a practical one, but it had no results; it may be hoped that at least the excursions to Eger Castle and Franzenbad as well as the obligatory celebration of brotherhood came off successfully.³⁵ A further meeting was to take place in the spring at Rumburk, but after the dissolution of the Imperial Parliament one constitutional society after another disbanded. If the Czech bourgeoisie did not exactly distinguish itself in 1848, its German counterpart did not emerge any better. On both sides, those who favored cooperation between the nationalities remained in the minority. Uffo Horn, Kirchberger, Sperling-

Dauscha all spoke to deaf ears when they pointed out that along with the nationality question, the social question was also in need of solution. Thus men like Löhner, Kuh, and Strache continued to hold the floor, to the great relief of Clary-Aldringen, Clam-Gallas, Nostitz, Lažanský and the rest, who at least were certain about one point: they were more interested in class questions than national ones, which they considered to be utterly beside the point.

IX

"The Army Takes Over the Protection of the Court and Government"

> We Czechs, Moravians,
>   and all Slavs
> Shall defend with body and spirit
>   the freedoms given us.
> We shall remain loyal
>   to the Imperial House
> As long as the King and Emperor
>   keeps his word.
>
> "A Song about the Latest Terrible Revolution in Vienna, Broken Out on October 6, 1848."

1. The Road to Olomouc

We shall leaf through Vojta Náprstek's diary one last time. When we left his narrative, he was describing his discussion with the Viennese radical Dr. Schütte, who appeared just a few weeks later on Windischgrätz's blacklist. The conversation took place on Friday, September 29, and Náprstek confessed his dream of a confederation of Slav republics. On Saturday he and his comrades promised that they would meet again in the year 1855, either in Prague at Slovanská Lípa, or, if it were by then the center of a Jugoslav republic, in Constantinople. On Sunday October 1, Náprstek spoke for the last time at the Bohemian-Moravian-Silesian Union on the subject of Slovakia and prepared to leave for America, were he intended to learn first-hand about the organization of a true republic. On October 6, however, he learned that there had been shooting in the station of the Northern Line as soldiers departed for the Hungarian battlefield. He made his way through the barricades to the building of the Imperial Parliament and met with its president Strobach. The next day he met his friends from The Seven in the pub "At the Sign of the Lamb," then left the city. On October 8 he arrived at Krasice in Moravia, then traveled through Přerov and Bohumín into Prussian Silesia, and on the 10th he was in Breslau with Čelakovský. From here he went by way of Berlin to Hamburg, were he sent a note to his mother. From the "Bohemian Elbe" he also wrote to *Národní noviny* to explain somewhat shamefacedly that he was leaving for America in order to acquaint himself with the most advance political and social organization in the world. His ship left Cuxhaven on October 28 and arrived in New York on December 16. Thus ended the "Fateful Year" of 1848 for Náprstek.[1]

His departure probably saved him from the wave of arrests which followed the defeat of the Viennese rebellion. It is likely that he would have adopted the stance of some of his friends, among the students especially P. V. Kleinert, who on October 10 declared that the student delegation had come to Vienna in order to fight. In Prague the students held a lengthy discussion about their attitude toward rebellious Vienna between October 13 and 15, and at a meeting in the Carolinum, even after speeches by Rieger, Št'ur and Hodža, it was resolved that "the delegates of the Prague Student Committee consider the struggle in Vienna to be a struggle for freedom against reaction, and they ask the help of all students for the people of Vienna." But they also declared that Kleinert and Jirgle, with their premature promises of the students' support, had greatly exceeded their authority. Rieger, Havlíček, Palacký, Bradka and Sabina all agreed that Kleinert, if not quite "ripe for hanging" as Havlíček said, should at the very least be hailed before the student tribunal. They repudiated the students' declaration, because in their view the struggle in Vienna was not "purely a struggle for freedom," and on October 15 Havlíček even expressed support for Windischgrätz. Most of the Prague students remained sympathetic toward the Viennese, and their colleagues frm Olomouc and Brno really did try to go to the aid of the Viennese rebellion.[2]

But the *Pražský vecerní list*, the organ of the Czech radical democrats, adopted a view of the rebellion which was quite similar to that of the conservative *Národní noviny*—even though not long before it had published the radical democratic program which included a demand that the poor be protected against the rich. Here too nationalism prevailed over the ideal of social justice, and the same was true on the German side. It is sufficient to read through *Der Radikale*, published by Becher and edited in Vienna by H. Jellinek, which is full of anti-Czech and anti-Slav sentiment. Even Gustav Freytag, correspondent of the *Grenzboten*, could not withstand the fever in his "Sermon on the Ferdinandsbrücke."[3]

While the programs of the Czech and German liberals and radical democrats were disfigured by ideological confusion, murky formulations, and nationalism, the proponents of reaction expressed themselves lucidly, crisply, and uncompromisingly. We do not know precisely what the greatest of the reactionaries Metternich was thinking in September and October of 1848, but his

Thoughts and Maxims expressed the premise that Austria is the guarantor of a renewed "order" in Europe which had been interrupted by revolution and certainly had nothing in common with Frankfurt. The task of "black-yellow" Vienna and "black-white" Berlin was to put an end to the "black-red-gold" demagoguery of Frankfurt.[4] It is probable that most of his supporters in Bohemia and Moravia viewed the "restoration of order" concretely as the defense of "feudal rights."

This is suggested by Edmund Clary-Aldringen's efforts to draw up a program for his Society of Landowners, which emerged at the Teplitz Congress. After these preliminary meetings held at the end of August, Clary-Aldringen called an assembly of the landowners on September 17. His threefold aim was to assure representation of the landowners' interests before the Imperial and Bohemian parliaments, the continued existence of the patrimonial courts, and the payment of compensation for the abolition of the *robota*.[5] Clary-Aldringen appears to have been disappointed at the outcome of the meeting. Albert Nostitz was elected president of the society, and Clary-Aldringen himself was not even placed on the steering committee, whose task, according to a bilingual declaration, was the "preservation and furtherance of the material and political interests of the landowners." By the end of the year, only 140 applications for membership were received, and even a lowering of property qualifications well below the original 300 acres failed to help. Most of the members came from northwestern Bohemia. The Czech minority included members of the Nádherný family, Václav Veith of Livěchov, and Palacký's father-in-law Měchura, who wrote an anonymous tract against the abolition of the *robota*.[6] When the steering committee met on January 6, 1849 it concluded that the organization's membership apparently could not be increased, but it drew up a list of by-laws and drafted petitions to Schwarzenberg's government and the Imperial Parliament. The petitions requested that the patent of September 7 be replaced with a law recognizing the Society as the spokesman of the former noble as well as the bourgeois and "general" domains; they also demanded that the government guarantee compensation for the *robota*. Still, they did not go as far as Windischgrätz, who was working not to amend the *robota* patent, as the Society was doing, but to annul it altogether. The Society relied not only upon the Imperial Parliament but upon the Bohemian parliament as well, and its existence came to an end with the collapse of constitutionalism.[7]

In the Imperial Parliament the discussions soon resulted in the Bohemian delegates' estrangement from Viennese public opinion. In the debate over *robota* compensation, the peasants' position was defended by Jan Sidon of Jičín, who had once urged the students there to go to the aid of Prague during the Whitsuntide uprising. Sidon was a teacher of religion at the Gymnasium, but it did not dampen his radicalism. On July 24 he warned of the danger of reaction, which after the Whitsuntide uprising began to put forth fresh buds; certainly he knew that at this time several lords were trying to collect dues and services from their former serfs.[8] The vote on a "reduced compensation" was 174 in favor, 144 against, with 36 abstentions. Of the 78 Czech-speaking delegates, 53 were in favor, 14 against, with 11 abstaining. Two thirds of the 36 abstentions came from Bohemian and Moravian delegates. Thus there was no "Czech" position on the question of the *robota*. It is true that in the final vote the majority was composed chiefly of Slavs and the minority chiefly of Germans. Most of the "peasant" delegates voted against compensation on August 31, which suggests that most of the Czech delegates voted against the interests of their rural constituents.[9] Why did they do it? Probably because they included landowners, as well as a number of lawyers who favored an orderly "reduced compensation" so that the patent would not stand merely as one of the results of revolution but as a lawful act fully binding upon both sides.

The suspicion that the Czech delegates were henchmen of the government was strengthened by the vote on a question that preoccupied Vienna at the beginning of September: did laws passed by the Parliament require the Emperor's approval? On September 2 Minister Bach defended the principle that approval was necessary; the Czech delegates Rieger and Trojan generally agreed, while the Moravian delegate Josef Demel spoke out against. The government won by a margin of 183 to 119, thanks to Czech and Galician support.[10]

The Czechs' alienation was completed by debate on the Hungarian question. Relations between Batthyány's Hungarian government and the central government and Court deteriorated rapidly. When Jellačić crossed the River Drava, the attack on Hungary was launched; it represented the beginning of a nationality struggle and a war between the governments at Vienna and Budapest. Batthyány's government fell, and the figure of Lajos Kossuth emerged. The Hungarian leaders who wished to avoid conflict but were unable to win over the Court sent their representatives to Vienna. When they were refused a hearing at Court, they asked to present their case before the Imperial Parliament.

In July a delegation of Croations applied to the Parliament for a similar hearing, but they were rebuffed.[11] It could not be assumed that the delegates of Slavic background would look with particular favor upon the demands of the Magyars, but the German Left and the Poles were both active sympathizers. The situation that now existed had not been envisaged when the parliamentary calendar was worked out; and now the question was whether to change it. Ludwig Löhner of the *Verein* spoke in support of the Magyar delegation. Anton Springer, who was later not particularly sympathetic to Czech bourgeois demands, wrote in his *History of Austria* that Löhner was motivated by blind hatred of the Slavs.¹² F. L. Rieger spoke against the Magyar delegation: "Why did they come? To declare that they wish to renew brotherly relations which they themselves broke off earlier? Not at all! Did they come to give assurances that they will give justice to all the nationalities of Hungary—Germans and Slavs—which until now they have cruelly suppressed? Did they come to announce that the nationalities may henceforth expect equality? Not at all."¹³

Rieger's most astute mention of the German minority in Hungary obliged Löhner to protest that it was not at all a question here of national struggle. "I promise you., gentlemen, that at this moment I have forgotten to which nationality I belong. I think and feel only as a member of Parliament." Löhner, unlike Rieger, did not speculate about what the Magyar delegation wished to impart to the Imperial Parliament. He admitted that the Magyars had made many mistakes. He did not even recommend that the Slavs follow the lead of the more mature Germans. Instead he spoke of the growing danger of military intervention, the increasing strength of the generals of whatever nationality. If we read through Rieger's and Löhner's speeches today, we must conlude that the latter behaved with greater forthrightness and less demagoguery. The Magyar request was opposed not only by the 78 Czech-speaking delegates but also by those from the Austrian lands and Galicia. The proposal was defeated 186 to 108, with only one abstention. The ten Bohemian delegates in favor were all Germans; still, most of the Bohemian Germans, too, had sided with Rieger against Löhner.¹⁴

At first glance the vote appeared to represent a great success for Rieger and Czech policy, but it was only a pyrrhic victory. Not all the Czechs, as Havlíček had to admit, were pleased with it. The *Pražský vecerní list* condemned the Magyars, to be sure, but neither was it pleased with Jellačić. At the end of September the fate of the Slovaks and other national minorities in Hungary caused great concern among the Czech public, as well as the radical democrats of Vojta Náprstek's stripe. The rejection of the Magyar petition worsened relations, if possible, between the Viennese radicals and the Czech liberal politicians, and particular enmity developed between the President of the Parliament Strobach, and Rieger, and Havlíček. The campaign of the Viennese press against the government and its lackeys the Czechs intensified; the political polarity merged with the persistent economic difficulties. The day before the debate of September 19 the government lowered the wages paid to the workers in public projects. Then events gathered momentum. Count Lamberg, the Imperial Commissioner dispatched to Hungary, was assasinated in Pest on September 28. The Government reacted with the decree of October 3, which dissolved the Hungarian parliament and invalidated its resolutions. The next day martial law was proclaimed throughout Hungary and all army units were placed under Jellačić's command. This meant open warfare.

The Viennese press responded with unheard-of vehemence to the appointment of a "Slav" general as commander of an army in charge of crushing Magyar resistance.[16] The targets were War Minister Latour and the entire army. After all, on September 13, the Parliament had rejected the text of a congratulatory letter to Radetzky's army, though it was at about this time that Grillparzer wrote his ode to the Field Marshal and the elder Strauss composed the march in his honor. The revolutionary fervor of the bourgeoisie gave way to patriotic ardor. On the other hand, the popular elements in Vienna were wholly on the side of the Magyars. The first conflict occurred on October 5, when grendiers of Ceccopieri's Italian regiment had to be forced by the cavalry to leave for the Hungarian front. They were to be followed by the grenadiers of Richter's infantry regiment the next day. Crowds tried to prevent their depatureure, and a sortie by one Galician company disintegrated when some of the soldiers mutinied. Street fighting broke out, and the National Guard from the suburbs and the Academic Legion intervened. The pro-monarchical National Guardsmen from the city center were overwhelmed, and the commander General Auersperg ordered them to disperse. Blood flowed in the streets and even in the Cathedral of St. Stephen. The Municipal Armory Am Hof was taken, and armed crowds moved towards the War Ministry in the Palace complex. Minister Latour, attempting to leave the building, was caught and lynched.[17]

This was the beginning of the Viennese October revolution. It was also the beginning of a new stage in the struggle between revolution and counter-revolution. We have detailed information in the papers of the Emperor's adjutant Josef Lobkowitz and Felix Schwarzenberg. Lobkowitz received his first reports of the fighting from the commander of the National Guard in the center of the capital at 10:45 in the morning of October 6.[18] According to the existing plan, he began to prepare for the Emperor's departure "under military escort." Radetzky sent Felix Schwarzenberg from his post in Milan to Vienna, perhaps to superintend a diplomatic solution to the situation in northern Italy. According to his biographer Baron Horwath, Schwarzenberg witnessed Auersperg's order to evacuate the center of the city. He supposedly wanted to prompt Auersperg to send a detachment from the units standing before the walls to save Latour. Then he took part in the struggle for Leopoldstadt and in the evening met with Minister Bach, who had barely managed to escape from the city. On October 7 Schwarzenberg saw the collapse of the Parliament's efforts to mediate, and on the 9th he made a personal contribution of 100,000 gulden to the war treasury. On the 11th, standing with his troops in the garden of Belvedere, he received an order to appear at the Imperial Court.[19] Windischgrätz had already offered him a Ministry through his agent Baron Langenau; now there came a more important opportunity.

But where was the Court on October 11? Accompanied by a brigade and artillery, it had set out early on the morning of the 9th from Schönbrunn on the road to Krems. Passing through Herzogenburg, it reached the monastery of St. Hypolite outside Znojmo on the 11th. Several days earlier the Court issued a proclamation in the Emperor's name "to the nations of my hereditary German and Slavonic lands," complaining of the "sad and bitter events, the work of a small but active party, which crush all freedom." It declared that the Emperor had left the capital once again for a place where he could "implement constitutional freedom as a permanent fact, to the well-being of his nations." The declaration was thus intended "to satisfy" those lands through which the Emperor passed.[20]

On October 12 the procession reached Pohořelice, where it was met by the head of the Brno police Count Buben. One company of Archduke Ludwig's regiment remained here, while two squadrons of Mengen's cuirassier regiment continued with the procession to Židlochovice, where the Court spent the night in the castle belonging to Archduke Albert. According to Lobkowitz's testimony, Schwarzenberg arrived here in the middle of the night.[21] The Court was awaited by a highly varied assembly: another company frm Mazzucheli's regiment, the Governor Count Lazanský, the Moravian Commander Prince Reuss, the bishop of Brno, representatives of the Imperial Parliament who had fled from Vienna, representatives of the city of Brno, Brno National Guardsmen, and finally a number of peasants. "The representatives from most of the communities of the Zidlochovice Domain, whom the Captain introduced, were assured by the Emperor that the *robota* and tithes would remain abolished in return for appropriate compensation.[22] Josef Lobkowitz saved the scrap of paper from which the mentally limited Emperor read his remarks, in broken Czech, to his Moravian subjects: "I am glad to see you, I shall consider your petitions. Just be patient. The old laws shall remain in force until new ones take their place."[23]

The Emperor was being used as a "father figure" to pacify the urban population by emphasizing constitutionalism, and the rural population by confirming the end to the *robota*. But just to be safe, the Court avoided the "eternally loyal city of Brno," continuing instead by way of Blučina, Telnice, and Sokolnice to the Olomouc road as far as Vyškov, where they stopped for the night. Mazzuchelli's infantrymen were relieved by troops from Khevenhüller's regiment. At the domain of Sokolnice the procession was joined by peasants on horseback, then by the National Guardsmen of Austerlitz. "His Majesty was moved by these constant signs of devotion and more than once remarked that he discovered anew the old fealty and love of the Moravians and intended to stand by his promise to grant constitutional rights."[24]

On October 14 the Court proceeded by way of Prostějov to Olomouc, where its welcome, especially on the part of the students, was ostentatiously cool. Lobkowitz wrote that the Emperor had had invited Feliz Schwarzenberg to appear at Court, but it is more likely that the invitation came from Schwarzenberg's brother-in-law Windischgrätz. On October 11, the same day that Felix Schwarzenberg received his order outside Vienna, Windischgrätz declared publicly that the anarchy in Vienna had imposed upon him a sacred duty to leave Prague with his soldiers to preserve the person of the Emperor as well as "the unity of the Constitutional Monarchy." Windischgrätz certainly looked very strange as the defender of constitutionalism, and the pose convinced neither the loyalist Czech delegates nor Palacký. Two delegates were sent to Olomouc to submit the opinion that the Imperial Parliament was no longer capable of functioning. There were thirty-six Czech and German delegates in Prague at the time. But not all the Czech delegates had left Vienna. Only the most prominent could have been in any danger—Strobach, Rieger, Palacký. According to the minutes, six Czechs were present for the session of October 13 (Sidon, Sadil, Loos, Šembera, Mokrý, Riegel) and the first four were still there on October 21, as were Pillersdorf and Doblhoff.[25]

Brauner and Helfert, a conservative delegate from Tachov, appeared at Court to argue that the dissolution of Parliament would be an unfortunate mistake. The manifesto of October 16 showed that the danger threatening Austrian parliamentarianism was a very real one. Windischgrätz, appointed Field Marshal and given command of all Austrian troops except Radetzky's southern army, now became in fact a military dictator as well as the superior of the "Slav General" Jellačič. Brauner was convinced that the aristocrats and soldiers wanted to dissolve Parliament, and he tried to convince the rising star Felix Schwarzenberg that Bohemia stood behind constitutionalism. Perhaps partly because of this, a further Imperial manifesto was issued three days later which stressed the ruler's "unalterable will" that "order and freedoms granted our nations, however they may have been misused by criminal individuals, ... are to remain in their full scope," and that the Imperial Parliament was to continue with its task of preparing a constitution.[26] Soon it was to be made plain that his was no more than a tactical manoeuver, worth less than the paper on which it was printed.

In fortified Olomouc, protected by strong contingents under the command of Windischgrätz's old comrade-at-arms Vice Marshal Sunstenau, the Court and government remained nearly a year. The mood of the inhabitants caused some anxiety—a fact corroborated, among others, by Sunstenau in his memoirs—but the troops' advantage was always absolute.[27] In the next few days Windischgrätz shifted contingents from the Bohemian and Moravian commands to Olomouc, amounting to about 60,000 men. From the 15th to the 19th he remained in the city himself, and afterwards he was represented by Felix Schwarzenberg, who assured him on October 20 that he would prevent the Court from negotiating with representatives of the Parliament, and that "nothing shall occur to threaten the progress of Your Highness or that of the Government."[28]

The day-to-day "military campaign against rebellious Vienna" may be traced in a number of sources: the papers of Alfred Windischgrätz, his letters from Vienna addressed to Schwarzenberg, and finally the partially ciphered letters that Adjutant General Lobkowitz received from Field Artillery Commander Grünne, Windischgrätz's political adviser and truly a grey eminence. Three military divisions were brought to Vienna: Jellačić blocked communication with the Hungarian border, Auersperg isolated the center of the city, and Serbelloni's forces were held in reserve for the moment. As a result of an earlier agreement, no military dictatorship was proclaimed, in spite of Kübeck's recommendation; instead, the fiction was preserved that the constitutional régime continued to exist and that the army had come to "liberate" the Imperial Parliament.

2 The Second Victory of the Counter-Revolution: Vienna in October 1848

The Parliament in Vienna actually continued to meet to the end of October, and it continued to make decisions, for two hundred delegates remained, well over the required majority. Under the presidency of the Pole Smolka, who replaced Strobach after the latter's flight to Prague, the Parliament's chief activity consisted in repeated attempts to mediate, to no effect whatever. Immediately on October 6 it issued a declaration to the nationalities of Austria reporting the Court's flight and the continued presence of Ministers Doblhoff, Hornbostel and Krauss, who would henceforth function as the government. Within a short time, however, Krauss was the only one left, and on October 12 he named Wenzel Caesar Messenhauser as provisional head of the National Guard.[29]

Messenhauser was a Moravian. He was born in 1813 in Prostějov, the son of a military musician and a servant girl. From the age of six he was raised in military schools, and at sixteen he enlisted in the army, reaching the rank of corporal within three years.[30] By dint of a remarkable energy he educated himself, particularly in history, and he became an instructor in the military academy in Wiener Neustadt. There he attracted the attention of the superintendent Colonel Zanini, the "revolutionarly" War Minister of March 1848, and won promotion to Second Lieutenant. Messenhauser then moved from one infantry regiment to another in Vienna and Galicia until the spring of 1847. The otbreak of the revolution found him in Lemberg, where he helped the burghers to organize a National Guard. At the end of March 1848 he was in Vienna, where he submitted his resignation from the army. Messenhauser was the author of military history textbooks, but his talents were more literary than strategic. Certainly they were not equal to defending Vienna. On October 14, probably with some relief, he announced that the command had been assumed by the Polish revolutionary Lieutenant General Jozef Bem, who had fought in the Napoleonic Wars and the revolutionary sruggles of 1830.[31]

On the 13th or 14th four members of the Frankfurt Left arrived in Vienna. They had been unable to secure a resolution of sympathy with the Viennese uprising from the Assembly, but still they wished to express their own sympathy. They were led by the Leipzig delegate Robert Blum; the others were gymnasium professor Julius Fröbel, Bohemian-German poet Moritz Hartmann, delegate from Leitmeritz, and Silesian delegate Albert Trampusch. On October 23 Blum spoke to the students in the aula of the University, declaring that "in place of the force which once held the various nationalities of the Austrian Empire together, a union of general freedom has been created, recognizing the equality of all nationalities. Shared freedom binds together far more effectively than mere force has been able to do in the past. If there still exist elements which wish to crush non-German nationalities by force, then they must be crushed themselves."[32] Three days later Blum and Fröbel entered the "élite corps" of the National Guard and were named captains. Only Blum participated in any actual fighting, in the neighborhood of the Sophia Bridge, but both men lay down their arms on the 29th, when peace negotiations began.

Between October 23 and 26, the Central Committee of Viennese Democratic Societies (replacing the Committee of Safety dissolved at the end of August) issued a series of resolutions against Windischgrätz. But Windischgrätz issued his own resolutions. The first, given on October 20 at Břeclav, promised an early defeat of the revolution and the pacification of Vienna. A second on the 23rd demanded the immediate delivery of Kossuth's Magyar collaborator Pulszky, with whom Leo Thun, General Bem, Messenhauser, and Náprstek's friend Schütte had negotiated the same day, when Windischgraätz moved into the suburb of Floridsdorff. On the 27th Windischgrätz demanded the capitulation of Vienna, and the attack on the center began the next day. A telegram which Lobkowitz received at Olomouc shortly after reported that Vienna was in flames. The fiercest fighting took place in the Jägerzeile, where Bem directed the defense. By evening Windischgrätz could report to Olomouc that he was in control of the city as far as the inner fortifications. The same evening the Hungarian troops led by General Móga, Görgey, and Kossuth arrived outside the city, just as negotiations were beginning for a truce, and on the 29th a municipal delegation informed Windischgrätz of the city's surrender. But on the 30th artillery could be heard in the distance: the Hungarian army had engaged Austrian contingents near Schwechat. Messenhauser misjudged the situation, and as the Magyars began their orderly retreat, he did not prevent a renewal of the conflict. On October 31 the city was attacked in the neighborhood of the Imperial Palace. The bombardment ceased late in the afternoon, and by half past six in the evening troops had penetrated as far as the square before St. Stephen's Cathedral. This marked the end of the armed defense.[34]

The struggle claimed heavy casualties on both sides. The army lost about 1,200 men, the defenders about 3,000. Martial law was proclaimed immediately. The National Guard, the Academic Legion and the political clubs were all dissolved, and the newspapers subjected to strict censorship. Most of the defenders of the city were arrested.[35] Together about 2,400 persons were detained, including Poles, Czechs, and Jugoslavs. About a half were released within a few months; 400 received long prison terms and 25 were executed. Among the first victims was Robert Blum, executed on November 9 as a challenge and a threat to the Frankfurt Assembly. Blum's friend Fröbel was also sentenced to death, but was later only deported. On the 16th Václav Caesar Messenhauser was executed, and one week later so were two radical journalists, Alfred Julius Becher, publisher of *Der Radikale*, and his editor Dr. Hermann Jellinek.[36]

Windischgrätz had achieved a second victory. The victor over rebelious Prague and Vienna was truly in a position to dictate, since Wessenberg's government had collapsed in October. Its Viennese member, Minister Krauss, let Messenhauser be executed, even though not long before he had named him commander of the National Guard; and Minister Bach did not even spare Blum. In November 1848 Windischgrätz was at the zenith of his personal power. The extensive correspondence that he conducted with the future head of the Government Felix Schwarzenberg richly reveals the Marshal's dominance, and only later did signs appear of an independent policy on Schwarzenberg's part. He, too, began to make his influence felt, even bofore his appointment as Prime Minister on November 21, but only in matters that could not bring him into conflict with his omnipotent brother-in-law. Windischgrätz was of course so preoccupied with plans for the third act of his campaign against revolution—this time in Hungary—that he was willing to leave most of the details of consolidation to Schwarzenberg. Windischgrätz's favor in the eyes of Nicholas I reached new heights. The Tsar had congratulated him on his defeat of Prague, and after the fall of Vienna he rewarded him with the order of St. Andrew. The Tsar's citation, together with the testimony of the Prussian ambassador von Rochow, show that Nicholas was concerned above all with the solidarity of the ruling class, the preservation of the old order, and that any flirtation with Panslavism was out of the question from his point of view.[37]

Something remains to be said about the attitude of Czech politicians to developments in Vienna, and this is certainly not one of the glorious chapters in the history of Czech bourgeois political thought. The Czech delegates who returned to Prague after October 6 naturally enough attempted to justify their action as the only correct thing to do—an implicit condemnation of the Viennese revolution. We have already seen that members of Slovanská Lípa as well as students were sent to Vienna after the first reports of fighting, and that the students in particular sided with the rebels. Before the deputation returned, the newly elected Prague city council met with Palacký and Rieger to discuss what position to take on the events in Vienna. The radical members yielded only after a "long and angry debate," so that the council endorsed a simplified view of the revolution as a struggle of Slavs against Germans and Magyars.[38] Yet this did not suffice to soothe consciences, and the memory of Windischgrätz's régime in Prague after the Whitsuntide uprising was still very much alive. Thus, without consulting the envoys, a delegation was sent to Olomouc with an offer of mediation, which was of course refused.

The delegation from Slovanská Lípa returned early in the morning of October 12, and they delivered their report at a meeting held that evening: "It is clear that the entire rebellion has a German-Magyar character. But there is every reason for us to take a stand against reaction. Thus, you defenders of freedom, and you, Czech nation, be on guard. If the wantonness of anarchy has been eliminated, we must not allow our rights to be abrogated by the wantonness of the army." But Rieger and Brauner discerned no such danger.[39] The next day at a meeting of the Slovanská Lípa executive committee the radical members' dissent was expressed by Ferdinand Viták, and they even demanded that the envoys be dispatched to Vienna once again. The suggestion was rejected, but at this juncture František Havlíček expressed the fateful dilemma in which the Viennese revolution had placed the Czech radicals: if Vienna won, the Monarchy would collapse; if Vienna fell, the Monarchy would become the puppet of the army.[40] In the end Slovanská Lípa stood against Vienna, but it did support the city council's efforts to mediate. We have already seen how Karel Havlíček helped to quash student sympathy for the Viennese revolution.

The *Pražský vercerní list* printed articles by Karel Sabina which were in many respects self-contradictory; but Sabina essentially represented a view that emerged in the discussions of Slovanská Lípa, that "freedom and nationality" are inseparable—which raised fears about what the defeat of Vienna might mean for Austria's youthful democracy.

Národní noviny, by contrast, could see no clouds on the horizon at all. It appears the at this point Karel Havlíček Borovský entered a fool's paradise. Perhaps he believed that if he repeated often enough that constitutionalism and freedom were in no danger, they would endure. But now he praised Windischgrätz and thereby helped secure his position—just as Löhner and the German radicals had done after the Whitsun uprising. The approval and delight which he expressed at Windischgrätz's execution of Robert Blum, who had been democratically elected to Frankfurt and was protected by parliamentary immunity, was not one of the peaks of his journalistic career.[41] Certainly the Czech delegates Brauner, Havlicek and Rieger had no cause to sympathize with Vienna. But their spiteful attitude towards the Viennese radicals was pathological, and they played directly into the hands of the reaction because they were unable to perceive the danger from that quarter. Their picture of the rebellion was distorted because it ignored the fact that German or Hungarian partisans were not the only ones fighting in the streets of Vienna. The deputy of Lieutenant Governor Mecséry was surprised and gratified indeed when his fears about the Bohemian reaction to Vienna's fall proved to be groundless. Aside from a few disturbances among the popular elements—especially the workers in Reichenberg—nothing happened at all.[42]

In Moravia, which was closer to Vienna, things were different. The Moravian parliament considered the events in Vienna on October 9 and received reports from Kajetan Mayer and Alois Pražák. The next day they unanimously declared their support for the Imperial Parliament. But then on the 13th a revised, more prudently worded declaration was issued which neither criticized nor supported Vienna. The Czech newspapers published in Moravia, *Týdenník* and *Moravské noviny*, were against Vienna, but in the next days and weeks there were several workers' demonstrations in Brno in its favor.[43]

If the defeat of Prague in June 1848 only roughly coincided with the suppression of the workers' uprising in Paris, the defeat of Berlin in October was a direct consequence of Windischgrätz's success in Vienna. The emboldened Prussian King took the offensive against his own revolutionaries, who between October 26 and 29 staged a great Democratic Congress in Berlin. There was a demonstration in support of Vienna in front of the Parliament building, but the Prussian Parliament merely passed along to the Frankfurt Assembly the demands for military aid to the Viennese revolutionaries. On November 1 the

King appointed as Prime Minister Frederick William von Brandenburg, an illegitimate son of Frederick William III. When the Parliament protested on November 9, it was suspended and transferred to the provincial town of Brandenburg. But it refused to comply. The *Bürgerwehr* refused to advance, and workers' clubs declared their support for Parliament. Yet their was no popular uprising. General Wrangel occupied Berlin on November 10 with 13,000 men, dissolved the *Bürgerwehr* and closed the workers' clubs. The Parliament building was occupied by the army, but no conflict erupted. Members of Parliament declared that they would refuse to pay taxes, but only the most radical citizens, including Karl Marx, followed suit. On November 26, 260 of the original 400 delegates assembled at Brandenburg. The government moved the dissolution of Parliament and at the same time issued a relatively liberal constitution which was obviously intended to be only a temporary arrangement to pacify the populace.[44]

Just as earlier in Prague, Milan, and Paris, so now in Vienna and Berlin the flame of constitutionalism was extinguished in October and November. The counter-revolution could now move directly against popular expressions of support for Vienna: demonstrations in Lemberg at the beginning of November were controlled without difficulty by General Hammerstein. Only Hungary and Venetia stood in the way of the complete triumph of counter-revolution. But their final defeat required that the situation in Austria be consolidated, and this was the task of Felix Schwarzenberg.

X
Austria's Future is Decided

1. When in March Emperor Ferdinand
    gave us a constitution
   Nobody thought that there would be
    such a revolution;
   For everybody wanted freedom
    like a platter of roast duck.
   But all of a sudden we found before us
    iron dumplings for the feast.

2. Here, it was said, the Czechs wanted
    to devour the Germans,
   There, again,
    the Serbs the Magyars.
   Now we know that the lords
    made fools of us.
   The nations rose against each other,
    and swooning from the brawl,
   They wanted no more of Freedom.

"A New Song, which we shall be singing in 1849."

1. *The Rise of Felix Schwarzenberg*

Felix Schwarzenberg shared the job of consolidating the counterrevolution with his colleagues General Grünne and Josef Lobkowitz. Throughout November they exchanged a number of telegrams which have been preserved by chance among Lobkowitz's papers. There is a dispatch of November 20: "Court Secretary Deutscher arrives certainly 22 this month," with Lobkowitz's marginal comment: "This is the slogan agreed upon by Grünne and Lobkowitz concerning the abdication of Emperor Ferdinand, originally set for November 22."[1] We do not know why the abdication was postponed, nor why it had been planned to coincide with the opening of the Imperial Parliament at Kremsier.

In any case, the previous day a new government had been named, headed by Windischgrätz's alter ego Felix Schwarzenberg. The second most significant appointment to the cabinet was Franz Stadion (who has sometimes been confused with Rudolf Stadion, former governor of Bohemia). Franz Stadion was a late-Josephine bureaucrat of Pillersdorf's type, already well known from his posts as governor in Pomerania and Galicia, and how he took over the Interior Ministry as well as the Ministry of Education. The former revolutionary Alexander Bach became Minister of Justice; Krauss took over Finance, and Von Cordon, former Commander of Vienna, the War Ministry. The new Minister of Trade was the Rhinelander K.L. Bruck, and the Minister of Agriculture and Mining Ferdinand Thinner. Stadion's efforts in the first days of December to bring a Czech into the government in the person of Rieger ended in failure, and the Ministry of Education eventually went to J.A. Helfert, a Bohemian German. Later the Croatian Baron Kulmer was to represent the Slav element as Minister-without-Portfolio. The average age of Schwarzenberg's government, which lasted until his death on April 5, 1852, was only 48.3 years, the youngest ever.

When the Imperial Parliament resumed its meetings on November 22 in Kremsier, only 332 of the 386 elected delegates ever arrived. The Czech delegates suggested that the Parliament be moved to Brno, but the demonstrations there in October had shown that the city was still too "unsettled." According to Bohuš Rieger, Kremsier had been suggested first by Palacký as a "slavonic city;" on the other hand, Helfert reported that he, Palacký and Pinkas learned for the first time on their trip to Olomouc that the site of the assembly had been fixed by the patent of October 22. We do not know to what extent the other delegates shared Helfert's opinion that Schwarzenberg was a "böhmischer Patriot." The judgement was just as mistaken as that which labeled Kremsier a "Czech" town, which in reality it was not. As for Schwarzenberg, he, like Windischgrätz or Clary-Aldringen, was above all an aristocrat.[2] The choice fell upon Kremsier because its lord Archbishop Sommerau-Beeck had often played host to various archdukes. His chateau was large enough and the town small enough to accomodate a parliament which would not become a thorn in the side of Windischgrätz or Kübeck, who believed in straightforward military dictatorship. Windischgrätz was willing to endure the constitutional fancy-dress only because he was so busy organizing the offensive against Hungary. Sommerau-Beeck was a conservative, against whom the students led by Vojta Náprstek had protested in the spring, and he had particularly good relations with Franz Josef's tutor, Father (later Bishop and Cardinal) Rauscher.[3]

On November 25 the government's program—the work of Stadion with stylistic revisions by Hübner—was published: "We want a constitutional monarchy sincerely and without reservation," the declaration read. Hübner noted that Schwarzenberg could not suppress a smile over a further phrase promising that the government would take the lead in pressing for a constitution.[4]

The Imperial Parliament received the declaration almost with enthusiasm. After all, the leftist delegates in particular had been afraid of arrest, and they expected the parliament to be dissolved at any moment. This was also why on the German side Schuselka took the place of Löhner. The composition of the parliament understandably was not greatly altered. There were 168 noblemen, 40 members of the predominantly German bourgeoisie (the most active of whom were members of Löhner's *Verein*), and 156 members of the intelligentsia.[5] The parliament's first task was to approve or reject the minutes of the last meeting in Vienna (October 28-31). The government of course favored rejection because the meeting had taken place in the midst of the uprising, and Rieger supported this point of view. The minutes were rejected by a vote of 143 to 124.[6]

Just how the government regarded the parliament is revealed in the process of Ferdinand's abdication on December 2. Only a few knew anything about it beforehand—Windischgrätz, Grünne, Lobkowitz, Schwarzenberg. Lobkowitz's archive contains the paper from which the unfortunate Emperor read in a scarcely audible voice at eight o'clock in the morning: "Important considerations have led me to the unalterable decision to give up the Imperial Crown. I empower the Prime Minister and Minister of the Imperial House to assign it to another."[7] The abdication had been planned since August, when Franz Josef reached the age of eighteen. The parliament was summoned on December 2 at noon. More than one delegate was convinced that dissolution was the issue. The announcement of the Emperor's abdication, whose name was bound with constitutional promises and reforms, aroused sincere grief, and a parliamentary delegation was sent to Olomouc to express sympathy. But it found only Ferdinand's young successor, who declared that the constitution depended entirely upon the parliament's success in working with the government. What was immediately striking was that the new ruler signed himself "by the grace of God," which Ferdinand had not done since March. The Emperor together with those closest to him then saw the delegation out to the train for Prague. In Hradčany, until recently Windischgrätz's headquarters, the delegation found Ferdinand.[8]

Schwarzenberg arrived an hour late for the session of parliament; the same evening he informed Grünne from Olomouc that the delegates had "received the news of the abdication as might be expected."[9] Complete agreement between Schwarzenberg and Windischgrätz lasted until the end of December. The Prime Minister was also in contact with Radetzky, who had no objection to the drift of events as long as he was left a free hand in Italy. Radetzky's chief of staff Lieutenant Field Marshal Hess believed that the Italian and Hungarian theatres were of roughly equal significance, but that Hungary would not have risen had it not been for Italy. It appears, however, that Schwarzenberg's good relations with the leader of the Southern Army were calculated to restrict the power of his brother-in-law.[10] His second source of support was the Catholic hierarchy. The intermediaries were the youthful Emperor's tutor Rauscher and the Prime Minister's brother Cardinal Archbishop Schwarzenberg of Prague. This was significant, because in the meantime there had been discussion at Kremsier of separating the Church from the state.[11] In any case, it had been rumored since December that the government was not going to accept the parliament's draft constitution under any circumstances. Windischgrätz and Kübeck concluded that the parliament, which did not include what they regarded as the cream of Austrian society, should be dissolved. Stadion rushed to prepare his own version of a constitution. In January he, too, was persuaded of the wisdom of dissolving the Parliament which in November he and Schwarzenberg had defended. At that time the Prime Minister still needed it as a counterweight to the Frankfurt Assembly, but he did not intend to suffer its existence one day longer than necessary.

The discussions about the draft constitution, which took place in Kremsier between January 4 and 10, 1849, did nothing to improve relations between the government and parliament. In Vienna the draft of a preamble to the constitution, composed by a three-member subcommittee, had not been formally accepted. Rieger's draft, which has not survived in its entirety, was composed with the help of Rotteck-Welcker's *Staatlexikon*, from which several elements of the French constitutions of 1791 and 1793 were lifted, along with a few from the constitution of the state of Texas. The work of a five-member committee which drew up the draft of an entire constitution was rejected, as was Palacký's own first draft, based on the Belgian constitution and proposing four groups of lands—Poland, Bohemia-Moravia, Illyria, and German Austria. It is worth noting that Palacký did not envisage a closer union of the Bohemian lands, as demanded by the first and second Prague petitions. Nor was his second draft accepted, which the commission considered between January 23 and February 3, 1849, and in which Palacký accepted the principle of ethnic geographical boundaries and suggested the creation of eight territories without regard to existing political boundaries. Essentially, then, he repeated Löhner's suggestion: the creation of a German-Austrian land, including the German parts of Bohemia, Moravia and Silesia, and a Czecho-Slovak land, which of course, was to be "compressed as far as possible." J.V. Frič regarded Palacký's draft constitutions as evidence of his treason. In any case the ethnic principle represented little more than a utopia in 1848. When his plan was rejected, Palacký resigned. His place was taken by Antonín Strobach, who like Pinkas belonged to the "moderates."[12]

But in their views on the franchise Strobach and Pinkas were not at all moderate; they were reactionary, because they supported the idea of a property qualification. In this regard Rieger was far more liberal, and even though he made it plain that he did not trust the "proletarians," he still defended the right of these potential "communists" to vote.[13]

The parliamentary debate at the beginning of January concerned only Article One of the draft constitution, and especially the revolutionary-sounding phrase announcing that all power originates in the people. Stadion objected strenuously, pointing to all the difficulties that had been caused in the past year by revolutionary rhetoric. Pinkas himself spoke against Stadion, and he was able to gather 178 signatures representing all shades of opinion in support of his protest. When it came to a vote, Pinkas's interpolation received 196 votes, while the government received only 99. On January 10 Rieger delivered a firey defense of his First Article, which was very well received. In the vote which followed, all the Czech delegates supported the government's recommendation that the article be tabled.[14]

This behavior raises the question of why the Czech delegates, who had been in opposition to Pillersdorf's and Wessenberg's bourgeois liberal governments, now supported Schwarzenberg's reactionary government. After all, in the 29 meetings which took place after January 10, the government benches were empty 14 times, and to the end of February the government left 29 questions unanswered. Palacký, Strobach, and Brauner, of whom some complained that they were beginning to behave like dictators, only rarely assumed an antigovernment posture, and then only in purely Bohemian matters. Their "realist" policy was in fact quite unrealistic. Havlíček, whose *Národní noviny* became merely an official mouthpiece, as late as February 18 was hotly denying rumors of parliament's impending dissolution. Yet some were already aware that on January 20 the government had decided to dissolve parliament and issue a paper constitution, just as had happened in Prussia in December, where the parliament had also been shifted from the capital to a small provincial town, then scattered by the army. It did not even matter that the draft constitution as signed by Fejfalík, Mayer, and Pinkas, a compromise between bureaucratic centralism and traditional federalism, was acceptable to the government and was also supposed to take effect also in war-torn Hungary and Venetia.[15]

The Imperial Parliament was dissolved by an Imperial Patent dated March 4 but not published until the 7th. It was executed by two companies under Count Huyn, whose two reports of the smooth proceedings reveal clearly the attitude of an aristocratic reactionary whose first concern was to initiate a hunt for leftist delegates. The Czech delegates, who according to Huyn were the most obdurate, were the only ones to issue a formal protest, in Prague on March 15. Their act had no more effect, of course, than the petition which had been circulated by Slovanská Lípa in support of the threatened parliament, which gathered over 40,000 signatures by March 1; and the final official act of the parliament's president had been to reply to a letter from the students of Prague expressing their support.[16]

On March 7 Stadion's version of the constitution was issued, along with a declaration of civil rights and a patent on *robota* compensation. It was a stillborn constitution since Windischgrätz had been opposed to it from the beginning. Its only result was the appointment of an Imperial Council, whose head became the reactionary Kübeck at the end of 1850. He, together with Grünne (Lobkowitz's replacement as Imperial Adjutant), Bishop Rauscher, and Empress Sophia, was able to control the young Emperor. Schwarzenberg regarded the constitution only as a means of power. Like the parliament's draft, this constitution was conceived for the whole Monarchy, which in Schwarzenberg's plan would become part of the German Union. The Frankfurt National Assembly rejected Schwarzenberg's proposal of March 9 and on the 27th accepted the German constitution, which did not count with Austria at all. This Little-German program was sabotaged in turn on April 5, when Frederick William IV of Prussia refused the Imperial Crown that was offered him.

The fate of the revolution in central Europe had been sealed by the end of the year 1848. What followed was merely the liquidation of its remnants. Its single legacy was the abolition of serfdom. Stadion's constitution never took effect, and its author retired from public life in July 1849 because of illness. The forces of counter-revolution also won in Italy, where the army of the King of Sardinia was routed at Mortara and Novara on March 21 and 23. Venice was the last to capitulate, on August 22. Windischgrätz, more talented as a politician than as a strategist, was relieved on April 14 after failures in Hungary.[17] Josef Lobkowitz, who at the end of 1848 returned to the army in Hungary as a brigade commander, entered the European stage once more when he was sent to St. Petersburg in April 1849 to arrange the details of Russian aid against the Hungarian revolution. A draft of his report of May 7 to Schwarzenberg recalls the reports which Friedrich Thun had sent to Ficquelmont more than a year before. Nicholas I mildly chided Lobkowitz for Austria's failure to give Russia sufficient help in 1830. Such things must not be repeated. Thus the Tsar made the occupation of Galicia a condition of sending his two armies into Hungary. He also concluded that there was nothing to fear from France, now controlled by Louis Napoleon.[18]

Thus the "Bohemian" aristocrats stood against social change in central

Europe at the end of the counter-revolutionary offensive just as they had at its beginning. With Schwarzenberg in the lead, they attained their goals. They found an unexpected ally in Alexander Bach, whose transformation from a revolutionary liberal into an authoritarian government minister was both rapid and thorough. The measures of May 1849 were backed by Schwarzenberg and Bach in Vienna, Mecséry and Khevenhüller in Prague.[19] The unresolved nationality question interested both Schwarzenberg and Bach, but only because they perceived that excessive Germanizing pressure might provoke the Austrian Slavs into a new revolution.[20] They agreed with Archduke Albrecht that it was necessary to take steps against the kind of journalism practised by A.H. Springer.[21] And when L.F. Rieger applied to Schwarzenberg for an interview in Dresden and assured him of his loyalty, the latter wrote to Bach that Rieger was a highly dangerous man, a student of revolution, and suggested that he be watched far more closely in the future.[22]

After Kübeck's arrival on the Imperial Council, nobody bothered to conceal the aim of jettisoning the awkward constitution. Schwarzenberg called it the "misconstitution," even while its author Stadion still lived. In Jauary 1850 Schmerling left the government, and in May he was followed by Bruck. On the other hand, Leo Thun-Hohenstein came into Bach's government somewhat later as clerical candidate for the office of Minister of Education and Culture. The Sylvester Patent of 1851, issued at Kübeck's initiative, meant the end of the forced constitution. From the ashes of the revolution there remained only a formal equality of citizens before the law, the abolition of the *robota*, and perhaps also a degree of administrative autonomy.

Schwarzenberg, following Metternich's lead, cared more for foreign policy than domestic affairs, which he left Alexander Bach to deal with—of course in the spirit of Kübeck's principles. The "procession to Olomouc" enabled him to garner another prestige victory over Prussia, eventually with the help of Russia. But the path which he embarked upon led eventually to Austria's isolation and defeat. Nevertheless, until April 5, 1852, when he suddenly died, Felix Schwarzenberg was the preeminent figure in the Austrian Monarchy, and the obituaries which pointed to his vast influence did not exaggerate.[24] On the other hand, it is noteworthy that when in June the archivist Aldolf Berger began to collect material from Schwarzenberg's colleagues for an official memorial volume, he received several contributions with which he cannot have been greatly pleased.

Anton von Prokesch-Osten, one of the ablest diplomats that the Monarchy ever had in its service, wrote that he opposed publication of the official biography even though he had contributed material for it. He believed that Schwarzenberg was a conservative and an aristocrat but not a patriot. His single aim was the creation of a conservative Austria through the restoration of the old order not only on the throne.[25] Berger and the other publicists, however, did not allow themselves to be discouraged, and they finished the laudatory volume. What is more remarkable is that after the Second World War more than one historian could be found, especially in the New World, who admired Schwarzenberg as the creator of a strong and united central Europe.[26] But then we already know that Schwarzenberg's teacher Metternich also has his admirers.

Schwarzenberg's death ended a transitional phase of development which evolved into what later became known as neoabsolutism—an effort to resurrect the absolute power of the ruler by relying on a coalition between the feudal landowners of whatever nationality and the predominantly German haute-bourgeoisie. Schwarzenberg of course was no ideologue, and he scarcely troubled himself about a theoretical justification for his method of government. He was even less interested in political theory than Metternich had been—at any rate he did not have his Genz. He parted with Windischgrätz because he considered the Marshal's efforts towards the complete eradication of 1848 and the restoration of the old patrimonial order in its entirety to be completely unreal. In 1848 he had parted company with Kübeck—though of course not with the Kübeck who had earlier written critical commentaries about Metternich's régime and defended large-scale enterprise—in order that he might meet with him once again later.

Schwarzenberg's attitude towards politics might be described as cynical. He purposely allowed Windischgrätz to fall, even though he owed him his career, and in human terms his treatment of Stadion was equally reprehensible. Did Prokesch-Osten judge him too harshly? Most of his papers were destroyed, and no real conclusions can be made from what remains. But it is certain that Felix Schwarzenberg was one of the pivotal figures in the military-landowning clique, composed largely of aristocrats with estates in Bohemia and Moravia who were grouped around the great General Windischgrätz in 1848. It had been Schwarzenberg's appointment as Prime Minister on November 21, 1848, which assured the victory of reaction and the end of the revolution.

2 Austria and the "Bohemian Question" at the End of 1848

The close of the year 1848 is in most ways a natural end to this narrative of revolution and counter-revolution in Austria in this "Annus mirabilis." From the Bohemian viewpoint, of course, this means that the history of the Kremsier Parliament and the May rebellion of 1849 do not fit within the parameters. But the sources that have been used in the foregoing narrative indicate that the fate of the Imperial Parliament was sealed as soon as Windischgrätz crushed the Viennese revolution and Schwarzenberg became head of the government.

It appears that in the future the significance of the Kremsier Parliament will have to be sought chiefly in its role in the creation of the modern Czech nation.[27] The May rebellion was a tragic attempt to undo what could not be undone, and it proved to be the last attempt for a long time on the part of a younger generation to reverse the results of counter-revolution. It should be studied not only in connection with Saxony or Germany as a whole, but also with similar efforts to overthrow the absolutist régimes of Windischgrätz, Welden, Haynau, and Geringer in defeated Hungary.[28]

The "Czech Revolution" of 1848 was one part of the powerful series of revolutions which shook practically the entire European continent. Therefore it cannot be understood, nor should it even be considered, in isolation from developments elsewhere in central Europe—the Habsburg Monarchy and its neighboring lands. How did contemporaries view the role of the revolution in solving the "Czech question"—that is, the fate of Czech national society?

From the viewpoint of the Viennese German-speaking bourgeoisie the revolution brought about a regrettable separatism in Bohemia just as it did in Hungary, Italy and Galicia. This was the view of the centralist A. Bauer, while according to the German radical Arnold Ruge, central Europe in 1848 was the stage of a conflict between revolution and counter-revolution whose favorable outcome could have been the creation of a democratic state which upheld freedom in a social sense. This is the dream which also haunted Robert Blum, and it is preserved for us on the pages of his police file.[29]

The author of the pamphlet "Two Burning Questions in Austria," on the other hand, believed that the Austrian Monarchy had its justification as a bulwark against social revolution.[30] In the spring of 1849 this view was not shared by Count Leo Thun, who concluded that "revolutions arise from feelings of oppression and opposition....Every revolution has cleansed the political organism from some kind of malady." What bothered Thun was the identification of political thought with nationalist ideology in Bohemia and the refusal of the Czech public ever to consider that it might become impossible to continue to work with the central government.[31] Anton Springer was aware of the detrimental effects of the connection between nationalism and politics.

> When in the autumn of 1848 the nationally conservative policies of the Magyars united with their politically liberal ideas and the nationally liberal demands of the Slavs became entangled with politically conservative ideas, ... the original motives remained unaltered, nor was the essential character of the war in any way modified: it was and remained until the spring of 1849 a war of the nationalities. It appears that just as religious war preceded religious freedom, so too destructive national

wars will have to be fought out before equality among nations can be realized.³²
But what was decisive for Springer was that "revolutions are only an expression of the reality that human development proceeds *in time;* to oppose them is to oppose history itself."³³

Nor did the former Prime Minister Ficquelmont doubt the existence of revolution. In his view, of course, the revolution of 1848 was the outcome of a moral crisis caused by conflict among the European great powers. The chief villains were hypocritical England and her competitor France. In England the social question was raised by the development of industry, in France by the ideology of "liberty." In both cases, the result was the destruction which engulfed nearly the entire continent.³⁴ Springer, however, had been the enemy of Ficquelmont's dogmas for a long time, and he thought it nonsensical to blame Palmerston for the revolutions in Europe. He believed that the difficulties in central Europe could be solved by a federal system such as had been established in North America.³⁵

Jakub Malý provided his translation of Mignet's *History of the French Revolution* with an introduction in which he declared that "the Revolution touched us also in its last phase--a revolution rich in consequences and not yet finished. The course of all revolutions is the same. ...Only peaceful reforms can be lasting... The comparison between the first French Revolution and the Revolution of 1848 is, I trust, confirmed by the turn of events in France. We too may be considerably enlightened by the bitter experiences of the past two years." But even the enlightened Jakub Malý was convinced that revolution is necessary when state and government "are unable to assure their citizens liberty and material well-being."³⁶

The "unenlightened" Anton Springer, on the other hand, concluded that "the real home of revolution is the inner consciousness, where truncheons cannot reach."³⁷ Little can be added to his assessment of 1848's significance for Bohemia and the western Slavs as a whole. "If before 1848 it was possible to doubt the political awareness, even the ultimate survival of the western Slavs—and we too had our doubts—since that time nobody can dispute that, should one path be closed to them, they will find another...."³⁸

But that was not all. Springer, one of the few real radical democrats in 1848, admitted his conviction that

> the Slavs are predestined by their pure character, their social sense, their penchant for federation and legal custom, to form a social state, and therefore they complement the efforts of the British, the French and the Germans. England, as we have seen, tries to free man from nature through industry; in France old social forms are destroyed as an example to the whole world; in Germany there originated a free, humane view of the world. But can social thought find its purely political expres-

sion? ... For this, it seems to me, the ground of history in all these lands is too exhausted. On the other hand, many indications lead me to conclude that eastern Europe is singled out for this task. Let Russia try with its might to prevent the world spirit from realizing this plan. Who knows? Perhaps it is just here that federative political forms, to which the future belongs, will be born first. What is certain is that political revolution will nowhere have greater social significance than in Russia....[39]

Anton Springer, in 1848 Viennese correspondent of the *Constitution Newsletter from Bohemia* and afterward docent in history in the University of Prague—one of the most important historians ever to work there—looked clearly into the future. After 1848 the Czech nation, in spite of all its disappointments and mistakes, re-formed itself as a political entity whose significance nobody could doubt—neither Thun. nor Schwarzenberg, perhaps not even Windischgrätz. But we have seen that this process of formation was not at an end in Bohemia, not to mention Moravia or Silesia. In a political sense, Czech society was not as solid as Thun, for understandable reasons, attempted to make it appear. Its liberal bourgeoisie was no worse—but no better, either—than the German bourgeoisie. It would be wrong to jump to simple conclusions about the progressive or reactionary character of national political entities that were inevitably divided into social classes. The Czech liberals later received recognition that they scarcely deserved. Their tragedy was that they began their struggle with the old Estates' society burdened with a decided inferiority complex and almost without any political experience at all. Their fear of the proletariat may have been feigned sometimes, and it certainly had its tactical background, but it was there nevertheless. The real struggle on the barricades in Prague, just as in Vienna, Milan, or Paris, was fought by the proletariat, the "common people," the nameless crowd for whom we have tried to find a name.

During 1848 people in Central Europe first broke through to radical democracy. Therefore it is certainly a false impression that at the beginning, behind the political events of March 1848, there stood some kind of secret society, whether it was called "Repeal" or something else. Institutionally there was nothing more solid than those organizations which brought together the economically or culturally or socially active members of the petite bourgeoisie, from whom grew the intelligentsia. The structure of this society was not yet clear, although there is no lack of sources which allow us to trace the origins of interest groups which appeared on March 11 and afterwards, a good decade in advance of the times.

If you were looking for a simple picture of the 1848 revolution, populated by heroes and villains etched in black and white, then you have probably been disappointed. Heroes and villains cannot be sought only on the Czech or the German side, nor on the liberal or the radical side. Heroes were not forthcoming from any of the "sides." They were the simple people whose views were mirrored in their songs—people who always knew that Windischgrätz was an enemy even though Mr. Havlíček first condemned him, then praised him. They were the people who, provoked by the soldiers, ran to erect the barricades on June 12, 1848. It was not their fault that they had neither the arms nor the consciousness which might have enabled them to halt the heavy step of the grenadiers who carried the counter-revolution on their bayonets.

For a Czech historian who wishes neither to write a panegyric to the "Fathers of the Nation" nor repeat paragraphs from the textbooks, to write about 1848 is neither a simple nor a particularly joyous task. Many of the questions can still only be posed, many remain unanswered, and it will be up to future generations to derive their own view of the problems of 1848. It is not a theme to elicit outbursts of national pride. Rather it prompts consideration of what patriotism means and where the roots of our own internationalism lie.

Not a few protagonists of the Czech national movement appear quite strange in retrospect. Some of their roles will appear ambiguous, some of the uniforms that have been invented for them will seem to have faded. Let us return once more to the words with which Anton Springer concluded his lectures on the revolutionary era:

Conditions unfortunately, were still such that the world spirit could continue along its path only through a devastated landscape. But we ought to keep several things in mind: what was lost either was not worthy of continued life or else was replaced a thousandfold; with the further spread of education the development of mankind will proceed more harmoniously; and finally, 'human life is not merely a joke, and history is carried forward by tragedy.'[40]

Epilogue: From the Revolution of 1848 to the Paris Commune and the First International

There is a substantial qualitative difference between bourgeois and socialist revolutions. Therefore it is not very fruitful to search for the "legacy of 1848" in our contemporary situation. But what we can and should trace is the fate of revolutionary traditions stretching from the time of the first conflict between the still unformed bourgeoisie and the representatives of the old feudal régime, to the beginning of the working-class movement. We have seen that this conflict was the thread running through the events of 1848, in which the leaders of neither the Czech, the German nor the Italian bourgeoisie distinguished themselves. Their attitudes towards the Austrian Monarchy differed, but the bourgeois nationalists were unable to repair their mutual relationships even when the danger of reaction was literally at their doorstep. And not one of them even attempted a solution to the second serious question: the social question.

What happened to the Czech bearers of revolutionary thought in 1848? After the tragic footnote provided by the May uprising in 1849, many were held in fortified prisons in Olomouc, Komarom, Kufstein, and Mukačeva; others were sent to Brixen or Lubljiana, as happened to Havlíček and Arnold. But what was suppressed at home resurfaced twenty years later in the larger cities—Vienna, Budapest, Prague—chiefly because these centers of the Czech and Slovak proletariat could count on the moral and occasionally the material support of the revolutionary and working-class emigration.[1] After 1848 the exiles were concentrated in Paris, Berlin, and London, and also across the sea in New York, Chicago, and St. Louis. Just as there existed an official Czech national policy laid down by conservative liberals like Palacký and Rieger, there also appeared other programs—that created by Sladkovský, Tieftrunk, Tonner, and Náprstek, and that represented by the democratic and working-class movement in exile. The Russian exiles have been closely studied by Soviet historians, and the significance of the German émigrés has been clarified by Karl Obermann.[2] The Czech revolutionaries who left their country also played their role in later years.

One of the problems that we are trying to approach through quantitative analysis of individual elements in the historical process is that of the extent and composition of the working-class emigration. One of the aids in the American sphere is an analysis of the composition of participants in the American Civil War.[3] The extensive memoirs and the wealth of biographical data contained, for example, in certain "national calendars" help us to answer a number of important questions. Material concerning nearly 400 Czech participants in the Civil War on the Union side includes the names of many members of the chiefly working-class emigration.[4]

Besides the many sons of participants in the events of 1848, there were eight who were themselves involved in the revolution. Three had participated in the struggles on the barricades: Ferdinand Horák, František Mráček, and Jan Posler. Horák was a law student who was sentenced in 184 in a trial with German participants in the May uprising. During his imprisonment in Komarom he became acquainted with J.V. Frič. In the American Civil War he was a sergeant in the Garibaldi Guard, the thirty-ninth infantry regiment from New York. František Mráček, born in 1825 at Nedakonice in Moravia, studied in the Prague Polytechnic in 1848. He was a friend of Frič and later tried to help him. He took part in the volunteer expedition to Slovakia, and in 1849 he was sentenced to twenty years in prison as a member of the Czech-Moravian Brotherhood. In New York he worked in a cigar factory; in St. Louis he edited the *Národní noviny;* then he went to Russia to search for a place to establish "New Bohemia" and died in Odessa in 1896. Jan Posler, born in 1823, arrived in Prague during the Whitsuntide uprising with the National Guard of Litomyšl and emigrated to America in 1856.[5]

Matěj Rybín of Strakonice, who had fought in Vienna in 1848, was a machine maker and soldier of the National Guard in St. Louis, where he was under the command of Marx's and Engels's collaborator Josef Weydemeyer. Edward Wratislaw was an officer under the Polish general Mieroslawski in Germany, then Engels's co-worker in 1849. Perhaps he came from the family of the same name which had been settled in England since the end of the eighteenth century. Jan Borecký and Franz Fallada also left Bohemia after having fought on the barricades. Borecký had been in Saxony and Hungary before leaving for St. Louis. Another of Frič's friends was Antonín Macal, who worked as a machine maker in Paris and in 1861 fought in Italy with Jindřich Podlipný and E. Rüffer in the "Hungarian Legion" under Garibaldi.

Two further veterans of the revolutionary wars deserve our attention: F.G. Přibyl and Pavel Hudek. Přibyl came from a family of Moravian gunsmiths, and before he joined relatives in America he worked in Brno and Vienna. We hear from him again in 1896, when he was among the volunteers to aid the Cuban Revolution. Hudek was born in 1833 and went to America in 1856. In the Civil War he served in the Chicago "Slavonic Artillerymen" of the twenty-

Epilogue

fourth Illinois infantry regiment. In 1884 he was a co-founder of the American Labor Party in Chicago, having been a candidate with L. Meilbek on the Socialist Workers' ticket. He also founded an organization called the "Bohemian Lincoln Rifles," which was expelled from the ranks of the Illinois National Guard when it refused to advance against the workers. Hudek then founded the "Bohemian Sharpshooters" who in 1886 were accused of collusion with the "anarchists" of the famous Haymarket massacre. But by this time Hudek was dead.[6]

Other Czech "48ers" also found refuge in America. We have mentioned one of them already, František Korbel, who was born in 1831 in Bechyně. On June 12, 1848, he is said to have fled from the house of the imprisoned Baron Villani, commander of Svornost in Příkopy, disguised as a footman. Then he may have taken part in the fighting on the barricades. He was in the Clementinum and left Prague to take part in the campaign to Slovakia, which was scattered at the end of September 1848. In October Korbel reached Vienna, where he was interrogated with the students, and finally left for America. He found no gold in California, but he cleared land in Sonoma County and established a vineyard. Korbel, Náprstek and Dr. Adolf Straka in London were to become the most prominent of the generation of 1848 emigrants.[7]

From this review it is also clear that in 1859-62 a number of Czechs took part in Garibaldi's revolutionary struggle for the unification of Italy. Their core was made up of the fifteen factory workers of Turin who took part in the famous campaign of the "Thousand" volunteers, when J.V. Frič was unable to form an independent unit. From Frič and also from the correspondence of F.L. Rieger we learn something of the activities of individuals and groups who in the 1850s and especially at the beginning of the 1860s were in London, Paris, and several German cities. As a whole, they lived upon the legacy of 1848. They called themselves "Beseda," "Slovanská Lípa," or "Slávie;" their journals were called *Národní noviny*, *Slávie*, or *Slovan*. A branch of Slovanská Lípa even existed in the twenty-second Illinois infantry.

The most significant of these organizations was perhaps the Paris *Beseda*, founded on October 16, 1862, at the initiative of J.V. Frič at the Café des Nations near the Palais Royal. The original twenty-one members included two with Polish names (J. and F. Oleszkiewicz); two signed their names in German, and there was one Frenchman, Léon Grillepoix. The most active of the Czechs were the tailor Josef Hulek, who supported all the new Czech arrivals; the painter B. Kroupa, later a close friend of Vojta Náprstek; Ladislav Vojáček, who acted as Frič's courier and brought him money from Prague; and F. Skorpil, whom Frič sent to Prague as a "workers' agent" to establish contact with workers' organizations and with Frič's friends, including the historian E. Tonner. The most important accomplishment of the Paris *Beseda* was the publication in 1867 of the first French language introduction to things Bohemian, which has already been mentioned.[8]

We know little of the other activities of this organization. In the records of the Paris police, who dissolved the *Beseda* after the fall of the Commune, something more can perhaps be found. On July 5, 1871, in Vienna the Minister of the Interior informed the Bohemian Governor that in Paris several Austro-Hungarian citizens had been arrested as participants in the Commune: Simon Deutsch, a banker from Vienna; Václav Skoda, a master tailor from Bohemia; André Lapczynski from Galicia; and Vincenz Schmidt, a journeyman baker from Bohemia. Simon Deutsch, who was well-known for his financial support of workers' organizations, was released with Schmidt; we know nothing about the fate of Václav Skoda. On August 13, 1871 the Paris officials informed Vienna that a number of individuals "seriously compromised in the Paris uprising" had fled to Austria. Among the Bohemians arrested in Paris, according to the report, there was one "Kratochvil, a representative of the International;" others were J. Hulek, F. Oleszkiewicz, H. Zýka, F. Beneš, A. Hadrbolec, F. Heller, Č. Jerman, F. Khain, J.N. Paradyski. Of these, Zýka, Heller, Hulek, and Oleszkiewicz were charter members of the Czecho-Moravian *Beseda*.[9]

It is of course possible that the French police did not take great trouble over identifying "Internationalists" and confused them with the leadership of the *Beseda*, which had recently been outlawed. It is for example unlikely that the master tailor Josef Hulek, one of whose customers was Napoleon III himself, was a committed revolutionary. But American sources show that the Paris *Beseda* provided some of the founders of the Czech Workers' Society in New York, including its leader Jiřík Slitr. From 1870 to 1872 the Czech Workers' Society comprised the Third (Bohemian) Section of the North American Federation of the First International. Together with workers' organizations in Chicago and St. Louis they were supporters of the Paris Commune and representatives of Czech national feeling and proletarian internationalism. Their organs, Paldov's *Národní noviny* and Klácel's *Slovan amerikánský*, were matched in Bohemia only by the journal *Dělník*.[10]

On April 1, 1871, J.B. Pecka published an article in *Dělník* about the Paris uprising, an eloquent defense of the young Commune but also a consideration of the role of revolutions as agents of historical change.

> If revolution ever wins, it certainly represents a great step forward. We see from history that wherever revolution has triumphed, the nation has gained. In Bohemia, we may compare the position of the nation before Hus and after. The nation became stronger with the war. It was not the fault of the Bohemian revolution that democratic institutions did not endure and that serfdom appeared around

Epilogue

1500: it was the fault of the Battle of Lípany. If the aristocracy had been defeated, the nation would not have been led to where it stood after 1620 with the defeat in the Battle of the White Mountain. Let us look at the state of the Dutch before their revolution and after; at the state of the French before 1790 and after.... There is no nation which can produce so many democratic elements as our own. Therefore those who presently enjoy happiness at the expense of democracy must always live in fear of 'dangerous innovations.' Thus is will be important just how all those who are truly in sympathy with the 'lower' classes will regard revolutionaries—whether they wish them luck or not. The social question must find its solution, and it shall: it is not inevitable that most of the people should become mere objects at the disposal of the rich.[11]

Pecka's article, which placed the Paris Commune in the company of revolutions beginning with the Czech Hussites, continuing through the Revolt of the Netherlands in the sixteenth century and the French Revolution of the eighteenth, has not yet found its place in the history of Czech historical consciousness. In its argumentation, of course, we find traces of Palacký's conception, which the "revolutionary docent" Dr. Bruna passed along in his lectures to the students of the University of Prague in 1848-9. But Pecka's article is closer to Louis Blanc than to Palacký. Its scope is wider than what was usual in Czech historiography. It recalls the words that Palacký wrote in 1848 in his introduction to the first volume of the *History of the Czech Nation*. "On the one hand, the researcher's industry unearths more and more historical sources which until now have been hidden; on the other, the scope of human awareness widens as the field of investigation becomes more solid." Pecka's breadth of vision was remarkable. Although he did not write directly in his article about the revolutionary year 1848, he did offer a concealed critique of the official Czech "national" policy, one of whose representatives, František Palacký, was outstripped by his own idea carried to its logical conclusions. The Czech bourgeoisie of 1848 was unable and unwilling to lead the struggle for a democratic revolution, since the "social question" was already taboo as far as it was concerned. Therefore the working class was left to lead this struggle to an eventually victorious conclusion.

Notes

Chapter I

1. *Die Prager Juni-Ereignisse in der Pfingstwoche des Jahres 1848. Nach den Ergebnissen der Hierüber gepflogenen gerichtlichen Untersuchung*, (Vienna 1849), 80 pp and map.
2. *Ibid.*, 3
3. *Ibid.*, 45
4. A.H. Springer, *Österreich nach der Revolution*, (Leipzig 1850) 102 pp.
5. *Ibid.*, 7.
6. *Ibid.*, 8-9.
7. *Ibid.*, 22-23.
8. *Ibid.*, 23-24.
9. *La Bohême historique, pittoresque et littéraire*, ed. Joseph Fricz et Louis Leger, (Paris 1867). See the chapter entitled "Le Congrès slave de Prague de 1848," 199-212.
10. J.V. Frič, *Paměti*, ed. K. Cvejn, 3 volumes (Prague 1957-1963). J. Heidler published a critique of Frič's memoirs in *Český časopis historický* (hereafter CCH) as early as 1912. See also the collection *Josef V. Frič a demokraticképroudy v české politice a kultuře* (Prague 1956) and most recently, V. Záček, "Josef V. Frič v Zahřebu," *Sborník Národního muzea* XVI (1971) 21 ff.
·11. *La Bohême historique...*, 199-201
12. *Ibid.*, 12.
13 *Ibid.*, 206-209.
14. A.H. Springer, *Op. cit.*, 65.
15. *Idem, Geschichte des Revolutionszeitalters, 1789-1848*, (Prague 1849). E. Hobsbawm, *The Age of Revolution* (London 1962). Compare also W.L. Langer, *Political and Social Upheaval, 1832-1852* (New York 1969).
16. J.A. Helfert, "Vlastní skušenosti a paměti," *Osvěta* XX, XXI, XXVI, XXVII (1890-91, 1896-97). Jakub Malý, *Naše znovuzrození*, (Prague 1880-84). J.J. Toužimský, *Na úsvitě nové doby*, (Prague 1898). Ludwig Brügel, *Geschichte der österreichischen Sozialdemokratie*, (Vienna 1924).
17. J. Toužimský, *Op. cit.*, 109.
18. F. Roubík, *Český rok 1848* (Prague 1948). *Idem*, "Ke vzniku úředních soupisu účastníků hnutí v letech 1848-1849," *Casopis společností přátel starožitností českých* LXX (1962) 150-156. K. Kazbunda, *České hnutí roku 1848*(Prague 1929).
19. J. Matoušek, *Karel Sladkovský a český radikalismus za revoluce a reakce* (Prague 1929). For Frič's memoirs, see above, n. 10.

20. Franz Schuselka, *Das Revolutionsjahr März 1848-März 1849*, (Vienna 1850), 97, 109, 185, 257, 307.
21. J. Fischer, *Myšlenka a dílo Františka Palackého*, 2 volumes (Prague 1926-27).
22. V. Cejchan, "M. Bakunin v Praze roku 1848," CCH XXXVIII (1932) 564-569.
23. E. Bass, *Ctenío roce osmačtyřicátém* (Prague 1940). Jan Jeník z Bratřic, *Z mých pamětí* (Prague 1945) 124.
24. J. Volf, *Dějiny novin v Cechách do roku 1848* (Prague 1930) 98-99, 150.
25. A. Klíma, *Rok 1848 v Cechách* (Prague 1948). V. Klimeš, *Ceská vesnice v roce 1848* (Most 1949). J. Macůrek, "The Achievements of the Slavonic Congress," Slavonic and East European Review (hereafter SEER) XXVI (1947-48) 329-340. See the bibliographical survey in *25 ans d'historiographie tehécoslovaque* (Prague 1960).
26. J. Purš, "K problematice průmyslové revoluce v CSR," *Ceskoslovenskýčasopis historický* (here after CSCH) IV (1956) 1-27. Idem, "The Industrial Revolution in the Czech Lands," *Historica* II (1960), 183-272. L. Kárníková, *Vývoj obyvatelstva v českých zemích, 1754-1914* (Prague 1965). J. Křížek, *Národnígardy v roce 1848* (Prague 1954).
27. V. Král, "F.A. Brauner za revoluce a reakce 1848-49," *Sborník archivních prací* (SAP) II (1952), 123-190. O. Říha, "O národním hnutí a národnostní otázce 1848-1918," CSCH II (1954) 47-68. Z. Samberger, "Die revolutionäre Zusammenarbeit der tschechischen und sächsischen Demokraten im Frühjahr 1849," in *Aus 500 Jahren deutsch-tschechoslowakischer Geschichte*, ed., K. Obermann and J. Polišenský (Berlin 1958). K. Kosík, *Ceská radikální demokracie* (Prague 1958).
28. F. Engels, *Germany: Revolution and Counter-Revolution* (Moscow n.d.). Idem, *Revolution und Kontrarevolution in Deutschland* (Berlin 1971). Marx-Engels, *Werke*, volume 8, 3-108.
29. Marx-Engels, *Die Revolution von 1848* (Berlin 1948); *Werke* volumes 5 and 6 (work from March 1848 to July 1849).
30. Marx-Engels, *Werke* 8, 3-108.
31. K. Kreibich, "Národnostníotázka v Ceskoslovensku," *Komunistická revue* (KR) (1924) 321-333.
32. J. Sverma, "Ceskáotázka v revolucí 1848," KR (1924) 321-333.
33. Idem, "Marx a českáotázka," KR (1928) 430-442.
34. Idem, "Karl Marx a českýnárod," KR (1933) 48-53.
35. K. Konrad, "Pražskýbřezen 1848," *Tvorba* 10 (1938) 114-116. J. Sverma, "Slovanská otázka v nasí české politice," *Cs. Listy* 3 (1943) 2-3. Z. Nejedlý, *Komunisté, dědici velkých tradic českého národa* (Prague 1950), 7-101.
36. A. Rothstein, "Británie a Ceskoslovensko 1848-1938-1948" *Nová Mysl* II (1948) 540-544.
37. Marx-Engels, *Vybrané spisy* I, 25.
38. Ibid., 32.
39. Ibid., 39-41.
40. Ibid., 36.
41. Ibid., 47.
42. Ibid., 44.
43. Ibid., 59.

44. *Ibid.*, 58.
45. *Studien über die Revolution*, ed. M. Kossok (Berlin 1969), VII ff.
46. *De zeven revoluties*, ed. I. Schöffer (The Hague, n.d).
47. K. Obermann, *Deutschland von 1815 bis 1849* (Berlin 1961).
48. S. Kieniewicz, "The Social Visage of Poland in 1848," SEER, XXVII (1948-49) 91-105. J. Blum, *Noble Landowners and Agriculture in Austria, 1815-1848* (Baltimore 1948). R.F. Leslie, "Polish Left-Wing Political Tactics, 1831-1846," SEER, XXXIII (1954), 120-139.
49. E.P. Thompson, *The Making of the English Working Class* (London 1965) 9 ff.
50. *Ibid.*, 189-190, 199, 787.
51. G. Rudé, *The Crowd in History. A Study of Popular Disturbances in France and England, 1730-1848* (London 1964). B.D. Parygin, *Sociální psychologie* (Prague 1968) 137 ff.
52. V. Král, *O marxistické koncepci národních dějin* (Prague 1971), 6-7.
53. J. Polišenský, *Obor historie na pražské universitě kolem roku 1848*, (AUC-Prague 1958) 113-130.
54. *Otázky studia obecných dějin* I (Prague 1957).
55. *Mémoires, Documents et Ecrits laissés par le Prince de Metternich*, ed. R. Metternich, 8 volumes (Paris 1880-1884). H. von Srbik, *Metternich, der Staatsmann und der Mensch*, 2 volumes (Munich 1925), volume 3 (Munich 1954) contains bibliography 1925-1952. G. Bertier de Sauvigny, *Metternich et son temps* (Paris 1959). More critical than Srbik and Bertier is K. Obermann, "Bemerkungen über die bürgerliche Metternich-Forschung," *Zeitschrift für Geschichtswissenschaft* (ZGW) VI (1958) 1327-1342. The most recent contribution, based essentially on Viennese sources, is by A. Palmer, *Metternich* (London 1972).
56. K. Obermann, "Bemerkungen,..." Idem, "Die Rossl der zaristischen Hilfs- und Interventionspläne gegen die Revolution in der ersten Hälfte des Jahres 1848," ZGW (1964) 179-212.
57. Acta Clementina (Metternich Family Archive—FA) *Inventory of the State Central Archive* (Prague 1966-1969).
58. Kolowrat-Liebsteinský FA, State Archive (SA) Zámrsk; and Althan-Khuen-Lützow FA, SA Brno contain what is left of Kolowrat's papers. Clam-Gallas FA is in SA Prague, Křivoklát branch. Other collections: Bellegard FA in SA Opava Deym FA in SA Zámrsk Hartig FA in SA Litoměřice.
59. Chotek FA in SA Prague, Benešov branch. Lažanský FA in SA Pilsen, Zlutice branch; Mittrovský FA in SA Brno. Jan of Neuberg's scanty papers are in the Cejetička collection in SA Prague. Nostitz-Rieneck in SA Pilsen, Zlutice branch. Salm-Reifferscheidt FA in SA Brno. Papers of Sylva family in the District Museum, Prostějov, with some material in Beaufort-Spontin FA in SA Pilsen, Zlutice branch. Sternberk and Vrtba FAs in SA Prague, Benešov branch. Papers of Christian Waldstein-Wartenberg and correspondence between Archduke Stephen and Josef Thun-Hohenstein are in SA Prague, Mnichovo Hradiště branch.
60. Ficquelmont's papers in Clary-Aldringen FA, SA Litoměřice. Děčín branch, chiefly cartons 263-275.

61. Edmund's papers, with his journal is in Clary-Aldringen FA, SA Litoměřice, Děčín branch. In the same repository are papers of Eduard Clam Gallas (cartons 177-184) and an inventory of the papers of Friedrich and Leo Thun.

62. Alfred Windischgrätz papers, SA Pilsen, Klatovy branch.

63. The remains of Felix Schwarzenberg's papers in Schwarzenberg FA, SA Třeboň, Krumlov branch.

64. J.M. Thun-Hohenstein papers in SA Pilsen, Zlutice branch, repository at Klášterec nad Ohří in the collection Thun-Hohenstein FA (Klášterec branch). Thun's apology in the papers of Josef Lobkowitz, SA Litoměřice, Zitenice branch. See V. Chaloupecký, "Hrabě Josef Matyás Thun a Slovanský sjezd v Praze," CCH (1913) 84-91.

65. Josef Lobkowitz's voluminous papers are in Lobkowitz of Dolní Beřkovice FA, SA Litoměřice, Zitenice.

66. Hübner's papers in Municipal Archive Bratislava. Sommerau-Beeck in the Archive of the Archbishops of Olomouc, SA Opava, Olomouc branch. F.V. Peřinka papers in District Archive, Kroměříž. Coudenhove FA in SA Pilsen, Klatovy branch. Stadion FA in SA Pilsen. Felix Lichnowsky papers in Lichnowsky FA, SA Opava.

67. J. Purš, Průmyslova revoluce (Prague 1973)

EM68. L. Neckářová, G. Mazzini a česká otázka (unpub. dissertation Charles University, Prague 1952). K. Novotný, "Hnutítypografického dělnictva v Praze r. 1848," Zápisky katedry československých dějin a archívní studia III (1958) 7-19. M. Hroch, "K problematice formováníbouržoazního národa v Evropě," CSCH (1961), 374-391. V. Vomáčková, "K. národnostní otázce v buržoazní revoluci 1848 v českých zemích,"CSCH 1961, 1-16. M. Myška, Počátky vytvářeníčelnické třídy v železárnách na Ostrovsku (Ostrava 1962).

69. M. Churán, Ohlas revoluce 1848 v českém tisku (unpub. dissertation, Charles University Prague 1954). L. Sumavská, Ohlas anglických a irských událostí v letech 1830-1848 (unpub. diss. Charles Univ. 1954).

70. K. Novotný, J. Polišenský, V. Vomáčková, Boje dělníku na stavbách našich prvních železnic (Prague 1957). J. Polišenský, Opavský kongres roku 1820 a evropská politika let 1820-1822 (Opva 1962). K. Obermann, Ctvrtý stav v revoluci (Prague 1961). J. Polišenský, "Rakousko, Prusko a Něecko 1850-1866," CSCH 1967 249-262.

71. R. Endres, Revolution in Österreich 1848 (Vienna 1947). A. Nowotny, 1848. Österreichs Ringen um Freiheit und Völkerfrieden vor hundert Jahren (Graz, Vienna 1948). M. von Ehnl, Wenzel Cäsar Messenhauser, Nationalgarde-Oberkommandant von Wien 1848 (Vienna 1948). R. Kozling et al., Die Revolution im Kaisertum Österreich 1848-1849 2 volumes (Vienna 1948, 1952). A. Wandruszka, Das Haus Habsburg. Die Geschichte einer europäischen Monarchie (Vienna 1956). H. Benedikt, Kaiseradler über dem Apennin (Vienna 1964).

72. H. Hantsch, Die Nationalitätenfrage im alten Österreich (Vienna 1954) Idem, Geschichte Österreichs (Vienna 1961).

73. Gestalter der Geschicke Österreichs (Vienna 1962 contains contributions by R. Lorenz on Bach and Schmerling, A. Nowotny on Franz Josef, and L. Jedlicka on Archduke Albert.

74. E. Priesterová, *Stručné dějiny Rakouska* (Prague 1954). E. Fischer, *Österreich 1848* (Vienna 1946).

75. K. Wessely, "Die Stellung Österreichs im Rahmen der Industrialisierung Europas," *Österreichische Osthefte* (1972) 125-136. F. Prinz, *Prag und Wien 1848*. Compare the views contained in the collection *Die Deutschen in Böhmen und Mähren*, ed. H. Preidel (Gräfelfing bei München 1952).

76. R.A. Kann, *The Multi-National Empire*, 2 volumes (New York 1950).

77. J.R. Rath, *The Viennese Revolution of 1848* (Austin 1957). S.Z. Pech, *The Czech Revolution of 1848* (Chapel Hill 1969). T.S. Hamerow, "History and the German Revolution of 1848," *American Historical Review* (1954) 27-44.

78. J. Droz, *Les révolutions allemandes de 1848* (Paris 1957). S. Fischer-Galati, "East Central Europe: Continuity and Change," Journal of International Affairs (1966) 1-8. V.L. Tapié, "Méthodes et problèmes de l'histoire de l' Europe Centrale," *Mélanges Pierre Renouvin* (Paris 1966) 33-49. Tapié's conception approaches that of W. Lorenz, *Monolog über Böhem* (Vienna 1964).

79. E. Winter, "Eine grundlegende Urkunde des Austroslavismus," *Zeitschrift für Slavistik* (1958) 107-124. E. Wolfgramm, "Böhmen im Widerstreit der Nationalitäten: zum tschechischdeutschen Verhältnis um 1848," *Wissenschaftliche Zeitschrift der K. Marx-Universität Leipzig* (1967) 137-141.

80. R. Averbuch, "Tsarskaya interventsia v borbe s vengerskoy revolutsiyey" (Moscow 1935). *K stoletiu revolutsii 1848 goda*, ed. B.F. Porshnev and A. Benedikov (Moscow 1948). I. Udalcov, *Aufzeichnungen über die Geschichte des nationalen und politischen Kampfes in Böhmen im Jahre 1848* (Berlin 1953). Averbuch's work has been the basis of E. Andics's *Die Habsburger und die Frage der Zarenhilfe gegen die Revolution* (Budapest 1960). Idem., *Das Büdnis Habsburg-Romanow* (Budapest 1963).

81. V. Záček, *Cechové a Poláci roku 1848* (Prague 1947). M. Novák, "Rakouská policie a politický vývoj v Cechách před r. 1848," SAP (1953) 43-167. M. Trapl, "Olomoucká universita v prvním (vzestupném) období revoluce 1848," *Sborník Vysoké školy pedagogické v Olomouci* 1957, 5-54. B. Sindelář, "Ohlas mad'arské revoluce 1848-49 na Moravě a ve Slezsku," *Rozpravy CSAV* (1957). *Slovanský sjezd v Praze roku 1848*, ed. Z.V. Tobolka and V. Záček (Prague 1958). F. Cervinka, Ceský nacionalismus v XIX. století, (Prague 1965).

82. J. Kočí, *Emanuel Arnold* (Prague 1964). M. Trapl, "Božena Němcová v revoluci let 1848 az 1849,"' *Sborník Pedagogického institutu* (Olomouc 1964) 85-102. Z. Simeček, "Josef Chovanetz: Osudy publicisty a novináře v dobe předbřeznové a v revoluci 1848," SMM 1966, 80-91. J. Havránek, "The Development of Czech Nationalism," *Austrian History Yearbook* III vol. 2, 233-260. M. Hroch, *Die Vorkämpfer des nationalen Erwachens* (Prague 1969).

83. J. Belda, *Liberec v revolucním roce 1848* (Liberec 1959). See also A. Hanke, *Die nationale Bewegung in Aussig von 1848-1914* (Prague 1943). F. Roubík, "Ke vzniku úředních soupisu účastníků hnutí v letech 1848-49," CSPS 1962, 150-156.

Chapter II

1. J.D. Durand, "The Modern Explosion of World Population," *Proceedings of the*

American Philosophical Society (1967) 136-159.

2. J. Lhomme, *La grande bourgeoisie au pouvoir, 1830-1880*, (Paris 1960), 51 ff.

E.M. Thompson, *English Landed Society in the Nineteenth Century* (London 1963), chapter 4. S.F. Wolley, "The Personnel of the Parliament of 1833," *English Historical Review* (EHR) 1938, 240-262.

3. J. Blum, *Noble Landowners...*, 25, 33. T.S. Hamerow, *Restoration, Revolution, Reaction* (Princeton 1958), ch. 3. M. Laran, "Nobles et paysans en Russie, 1762-1861" *Annales* 1966, 11-140.

4. J. Polišenský, *Opavský kongres...*, 10, 25, 104, 123-24, 133-141. B. Gille, *Histoire de la maison Rothschild, Tome I, Des orgines à 1848* (Paris, Geneva 1965) 47 ff.

5. W.O. Aydelotte, "The House of Commons in the 1840's," *History* (1954) 249 ff.

6. J. Polišenský, V. Vomácková, K. Novotný, *Boje dělníků...*, 40 ff.

7. G. Candeloro, *Storia dell' Italia Moderna*, volume 1 (Milan 1958) 246 ff, 322 ff. T.W. Freeman, *Pre-Famine Ireland* (Manchester 1957).

8. R.N. Salaman, *The History and Social Influence of the Potato* (Cambridge 1949).

9. W.F. Adams, *Ireland and Irish Migration to the New World from 1815 to the Famine* (New Haven 1932). K.H. Connell, *The Population of Ireland, 1750-1845* (Oxford 1950), 24 ff.

10. F.X. Coquin, "Faim et migrations en Russie au XIXe siècle," *Revue d'histoire moderne et contemporaine*, 1964, 127-144.

11. A. de Tocqueville, *Werke und Briefe*, ed. Burckhardt (Frankfurt 1956). C. Thienen-Adlerflycht, *Graf Leo Thun im Vormärz* (Graz-Köln 1967) 195 ff. I. Gál, "Széchenyi and the Czechs," *Studia Slavica Hungarica* 1972, 129-145.

12. P.J. Mantoux, *The Industrial Revolution in the Eighteenth Century* (London 1948). T.S. Ashton, *The Industrial Revolution 1760-1830* (London 1948).

13. W. Langer, *Social and Political Upheaval...*, 25 ff.

14. P. Deane, *The First Industrial Revolution* (Cambridge 165).

15. L. Jeníček, J. Krulis, *British Industry of the Industrial Revolution in the Iron and Steel Industry in Czechoslovakia* (Prague 1968) 15. K. Wessely, *Die Stellung Österreichs...*, 130 ff.

16. L. Jeníček, J. Krulíš, *British Industry...*, 10-13. Myska, *Založení a počátky Vítkovických železáren* (Ostrava 1960).

17. Klein FA, SA Opava, Janovice branch. V. Vomácková, "Podnikatelskáfirma bratří Kleinů a její starosti roku 1848," CMM 1952..

18. L. Jeníček, J. Krulíš, *British Industry...*, 50.

19. Beaufort FA, SA Pilsen, Zlutice branch.

20. *Geschichte der Eisenbahnen der österreichisch-ungarischen Monarchie*, volume 1 (Vienna 1897). See also J. Polišenský et al., *Boje delníku...* 42 ff.

21. B. Michel, "La révolution Industrielle dans les pays tchèques au XIXe siècle," *Annales*, 1965-1005.

22. A. Briggs, "The Language of 'Class' in Early 19th Century England," *Essays in Labour History*, A. Briggs and John Saville ed. (London 1960) 43-74.

23. S. Pollard, "Nineteenth Century Cooperation," in the collection cited above, n.

22. M. Dob, *Studies in the Development of Capitalism* (London 1947).
24. J. Polišenský, S. Hart, *Praha a Amsterodam v 17. a 18. století* (Prague 1967).
25. E. Hobsbawm, "En Angleterre: Révolution industrielle et vie matérielle des classes populaires," *Annales*, 1962, 1047-1061.
26. See W.L. Langer, 197 ff.
27. H. Mottek ed., *Studien zur Geschichte der industriellen Revolution in Deutschland* (Berlin 1960) 65-143.
28. J. Kuczynski, *Bürgerliche und halbfeudale Literatur aus den Jahren 1840-1847 zur Lage der Arbeiter* (Berlin 1960). See also Langer, 205 ff.
29. Viktor Andrian, *Oesterreich und dessen Zukunft* (Hamburg 1843). See J. Heidler, *Cechy a Rakousko v politických brožurách předbřeznových* (Prague 1920) 81 ff.
30. *Oesterreich und Russland* (Leipzig 1844). Heidler, 203.
31. Heidler, 53-54.
32. *Germany: Revolution and Counter-Revolution*.
33. *Hof-und Staats-Handbuch des österreichischen Kaiserthumes* (Vienna 1847) volume 1, 3, 185, 363.
34. F. Walter, *Kaiser Franz I.* A. Nowotny, "Staatskanzler Clemens Wenzel Fürst Metternich," *Gestalter der Geschicke Österreichs* Hugo Hantsch ed (Innsbruck 1962). 295-312, and an extensive bibliography 333-342.
35. *Hof-und Staats-Handbuch...* I, I-XII. A. Wandruszka, *Das Haus Habsburg*, 171 ff.
36. Habsburg of Tuscany FA, State Central Archive, Prague.
37. L. Jedlicka, "Erzherzog Carl," *Gestalter...*, 313-322.
38. L. Jedlicka, "Feldmarschall Erzherzog Albrecht," *Gestalter...* 389-396.
39. F. Popelka, "Erzherzog Johann von Österreich," *Gestalter...* 343-358.
40. F. Walter, "Kaiser Franz I.", *Gestalter...* 307. A. Lhotsky, *Österreichische Historiographie* (Vienna 1962) 211 ff.
41. *Hof-und Staats-Handbuch...* I, 287 ff, 593 ff. J. Jedlicka, "Feldmarschall Josef Radetzky," *Gestalter....* 371-378.
42. See J. Polišenský et al., *Boje dělníků...*, 23 ff.
43. *Ibid.* J. Purš, "K problematice průmyslové revoluce...", 26.
44. *Ibid.*, 32 ff.
45. *Handbuch des Königreichs Böhmen für das Jahr 1844* (Prague n.d.).
46. *Dějiny české literatury II, Literatura národního obrození* (Praha 1960) 603 ff.
47. M. Hroch, "The Social Composition of the Czech Patriots in Bohemia, 1827-1848," *The Czech Renascence of the 19th Century* (Toronto 1970) 33-52. "Vlastenci bez národa," *Naše živá i mrtvá minulost* (Prague 1968) 107-135. "Místo českého obrození v procesu formování novodobých evropských národu," *Studie z obecných dějin UK* (Prague 1972) 47-62.
48. S. Pech, *The Czech Revolution...*, 17-18, 291-308.
49. J. Polišenský et al., *Boje Dělníků...*, 37 ff.
50. *Ibid.*, 40 ff. M. Trapl, *Novinář Jan Ohéral* (Ostrava 1969) 12, 42, 98.
51. V. Vomáčková, J. Polišenský, "Stávka železničních dělníků před Prahou 6. VII. 1844," CSCH 1953. This was the first study of the episode. Here the narrative has been

augmented with material from SCA Prague (PG 1841-45, PP 1844, TS fasc. 11439). Municipal Archive, Prague (AMP Protocollum exhibitorum 1844).
52. *Handbuch des Königreichs Böhmen...*, 628-629.
53. J. Polišenský et al., *Boje dělníků...*, 63, 65, 67.
54. *Ibid.*, 77 ff
55. *Ibid.*, 88-89.
56. *Ibid.*, 82
57. *Ibid.*, 87 ff.
58. *Ibid.*, 88.
59. *Ibid.*, 128.
60. M. Hroch, "Vlastenci...," 107-108.
61. *Ibid.*, 121
62. G. Winter, *Očima Západu* (London n.d.) 25 ff.
63. *Ibid.*, 30
64. *Ibid.*, 27-28.
65. C. Kříž, *Ci conosciamo da undici secoli* (Prague 1966) 65 ff. With bibliography on Czech-Italian relations. Marx-Engels, *Sul Risorgimento Italiano*, ed. E. Ragionieri (Editori Riuniti 1959) 7-41.
66. C. Kříž, *Ci conosciamo...*, 70 ff. A. Cronia, *Cechy v dějinách italské kultury*, (Prague 1936) 91-98.
67. C. Kříž, *Ci conosciamo...*, 96 ff.
68. W. Giusti, *Mazzini egli Slavi* (Milan 1940). A. Cronia, *Cechy v dějinách...* 100-101.
69. A. Cronia, *La conoscenza del mondo slavo in Italia* (Padua 1058) 395 ff. See A. Balli, *La Boemia* (Milan 1837).
70. A de Gorowski, *Le panslavisme, son histoire, ses véritables éléments religieux, sociaux, philosophiques et politiques* (Florence 1848). See A. Cronia, *La conoscenza...*, 401 ff.
71. J. Polišenský, *Le "problème tchèque" et la France de 1789 à 1848* (AUC Prague 1966). M. Bignon, *Du Congrès de Troppau* (Paris 1821).
72. A.C. Thibaudeau, *La Bohême. Roman historique* (Paris 1834) E. Quinet, "Stimme eines Ausländers über Böhmen," *Panorama des Universums* (1834). See also *Révue Britannique*, 1837, 1839, 1843. *Univers pittoresque*, 1842. *Révue des Deux Mondes*, I, II, IV (1842-1845). *Magasin pittoresque* 1846-7.
73. J. Polišenský, *Le 'problème tchèque'...*, contains bibliography.
74. C. Dickens, *Střdrý vecer..., zčeštěno od M. Fialky* (Prague 1846). F. Klácel, "Shakespeare, Goethe a Schiller," CCM 1847, 250 ff.
75. M. Sova, "Sir John Bowring and the Slavs," SEER 1943, 128-144.
76. J. Strong, *Cultural Aspects 1831* (London 1831)
77. Jan Jeník Bratřic, *Z mých pamětí...*, 47-48.
78. See J.V. Polišenský, *Britain and Czechoslovakia* (Prague 1968) 50 ff.
79. K. Slavíček, *Tajná politická společnost český Repeal v roce 1848* (Prague 1947). Náprstek's diary is in the Náprstek Museum, Prague.
80. J. Polišenský, *Britain...* 80.

81. Idem, "America and the Beginnings of Modern Czech Political Thought," in *The Czech Renascence...*, 215-223.
82. J.S. Tomíček, "Počátek a vznik severo-amerického soustátí," *Ceskávčela* 1835, 26-35.
83. J. Malý, "Povstání a nynejsí stav svobodného státu Texase," CCM 1842, 62-80. "Texas a Spojené obce Severo-americké," *Ceskávčela* 1844, 82-83. J. Benoni, "O Americe vubec a severoamerických obcích zvlášt'," *Poutník* 1847, 227 ff.
84. H. Rokyta, *Die böhmischen Länder. Handbuch der Denkmäler und Gedenkstätten europäischer Kulturbeziehungen in den böhmischen Ländern* (Salzburg 1970). This is the best survey of German Literature in Bohemia.
85. See E. Schremmer, "Das Schrifttum der Sudetendeutschen," in *Die Deutschen in Böhmen...*, 185. F. Martini, *Deutsche Literaturgeschichte* (Stuttgart 1968).
86. F.L. Loewenheim, "German Literature and the Czech Renascence: Ignaz Kuranda, *Die Grenzboten*, and Development in Bohemia 1845-1849," in *The Czech Renascence...* 146-157.

Chapter III

1. See K. Obermann, "Bemerkungen...," 1327-1342. *Deutschland von 1815...,passim*. "Unveröffentlichte Materialen über die Tätigkeit Metternichs in der Revolution von 1848-1849," *Mitteilungen des Österreichischen Staatsarchive* 1968, 214 ff. Obermann used only part of the inventories for the recatalogued Metternich collection in the State Central Archive, Prague.
2. C. Thienen- Adlerflycht, *Graf Leo Thun im Vormärz* (Graz 1967) 123.
3. H. Kissinger, *A World Restored* (New York 1964).
4. *Ibid.*, 324 ff.
5. For Knoll, see Polišenský, *Obor historie...*, 113-130.
6. *Ibid.*; K. Vietz, *Das Studium der allgemeinen Geschichte*, (Prague 1844) 107 ff.
7. Metternich to Hartig, 7.VII.1843, French, Hartig SA Litoměřice, Zitenice branch.
8. J.M. Thun-Hohenstein's fragmentary papers (SA Pilsen) include personal papers from 1848, correspondence and literary MSS, chiefly translations from Czech into German. L. Kubíkdeník, "Hrabě Leo Thun a jeho český," *Z minulosti Děčínska* 1965 259 ff.
9. F. Deym's papers (SA Zámrsk) contain documents of an economic character, and nothing from 1848. Hartig's papers include a MS *Genesis der Revolution* (1848), *Nachtgedanken* (1851), and other materials for 1848-49, as well as numerous letters from Ficquelmont and Krauss, Rothschild and Metternich (SA Litoměřice, Zitenice branch).
10. Kolowrat's important papers are in the Family Archives of Althan and Khuen-Lützow, SA Brno.
11. Chotek's journal is in SA Prague, Benešov branch.
12. Friedrich Schwarzenberg, *Aus dem Wanderbuch eines verabschiedeten Lanzknechten* (Vienna 1843) Original in Schwarzenberg FA, SA Třeboň. See J.B. Novák, "Ze Zápisku posledního lancknechta," CCH 1925.

Notes

13. Felix Lichnowsky's papers (SA Opava) contain reports of Carlist activity in Spain and France.

14. See the admiring biography by A. Schwarzenberg, *Prince Felix zu Schwarzenberg, Prime Minister of Austria* (New York 1946).

15. F. Palacký, *Popis královstvíčeského* (Prague 1848).

16. See J. Polišenský, F. Snider, "Změny ve složení české šlechty v 16. a 17. století," CSCH 1972, 515-526.

17. See E. Berndorfová, *Sociální základna české šlechty v době posledního stavovského odboje proti Habsburkum 1741-1742* (dissertation Charles Univ. 1972).

18. J. Polišenský, *Obor historie...*, 120 ff.

19. H. Srbik, *Metternich...*, II, 185-189.

20. There are interesting reports of Joinville's plans in Beaufort FA, SA Pilsen.

21. On the situation in the Austrian lands, see E. Violand, *Die soziale Geschichte der Revolution in Österreich* (Leipzig 1850). Srbik, *Metternich...*, II 207 ff. R. Lorenz, "Anton Ritter von Schmerling und Alexander Freiherr von Bach," in *Gestalter...* 407 ff. H. Sturmberger, *Der Weg zum Verfassungsstaat. Die politische Entwicklung in Oberösterreich von 1792 bis 1861* (Vienna 1962) 47 ff.

22. H.v. Srbik, *Metternich...* II, 242, 244.

23. S. Ostrovská, *Rakouská politika v Itálii v předvečer revoluce 1848* (dissertation, Charles Univ. 1960) is still the fullest work on Ficquelmont.

24. Polišenský, *Opavský kongres...*, 11, 106.

25. First mention of Mazzini's Young Italy: register of the Moravian-Silesian Governorship (SA Brno). In the same repository are the papers of Rudolf Lützow, and there is further material in the Dubský FA, SA Opava. See A. Saitta, *Il cammino umano*, volume III (Florence 1970) 138 ff, for a Marxist interpretation. H. Benedikt, *Kaiser-adler...*, wrote from an old-fashioned liberal point of view.

26. *Aus Metternichs nachgelassenen Papieren*, ed. Richard Metternich, 7 volumes (Vienna 1883).

27. Report from E. Clam-Gallas to Windischgrätz, 11. II 1848, German, Windischgrätz FA, SA Pilsen.

28. reproduced in *Aus Metternichs...*, vol. 7, 535-36.

29. *Ibid.*, 532.

30. For the February Revolution, see J. Bruhat, *Les journées de février* (Paris 1948). G. Duveau, *1848: The Making of a Revolution* (New York 1967). J. Tullard, *La préfecture de police sous la Monarchie de Juillet* (Paris 1964) 168 ff. J. Vidalenc, "L' Armée francaise sous la monarchie constitutionelle," *Information hostique* 1949, 57-62.

31. M. Dommanget, *La Révolution de 1848 et le drapeau rouge*, (Paris 1948). P. Loustau, *Louis Blanc à la commission du Luxembourg* (Paris 1908).

32. Supplement to the report of the Police Council, State Central Archive Prague.

33. E. Andics, *Die Habsburger...*, 55.

34. *Aus Metternichs...*, 7, 533. "La Russie considérée pour le rapport réligieux" 12.III.1848, Ficquelmont FA, SA Litoměřice, Děčín branch.

35. "Geheime Mission des Grafen Friedrich Thun in St. Petersburg zur Darlegung der revolutionären Verhältnisse in Österreich, 5-13. IV. 1848." Friedrich Thun Papers,

Thun-Hohenstein FA, SA Litoměřice, Děčín branch (hereafter cited as F. Thun).
36. Ficquelmont to Thun, 21.III.1848, Vienna, reproduced by E. Andics, AVPR 15, 49.
37. Thun to Ficquelmont 5.III.1848, SPb, French, Ibid., D111-1.
38. Nesselrode to Count von Medem, 5.III.1848, SPb, French copy, Staatskanzlei 136, Russland III, f. 109-111a. I thank Noreen Gallagher for a photocopy of this document.
39. Thun to Ficquelmont, 13.IV.1848, SPb, French draft, D 111-2, Fair copy in Staatskanzlei 136, Russland III, f. 141a-147.
40. F. Thun to Ficquelmont, 13.IV.1848, SPb, French draft, D 111-3. Original in Staatskanzlei 136, Russland III, 149-154.
41. Thun to Metternich, 2.V.1848, Stockholm, German draft, D 70-1. Answer from 13.V. 1848, London, Ibid., D.70-2. The diplomatic correspondence among the capitals shows that the machinery continued to function unimpeded.

Chapter IV

1. See A. Schmidl, *Wien und seine nächsten Umgebungen* (Vienna 1847) 162 ff. K. Weiss, *Geschichte der Stadt Wien*, vol. 2 (Vienna 1872) 239 ff. *Hof-und Staats-Handbuch*...I, 577 ff, 593 ff.
2. E.v. Zenker, *Die Wiener Revolution in ihren sozialen Voraussetzungen und Beziehungen*, (Wien 1897) 112 ff. The military side of the conflict is best reported by R. Kiszling, *Die Revolution im Kaisertum Oesterreich* (Vienna 1948) vol. 1, 35 ff.
3. J. Zeyer, *Vojta Náprstek*(Prague 1896). R. Tyršová, *Vojta Náprstek* (Prague n.d.). B. Lifka, "Český revolucionář mezi třemi světadíly," CCM (1964) 83 ff. An adequate biography has not yet appeared. Zeyer wrote a commentary on his selection from Náprstek's journal: *Kostra k denníku Vojty Náprstka*, MS in Náprstek Museum, Prague.
4. *Kostra*..., 65 ff.
5. *Ibid.*, 73, 81-82, 93-94.
6. *Aus Metternichs*..., 7, 833 ff.
7. H.v. Srbik, *Metternich*..., II, 258 ff. See "Notizen über die Ursachen und den Gang der ständischen Bewegung...," Acta Clementina 33, for January and February, Metternich FA, State Central Archive, Prague.
8. Metternich's correspondence with Appónyi, Trautmannsdorf, the Prussian Crown Prince: Acta Clementina 5, 11. Correspondence with William of Württemberg, Ficquelmont, Archduke Johann, Colloredo, Esterházy, Acta Clementina 1, 4-7, contains references to the February revolution.
9. *Aus Metternichs*..., 7, 539.
10. Srbik, *Metternich*,..., II, 280 ff. *Aus Metternichs*..., 7, 533 ff. See P. Müller, *Feldmarschall Fürst Windischgrätz* (Vienna 1934) 66, 88-89.
11. *Letáky z roku 1848*, ed. M. Novotný (Prague 1948) 25, 28 ff. J.J. Toužimský, *Na úsvitě nové doby*..., 108 ff.
12. The latest biography of Windischgrätz, by F. Schuster, *Tachau-Pfrauenberger Heimat* (Weiden 1962), is still full of praise for the "victor over three revolutions."

Notes

Windischgrätz's papers from 1848 (Win.FA, Section III, SA Pilsen, Klatovy branch) contain no mention of the miniature dictatorship in March 1848.

13. "Denkschriften über die Wiener Revolution 1848," Acta/Clementina 33, contains copies of reports and memoranda. H. Meyer, *1848: Studien zur Geschichte der deutschen Revolution* (Darmstadt 1949), contains valuable information about the Viennese radicals.

14. M. Britovšek, *Anton Füster in revoljucija 1848 v Avstrii* (Maribor 1970).

15. H.v. Srbik, *Metternich...*, II, 289-290.

16. See B. Spuler, *Regenten und Regierungen der Welt, Teil II* (Würzburg 1962) 284 ff. *Hof-und Staats-Handbuch* I., 225 ff, for comparison with the situation in 1847.

17. *Valtice* (Brno 1970), 106. Collection "Městeký úřad Valtice" District Archive Břeclav at Mikulov).

18. *Aus Metternichs...*, 8, 6. Srbik, *Metternich...*, II, 292 ff.

19. Metternich's correspondence after his flight from Vienna is in Clementina, 7, 9, 10. Metternich to Ficquelmont, 20.III.1848, Valtice., Clementina 51.

20. Metternich to S. Rothschild, 3..IV.1848, Arnheim, clementina 20, F. 61ff. See C. Corti, *Der Aufstieg des Hauses Rothschild* (Munich 1927).

21. *Letáky...*, 81-87.

22. J.A. v. Helfert, *Mailand und der lombardische Aufstand, März 1848* (Frankfurt 1856), 5 ff. A. Saitta, *Op.cit.h.*, 200 ff.

23. See n. 21.

24. G. Candeloro, *Storia d'Italia moderna*, vol. 3, (Milan 1960) 165ff. H. Kerchnawe, *Radetzky* (Vienna 1944), 62 ff. P. Pieri, *Storia militare del Risorgimento* (Turin 1962) 187 ff.

25. V. Marchesi, *Storia documetata della rivoluzione e della difesa di Venezia negli anni 1848-1849* (Venice 1913). See Saitta, *Op.cit.*, II, 201.

26. Italian documents and the text of Ficquelmont's report of March 18, 1848, in Clementina 33, SCA Prague. F. Hartig also wrote reports about the Austrian régime in Lombardy-Venetia and sent them to Metternich: Clementina 7 f. 10 ff.

27. Report of rudolf Count Lützow, 24.XII.1849, Vienna, French draft, Dubský FA, SA Opava, Janovice branch.

28. A. Schwarzenberg, *Prince Felix...*, 8 ff. See R. Kiszling, "Fürst Felix zu Schwarzenberg," in *Gestalter...*, 359-370. Schwarzenberg's papers (hereafter FS) in S.FA, 548, 547a.

29. FS, *Ibid.*, 547a. The so-called Geheime Korrespondenz with material about his stay in Petersburg and England: FS 36-37 (547a).

30. L. Blanch, *The Wilder Shores of Love* (London 1959) Schwarzenberg FA 547a, FS 37 (letters from England, 1827-29).

31. Diplomatische Mission nach Haag, 2.IX.-27.X.1833, *Ibid.*, 547a, FS 32, correspondence with Wessenberg of October 1833, FS 33.

32. Schwarzenberg's correspondence with F. Thun 1841-44 from Naples is in Thun FA, SA Litoměřice, Děčín branch D 96, 1-15.

33. Papers of Frederick, Charles and Edmund in Schwarzenberg FA Třeboň.

34. Reports of suppression of the uprising in Cremona in Coudenhove FA, 65, SA

227

Pilsen, Klatovy branch. Schwarzenberg FA, FS 25, contains report by L. Reindl of the personal participation of Felix Schwarzenberg.

35. Clementina 33 contains copies of Radetzky's letters to Wellington and Hartig's letters to Radetzky.   36. J.J. Toužimský, 50-52.

37. K. Slavíček, Tajná politická společnost..., 119 ff.

38. Toužimský, 65-66. S. Pech, "The Czech Working Class in 1848,"Canadian Slavonic Papers (1967) 59-74.

39. Boj za právo, Sborník aktů politických u věcech státu a národu českého od roku 1848, J.M. Černý ed., (Prague 1893) 12-17.

40. Zusammenstellungen der Relationen über die am 11. März staatgefundene Versammlung, 12.III.1848. Report by Heyde, SCA Prague, PG 1846-1849, 15c/3 No 1668-1848. See Kazbunda, 362-363. For reports sent from Brno the same day by Lažanský to Kolowrat, Ibid., 375-76.

41. The original reply to the petition is in Kazbunda, 364-365. Rudolf Stadion to Pillersdorf 28.III.1848, Ibid., 366.

42. Czech version of the Prague petition of March 29 is in Prinz, Prag und Wien..., 109-112, 112-114. On Müller, see Janáček, Vyprávění o Staroměstské radnici (Prague 1961) 213 ff.

43. Stadion to Pillersdorf 29,III,1848, Kazbunda, 369; 370-71.

44. Fragment of Stadion to Pillersdorf, 3 IV.1848, Ibid.371.

45. Archduke Ferdinand: Kazbunda 367-368; 372 ff contains several of the leaflets. Ferdinand to Pillersdorf 8.IV.1848, reply to the petition, Prinz, 115-117.

46. M. Trapl, A. Přichystal, České národní obrození na Moravě v době předbřeznové a v revolučních letech 1848-1849 (Olomouc 1970).

47. Protocols of the Gubernium Commission, Kazbunda, 376-382.

48. G. Čechová, J. Martínek, "Národní výbor v roce 1848," Sborník archívních prací (SAP) 1954, 10 ff.

49. L. Namier, 1848: The Revolution of the Intellectuals, (London 1944) 258, 263.

Chapter V

1. F. Schuselka, 97

2. Ficquelmont's papers after 15 March are in cartons 74, 76 in the Clary-Aodringen FA, SA Litoměřice, Děčín, hereafter cited "Ficquelmont."

3. L. Graf Ficquelmont, Aufklärungen über die Zeit vom 20.III bis zum 4. Mai 1848 (Vienna 1859) 4, 12.

4. E. Zöllner, Geschichte Oesterreichs, 350-357. Ficquelmont, Aufklärungen..., 68.

5. J. Droz, Les révolutions allemandes..., 227-235.

6. L. Ficquelmont, Aufklärungen..., 53, 55.

7. Ibid., 59-60.

8. Ibid., 65.

9. Kazbunda, 245 cites the decisions of the General Command at the end of March after the Vienna Feldakten (1848-6-6 1/3).

10. The Czech text of the cabinet memorandum is reprinted in Minulost našeho státu

v dokumentech, A. Míka ed., (Prague 1971) 202.
11. J. Droz, *Les révolutions allemandes*..., 242-251.   12. *Ibid.*, 236-242. J.N. Hawgood, "1848 in Central Europe," *The Slavonic Review* (1948) 314-328.
13. M. Morris, *From Cobbett to the Chartists* (London 1948) 194-198. F.C. Mather, "Chartism"Hist. Assoc. London (1965)
14. L. Ficquelmont, *Aufklärungen*..., 105-111.
15. *Ibid.*, 113-118.
16. *Ibid.*, 74-76, 88, 99. E. Zöllner, *Geschichte Österreichs*, 357.
17. For the end of Ficquelmnot's Government, see F. Schuselka, *Op.cit.*, and W. Langer, 355. P. Burian, *Die Nationalitäten in "Cisleithanien" und das Wahlrecht der Märzrevolution, 1848-1849* (Graz 1967) 219 ff.
18. J. Blum, *Noble Landowners*..., 232 ff. V. Klimeš, *Česká vesnice v roce 1848*(Most 1949). J. Kočí, "Příspěvek k rolnickéotázce v Cechách v roce 1848," CSCH 1957, 59-85. *Petice venkovského lidu z Cech k Národnímu výboru z roku 1848* (Prague 1954, F. Roubík ed.). *Petice moravského lidu ke sněmu roku 1848*, ed. J. Radimský, M. Wurmová (Brno 1955).
19. *Die Geschichte Ungarns*, ed. E. Pamlényi (Budapest 1971) 299 ff for recent bibliography.
20. Z.I. Tóth, "The Nationality Problem in Hungary in 1848-1849" (Budapest, *Acta Historica* 1955) 235-277. G.E. Ruthenburg, "Jellačič, the Croatian Military Border and the Intervention against Hungary in 1848," *Austrian History Yearbook* 1965, 45-67.
21. D. Stranjakovič, "La collaboration des Croates et des Serbes en 1848-1849," *Le monde slave* (1935) 394-404. L. Makkai, *Histoire de Transylvanie* (Paris 1946) 310 ff. V. Cherestesiu, "Die internationale Bedeutung der Revolution im Jahre 1848," *XIIe Congrès International des Sciences Historiques, Rapports I, Grands thèmes* (Vienna 1965) 257 ff.
22. V. Záček, "České a jihoslovanské Slovanské lípy v roce 1848," *Literární archiv PNP* (1971) 195-239. F. Prinz, 20-24.
23. K. Kazbunda, 120-123. S. Pech, *The Czech Revolution*..., 309-318. *Stručnédějiny University Karlovy* (Prague 1964) 179-190.
24. Archbishop M.J. Sommerau-Beeck to the Ministry of the Interior, after 30.IV.1848, Kroměříž, German draft, SA Opava, Olomouc branch, AO, Volná akta 1848.
25. F. Jílek, *Pražská polytechnika*..., 268-366.
26. F. Svátek, *Svatováclavský výbor a dělnická otázka v Praze na jaře 1848* (dissertation Charles University 1959). K. Novotný, "První český časopis pro dělnictvo: Kampelíkův "Hlásník z r. 1848," *Novinářský sborník* (1965) 174 ff.
27. S. Pech, 294.
28. *Ibid.*, 295 ff.
29. K. Griewank, "Ursachen und Folgen des Scheiterns der deutschen Revolution von 1848," *Historische Zeitschrift* (1950) 495-523. Evidence of interest in events in Frankfurt is in the collection Gub.Pres. 1782-1850, B 13/1a, SA Brno.
30. A. Fischer, "Deutschland ohne Österreich? Österreich ohne Deutschland?" (Olomouc, after 2.IV.1848)

31. An address of Bohemian Germans to the Ministry of the Interior, 9.IV.1848, Vienna. Aldringen FA, SA Litoměřice Děčín branch. F. Prinz, 27 ff. E.K. Sicher, *Ludwig von Löhner* (Munich 1965).
32. F. Prinz, 27-28.
33. F. Palacký, "Eine Stimme über Österreichs Anschluss an Deutschland. An den Fünfziger Ausschuss z. H. dem Herrn Präs. Soiron in Frankfurt am Main," (Prague 1848), printed copy in Clary-Aldringen FA. See V.V. Tomek, Paměti..., I, 267.
34. F. Schuselka, 106-110.
35. F. Prinz, 33. *Pražské noviny*, 17.V.1846, 12.III.1848. *Národní noviny* 19.III.1848.
36. F. Prinz, 34-35.
37. *Der Volksfreund*, 22.IV.1848. Beilage: Die Adresse der Deutschen Böhmens, Mährens und Schlesiens, 9.IV.1848. "An die Deutschen in Böhmen," leaflet 18.IV.1848. Clary-Aldringen FA, Angelegenheiten des Deutsch-Böhm. Vereins in Wien, SA Litoměřice, Děčín.
38. Löhner to Edmund Clary-Aldringen, 20.IV.1848, Ger. original, Clary-Aldringen FA.
39. E. Clary-Aldringen, German draft for speech to *Deutsch-Böhm. Verein*, Clary Aldringen FA.
40. E. Clary-Aldringen to J.A. Schwarzenberg (n.d.) in P. Molish, *Briefe zur deutschen Politik in Österreich von 1848 bis 1918* (Vienna 1934) 1-2.
41. Löhner to Clary-Aldringen (n.d.) Vienna, Ger. orig., Clary-Aldringen FA.
42. Minutes of Ministerial Council meeting of 26.IV on Frankfurt elections in Prinz, 30-37. See also A. Springer, *Geschichte Oesterreichs seit dem Wiener Frieden II. Theil* (Leipzig 1865) 270. Prinz, 38-39. *Von dem Vereine...*, German pamphlet, Clary-Aldringen FA.
43. Latour's correspondence with Windischgrätz is in Windischgrätz FA, SA Pilsen, Klatovy branch, Section III, 13, carton 323. Kazbunda, 168-78.
44. *Ibid.*, 135 ff, 210-213. Prinz, 40-42.
45. "Vom Vereine der Deutschen aus Böhmen, Mähren, Schlesien zur Auferhaltung ihrer Nationalität. Liebe Landsleute!" pamphlet in Clary-Aldringen FA.
46. "Landsleute und Brüder!" (18.IV.1848). "Wahl-Manifest der Deutschen aus Böhmen..." pamphlet, Clary-Aldringen FA.
47. "Freunde und Landsleute!" 4.IV.1848, pamphlet.. Reply to article of 18.VI.1848, untitled pamphlet, n.d. "Programm zu der auf dem 19. Juni dJ. anberufenen Versammlung böhmischer und sächsischer Grenznachbarn auf dem Grossen Winterberge...," 11.VI.1848, Königstein, pamphlet, Clary-Aldringen FA, as well as two further pamphlets: "Deutsche Brüder aus Böhmen!" (VII1848, Dresden). and "Deutsche Brüder aus Österreich!" (VII.1848, Dresden).
48. F. Jílek, *Pražská polytechnika...*, 319-320. J. Koci, *Emanuel Arnold*, 36 ff.
49. J. Palacký, "Intimní vzpomínky na Fr. Palackého," *Pamatník na oslavu stých narozenin Frant. Palackého* (Prague 1898) 129.

Chapter VI

1. F. v. Biedenfeld, *Feldzug der Oesterreicher in Italien* (Weimar 1849) 120-121, 136

ff. P. Pieri, *Storia militare del Risorgimento*. . ., chapters 7 and 8.
2. D. Demarco, *Il crollo del Regno delle Due Sicilie* (Naples 1960) 152 ff. G. Paladino, "Il governo napoletano e la guerra del 1848," *Nuova rivista storica* (1919) 565-600.
3. H. Kerchnawe, *Radetzky*. . ., 70-72.
4. V. Bariberi, "I tentativi di mediazione anglo-francesi durante la guerra del 1848," *Rassegna storica del Risorgimento* (1955) 206-217. R. Kiszling, *Fürst Felix zu Schwarzenberg* (Graz 1952) 34 ff.
5. H. Kerchnawe, *Radetzky*. . ., 7, 102.
6. *Ibid.*, 70-82.
7. K. Kreibich, "Němci a česká revoluce r. 1848," *Nová mysl* (1948) 497-512. Windischgrätz FA, Section XIIId, Von der Italienischen Armee, carton 323, SA Pilsen, Klatovy branch (hereafter Windischgrätz FA)
8. Count L. Thun to J. Lobkowitz, 13. V. 1848, Prague, notice of appointment, German original, Lobkowitz FA, SA Litoměřice, Zitenice branch, (hereafter Lobkowitz FA)
9. Entwurf zu einem Dienst- und Abrichtungs-Reglement für die Nationalgarde, Lobkowitz FA Ia 17.
10. Windischgrätz to Lobkowitz, 2.VII.1848, Prague, German original Lobkowitz FA Id 15.
11. "Ceským bratrum!" pamphlet V.1848, printed in Kazbunda, 382. J. Křížek, *Národní gardy*. . ., 89-95.
12. *Ibid.*, 253-260.
13. K. Obermann, *Flugblätter der Revolution* (Berlin 1970)) 256-259.
14. B. Bretholz, *Geschichte Böhmens und Mährens*, volume 4, (Reichenberg 1925) 993 ff.
15. "Hlavní dásady pro návrh ústavy království českého," in *Minulost našeho statu*. . ., 211-214.
16. A.J. Becher, "Offener Brief des "Radikalen" an den Ausschuss der Bürger. . ., 5.VI.1848, Vienna, in K. Obermann, *Flugblätter*. . ., 293-295. "Programm des Zentral-Wahl-Komitees für den bevorstehenden konstituierenden Reichstag," VI.1848, Vienna, *Ibid.*, 296. "An die Arbeiter!" 11.VI.1848, Vienna, *Ibid.*, 297. "Wie wird die Majestät des Volkes," n.d., *Ibid.*, 298-300.
17. Prinz, 46-48.
18. Report by Thun to Pillersdorf, 24.V.1848, Prague, German draft, printed in Prinz, 48-49.
19. "Das Gründungsprotokoll der Prager provisorischen Regierung. . .," 28.V.1848, Prague, in Kazbunda, 387.
20. L. Thun to the Emperor, 29.V.1848, Prague, in Prinz, 50. "Entwurf einer provisorischen Regierungsvollmacht für Grafen Thun," 29.V.1848, Prague, Prinz, 50-51. See also Kazburída, 214-218, 234-235.
21. Pillersdorf to Thun, 1.VI.1848, Vienna, German draft, Prinz, 58-61, 125-127.
22. Pillersdorf to Thun, 4.VI.1848, Vienna, German draft, see Prinz, 52-55.
23. Thun to Pillersdorf, 6.VI.1848, Prague draft from Thun Hohenstein FA.

Pillersdorf to Thun 7.VI.1848, German copy.
24. Wessenberg and Doblhoff to the Emperor 9.VI.1848, Innsbruck, in Kazbunda, 388-390, and Prinz, 62. Protocol of Ministerial Council 14.VI.1848, Vienna, see Prinz, 69-70.
25. V.Cejchan, "Ke vzniku myšlenky slovanského sjezdu r. 1848,"*Slovanský přehled*(1928) 401 ff. *Slovanský sjezd v Praze roku 1848*, ed. V. Záček and Z.Tobolka (Prague 1958).
26. S.Pech, 127.
27. V. Záček. *Cechové a Poláci roku 1848* (Prague 1947-48) Pech, 135 ff.
28. Pech, 131.
29. *Slovanský sjezd.* . ., 365-368, 370-375.
30. "Manifesto of the Slavonic Congress to the European Nations," in *Minulost našeho státu*. . ., 215-219. See *Slovanský sjezd*. . ., 358-361.

Chapter VII

1. J. Sekavec, *Dvanáctý červen* in Novotný, *Letáky*. . ., 249 ff, with biographical information about the author.
2. *Národní noviny*, 24.VI.1848, see Křížek, 98-99.
3. Kazbunda, 245 ff.
4. Tyršová, *Vojta Náprstek*. . ., 1-2. Kazbunda, 248. Toužimský, 549.
5. F. Jílek, *Pražská polytechnika*. . ., 273-275.
6. Ernst, *Die Prager Juni-Ereignisse*. . ., 75 ff.
7. Jíek, 319.
8. *Die Prager Ereignisse*. . ., 8.
9. Kazbunda, 249.
10. *Letáky*. . ., 259, 261-269.
11. F. Jílek, *Pražská polytechnika*, 323-344.
12. Chapter 4, n.3.
13. *Kostra k denníku*. . ., 95-96.
14. *Ibid.*, 101.
15. *Ibid.*, 102.
16. My thanks to the archivists in the Prague Municipal Archive, who procured for me nearly all the Catholic parish registers for 1848. The Protestant parish registers are not in the archive.
17. Toužimský's narrative is essentially correct, see 549 ff.
18. Register of Our Lady of the Snows II, Prague Municipal Archive (hereafter PMA) Z 3, 12.VI.1848.
19. Registers: St. Apolinář, Z 11. St. Gall, Z 8, Týn Z 8, Brothers of Mercy Z 3, St. Peter in Poříčí Z 9, Our Lady of Victory Z 0, St. Thomas Z 4, Holy Trinity in Spálená, Z 3.
20. Register St. Thomas in Lesser Town, Z 4 12.VI.1848.
21. The dead of June 13 are recorded in registers of St. Apolinář, St. Gall and St. Henry.

22. The five dead for 14 June are in register of St. Apolinář.
23. Two of the dead were victims of the bombardment, recorded in St. Francis and Brothers of Mercy. Radtner fell in Střelecký Island, recorded in Our Lady of Victory, F. Adamovský recorded in St. Thomas.
24. On June 16 the following were brought to hospital and died in the next days: Josef Beránek, Josef Fejtek, Josef Tobias. Registers of St. Apolinář and the Brothers of Mercy PMA.
25. Registers- St. Apolinář, St. Henry, St. Thomas. See "Die Opfer der Prager Pfingsten," *Vierteljahrschrift für praktische Heilkunde* (1848) 144-145. *Bohemia*, 1.X.1848.
26. V.V. Tomek, *Paměti z mého života*, volume 1 (Prague 1904) 294 ff.
27. "Die Opfer der Prager Pfingsten. . .," 145. Only 41 dead (38 men, 3 women) are listed in the parish registers. It is surprising that no dead are recorded in the registers of parishes in Smíchov, in Holy Trinity Podskálí, Vyšehrad, or Karlín-Olšany.
28. The results of this analysis do not confirm the conclusions of the most recent study, by S. Pech, 148-149, 320-321, who relied on published material.
29. See A. Bajerová, *Svatodušníbouře v Praze r. 1848 ve světle soudního šetřování* (Pilsen 1920) 74-75. Olšany Cemetery, monument "Den braven in den Junitagen gefallenen Soldaten."
30. G. Rudé, *The Crowd in History*, 109-178.
31. Nicholas to Windischgrätz, 15.VI.1848, French original, Windischgrätz FA, carton 323 III/13 no. 55b.
32. Ministerial Council 13.VI; see Kazbunda 390-393; Prinz, 68-69. For the outcome of the meetings, Kazbunda 393-396, 397.
33. Ministerial Council 16.VI.1848. See Prinz, 70-71.
34. Windischgrätz to the Emperor (?), 17.VI.1848, Prague-Hradčany, printed in Kazbunda, 404-410.
35. See Kazbunda, 411-413; Prinz, 72-74; K. Sieber, 81 ff; Schuselka, 185-186.
36. Ministerial Council, 17.-18.VI.1848, see Prinz, 127-128; L. Thun to the Minister of the Interior between 19 and 26. VI.1848, Prague, *Ibid.*, 132-133; Same to same, 20.VI.1848 Prague, *Ibid.*, 135; Minister of the Interior to Thun, 21.VI.1848, Vienna, *Ibid.*, 75. Pillersdorf to Thun, 21.VI.1848, *Ibid.*, 65. Thun to Ministerial Council, 21.VI., *Ibid.*, 77. Report of the Committee of Safety to the Ministerial Council, *Ibid.*, 78-79, 128-130, with a draft of Pillersdorf's reply.
37. Kazbunda, 398-404, for the unpublished portions of the commissioners' reports of their mission to Prague.
38. Thun to Pillersdorf, 25.VI.1848, Kazbunda 414-416. Pillersdorf to Thun, 26.VI.1848, *Ibid.*, 416. See also Prinz, 134-135, 138, 139-140. Thun's report of the Prague events are in Prinz, 140-151.
39. Thun to Lobkowitz, 19.VI.1848, Lobkowitz FA, I d 16-19. Chaloupecký, "Hrabě Josef Matyáš Thun. . .," 84 ff. Report by Komers to Latour, 4.VII.1848, Kazbunda 418-420.
40. *Prager Zeitung* 19.VII.1848. *The Times* 22.III.1848. My thanks to Aloys Skoumal for photocopies. D. Svoboda, Z. Svoboda, "Neznámý židovský deník z roku 1848," *Sborník národního muzea v Praze* (1966) 281-311. See also *The Times*, 27. III.1848.

233

41. *The Times,* 12.V, 20.V., 28.V.1848.
42. *The Times,* 27.V., 30.V.1848.
43. *The Times,* after 14.VI.1848.
44. *The Times,* 21.VI.1848. Bohemia, 23., 24.VI.1848.
45. A Rothstein, "Británie a Ceskoslovensko...," 540-544. F. Loewenheim, "German Liberalism and the Czech Renascence," in *The Czech Renascence.* . ., 165 ff.
46. *Neue Rheinische Zeitung,* 17.VI.1848. I.I. Udalcov, *Z dějin národních a politických boju v Cechách roku 1848* (Prague 1954) 166-168.

Chapter VIII

1. *Kostra denníku.* . ., 106-107.
2. *Ibid.,* 118-121. V.V. Tomek, *Paměti.* . ., I, 302 ff.
3. *Kostra denníku.* . ., 122-128.
4. Toužimský, 669 ff. J. Kočí, *Emmanuel Arnold,* 43 ff. L. Dvořák, *Josef Perwolf* (Prague 1972) 8-11.
5. Metternich to Wessenberg, 3-18.VIII.1848, Clementina 10, f. 4 ff.
6. R. Lorenz, "Anton Ritter v. Schmerling und Alexander Freiherr v. Bach. . .," *Gestalter.* . ., 407-430.
7. O. Meister, "Ernst von Schwarzer, ein mährischer Achtundvierziger, Minister und Journalist," *Zeitschrift des Deutschen Vereines für die Geschichte Mährens und Schlesiens* (ZDVGMS), 1937.
8. My thanks to Dr. R. Neck for materials from the Austrian State Archive, Vienna, collection "Oesterreichischer Reichstag 1848-1849" (XVI/3, 35/11, 35/13, 35/14). See *Verhandlungen des österreichischen Reichstages nach der stenographischen Aufnahme* (Vienna 1848-49), hereafter *Verhandlungen,* and A. Springer, *Geschichte Oesterreichs.* . ., II, 400 ff.
9. R. Till, *"Innenminister Franz Graf Stadion,"* Gestalter. . ., 379-387.
10. See *Minulost našeho statu.* . ., 226-228.
11. *Ibid.,* 220-225.
12. F. Jílek, *Pražská polytechnika.* . ., 345-347, 349-350.
13. J. Toužimský, 713-714.
14. P. Pieri, *Storia militare.* . ., 258 ff. A. Saitta, *Il cammino umano,* volume III, 211 ff.
15. V. Balbieri, *I tentativi di mediazione.* . ., 683 ff. A.J.P. Taylor, *The Italian Problem in European Diplomacy, 1847-1849* (Manchester 1934) 120 ff.
16. E. Valsecchi, *"Le classi popolari e il Risorgimento,"* Cultura e scuola (1965), 82-93. A. Soboul, "Risorgimento et révolution bourgeoise," *La Pensée* (1961), 63-73. Saitta, 213-214.
17. The "Great-Austrian" viewpoint is expressed in Jedlicka's study of Radetzky in *Gestalter.* . ., 371-77, 389-395. See also Kiszling on Swarzenberg in the same collection, 349-370.
18. Toužimský, 762-763. His suspicion is confirmed by documents in Windischgrätz FA, carton 323, III, 13.

19. Eduard Clam-Gallas to Windischgrätz the younger, 20.II.1866, Prague, German original, Windischgrätz FA, 323, III, 13 d, 8-18.
20. M. von Angeli, *Eduard Graf Clam-Gallas. Ein...Lebensbild* (typewritten biography) Clam-Gallas FA, SA Litoměřice, Děčín branch, VII/6, no. 1. 181. See also no. 180 Feldzüge 1844-1866, VII/5-6. 184 Militaria VII/9.
21. J. Lobkowitz, "Notizen über meine Dienstleistung als General-Adjutant bei Seiner Majestät dem Kaiser Ferdinand im Jahre 1848," German original, Lobkowitz FA I b 1, f. 1-13. Lobkowitz's appointment carried the date 14.IX.1848: *Ibid.*, German original, I b 1, 9-10.
22. V. Vomáčková, "K národnestní otázce v buržoasní revoluci 1848 v českých zemích,"CSCH IX (1962), 1-16. "Oesterreich und der deutsch Zollverein," *Historica* (1963) V. Pstová-Vomáčková, *Připojení Rakouska k německému celnímu spolku v roce 1848* (Prague 1970). *Stenografischer Bericht über die Verhandlungen der am 28 August 1848 in Teplitz im Namen deutscher Städte, Gemeinden und konstitutioneller Vereine Böhmens zusammengekommen Vertrauensmänner* (Teplitz 1848), 62 pp.
23. *Gedenkbuch der Stadtvertretern vom Jahre 1848 über wichtige Sachen*, District Archive, Teplice 1250 Hb 59. *Jahrbücher der Stadt Töplitz*, VIII. BD., 434 ff. E. John, *Licht und Schatten*, (Teplitz 1864). *Idem, Zeiterignisse...*, Teplice District Archive. Clary-Aldringen's journal in Clary-Aldringen FA, SA Litoměřice, Děčín branch. My thanks to Přemysl Peer for these materials.
24. For Clary-Aldringen's relations with Löhner and the Viennese *Verein*, see n. 23. P. Molisch, *Briefe...*, 1-2.
25. *Stenographischer Bericht...*, 2-9. Clary's diary for 28.VIII.1848.
26. *Stenographischer Bericht...*, 10-21, Clary's diary 29.VIII. on the congress's second meeting.
27. *Stenographischer Bericht...*, 21-26. Clary, 29.VIII.
28. *Stenographischer Bericht...*, 27-38. Clary, 30.VIII.
29. *Stenographischer Bericht...*, 30.VIII, 38-45. Strache's speech, 44-45.
30. *Stenographischer Bericht...*, 31.VIII, 46-57. Clary, 31.VIII.
31. *Stenographischer Bericht...*, 57 ff. Clary 31.VIII.
32. *Ibid.*
33. Clary-Aldringen to *Prager Zeitung*, 6.IX.1848. *Jahrbücher der Stadt Töplitz*, VIII.
34. "Wiedergabe aus einem Gedenkbuch des J. 1848," in *Gedenkbuch...*, Teplice District Archive 1250 Hb 59.
35. Descriptions of the Eger congress in Bohemia, *Prager Zeitung* and *Národní noviny*, 2.XII.1848.

Chapter IX

1. *Kostra denníku...*, 128-130.
2. F. Jílek, *Pražská polytechnika...*, 349-358.
3. "Ctenář um našim,"*Pražský večerni list* 30.IX.1848.
G. Freytag, "Eine Predigt auf der Ferdinandbrücke," *Gessamelte Werke* 7 (Leipzig

n.d.) 111 ff, 130 ff.
4. "Pensées et Maximes," Clementina 25.
5. "Projekt zu einem Programm für die Versammlung des 17. Sept. 1848," German draft. Eröffnung der Grossgrundbesitzer-Versammlung am 17. Sept. 1848. Clary-Aldringen FA.
6. "Von der Versammlung. . .," 12.XI.1848.
7. Protocols of the meetings 6.I. and 13.I.1849, Ibid., in the collection entitled "Gutsbesitzer-Verein 1848. Nicht zu Stande gekommen."
8. Verhandlungen. . ., II, 48. S. Pech 176.
9. A. Springer, Geschichte Österreichs. . ., II, 426, J. Koči, "Příspěvek k rolnické otázce. . .," 250-251. Verhandlungen, II., 163-164.
10. Verhandlungen. . ., II, 212. S. Pech, 179-180.
11. J. Sidak, "Poslanstvo hrvatskog sabora avstrijskom parlamentu g. 1848," Rad na Filozofskog fakulteta u Zagrebu Odsjek za povijest, (1960) 1-33.
12. A. Springer, Geschichte Österreichs. . ., II, 407 ff.
13. Verhandlungen. . ., II., 472.
14. S. Pech, 185-186. See Springer's commentary in Constitutionelles Blatt f. Böhmen (hereafter CBB), supplements to no. 72, 22.IX.1848.
15. Die Geschichte Ungarns. . ., 314.
16. Ibid., see also W.L. Langer, 474.
17. J.-Rath, The Viennese Revolution of 1848. . ., 323 ff.
18. Rapport an den Gen. Adj. Lobkowitz, 6. Oktober 1848, 10 3/4 Morgen, Wien, German original, Lobkowitz FA I b 1, f 17-18.
19. Baron Horwat, "Aufzeichnungen über das Auftreten das Fürsten Felix Schwarzenberg während der Oktobertagen 1848 in Wien," (written in Prague in June 1852), Ibid. FS 38.
20. "K národ um mých dědičných zemí německých a slovanských." 8.X.1848 Czech-German printed text, Herzogenburg.
21. Josef Lobkowitz to Alfred II. Windischgrätz, 20.XII.1870 German draft, Lobkowitz FA b 1, F. 21-24.
22. "Oznámení mor.-slez. místodržitelství," 15.X.1848, Czech-German poster: "Oznámení, jak Jeho Milost Císař Pán v brněnském kraji přivítán byl."
23. Kaiser Ferdinand an die Häusler in Mähren, 12.X.1848, German original, Lobkowitz FA, I b 1, F. 25.
24. "Oznámení. . .," see n. 22.
25. A. Springer, Geschichte Österreichs. . ., I., 560. Pech, 193. Both criticize the flight of the Czech delegates.
26. J. Heidler, Příspěvky k listáři Dra. Frant. Riegra I, (Prague 1924) 46.
27. M. Trapl, "Olomouc v revolučním roce 1848," Sborník krajského vlastivědného muzea v Olomouci, IV (1956-1958) 69-101. Das hundert-jährige Entstehungs-Jubiläum der kg. Hauptstadt und Reichsgrenzfestung Olmütz (Olomouc 1958).
28. Felix Schwarzenberg to Windischgrätz, 20.X.1848, Olomouc German original, Windischgrätz FA, F.M. III/1, 1, carton 315, f. 1-2. Ibid., Feldzug gegen die insurgierte Residenz und die aus Ungarn erschienene Rebellen-Armee, 320, III/7 (VI).

Notes

29. "Völker Oesterreichs!" 7.X.1848 Vienna, printed in K. Obermann, *Flugblätter*..., 321. Krauss to Messenhauser, 12.X.1848., in Brügel, *Geschichte der österr. Sozialdemokratie* 63 ff. E. Priesterová, *Stručné dějiny Rakouska*, 422 ff.

30. M. von Ehnl, *Wenzel Cäsar Messenhauser. Nationalgarde-Oberkommandant von Wien 1848* (Vienna 1948)). See also W. Ethen's sketch of Messenhauser in *Ročenka muzea v Prostějově (1929)*.

31. "Höchst wichtig! Mitbürger!" *14.X.1848, Vienna, in Flugblätter*..., 324.§ "Bekantmachung," 14.X.1848, *Ibid.*, 325-6.

32. L. Brügel, *Geschichte*..., supplement, 17. S. Schmidt, *Robert Blum. Vom Leipziger Liberalen zum Märtyr der deutschen Demokratie*, (Weimar 1971).

33. "An die Bewohner von Wien," 23.-26. X.1848, in *Flugblätter*, 316, 327-331. L. Brügel, *Geschichte*..., supplement, 63.

34. Telegraphische Depeschen, Lobkowitz FA I b 1 (7), f. 31-41.

35. "Kundmachung. Vom Gemeinderat der Stadt Wein," 4.XI.1848, in *Flugblätter*..., 332.

36. For Blum's execution see Brügel, 23, where he also discusses the executions of Messenhauser and Jellinek.

37. Schwarzenberg to Windischgrätz, 20.X.1848, Olmütz, German original, Windischgrätz FA, F.M. III/1, (Schwarzenberg's correspondence F. 1-154)) In Section III/2 are letters from General Grünne and Franz Josef. Correspondence with Tsar Nicholas I., Section XIII b, carton 323. See also von Rochow's report from Petersburg and A. Scharf, *Die europäischen Grossmächte und die deutsche Revolution* (Leipzig 1942).

38. S. Pech, 195 ff.

39. *Ibid.*, 197, after the minutes of the meeting of 12.X.1848 in LA PNP.

40. Minutes of 13.X.1848. See Pech, 197.

41. *Národní noviny*, 14.XI.1848. Pech, 202.

42. J. Belda *Liberec v revolučním roce 1848* (Liberec 1959)

43. B. Šindelář, "O úloze lidových mas v revolučním dění roku 1848 na Moravě a ve Slezku," CSCH (1956) 389 ff.

44. K. Obermann, *Flugblätter*, 391 ff.

Chapter X

1. Grünne to Lobkowitz, 20.XI.1848, German original, Lobkowitz FA I b 1 (2), 43.

2. B. Bretholz, *Geschitchte Böhmens und Mährens*..., IV. Bd. 113. Pefinka's papers, District Archive Kroměříž, Holešov depository.

3. Archbishop Sommerau-Beeck's papers, SA Opava, Olomouc branch, VA 479-488. See also Kroměříž Municipal Archive 76 Protocol, 74, 68. O. Odložilík, *Na kroměřížském sněmu 1848 a 1849* (Prague 1947). J. Spáčil, *Veškerá moc ve státě vychází z lidu*..., (Kroměříž 1948).

4. B. Bretholz, *Geschichte Böhmens und Mährens*, 113.

5. Peřinka papers, Kroměříž District Archive.

6. *Verhandlungen des österr. Reichstages*..., II. 5 ff.

237

7. Entsagungsworte des Kaisers Ferdinand, 2.XII.1848 Olomouc German text, Lobkowitz FA, I b 1 (10), 49 (939).
8. Pech, 211.
9. F. Schwarzenberg to Grünne, 2.XII.1848, Olomouc, German copy, Lobkowitz FA I b 1 (11), 52.
10. Radetzky to the Emperor, 30.XII.1848, German copy, Schwarzenberg FA, 547 a, FS 1-3, 5. F. Schwarzenberg to Radetzky, 21.XII.1848, *Ibid.* Hess to Schwarzenberg 27.II.1849, Milan, German original, *Ibid.* FS 6.
11. F. Schwarzenberg to his brother Cardinal Schwarzenberg 6.I.1849, Olomouc, German original, *Ibid.* 547a, FS 4. See R. Till, "Kardinal Josef Othmar Rauscher," *Gestalter...*, 397-406. Bretholz, 114 ff.
12. *Die Protokolle des Verfassungsausschusses im österreichischen Reichstage 1848-1849*, A. Springer ed., (Leipzig 1865), 4 ff.
13. *Die Protokolle des Verfassungauschusses über die Grundrechte*, A. Fischel ed. (Vienna 1912) 181 ff.
14. *Verhandlungen...*, IV., 267 ff, 354 ff.
15. *Entwurf der Constitution-Urkunde* (Kremsier 1849), 32 pp. See *Minulost našeho státu...*, 231-247.
16. B. Bretholz, *Geschichte Böhmens und Mährens...*, 118 ff. S. Pech, 320 ff.
17. Rechberg to F. Schwarzenberg, 24.III.1849, Novara, German original, Schwarzenberg FA 547a, FS 8. *Die Geschichte Ungarns*, 327.
18. Windischgrätz to General Lobkowitz, 2.I.1849, Trnava, German original, Lobkowitz FA, I a 15, N.6 (Präsidialbefehle an alle Generäle der 3. Armee). Report by J. Lobkowitz from Petersburg, 7.V.1849, French original, Lobkowitz FA I c 1, f. 28v-29 (Mission nach St. Petersburg, 30.IV-18.V.1849).
19. A. Bach to Schwarzenberg, 10.V.1849. Vienna, German original, Schwarzenberg FA, 547a, FS 99.
20. F. Schwarzenberg to A. Bach, 2.II.1850, *Ibid.* 547 a, FS 11 (also "Memorandum eines echten Russen über die Zukunft unserer slawischen Stämme" is attached.)
21. Archduke Albrecht to Schwarzenberg, 19.IX.1850, Prague German original, *Ibid.* 547a, FS 13.
22. F. Schwarzenberg to A. Bach, 24.XII.1850, Dresden, German original, *Ibid.* 547a FS 17.
23. Documents concerning the death of F. Schwarzenberg and his burial at Třeboň, *Ibid.* 547a, FS 23-27.
24. Necrology from Austrian and German newspapers, after 2.IV.1852, *Ibid.*, PS 24. O. Halferstorfer, "Rede zu Trauerfeier in der Pfarrkirche am Hof in Wien" (Vienna 1852), *Ibid.*, FS 23.
25. Anton v. Prokesch-Osten to the Archivist A. Berg, 11.VI.1852, Berlin, German original, *Ibid.* FS 20.
26. A.F. Berger, *Felix Fürst zu Schwarzenberg. Ein Biographisches Denkmal* (Leipzig 1853). F. Stökl, *Ahnensaal der Fürsten zu Schwarzenberg* (Vienna 1853). See A. Schwarzenberg, *Prince Felix zu Schwarzenberg...*, (New York 1946). R. Kiszling, *Fürst Felix zu Schwarzenberg* (Graz 1952) F. Engel-Janosi, "Ein Kampf um Österreich

in Berlin und Frankfurt, 1849-1855." *Geschichte auf dem Ballhausplatz* (Graz 1963) 65-102.
27. O. Odložilík, *Na kroměřížském sněmu*. . ., 40.
28. *Die Geschichte Ungarns*, 341, 349.
29. A. Bauer, *Ist das Kaisertum Oesterreich bloss ein Länder-Complex, oder ein Staatsbild, oder ein Bundesstaat, oder eine mittelbare Monarchie?* (Vienna 1848). A. Ruge, *Die Gründung der Demokratie in Deutschland, oder: der Volksstaat und der socialdemokratische Freistaat* (Leipzig 1849).
30. *Zwei brennende Fragen in Oesterreich* (Vienna 1852).
31. Leo Graf Thun, *Betrachtungen über Zeitverhältnisse, insbesondere im Hinblick auf Böhmen (Prague 1849)*, 9.
32. A. Springer, *Oesterreich nach der Revolution*. . ., 65.
33. Idem, *Geschichte des Revolutionszeitalters*. . ., 721.
34. K.L. Graf Ficquelmont, *Lord Palmerston, England und der Continent* (Vienna 1852), 2 volumes, 270-271.
35. A. Springer, *Oesterreich, Preussen und Deutschland. Mit einem Sendschreiben an den Grafen L. Ficquelmont* (Leipzig 1851), 5, 13, 78. See H. Abeken, *Die Republik in Nord-Amerika und der Plan einer demokratisch-republikanischen Verfassung in Deutschland*, (Berlin 1848).
36. F.A. Mignet, *Historie revoluce francouzské od 1789-1814* translation by J.B. Malý, volume II (Prague 1850) 369.
37. A. Springer, *Geschichte des Revolutionszeitalters*. . ., 721.
38. Idem, *Oesterreich nach der Revolution*, 100.
39. Idem, *Geschichte des Revolutionszeitalters*. . ., 719.
40. Ibid.

Epilogue

1. See J. Polišenský, "Old revoluce roku 1848 k Pařížské komuně a První internacionále," in: *Mikulovské symposium III* (Mikulov 1972) 1-6.
2. K. Obermann, "Die amerikanische Arbeiterbewegung vor dem Bürgerkrieg im Kampf für Demokratie und gegen die Herrschaft der Sklavenhalter," ZGW (1962) 103-135. *Začiatky českej a slovenskej emigrácie do USA* ed M. Gosiorovský and J. Polišenský (Bratislava 1970).
3. K. Obermann, *Joseph Weydemeyer. Ein Lebensbild* (Berlin 1968).
4. V. Dolínek, *Účast Cecu v americké občanské válce* (unpub. candidature dissertation, Czechoslovak Academy of Sciences 1972).
5. T. Capek, *Naše Amerika* (Prague 1926) 203 ff.
6. See n. 4.
7. A. Seifert, "Za starým osmačtyřicátníkem Fr. Korbelem," *Naše zahraničí* (1920) 9-14.
8. *La Bohême historique et littéraire*. . .
9. J. Vrbata, "Ohlas Pařížské komuny v českých zemích," *Společenské vědy ve škole* (1971), 76-80.

10. J. Polišenský in *Začiatky českej a slovenskej emigrácie*. . .
11. *Dělník*, 1.IV.1871.

Index

Academic Legion of Prague, 113,174
Acta Clementina, 23
Aix-la-Chapelle, Congress of, 31
Albert, Archduke, 95,98-9,176
Allgemeine Zeitung of Augsburg, 59
Amerling, Karel Slavomil, 66
Andics, Erszébet, 90
Andrian-Werburg, Viktor, 40,83-4
Arnold, Emanuel, 4,127,134
d'Aspre, Constantin, 136,138,176
Auersperg, Charles, 190
d'Azeglio, Massimo, 85

Bach, Alexander, 172,188,190,205
Baillet-Latour, Theodore (see Latour)
Bakunin, Mikhail Alexandrovich, 146,154,156
Balbo, Cesare, 64
Bass, Edward, 9
Bastide, Jules, 175
Batthyány, Lajos, 124
Bauer, A., 207
Baumgartner, Andrew, 123
Beaufort-Spontin family, 36
Becher, Alfred Julius, 195
Beidtel, Karel (see Tebeldi, Albrecht)
Bem, Józef, 194-5
Berger, J.N., 166
Beseda of Paris, 213-4
Bignon, M., 64
Blanc, Louis, 89
Bloudek, Bedřich, 155
Blum, Robert, 194,197,207
Bolzano, Bernard, 52,68
Bombelles, Charles Louis de, 43
Borecký, Jan, 212
Borrosch, Alois, 142,150
Bowring, John 65-6
Bracegirdle, Thomas, 35
Bradka, A., 127,134

Brauner, Franz August, 111,113,196,197
Brentano, Clemens, 69
Breycha-Vauthier, 23
Buquoy, George Franz, 4,168
Burian, Tomáš, 96,98,102

Carlyle, Thomas, 38
Caroline of Wittelsbach, 43
Casati, Gabrio, 103-4,105
Castiglione, Jan, 138
Cattaneo, Carlo, 104,137
Cavaignac, Eugene, 175
Čelakovský, F.L., 66
Charles, Archduke, 43-4
Charles X of France, 64
Charles Albert, King of Sardinia, 85, ,105,136,137,138,175
Charles Ferdinand, Archduke, 114
Chartists, 120
Chotek, Rudolf, 78,82
Clam-Gallas, Edward, 24,176-7
Clam-Martinitz, Heinrich Jaroslav, 167
Clary-Aldringen, Edmund, 24,131-2, 178-84,187
Clary-Aldringen family, 102
Colloredo, Ferdinand 117
Committee of Safety (Sicherheitsausschluss) 123-4
Cooper, James Fenimore, 39
Cordon, Franz von, 200
Coudenhove, Theofil, 109
Czapka, Ignaz, 94

Demel, Josef, 188
Deutsch, Simon, 214
Deym, Fridrich, 41,75,109
Deym, Vojtěch (Adalbert), 112,143
Dickens, Charles, 33,65
Disraeli, Benjamin, 39-40

Doblhoff-Dier, Anton, 101,143-4,172
Doborovský, Josef, 63
Dom Miguel, 107
Durando, Giacomo, 137,175

Ebert, Karl Egon, 142
Ellenborough, Edward Law, 107
Ellenborough, Jane, 107-8
Engles, Friedrich, 12-22,61,62,120
Erben, Karel Jaromír, 81
d'Este, Ferdinand, 85

Faster, Petr, 110,154,160,168
Ferdinand V, 42-3,191-2,201
Ferdinand of Naples, 105-6,137
Ferdinand of Tuscany, 43
Fialka, Mořic, 65,162
Ficquelmont, Karl Ludwig, 24,84-7,90-2,103, 117-9,121-2,143,208
Fischer, Adolf, 128-9
Fischer, Josef, 179
Fischhof, Adolf, 123-4
Francis I, 42
Franz Josef I, 201
Francis Stephen of Lorraine, 37
Frič, Josef, 113
Frič, Josef Václav, 3-6,66,127,145,154, 156,202,213
Frederick William IV, 119,197-8,204
Fröbel, Julius, 194,195
Füster, Anton, 117

Gaj, Ludovit, 125
Garibaldi, Giuseppe, 175
Gaskell, Elizabeth, 40
Gauč, Vilém, 110,112
Gerstner, František Antonín, 34
Gindely, Anton, 68
Gioberti, Vincenzo, 85
Giusti, Giuseppe, 63
Gleig, G.R., 67
Goethe, Johann Wolfgang, 63
Gorowski, A. de, 64
Göschen, J.F.L., 179,180,181-3
Grenzboten, Die, 69-70,120,168,186
Grillparzer, Franz, 69
Grünne, Karl, 193,199,201,204

Haas, Andrew, 133-4
Haas, Antonín, 23
Hallaschka, F.K., 45,96
Hardegg, Johann Ignaz, 45,87
Hartig, Franz, 75,109
Haupt, Moritz, 179
Havlíček, František, 183,196
Havlíček Borovský, Karel, 67,130,160,170, 197,203
Heine, Heinrich, 62-3
Helfert, J.A., 8,68,109,130,200
Hess, Heinrich, 47,201-2
Heyde, Josef, 89-90,111
Hobsbawm, Eric, 7
Hodža, Milan, 171,186
Homoláč, J.V., 34
Horák, Ferdinand, 212
Hormayr, Josef, 73
Horn, Uffo, 69,126,179-84
Hornbostel, Theodor, 172
Horský, František, 95-6
Hoyoš, Johann, 122
Hroch, Miroslav, 61
Hübner, A., 87,172,200
Hübner, Alois, 102
Hudek, Pavel, 212-3
Hulek, Josef, 213-4
Hummelhauer, Karle, 138
Hye, Anton, 97

Inzaghi, Johann, 45,60,84
Irving, Washington, 67

Jellačić, Josef, 125,138,174,178,188,189, 192,193
Jellinek, Herman, 195
Jeník of Bratřice, Jan, 9-10,66
Johann, Archduke, 44,173
John, Edward, 178,183
Josef, Archduke, 44
Jungmann, Josef, 4,65

Kafka, Franz, 69
Kampelík, Fratišek Cyril, 41,52,128,151
Kerchnawe, H., 138
Kissinger, Henry A., 23,72
Klácel, František Matouš, 65
Klar, Pavel Alois, 55-8

Index

Kleczansky, Josef, 145,155,165,166
Klein brothers 34-5,53,59
Kleinert, Pavel Václav, 186
Klier, František, 179-82
Klinkowström, Alfons, 103
Knoll, Josef Leonard, 72-3
Kölnische Zeitung, 167
Killár, Jan, 63
Kolowrat-Krakovský, Hanuš, 95
Kolowrat-Liebšteinský, Anton, 23-4,41, 44,76,101,117,118
Kolowrat-Liebšteinský family, 23-4,76
Komers, Anton Emanuel, 167
Korbel, František, 213
Kossuth, Lajos, 124-5,188
Kraus, Karl, 69
Kraus, Filip, 119,123,131,200
Kreibich, Karel, 12,138
Kremsier (Kroměříž) Parliament, 199-200, 202,206-7
Krombholz, Dean of Česká Lípa, 182
Krtička of Jaden, Jan, 45
Kübeck, K.F., 41-2,45,60,71,101,188, 204,205-6
Kudlich, Hans, 173
Küttenbrugg, 179,183
Kuranda, Ignaz, 69-70,130,165

Lamberg, Franz Phillip, 189
Lambl, Dušan, 170
Langenau, Ferdinand, 150
Latour, Theodore, 47,121-2,123,133, 139,144,190
Lažanský of Buková, Leopold, 48,180
léger, Louis, 4
Lelek, Cyprián, 132
Lenin, Vladimir Ilyich, 9
Libelt, Karol, 145-6
Lichnowsky, Felix, 76
Liechtenstein family 101
Lichtner, A., 53
List, Friedrich, 35
Lobkowitz, Josef, 25,139,149,150,151,153, 177,190,191,204
Löhner, Ludwig von, 129,132,178-80,188-9
Louis Philippe, 87-9
Ludwig, Archduke, 44
Lützow, Rudolf, 85-6,105-6,126

Lützow family, 24,76

Macal, Antonín, 212
Mácha, Karel Hynek, 65
Malý, Jakub, 65,68,208
Manin, Daniel, 175
Maria Anna, Wife of Ferdinand V, 43
Maria Louisa, sister of Ferdinand V., 43
Marx, Karl, 12-21,120,134-5,164,168
Matauschek von Benndorf, Josef, 95
Matice Česká,50
Maux, Maximilian, 127,152,159
Mazzini, Giuseppe, 63-4,85,137
Mechura, Leopold, 81,187
Meissner, Alfred, 69
Mensdorff, Emmanuel, 155,166
Mensinger, Karel, 63,104
Messenhauser, Václav Caesar, 8,193-4,195
Metternich, Clemens Lothar, 23,30-1,42, 71,82-4,98-100,101-3
Metternich, Melanie, 87-8,98,101,103
Metternich, Richard, 23,102
Mieroslawski, Ludwik, 119,120
Mittrowsky, Anton Friedrich, 73,74
Montecuccoli, Albert, 98
Montenuovo, Wilhelm Albrecht, 43
Mráček, František, 212
Müller, Josef, 111
Müller, Major, 158
Muth, Petr, 54-5,95

Náprstek, Vojtěch, 67,95-7,99,154-6, 169-71,185
Národní noviny, 104,130,140,186,190,203
National Committee, 115,126,142,143
National Guard of Prague, 6,113,151,158
Němcová, Božena, 95
Neruda, Jan, 62
Nesselrode, Karl Robert, 90-2
Neuberg, Jan of, 161
Neue Rheinische Zeitung, 120,176
Nicholas I, 42,91-2,165,196,204
Nieperg, Adam von, 42
Nostitz, Albert, 143-4,187

Obermann, Karl, 23,26,211
Ohéral, Jan, 52
Opitz, Filip Maximilián, 52

243

Paget, John, 66
Palacký, František, 9,62,63,76-7,82,112,120, 128,129-30,133-4,135,146, 173,202,215
Palacký, Jan, 135
Palmerston, Henry, 137-8
Paris Revolution of 1848, 87-9
Parsons, Talcott, 20,72
Pecks, Josef Boleslav, 214-5
Palzel, Ludvík, 156,169
Pepe, Guglielmo, 137
Perner, Jan, 53,60
Pfitzner, Josef, 72-3
Pillersdorf, Franz, 41,101,121,122-3,132, 133,134,144,165,166,172
Pinkas, Adolf Maria, 126,203
Pius IX, 85,137
Polák, Milota Zdirad, 63,96
Posler, Jan, 212
Pražské noviny, 64,130,144
Pražský večerní list, 186,189,190
Prinz, Friedrich, 129,133
Prokesch-Osten, Anton von, 205-6

Radetzky, Josef Wenzel, 48,86,103,104-5,136, 137,138,139,174-5,190,201-2
Der Radikale, 186
Rainer, Archduke, 44
Rank, Josef, 129
Rath, R. John, 27
Rauscher, Josef Othmar, 202,204
Repeal Club of Prague, 67
Rieger, František Ladislav, 63,143-4,170, 188,189,196,197,200,203
Riepl, Franz Xavier, 34
Rilke, Rainer Maria, 69
Rössler, F.E., 129
Rothschild, Salomon, 53,101,102
Rothstein, A., 12
Rudolf of Habsburg, Archbishop of Olomouc, 34,38
Ruge, Arnold, 207
Ruppert, Ludvík, 110,112
Rybín, Matěj, 212

Sabina, Karel, 4,66,110,112,197
Šafařík, Pavel Josef, 63
Salm, Reiffersheidt, Franz Hugo, 34
Sand, George, 64-5

Sardagna, General, 122
Schnabel, G.N., 49
Schütte, General, 171
Schuselka, Franz, 8,116,130,142,166,201
Schwarzenberg, Felix, 24,76,106,175,190, 195-6,199,200,201,204-6
Schwarzenberg, Friedrich, 76,109
Schwarzenberg, Johann Adolf, 132
Schwarzenberg, Josef, 202
Schwarzenberg, Karl, 139
Schwarzenberg, Mathilde, 107
Schwarzer, Ernst, 172
Sealsfield, Charles (K.A. Postl), 68
Sedlnitzky, Josef, 45,117
Sekavec, Jan, 148-9
Serre, Marcel de, 64
Sladkovský, Karel, 127,150,151,153,155,160,170
Slavia, 113,127,151
Šlitr, Jiřík, 214
Slovanská Lípa, 113,126,196-7,204
Sommaruga, Franz, 101,119,121,123
Sommerau-Beeck, M.J., 102,127,200
Špitzner, Jindřich, 8
Springer, Anton, 1-3,6-7,188-9,207-9,210
Stadion, Franz, 131,173,199-200
Stadion, Rudolf, 82,111,113,203,204
Stephen, Archduke, 48,60,82
Stradal, Franz, 179,183
Stradal, Johann, 179
Strache, Edward, 179,181,183
Straka, Adolf, 213
Strauss, Johann, 190
Strobach, Antonín, 132,202-3
Strong, John, 166
Šťur, Ludovit, 5,186
Sue, Eugene, 39,40
Sunstenau, General, 192
Šverma, Jan, 12
Svornost, 113
Szechényi, István, 75

Taaffe, Ludwig, 45,101,119,121
Talatzko ofJeštětice, Jan, 48,98,131
Tebeldi, Albrecht (Beidtel, Karl), 97
Tedesko, K., 179,182
Teplitz, Congress of, 31
Thackeray, William Makepeace, 66

Thierry, Augustin, 82
Thomas, Edward and James, 35
Thun-Hohenstein, Friedrich, 24,90
Thun-Hohenstein, Josef Matthias, 25,75,
  146,166-7
Thun-Hohenstein, Leo, 41,71,75,132,
  133,142-5,149,150,153,155,167,171-2,207
Tieftrunk, Václav, 99,150,155,156
Times of London, 167,168
Tocqueville, Alexis de, 164
Tomíček, J.S., 68
Troján, Alois Pravoslav, 111
Troppau, Congress of, 26,31

Vegezzi, Ruscalle, 64
Verein der Deutschen aus Böhmen,
  Möhren und Schlesien, 129,131-2,
  133-4,165,178-84
Verein für Aufrechterhaltung der öffentlichen
Ordnung, 152,153
Vienna, Congress of, 31
Vietz, Karl, 74
Villani, K.D., 155,168,213
Viták, Ferdinand, 196
Vojáček, Ladislav, 213
Výšek, Antonín Dobroslav, 103,104

Wallmoden, Ludwig Georg, 136
Wanka, Wenzel, 150-1,161,165
Weber, Max, 20,72
Wellington, Arthur Wellesley, 46
Werfel, Franz, 69
Wessenberg, Johann Philip, 109,123,144,172
Wiener Zeitung, 166,167,168
Windischgrätz, Alfred, 1,5,59,87,100,106,
  118,133,135,138,139-41,143-4,149-
  51,153,
  157,159,165,171-8,192-3,194-6,204,206
Windischgrätz, Eleonora, 159
Winter, Edward, 62
Wratislaw, Edward, 212

Zach, František, 146,155
Zanini, Peter, 101,119,121,194
Zdekauer, Moříc, 53

LIBRARY OF DAVIDSON COLLEGE

Books on regular loan may be checked out for **two weeks.** Books must be presented at the Circulation Desk in order to be renewed.

A fine is charged after date due.

Special books are subject to special regulations at the discretion of the library staff.

MAY -4.1987